W9-CKU-880

HISTORICAL ATLAS OF THE HOLOCAUST

HISTORICAL ATLAS OF THE HOLOCAUST

UNITED STATES
HOLOCAUST MEMORIAL MUSEUM

Macmillan Publishing USA
Simon & Schuster Macmillan
New York

Prentice Hall International
London Mexico City New Delhi Singapore Sydney Toronto

Macmillan Publishing USA
An Imprint of Simon & Schuster Macmillan
1633 Broadway
New York, New York 10019

Library of Congress Catalog Card Number: 95-9354

Printed in the United States of America

Printing Number
    3 4 5 6 7 8 9 10

Library of Congress Cataloging-in-Publication Data
Historical Atlas of the Holocaust / United States Holocaust
Memorial Museum
        p.   cm.
        Includes bibliography and index.
        ISBN: 0-02-897451-4 (alk. paper)
1. Holocaust, Jewish (1939-1945)—Maps. 2. Holocaust, Jewish
(1939-1945) 3. Historical geography—Maps I. U.S. Holocaust
Memorial Museum.
G1797.21.E29H5 1995   95-9354
940.53'18'0223—dc20   CIP
                            Map

CONTENTS

7   Preface
8   Acknowledgements
9   Introduction

SECTION 1	EUROPE BEFORE THE WAR

12   Europe 1933
14   European Jewish Population Distribution circa 1933
15   Jewish Communities in Germany, Austria, and Czechoslovakia circa 1933
16   European Romani (Gypsy) Population Distribution circa 1939
17   German Territorial Losses, Versailles Treaty 1919
18   Remilitarization of the Rhineland and "Anschluss" with Austria 1936-1938
18   German Annexation of the Sudetenland 1938
19   Partition of Czechoslovakia 1938-1939
20   German Territorial Gains before the War, August 1939
21   Nazi Concentration Camps 1933-1934
22   Nazi Concentration Camps 1939
23   Identification Patches and Camp Badges (illustration)
24   "Kristallnacht": the Nationwide Pogrom of November 9 and 10, 1938
25   Voyage of the SS *St. Louis*, May 13-June 17, 1939
26   Jewish Emigration from Germany 1933-1940
28   "Euthanasia" Centers, Germany 1940-1945

SECTION 2	THE HOLOCAUST IN EASTERN EUROPE

30   Axis Alliance 1939-1941
31   Eastern Europe after the German-Soviet Pact 1939-1940
32   German Conquests in Europe 1939-1942
33   German Administration of Europe 1942
34   German Administration of Poland 1942
35   German Administration of Eastern Europe 1942
36   Ghettos in Occupied Poland 1939-1941
37   Warsaw Environs 1940
38   Warsaw Ghetto 1940
39   Deportations to Warsaw Ghetto 1941-1942
        Inset: East Europe 1941
40   Deportations from Warsaw Ghetto 1942
41   Warsaw Ghetto Uprising 1943
42   Deportations to Lodz Ghetto 1941-1942
43   Lodz Environs 1940
44   Lodz Ghetto 1940-1944
45   Nazi Camps in Occupied Poland 1939-1945
46   Krakow Environs 1942-1944
47   Krakow Ghetto, May 1942
48   Plaszow Concentration Camp, January 1944
49   "Erntefest," November 3, 1943

50   Invasion of the Soviet Union 1941-1942
51   Einsatzgruppen Massacres (Mobile Killing Units) in Eastern Europe, June 1941-November 1942
52   Deportations to Kamenets-Podolski 1941
53   Babi Yar Massacre in Kiev, September 29 and 30, 1941
54   Ghettos in Occupied Eastern Europe 1941-1942
56   Minsk Environs 1941-1942
57   Minsk Ghetto, July 1941
58   Bialystok Environs 1941
59   Bialystok Ghetto 1941-1943
60   Vilna Environs 1941-1943
61   Vilna Ghetto 1941-1943
62   Lvov Environs 1941-1942
63   Janowska Labor Camp, Fall 1942
64   Ghettos in the Baltic Countries 1941-1943
65   Nazi Camps in the Baltic Countries 1941-1945
66   Riga Environs 1941-1942
67   Riga Ghetto 1942
68   Kovno Environs 1941-1944
69   Kovno Ghetto 1941-1944
70   Romania 1941
70   Romania 1942
71   Romanian Camps and Ghettos 1942
72   Romanian Deportations to Transnistria 1941-1942
72   Romanian Participation in Massacres 1941-1942
73   Odessa Environs 1941-1944
74   Romanian-Occupied Odessa 1941-1944

SECTION 3	NAZI EXTERMINATION CAMPS

76   Extermination Camps in Occupied Poland 1942
77   Extermination Camps 1942
78   European Rail System 1939
80   Chelmno Environs, Spring 1942
81   Chelmno, Spring 1942
82   Major Deportations to Chelmno 1941-1944
83   Aktion Reinhard in the Generalgouvernement 1942
84   Belzec Environs, Winter 1942
85   Belzec Camp, Winter 1942
86   Major Deportations to Belzec 1942
87   Sobibor Environs, Spring 1942
88   Sobibor Camp, Spring 1942
89   Major Deportations to Sobibor 1942-1943
90   Treblinka Environs, Spring 1943
91   Treblinka Camp, Spring 1943
92   Major Deportations to Treblinka 1942-1943
93   Auschwitz Environs, Summer 1944
94   Auschwitz Development Zone

CONTENTS

95   Auschwitz I Camp 1944

96   Auschwitz II (Birkenau) Camp, Summer 1944

97   Auschwitz III (Monowitz) Camp 1944

98   Major Deportations from Ghettos in Poland to Auschwitz 1941-1944

99   Major Deportations to Auschwitz 1941-1944

99   Auschwitz Subcamp System, Upper Silesia 1941-1945

100   Majdanek Environs, Fall 1943

101   Majdanek Camp, Fall 1943

102   Major Deportations to Majdanek 1941-1944

SECTION 4 | THE HOLOCAUST IN WESTERN EUROPE

104   German Invasion of Western Europe 1940

104   Occupation of Western Europe 1940

105   Occupation of Western Europe 1944

106   Camps in France 1942

107   Major Deportations from France 1942-1944

107   Deportation of Jews from Paris

108   Paris Environs 1943

108   Central Paris 1943

109   Drancy Transit Camp 1943

110   Gurs Environs 1942

111   Gurs Camp 1942

111   Major Deportations of Jews to Gurs 1940-1943

112   Camps in France 1944

112   Occupation of Southern Zone, November 1942

113   Natzweiler-Struthof Environs, Spring 1944

114   Natzweiler-Struthof Camp, Spring 1944

115   Natzweiler-Struthof Subcamps 1942-1945

116   The Low Countries 1939

117   Nazi Camps in the Low Countries 1940-1945

118   Major Deportations from the Low Countries 1942-1944

119   Amsterdam Environs 1942

120   Amsterdam 1942

121   Anne Frank 1929-1945
      Inset: Hiding in Amsterdam 1942-1944

122   Westerbork Environs 1942

123   Westerbork Transit Camp 1942

124   Breendonk and Mechelen Environs 1942

125   Mechelen Transit Camp 1942

126   Breendonk Internment Camp 1942

SECTION 5 | THE HOLOCAUST IN CENTRAL EUROPE

128   Deportations of Jews from Germany 1941-1944

130   Berlin Environs 1942

131   Deportations of Jews from Berlin 1941-1943

132   Vienna Environs 1942

133   Deportations of Jews from Vienna 1941-1945

134   Theresienstadt Environs 1944

135   Theresienstadt Ghetto, Summer 1944

136   Deportations to Theresienstadt from Bohemia and Moravia 1941

136   Deportations from Theresienstadt 1942-1944

137   Greater Germany 1944

138   Greater Germany Major Nazi Camps 1944

140   Europe Major Nazi Camps 1943-1944

142   Persecution of Roma (Gypsies) 1939-1945

143   Nazi Medical Experiments 1942-1945

144   Dachau Environs 1944

145   Dachau Concentration Camp 1944

146   Dachau Subcamps 1938-1945

147   Buchenwald Environs 1945

148   Buchenwald Concentration Camp, Spring 1945

149   Buchenwald Subcamps 1938-1945

150   Mauthausen Environs, April 1945

151   Mauthausen Concentration Camp, April 1945

152   Mauthausen Subcamps in Former Austria 1938-1945

153   Ravensbrueck Environs 1945

154   Ravensbrueck Concentration Camp 1945

155   Ravensbrueck Subcamps 1941-1945

156   Gross-Rosen Environs 1945

157   Gross-Rosen Concentration Camp 1945

158   Gross-Rosen Subcamps 1940-1945

159   Stutthof Environs 1944

160   Stutthof Concentration Camp, Fall 1944

161   Stutthof Subcamps 1939-1945

162   Dora-Mittelbau Environs 1945

163   Dora-Mittelbau Concentration Camp 1945

164   Dora-Mittelbau Subcamps 1943-1945

165   Bergen-Belsen Environs 1944

166   Bergen-Belsen Concentration Camp 1944

SECTION 6 | THE HOLOCAUST IN SOUTHERN EUROPE AND HUNGARY

168   Invasion of the Balkans, April 1941

169   Partition of Yugoslavia 1941

169   Occupation of Greece 1941

170   German Administration of Southern Europe 1943

172   Major Nazi and Axis Camps in Southern Europe 1941-1944

174   Deportations from Southern Europe 1941-1944

176   Jasenovac Environs 1942

177   Jasenovac III Concentration Camp 1942

178   Salonika Environs 1942-1943

179   German-Occupied Salonika 1942-1943

180 Italy 1939
180 Italian-Occupied Areas in Southern Europe 1942
181 German-Occupied Areas of Italy 1943
182 Deportations from Italy 1943-1944
183 Rome Environs 1943
184 German-Occupied Rome 1943
185 Hungary 1937
186 Hungarian Expansion
186 Forced-Labor Camps for Jews in Occupied Hungary 1944
187 Major Ghettos in Occupied Hungary 1944
188 Deportations from Hungarian Ghettos 1944
189 Budapest Environs 1944
189 Budapest Ghetto 1944
190 Death March from Budapest 1944

SECTION 7 — RESCUE AND JEWISH ARMED RESISTANCE

192 Escape Routes from German-Occupied Europe 1942
194 Rescue of Danish Jews, Fall 1943
195 Escape Routes from Norway 1942-1943
196 Voyage of the *Struma,* December 12, 1941-February 24, 1942
197 Rescue in Budapest 1944-1945
198 Jewish Partisan Activity in Eastern Europe 1942-1944
199 Jewish Partisan Activity in Western Europe 1942-1944
200 Jewish Armed Resistance in Ghettos and Camps 1941-1944
201 Jewish Parachutists from Palestine 1943-1945
202 Jewish Brigade Group 1944-1945

SECTION 8 — DEATH MARCHES AND LIBERATION

204 Major Death Marches and Evacuations 1944-1945
205 Major Death Marches from Auschwitz January 1945
206 Evacuations and Death March from Stutthof, January-April 1945
    Inset: Death March to Lauenburg (Lebork)
207 Death Marches from Gross-Rosen 1945
207 Death Marches from Buchenwald, April 1945
208 Death March from Dachau to Tegernsee, March 1945
209 The Liberation of Major Nazi Camps 1944-1945
210 The Defeat of Nazi Germany 1942-1945
212 Battle of Berlin, April 1945

SECTION 9 — POSTWAR EUROPE 1945-1950

214 Europe in 1945
215 Eastern Europe in 1945
215 Occupation of Germany 1945
216 Major European War Crimes Trials 1943-1947
217 Major Camps for Jewish Displaced Persons 1945-1946
218 Jewish "Illegal" Immigration 1945-1947
220 Detention Camps in Cyprus, August 1946-February 1948
220 The State of Israel, Boundaries as of 1949
221 European Jewish Population Distribution circa 1950

222 European Regions and German Administration Units
224 Glossary
227 Bibliography
233 Gazetteer

The compilation of the maps for the *Historical Atlas of the Holocaust* involved a number of rare and little-used sources. In producing the atlas, the cartographic research and development team worked extensively with combinations of primary sources, each used to complement the information provided by another.

German army (Wehrmacht) maps captured by American forces during and after World War II constituted the principal map sources used in the atlas. Further, photographs—especially aerial photography taken by both Allied and German forces—were an invaluable source in compiling accurate plans of Nazi concentration camps. Political and strategic maps from the United States government and topographic and transportation maps from most European countries were essential resources for the country and city plans included in the atlas. All map sources used are from the time period 1933 to 1950. The construction of the maps also relied heavily on textual materials, primarily court records, memorial books, captured German records, and secondary works such as scholarly journals and survivor testimonies in German, French, and English.

The compilation of the Drancy transit camp plan (p. 109) illustrates the range of sources used. Located in a suburb of Paris, Drancy was the principal camp used during the deportation of Jews from France. German installations in Drancy were plotted through the use of military maps provided to German occupation forces. The alignment and names of streets were pinpointed through the use of period French civilian maps, which also identified French installations in the area. Camp features were added with the aid of contemporary photographs of the camp. Such photographs identified the structure of Drancy itself, the German headquarters situated next to the camp, the streets falling within the bounds of the camp, and the buildings used for manufacturing operations at Drancy. These features were confirmed, whenever possible, in documents, survivor testimonies, and secondary literature.

The range of rare sources used in the compilation of the atlas is further illustrated by the map of Babi Yar (p. 53), a ravine near Kiev where Einsatzgruppen (mobile killing unit) detachments massacred more than 33,000 Jews in late September 1941. Aerial photographs taken by both Allied and German air forces, civilian Soviet maps, and German military maps were complemented by the use of other photographs to identify features plotted on the map. The ravine itself and the road system leading to it were located through the use of a Soviet military topographic map. A German army map provided the plan of Kiev and the road network of the city.

Finally, a word about the place names used on the maps in the atlas. Many European town or city names had and continue to have several accepted forms. The borders of many European countries changed radically before, during, and after World War II, further complicating the choice of place names. In the atlas, cities and towns are generally named according to the language of the country in which they were located before World War II. German designations are used for Nazi concentration camps. No diacritics are used. A gazetteer listing alternative place names has been included (beginning on p. 233) to facilitate use of the atlas.

The Wexner Learning Center

The *Historical Atlas of the Holocaust* presents maps produced for the Wexner Learning Center of the United States Holocaust Memorial Museum.

The Center is an interactive computerized facility developed with funds donated by Mrs. Bella Wexner and Mr. and Mrs. Leslie H. Wexner of Columbus, Ohio. It offers Museum visitors historical information based on articles from the Macmillan *Encyclopedia of the Holocaust* and the Macmillan *Encyclopedia of the Third Reich* as the organizing "spine" of this multimedia, on-line program. To enrich and appropriately illustrate the articles drawn from the encyclopedias, the Center created databases of relevant supplementary materials: documentary photographs, film footage, videotaped eyewitness testimonies, musical materials, and, of course, maps. More than 500 maps have been incorporated into the Center's system; over 230 from among them constitute this atlas.

The maps, prepared by the Center's cartographer Dewey Hicks and its historian William Meinecke, are based on extensive research into primary sources: for example, period maps from the German army mapping service; Allied and German aerial photographs; political and strategic maps from the U.S. State Department and the Office of Strategic Services (OSS); railway and city maps from various European countries; and a great number of textual records.

The Holocaust took place across more than 20 European countries which during World War II were in the grip of Nazi Germany. During this period political boundaries changed, states were dismantled, new states established, and hundreds of place names, which before the war were unknown even to educated people, suddenly assumed great historic importance. Who would know the location of towns like Auschwitz, Treblinka, or Chelmno were it not for the death camps established there by the Germans? Who would know the location of geographic regions like the Sudetenland or Transnistria, the location of Nazi concentration camps like Dachau, Buchenwald, and Bergen-Belsen, had he not learned the history of the Nazi regime and the Holocaust? Conversely, it is impossible to learn and understand Holocaust history without complementing the chronological description and analysis of the events with adequate information on the geography underlying this chapter of modern history.

The sequence of maps in the atlas follows the chronology of the historic Holocaust-related events from 1933 to 1950. Since each map comes with detailed textual background information, the atlas can be regarded as a condensed history of the Holocaust, presenting the geographical aspects of the historic events.

The atlas is published both in book form and as a CD-ROM by Macmillan Publishing USA in association with the United States Holocaust Memorial Museum. It is an important scholarly publication of the Museum's Holocaust Research Institute, another contribution of the Museum to the field of Holocaust studies. It is an indispensable source of information for anybody who is interested in this tragic chapter of human history.

Jeshajahu Weinberg, Founding Director
United States Holocaust Memorial Museum

United States Holocaust Memorial Council
Miles Lerman, Chair
Ruth B. Mandel, Vice Chair

United States Holocaust Memorial Museum
Jeshajahu Weinberg, Founding Director
Walter Reich, Director

Review
Michael Berenbaum, Director, United States
        Holocaust Research Institute
Sybil Milton, Senior Historian, United States
        Holocaust Research Institute
Richard Breitman, Professor of History, The American
        University

Concept Development
Jeshajahu Weinberg
Yechiam Halevy

Atlas Design and Production
Jennifer Loew Mendelson, Director
Dewey G. Hicks, Cartographer
William F. Meinecke Jr., Historian
Sandra Kaiser, Editor

Cartography
Amy B. Gorman, Cartographic/Graphic Artist
Eric Smith, Technician
Thach Nguyen, Graphic Artist
Bertram Rothenberg, Editor
Jack Michaelson, Researcher
Rachel Kreiger, Aide
Mounir Murad, Color Separation

Research
Steven Luckert, Historian
Anne Molineu, Researcher
Elizabeth Soloway Snider, Editor

Database Development and Technical Support
Galia Steinbach

Project Coordination
Susan Graber, Coordinator
Deborah L. Gaffin, Coordinator

The Museum acknowledges with gratitude the contributions of the staff of its Research Institute, especially those working in the archives and library, and the staff of the Museum's Department of Technical Services. In addition, the Museum is grateful for the help of the following organizations:

Map Library, Library of Congress, Washington D.C.
Map Archives, National Archives, Washington D.C.
Defense Mapping Agency, Department of Defense,
        Washington D.C.
Defense Intelligence Agency, Department of Defense,
        Washington D.C.

The Museum also acknowledges the contributions to the production of the atlas of the following:

Cathy Chappell
Peter Fink
Wesley A. Fisher
Michael E. Garvey
Anna Gedrich
Margaret A. Gorman
Jack Harris
Patricia Heberer
William Hess
Radu V. Ioanid
Michelle Isenberg
Nancy Kellman-Maddocks
Robert W. Kesting
Arnold Kramer
Harry Lee
Yelena Luckert
Brad McKelvey
Barbara A. Meinecke
Joel H. Mendelson
Dana Ellyn Miller
Carl J. Modig
Jacek M. Nowakowski
John O'Keefe
Kathleen Samiy
Gerald L. Smith
Ikon Graphics
Thunderwave, Inc.
The Publishers Service Bureau

This atlas presents in specific detail—country by country, place by place, process by process—the evolution of the Holocaust. The importance of the *Historical Atlas of the Holocaust* lies in its emphasis on the specific; but specific events, places, and processes must be viewed in the context of the whole. This brief introduction is intended to tell the story of the Holocaust in an overview.

Throughout the atlas, "the Holocaust" means the systematic, state-sponsored murder of six million Jews and millions of non-Jews by the Nazis and their collaborators during World War II.

In his monumental work *The Destruction of the European Jews*, Raul Hilberg outlines six stages in the destruction process: definition, expropriation, concentration, mobile killing units, deportation, and killing centers. These stages are a useful way to think about the Holocaust.

In Germany, the Nuremberg legislation of 1935 defined the Jews; Jews were identified not by the religion they professed, the values and beliefs they avowed, the rituals they practiced, or the identity they affirmed, but biologically based on the religion of their grandparents. Civil liberties for Jews were abridged and then violated. Once established, this definition of the enemy was applied in country after country as the German Reich expanded its borders and occupied other lands.

Homes, businesses, possessions, synagogues, public institutions, and private property were taken from the Jews. At first, this was an effort to force them to emigrate, to make Germany free of Jews; later, confiscation and expropriation became an essential part of the "Final Solution."

During the war, Germany concentrated Jews, forcing them to live together in confined areas such as ghettos in Poland and the occupied territories in the east, and transit camps in the west. To the killers, these were temporary measures, pending some final policy. The victims thought the ghettos would endure and imagined some sort of underclass existence, at least until the end of the war.

With the invasion of the Soviet Union in June of 1941, the slaughter by Einsatzgruppen (mobile killing units) began. Accompanying advancing German forces, the Einsatzgruppen entered towns, villages, hamlets, even large cities, and rounded up and shot the Jews, Roma (Gypsies), and Soviet Commissars. This process continued as the army advanced. When the military situation permitted, the Einsatzgruppen returned to the larger Jewish communities to finish off what had been left undone.

The killing was difficult, even for the killers. They drank heavily; alcohol somehow made the work more bearable. Yet the killers themselves were marked. Heinrich Himmler was told by one of his Einsatzgruppen commanders that "these men are finished for the rest of their lives. What kind of followers are we training here? Either neurotics or savages."

To deal with this problem, a more impersonal method of killing was sought. The victims would be brought to the killers and dispatched in a way that kept the victims at a distance. Thus, a second form of killing was developed: the death camp, where the killing was done by gas and the bodies burned.

Railroads were the essential link in the killing process. And deportation transformed the ghetto into a transit camp, a way station to contain the captive population until the killing centers were developed and opened. Deportation meant the loss of home, the collapse of families, the beginning of a journey to death. The timetable was swift. The policy was announced in January 1942 at Wannsee; the killing centers were developed in the winter and spring, and by the summer of 1942 deportations had begun. By 1943, most of the Jews who were killed in the Holocaust were already dead.

Four camps were only for killing: Chelmno, Belzec, Sobibor, and Treblinka. Auschwitz and Majdanek served multiple functions: forced-labor camp, concentration camp, and killing center. Other concentration camps were not solely dedicated to killing, though conditions were so harsh, forced labor so intense, and food so scarce that hundreds of thousands of people died or were killed in them.

The progress of World War II had a significant impact on the Holocaust. With each German advance more Jews came under Nazi domination. Impending German losses often intensified the pace of destruction. Each area liberated from German control brought relief to its endangered population—none more endangered than the Jews.

Though the destruction of the Jews was at the center of Nazi ideology, Jews were not the only victims of Nazi Germany. Nazi racism was directed against a mosaic of victims. In the early years, trade unionists and political dissidents were incarcerated along with clergy who spoke out. Jehovah's Witnesses were imprisoned because they would not swear allegiance to the state, would not register for the draft, would not utter the words "Heil Hitler." German male homosexuals were targeted and arrested because they were an affront to the Nazi macho image: they would not breed the master race. Nazi propaganda demonized these targeted groups so as to facilitate their elimination. During the war, most especially in the early days of victory, the Germans also targeted Soviet prisoners of war for extinction. Further, Slavic nations were to be enslaved by the "master race."

The Germans systematically killed two other groups. Mentally retarded, physically handicapped, and emotionally disturbed Germans were killed in a "euthanasia" program. They were an embarrassment to the concept of the German master race. Gas chambers and crematoria were developed to kill these Germans and some physicians who presided over their destruction later staffed the Nazi killing centers. Darwinian ethics were taken to the extreme by the Nazis, who believed in survival of the fittest but were unwilling to wait for natural selection. Certain groups were defined as "life unworthy of living."

Roma (Gypsies) were also targeted and killed systematically. Their fate most closely paralleled that of the Jews. They were confined in ghettos such as Lodz and Warsaw. Romani men, women, and children were killed by the Einsatzgruppen and in the gas chambers of Auschwitz-Birkenau.

In the final months of the war, as camps in the east were being overrun, the Nazis instituted a series of forced evacuations by foot and by rail, hasty retreats of concentration camp populations. Few if any provisions were supplied. The marches, known as death marches, took place in the dead of winter, the last-ditch effort to keep the living witnesses from being freed by the Allies. For the victims, the struggle was no longer against the Nazis, but against death itself as they were forced to draw upon reservoirs of strength, pushed beyond the limits of endurance.

I have told the story in a brief outline. Before you are the geographical details—precise, small, anguishing. They tell another part, an essential part of the story. What remains unsaid in these details, and what you must bring to this atlas, is an understanding of the human tale: the anguish of the victims, the courage of the resisters, the morality of the rescuers, and the depravity of the perpetrators.

Michael Berenbaum, Director
United States Holocaust Research Institute

EUROPE BEFORE THE WAR

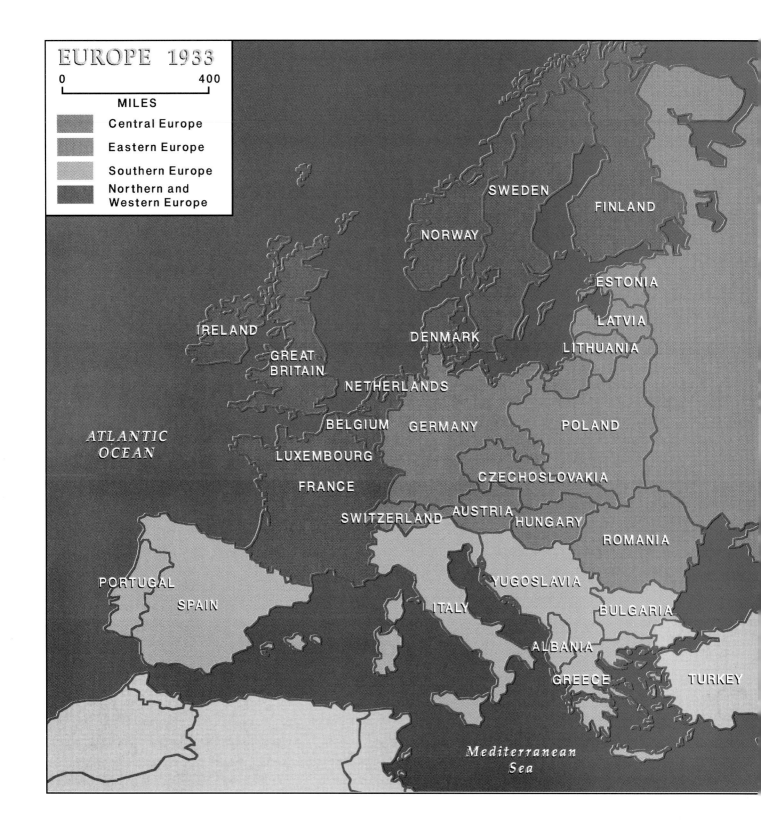

EUROPE 1933

0 _____ 400

MILES

Central Europe

Eastern Europe

Southern Europe

Northern and
Western Europe

SWEDEN

FINLAND

NORWAY

ESTONIA

LATVIA

IRELAND

DENMARK

LITHUANIA

GREAT
BRITAIN

NETHERLANDS

BELGIUM   GERMANY   POLAND

ATLANTIC
OCEAN

LUXEMBOURG

CZECHOSLOVAKIA

FRANCE

SWITZERLAND   AUSTRIA   HUNGARY

ROMANIA

PORTUGAL

YUGOSLAVIA

SPAIN

ITALY   BULGARIA

ALBANIA

GREECE   TURKEY

*Mediterranean
Sea*

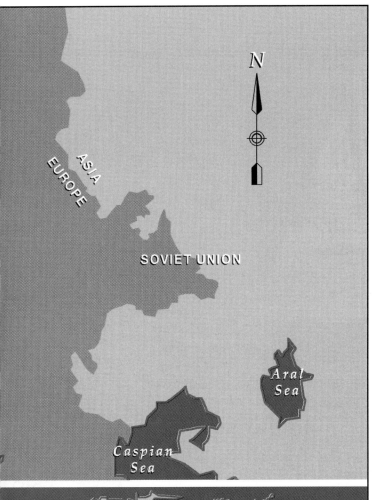

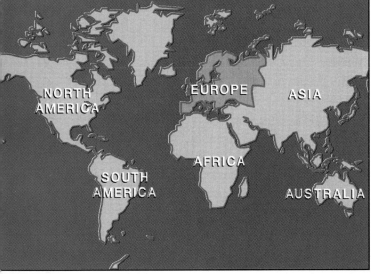

JEWS IN EUROPE BEFORE THE HOLOCAUST

Jews have lived in Europe for more than two thousand years. They trace their origins to the patriarch Abraham, who lived in the Middle Eastern kingdom of Mesopotamia in the seventeenth century B.C.E. Their religion is shaped by the Exodus from bondage in Egypt and the revelation to Moses at Sinai. Jews are monotheists, believing in one God. Their religious beliefs are contained and preserved in the Hebrew Bible.

When the Roman Empire sacked Jerusalem in 70 C.E., Jews were scattered to the far reaches of the empire, from present-day Portugal to Romania. The devastating defeat in Jerusalem and the break between Judaism and Christianity that followed it had a tremendous impact on the history of the Jews in Europe. For centuries, Christianity regarded Judaism and the Jews with hostility. From Augustine in the fifth century to Luther in the sixteenth century, Jews were demonized and lambasted as evil. As Christianity became the dominant religion of Europe, Jews were forced to the margins of society and treated as outsiders, with few civil rights.

Until the French Revolution of 1789, the status of Jews on the Continent remained tenuous. After 1789, France was in the vanguard of the emancipation movement, which gave civic and legal equality to the Jews. Even in France, however, emancipation did not diminish antisemitism. Across Europe, antisemitism took on racial overtones and became a powerful tool to mobilize political support. Jews became the target especially of conservative right-wing parties. Although civil equality for Jews was guaranteed by law by the early twentieth century, European Jewry was still beset by antisemitism and social discrimination.

The *American Jewish Yearbook* placed the total Jewish population of Europe at about 9.5 million in 1933. This number represented more than 60 percent of the world's Jewish population, which was estimated at 15.3 million. Most European Jews resided in eastern Europe. The largest Jewish communities in eastern Europe were in Poland, with about 3,000,000 Jews; the European part of the Soviet Union, with about 2,525,000; Romania, with about 980,000; and the three Baltic states combined, with about 255,000 (about 95,000 in

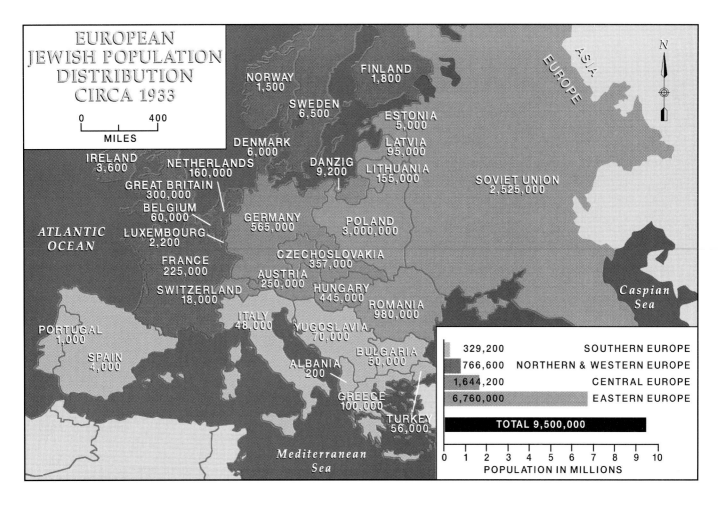

EUROPEAN
JEWISH POPULATION
DISTRIBUTION
CIRCA 1933

0   400
MILES

329,200	SOUTHERN EUROPE
766,600	NORTHERN & WESTERN EUROPE
1,644,200	CENTRAL EUROPE
6,760,000	EASTERN EUROPE
TOTAL 9,500,000	

0 1 2 3 4 5 6 7 8 9 10
POPULATION IN MILLIONS

Latvia, 155,000 in Lithuania, and 5,000 in Estonia).

The largest Jewish community in prewar central Europe was in Germany, with about 565,000 members according to the 1925 census. This was followed by Hungary with about 445,000, Czechoslovakia with about 357,000, and Austria with about 250,000. In western Europe the largest Jewish communities were in Great Britain, with about 300,000 Jews; France, with about 225,000; and the Netherlands, with about 160,000. In southern Europe, Greece had the largest Jewish population, with about 100,000 Jews. There were also significant Jewish communities in Yugoslavia (about 70,000), Bulgaria (about 50,000), and Italy (about 48,000).

Before the Nazi takeover of power in 1933, Europe had a dynamic and highly developed Jewish culture. In little more than a decade, most of Europe would be conquered, occupied, or annexed by Nazi Germany and most European Jews—two out of every three—would be dead. This immense tragedy extinguished a vibrant Jewish culture.

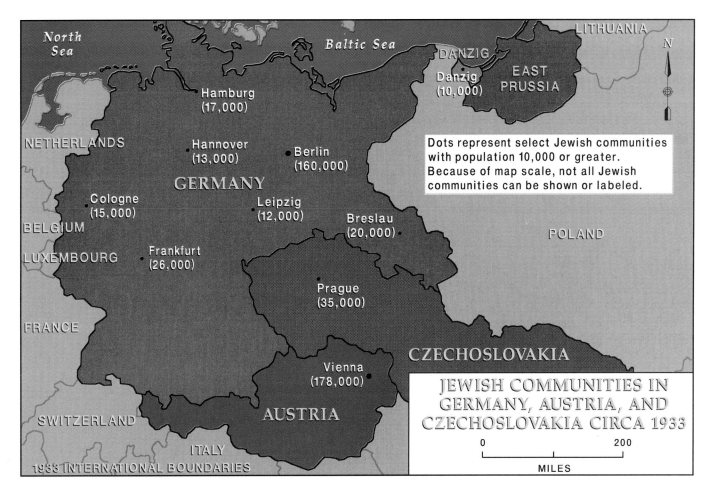

North Sea

Baltic Sea

LITHUANIA

N

DANZIG

Danzig
(10,000)

EAST
PRUSSIA

Hamburg
(17,000)

NETHERLANDS

Hannover
(13,000)

Berlin
(160,000)

Dots represent select Jewish communities
with population 10,000 or greater.
Because of map scale, not all Jewish
communities can be shown or labeled.

GERMANY

Cologne
(15,000)

Leipzig
(12,000)

Breslau
(20,000)

POLAND

BELGIUM

LUXEMBOURG

Frankfurt
(26,000)

FRANCE

Prague
(35,000)

CZECHOSLOVAKIA

Vienna
(178,000)

JEWISH COMMUNITIES IN
GERMANY, AUSTRIA, AND
CZECHOSLOVAKIA CIRCA 1933

SWITZERLAND

AUSTRIA

0   200

ITALY

MILES

1933 INTERNATIONAL BOUNDARIES

JEWISH COMMUNITIES: GERMANY, AUSTRIA, AND CZECHOSLOVAKIA

According to the census of June 16, 1933, the Jewish population of Germany, excluding the Saar region, totaled 499,682 people (a reduction from the 1925 figure due to emigration, especially following the Nazi takeover of power in January 1933). Jews represented about 0.8 percent of the total German population of about 62 million people. Separate figures were compiled for the Saar region, which was under the administration of the League of Nations until 1935. In the Saar region there were about 5,000 Jews as of January 1, 1933, about 0.56 percent of the total population.

Unlike ordinary census-taking methods, the Nazi racist criteria codified in the Nuremberg Laws of 1935 and subsequent ordinances identified Jews according to the religion practiced by an individual's grandparents. Consequently, the Nazis classified as Jews thousands of people who had converted from Judaism to another religion, among them even Roman Catholic priests and nuns and Protestant ministers whose grandparents were Jewish.

Eighty percent of the Jews in Germany (about 400,000

people) held German citizenship. The remainder were mostly Jews of Polish citizenship, many of whom were born in Germany and who had permanent resident status in Germany.

In all, about 70 percent of the Jews in Germany lived in urban areas. Fifty percent of all Jews in Germany lived in the 10 largest German cities. The largest Jewish population centers were in Berlin (about 160,000), Frankfurt am Main (about 26,000), Breslau (about 20,000), Hamburg (about 17,000), Cologne (about 15,000), Hannover (about 13,000), and Leipzig (about 12,000). According to the census of 1929, slightly over 10,000 Jews lived in the Free City of Danzig, representing 2 percent of the population.

According to the census of 1931, Austria had a Jewish population of 250,000, representing almost 4 percent of the total Austrian population of about 6.7 million people. The overwhelming majority of Jews in Austria, some 178,000, lived in the capital city, Vienna. According to the 1930 census, Czechoslovakia had a Jewish population of 357,000, representing about 2 percent of the population. The largest Jewish community in Czechoslovakia was in Prague, the capital city, with 35,000 people.

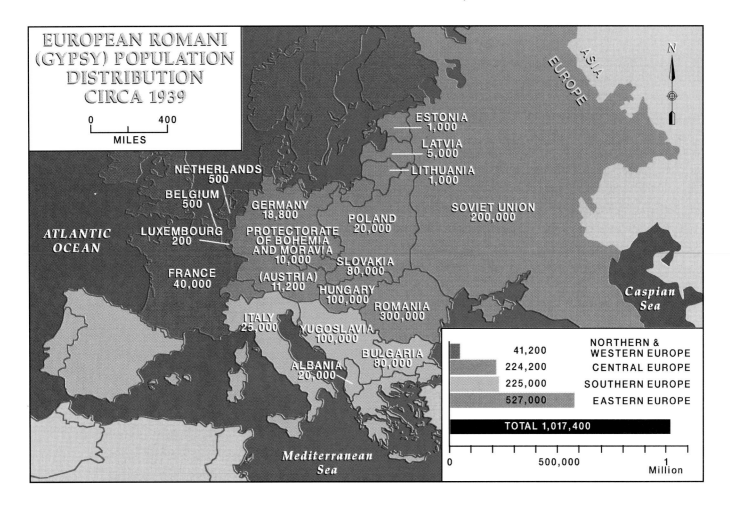

EUROPEAN ROMANI (GYPSY) POPULATION DISTRIBUTION CIRCA 1939

0   400
MILES

NETHERLANDS
500
BELGIUM
500
GERMANY
18,800
LUXEMBOURG
200
PROTECTORATE
OF BOHEMIA
AND MORAVIA
10,000
POLAND
20,000
SOVIET UNION
200,000
SLOVAKIA
80,000
ATLANTIC
OCEAN
FRANCE
40,000
(AUSTRIA)
11,200
HUNGARY
100,000
ROMANIA
300,000
ITALY
25,000
YUGOSLAVIA
100,000
BULGARIA
80,000
ALBANIA
20,000
ESTONIA
1,000
LATVIA
5,000
LITHUANIA
1,000
Caspian
Sea
Mediterranean
Sea

41,200	NORTHERN & WESTERN EUROPE	
224,200	CENTRAL EUROPE	
225,000	SOUTHERN EUROPE	
527,000	EASTERN EUROPE	
TOTAL 1,017,400		

0   500,000   1 Million

ROMANI (GYPSY) COMMUNITIES IN 1939

Roma (Gypsies) originated in India as a nomadic people and entered Europe between the eighth and tenth centuries C.E. In 1939, about a million Roma lived in Europe. Most European Roma lived in Romania (about 300,000), the Soviet Union (about 200,000), Hungary (about 100,000), and Yugoslavia (about 100,000). In southern Europe, approximately 20,000 Roma lived in Albania, 25,000 in Italy, and 80,000 in Bulgaria. About 90,000 alone lived in the Bohemian, Moravian, and Slovakian regions of Czechoslovakia. In Greater Germany there were about 30,000 Roma, most of whom held German citizenship; about 11,200 of this number lived in Austria. Relatively few Roma lived in western Europe: some 40,000 lived in France, 500 in Belgium, and 500 in the Netherlands.

Persecution of Roma in Germany, and indeed in all of Europe, preceded the Nazi takeover of power in 1933. As early as 1926, Roma were required to register with the police in Bavaria, Germany, and a commission to coordinate police action against Roma was established in Munich. In 1933, police in Germany began more rigorous enforcement of pre-Nazi legislation against those who followed a lifestyle labeled "Gypsy." The Nazis judged such people to be racially "undesirable" and, after Adolf Hitler's seizure of power, subjected them to most of the racial laws and persecutions. Throughout most of German-occupied Europe, Roma were interned, deported to concentration and extermination camps, and killed. In this way, the experience of Roma closely paralleled that of the Jews. While exact figures or percentages cannot be ascertained, historians estimate that the Germans and their allies killed between 25 and 50 percent of all European Roma.

GERMAN TERRITORIAL LOSSES
VERSAILLES TREATY 1919

0   100
MILES

GERMAN EXPANSION WITHOUT WAR
1933-1939

Territorial Losses Under the Versailles Treaty

In the 1919 Treaty of Versailles, the victorious powers of World War I (the United States, Great Britain, France, and other allied states) imposed punitive territorial, military, and economic treaty terms on defeated Germany. German representatives were not permitted to participate in the treaty negotiations and the terms were non-negotiable. Under protest and the threat of invasion, Germany signed the Treaty of Versailles on June 28, 1919.

The terms of the treaty required Germany to make territorial concessions, to pay reparations, and to restrict its military forces and installations. Under the territorial provisions of the treaty, Germany's national boundaries were reduced. In the west, Germany returned Alsace-Lorraine to France (Germany had annexed Alsace-Lorraine after the Franco-Prussian War of 1870-1871); Belgium received Eupen and Malmedy; the Saar region was placed under the administration of the League of Nations for 15 years; and Denmark received Northern Schleswig. In the east, the partitions of Poland during the eighteenth century were reversed. Poland,

restored, received parts of West Prussia and Silesia from Germany. In addition, Czechoslovakia received the Hultschin district from Germany; the largely German city of Danzig became a free city under the protection of the League of Nations; and Memel, a small strip of territory in East Prussia along the Baltic Sea, was ultimately placed under Lithuanian control. Outside Europe, Germany lost all its colonies. In sum, Germany forfeited 13 percent of its European territory (more than 27,000 square miles) and one-tenth of its population (between 6.5 and 7 million people).

Among the military provisions of the treaty were the demilitarization of the Rhineland, strict limits on the size and composition of Germany's armed forces (100,000 men, no aircraft, tanks, or submarines), and the prohibition of military conscription. Financially, Germany was to make reparations for war damages and payments to surviving relatives of those killed in World War I.

The Treaty of Versailles took effect on January 10, 1920, and many Germans viewed the treaty as a "victors' peace." Demands for its repudiation became a central theme among radical right-wing parties, such as the Nazi party, which blamed democratic parties for accepting the terms of the treaty.

REMILITARIZATION
OF THE RHINELAND
AND "ANSCHLUSS" WITH
AUSTRIA 1936–1938

0   150
MILES

German Military Movement

Austria "Anschluss" 1938

Demilitarized Zone 1919

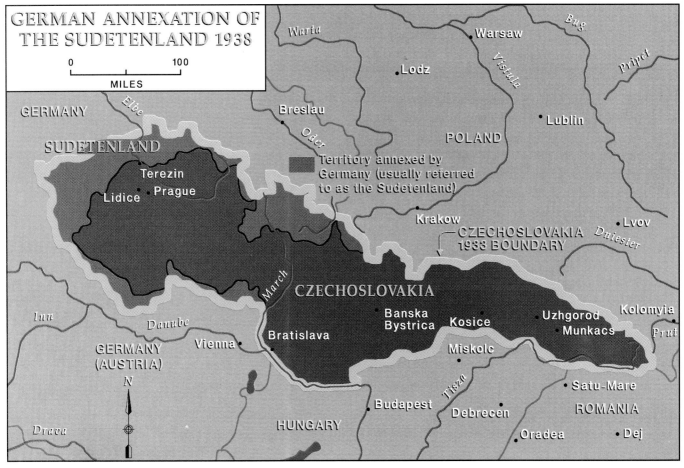

GERMAN ANNEXATION OF
THE SUDETENLAND 1938

0   100
MILES

Territory annexed by
Germany (usually referred
to as the Sudetenland)

CZECHOSLOVAKIA
1933 BOUNDARY

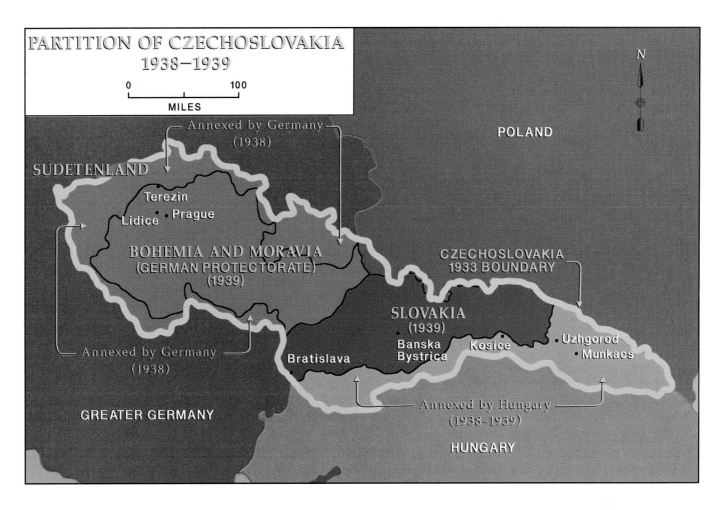

PARTITION OF CZECHOSLOVAKIA
1938–1939

0   100
MILES

POLAND

SUDETENLAND

Annexed by Germany
(1938)

Terezin
Lidice   •Prague

BOHEMIA AND MORAVIA
(GERMAN PROTECTORATE)
(1939)

CZECHOSLOVAKIA
1933 BOUNDARY

SLOVAKIA
(1939)
Banska   Kosice   •Uzhgorod
Bystrica   •Munkacs

Annexed by Germany
(1938)

Bratislava

GREATER GERMANY

Annexed by Hungary
(1938–1939)

HUNGARY

Remilitarization of the Rhineland and the "Anschluss"

At the Lausanne Conference of 1932, Germany, Britain, and France agreed to the formal suspension of reparations. Thus, when Adolf Hitler became chancellor of Germany in January 1933, the financial provisions of the Treaty of Versailles had already been revised. Hitler was determined to overturn the remaining military and territorial provisions of the Versailles treaty and include ethnic Germans in the Reich as a preliminary step toward the restoration of German power and the creation of a German empire in Europe.

The German armed forces engaged in secret rearmament even before the Nazi takeover of power. Thereafter, the Nazis supported rearmament and rapidly expanded arms production. Military conscription was introduced on March 16, 1935, in open violation of the Treaty of Versailles. At the same time, Hitler announced the expansion of the German army to more than 500,000 men.

In 1935, a plebiscite was held in the Saar region to determine the region's future sovereignty. The overwhelming-ly German population voted decisively for the return of the area to German rule.

In the 1925 Treaty of Locarno, Germany had recognized both the inviolability of its borders with France and Belgium and the demilitarization of the Rhineland. On March 7, 1936, however, Hitler repudiated the Treaty of Locarno and ordered the German armed forces (Wehrmacht) into the demilitarized Rhineland. Hitler's action brought condemnation from Britain and France, but neither nation intervened against this flagrant violation of the treaties of Locarno and Versailles.

After a prolonged period of intense propaganda inside Austria, German troops entered the country on March 12, 1938, receiving the enthusiastic support of most of the population. Austria was incorporated into Germany on the following day. In April, this German annexation was retroac-tively approved in a plebiscite that was manipulated to indicate that about 99 percent of the Austrian people wanted the union (known as the "Anschluss") with Germany. Neither Jews nor Roma (Gypsies) were permitted to vote in the plebiscite.

GERMAN TERRITORIAL GAINS
BEFORE THE WAR
AUGUST 1939

0   150
MILES

Munich Agreement and Partition of Czechoslovakia

In 1938, Hitler threatened to unleash a European war unless the Sudetenland, a border area of Czechoslovakia containing an ethnic German majority, was surrendered to Germany. The leaders of Britain, France, Italy, and Germany held a conference in Munich, Germany, on September 29-30, 1938, in which they agreed to the German annexation of the Sudetenland in exchange for a pledge of peace from Hitler. Czechoslovakia, which was not a party to the Munich negotiations, had little choice but to agree.

On March 15, 1939, Hitler violated the Munich agreement and moved against the Czechoslovak state. The Czech provinces of Bohemia and Moravia became a German protectorate and were occupied by German forces. Slovakia became

an independent state, closely allied with Germany. Germany's ally, Hungary, annexed the Transcarpathian Ukraine and strips of territory in southern Slovakia. Czechoslovakia ceased to exist as an independent nation.

Little more than a week later, on March 23, 1939, German troops suddenly occupied Memel. Lithuania was unable to prevent this occupation. Hitler also raised territorial demands on Poland in the spring of 1939. He demanded the annexation of the Free City of Danzig to Germany and extraterritorial access for Germany across the Polish frontier to East Prussia.

Convinced that Hitler could not be trusted to negotiate in good faith, Britain and France guaranteed the integrity of Polish territory against German aggression. Europe was on the brink of war.

Solid squares represent select camps. Because of map scale, not all camps can be shown or labeled.

NAZI CONCENTRATION CAMPS 1933–1934

CONCENTRATION CAMP SYSTEM 1933-1939

The term "concentration camp" refers to a camp in which people are detained or confined, usually under harsh conditions and without regard to due process and the legal norms of arrest and imprisonment. Concentration camps (Konzentrationslager; KL) were an integral feature of the Nazi regime between 1933 and 1945.

The first concentration camps in Germany were established soon after Hitler's appointment as chancellor in January 1933. The SA (Storm Troopers) and the police established concentration camps beginning in February 1933. These camps were set up on an ad hoc basis to handle the masses of people arrested as alleged political opponents of the regime and were established on the local level throughout Germany. For example, camps were located in Oranienburg, north of Berlin; Esterwegen, near Hamburg; Dachau, north of Munich; and Lichtenburg, in Saxony. Columbia Haus in Berlin was used for certain prisoners under investigation by the Gestapo (the German secret state police) and operated until 1936. Gradually, most of these early camps were disbanded and replaced by centrally organized concentration camps under the exclusive jurisdiction of the SS (Schutzstaffel; the elite guard of the Nazi state).

Dachau, the only concentration camp opened in 1933 that remained in operation until 1945, was the model for the Nazi concentration camp system that replaced the earlier camps. The daily routine at Dachau, the methods of punishment, and the duties of the SS guards became the norm, with some variation, at all German concentration camps.

By 1939, seven large concentration camps had been established. Besides Dachau, they were Sachsenhausen (1936), Buchenwald (1937), Neuengamme (1938), Flossenbuerg (1938), Mauthausen (1938), and Ravensbrueck (1939). As production in war industries intensified, Germany increased the exploitation of concentration camp prisoners for forced labor. After 1939, with new territorial conquests and larger groups of potential prisoners, the concentration camp system expanded rapidly.

CLASSIFICATION SYSTEM IN NAZI CONCENTRATION CAMPS

The Nazis victimized many groups. Among the first victims of persecution in Nazi Germany were political opponents—primarily Communists, Social Democrats, and trade unionists. Jehovah's Witnesses refused to serve in the

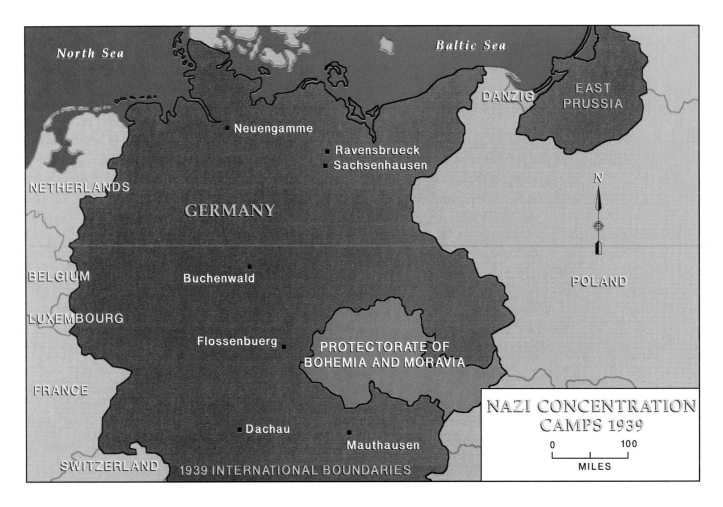

NAZI CONCENTRATION CAMPS 1939

0   100
MILES

German army or salute Adolf Hitler and consequently were targeted for persecution. The Nazis also persecuted German male homosexuals, whose sexual orientation was considered a hindrance to the preservation of the German nation. "Chronic" homosexuals were deported to jails and prisons; some were later remanded to the camps.

The Nazis persecuted those they considered to be racially inferior. Nazi racial ideology vilified above all Jews, but also propagated hatred for Roma (Gypsies) and blacks. The Nazis viewed Jews as racial enemies and consequently many were arbitrarily arrested and interned. Roma were also singled out on racial grounds for persecution. The Nazis viewed Poles and other Slavs as inferior, and slated them for subjugation and forced labor.

Jewish prisoners were singled out for the most brutal treatment in Nazi concentration camps. From 1938, Jews in the camps were identified by one yellow triangle placed over another, in the shape of a star, sewn onto their prison uniforms. After 1939 and with some variation from camp to camp, the categories of prisoners were easily identified by a marking system combining a colored inverted triangle with letters. The badges sewn onto prisoner uniforms enabled SS guards to readily identify the alleged grounds for incarceration.

Criminals were marked with green inverted triangles, political prisoners with red, asocials (including Roma, nonconformists, vagrants, and some other groups) with black or—in the case of Roma in some camps—brown triangles. Homosexuals were identified with pink triangles and Jehovah's Witnesses with purple ones. Non-German prisoners were identified by the first letter of the German name for their home country, which was sewn onto their badge. The two triangles forming the Jewish badge would both be yellow unless the Jewish prisoner was included in one of the other prisoner categories. A Jewish political prisoner, for example, would be identified with a yellow triangle beneath a red triangle. Further, the Nazis required Jews to wear yellow badges not only in the camps, but throughout most of occupied Europe.

IDENTIFICATION PATCHES AND CAMP BADGES

IDENTIFICATION PATCHES

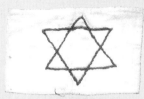

Armband, Generalgouvernement

Bulgaria (button)

Hungary

The Netherlands

Czechoslovakia

France

Polish ID
in the German Reich

CAMP BADGES

German
(Security Risk)

Italian

SYMBOL KEY

Jehovah's Witness

Homosexuals

Criminals

Jews

Gypsies and "Asocials"

Political Prisoners

Czech

Hungarian

Monowitz,
Poland

Belgian
Homosexual

French

Prisoner Number
Ravensbrueck, Germany

Prisoner Number
Sachsenhausen, Germany

Armband, Labor Subcamp
Malchow, Germany

Identification Tag
Radom, Poland

Not Actual Size

Photography by Arnold Kramer

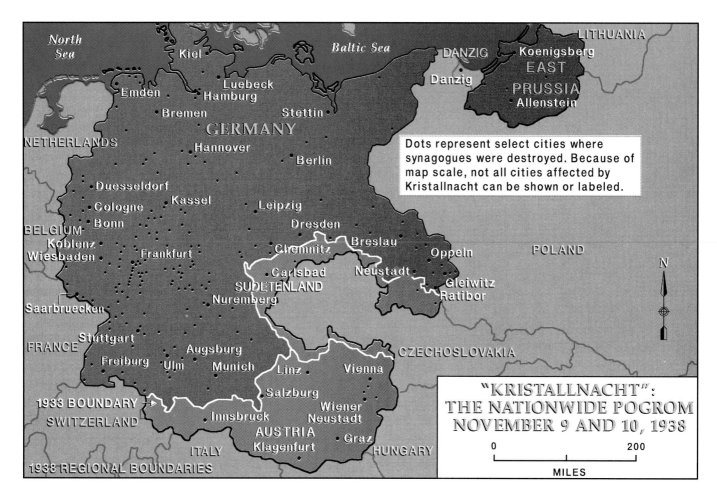

Dots represent select cities where synagogues were destroyed. Because of map scale, not all cities affected by Kristallnacht can be shown or labeled.

"KRISTALLNACHT":
THE NATIONWIDE POGROM
NOVEMBER 9 AND 10, 1938

0   200

MILES

"KRISTALLNACHT": THE NATIONWIDE POGROM OF NOVEMBER 9 AND 10, 1938

"Kristallnacht"—literally, "Crystal Night"—is usually translated from German as the "Night of Broken Glass"; it refers to the violent anti-Jewish pogrom of November 9 and 10, 1938. The pogrom occurred throughout Germany, which by then included both Austria and the Sudetenland region of Czechoslovakia. The name "Kristallnacht" referred to the broken windows of synagogues, Jewish-owned stores, communal centers, and homes plundered during the pogrom. Although frequently used, the term has come to be regarded as a euphemistic way to refer to this brutal pogrom.

The Germans officially presented "Kristallnacht" as a spontaneous outburst of public rage in response to the assassination of Ernst vom Rath, third secretary at the German embassy in Paris. A young Polish Jew named Herschel Grynszpan shot vom Rath on November 7, 1938. Grynszpan was apparently motivated by the plight of his parents who, like tens of thousands of Jews of Polish citizenship living in Germany, had been expelled from Germany but denied entry into their native Poland. Grynszpan's parents, and thousands of expelled Polish Jews, were stranded in a refugee camp near

the town of Zbaszyn in the border region between Poland and Germany. Grynszpan knew of his parents' plight through a letter he received from them.

Vom Rath died on November 9, 1938, two days after he was shot. As reprisal for vom Rath's death, the Nazis organized a massive pogrom against Jews throughout Germany. The pogrom was conducted primarily by the SA.

Hundreds of synagogues all over Germany, including Austria and the Sudetenland, were attacked, vandalized, looted, and destroyed. Many were set ablaze. Firemen were instructed to let the synagogues burn but to prevent the flames from spreading to nearby structures. The shop windows of thousands of Jewish-owned stores were smashed and the wares within looted. Jewish cemeteries were desecrated. Many Jews were attacked by mobs of SA men.

While not directly involved in the pogrom, the SS and the Gestapo used it as a pretext for the arrest of about 30,000 Jews, who were sent to the Dachau, Buchenwald, and Sachsenhausen concentration camps. Most of these Jews were treated brutally but released after a few weeks, on the condition that they were to begin the process of emigration from Germany.

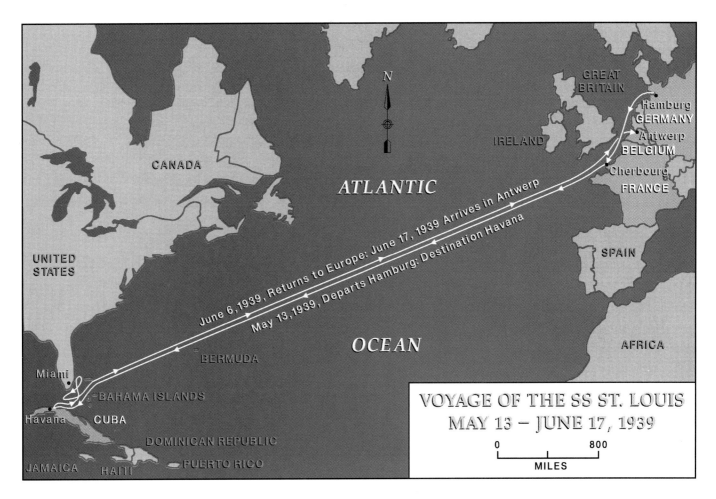

VOYAGE OF THE SS ST. LOUIS
MAY 13 – JUNE 17, 1939

0 — 800 MILES

The Nazis immediately claimed that the Jews were to blame for the pogrom and imposed a fine of one billion Reichsmarks (some 400 million U.S. dollars at 1938 rates) on the Jewish community of Germany. The state confiscated all the insurance payments that were to have been paid out to Jewish store owners as compensation for the damage. Jewish store owners were thus made responsible for the cost of all repairs to their businesses.

The November pogrom heralded a new wave of anti-Jewish legislation designed to further restrict Jewish life in Germany, to force the "Aryanization" (transfer to non-Jewish ownership) of Jewish-owned property, and to encourage Jewish emigration from Germany. Such measures demonstrated the uncertain fate confronting Jews in Germany.

JEWISH EMIGRATION FROM GERMANY
1933-1939

Between 1933 and 1939, Jews in Germany were subjected to arrest, economic boycott, the loss of civil rights and citizenship, incarceration in concentration camps, random violence, and the state-organized "Kristallnacht" ("Night of Broken Glass") pogrom. Jews reacted to Nazi persecution in a

number of ways. Forcibly segregated from German society, German Jews turned to and expanded their own institutions and social organizations. However, in the face of increasing repression and physical violence, many Jews fled Germany. At first, the German government encouraged Jews to emigrate and placed few restrictions on what possessions they could take. Gradually, however, the Nazis sought to deprive Jews fleeing Germany of their property by levying an increasingly heavy emigration tax and by restricting the amount of money that could be transferred abroad from German banks.

There were three major phases of Jewish emigration from Germany between 1933 and 1939. All were in reaction to heightened anti-Jewish violence and increasing legal restrictions on Jews in Germany. The first phase, in 1933, was in reaction to violent attacks on Jews during the jubilation over the Nazi takeover of power. Those Jews who were politically active fled quickly to adjacent European countries. Other measures that spurred decisions to emigrate at this time were the dismissal of Jews from the civil service and the Nazi-sponsored boycott of Jewish-owned stores. The second phase was in reaction to the Nuremberg Laws of September 1935 and subsequent related ordinances that deprived Jews of

German civil rights and prohibited marriage or sexual relations between German non-Jews and Jews. In the third phase, Jewish emigration increased dramatically in response to the German annexation of Austria and "Kristallnacht." After "Kristallnacht," the German state moved to confiscate Jewish-owned property and exclude Jews from the German economy. Many Jews decided that there was no longer a future for them in Germany and resolved to leave. Emigration was at that point the official Nazi policy regarding Jews in the attempt to render Germany "free of Jews" (judenrein).

According to the *American Jewish Yearbook*, about 432,000 Jews emigrated from Germany between 1933 and 1940. This figure includes Jews from Germany (282,000) and from countries and regions annexed by Germany before the

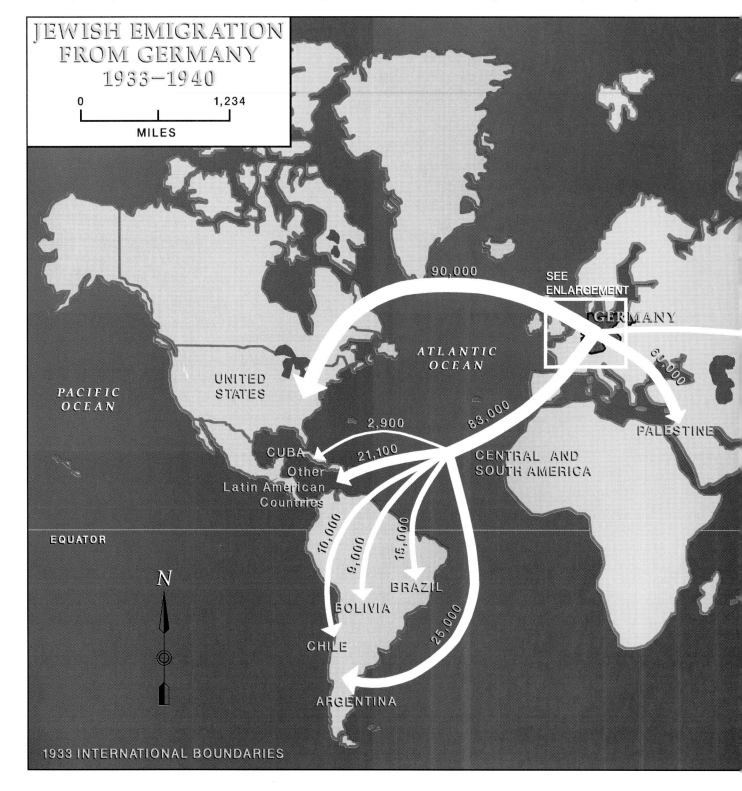

JEWISH EMIGRATION FROM GERMANY 1933–1940

0   1,234
MILES

90,000

SEE ENLARGEMENT

GERMANY

60,000

PACIFIC OCEAN

UNITED STATES

ATLANTIC OCEAN

PALESTINE

2,900   83,000

CUBA
Other Latin American Countries

21,100

CENTRAL AND SOUTH AMERICA

EQUATOR

10,000   9,000   15,000

BRAZIL

N

BOLIVIA

25,000

CHILE

ARGENTINA

1933 INTERNATIONAL BOUNDARIES

war (for example, 117,000 from Austria). Both individuals and entire families became refugees. More than 100,000 German-Jewish emigres traveled to western European countries, especially France, Belgium, and the Netherlands. Some 8,000 entered Switzerland and about 48,000 went to Great Britain and other European countries. About 90,000 German-Jewish refugees were able to emigrate to the United

States and 60,000 to Palestine, which was then under British mandate. About 83,000 German-Jewish refugees emigrated to Central and South America, with the largest numbers entering Argentina (25,000), Brazil (15,000), Chile (10,000), and Bolivia (9,000). Between 15,000 and 18,000 people were able to find refuge in Shanghai, China. Tens of thousands of German-Jewish refugees entered other countries. More Jews would have left Germany had such countries as the United States and Britain been more willing to admit them.

The Evian Conference on the question of Jewish refugees took place in Evian, France, in July 1938. Delegates from 32 countries, including the United States, Great Britain, France, Canada, and Australia, announced their countries' refusal to accept additional Jewish refugees. The plight of German-Jewish refugees, persecuted at home and unwanted abroad, is illustrated by the voyage of the *St. Louis*.

On May 13, 1939, the SS *St. Louis*, a German passenger ship, left Germany with almost a thousand Jewish refugees on board. The refugees' destination was Cuba, but before their arrival the Cuban government revoked their permission to land. The United States also refused the refugees permission to land. The *St. Louis* was forced to return to Europe in June 1939. During the return voyage, Great Britain, France, Belgium, and the Netherlands agreed to accept the stranded refugees, thanks to the efforts of the American Jewish Joint Distribution Committee. After German forces occupied the Netherlands, Belgium, and France in 1940, many *St. Louis* passengers and other Jewish refugees who had entered those countries were caught up in the "Final Solution," the Nazi plan to murder the Jews of Europe.

"EUTHANASIA" PROGRAM

The term "euthanasia" usually refers to the inducement of a painless death for a chronically or terminally ill individual. In Nazi usage, however, "euthanasia" referred to the systematic killing of those Germans whom the Nazis deemed "unworthy of life" because of alleged genetic diseases or defects. Hitler ordered the establishment of the "Euthanasia" Program in October 1939, but backdated the order to September 1, 1939, the first day of World War II. The secret operation was code-named T4, in reference to the street address (Tiergartenstrasse 4) of the program's coordinating office in Berlin. Six gassing installations were eventually established as part of the "Euthanasia" Program: Bernburg, Brandenburg, Grafeneck, Hadamar, Hartheim, and Sonnenstein.

The victims of the "Euthanasia" Program included the mentally retarded, the mentally ill, the physically handicapped,

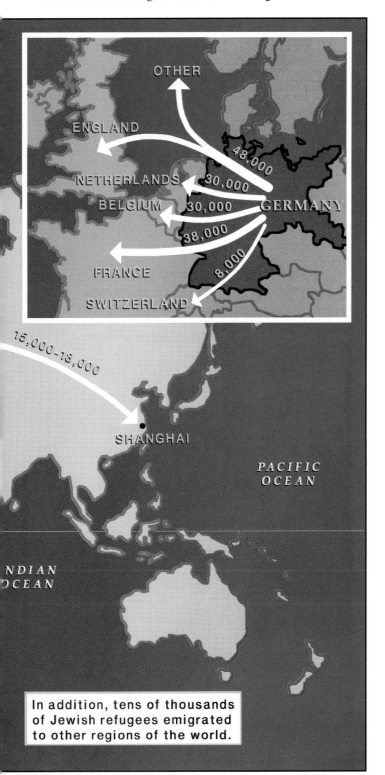

In addition, tens of thousands of Jewish refugees emigrated to other regions of the world.

chronically ill or deformed children, and the elderly residents of nursing homes. Patients were selected by their doctors for death. Doctors did not examine the patients in this process, but based their decisions on medical files. Those selected for "euthanasia" were transported by health-care workers to the sanitoria that served as central gassing installations. The victims were told they would undergo a physical evaluation and take a disinfecting shower. Instead, they were killed in gas chambers using carbon monoxide gas. Their bodies were immediately cremated and their ashes placed in urns without regard for accurately labeling the urns. One such urn was sent to each victim's family, together with a death certificate listing a false cause of death. The sudden death of thousands of chronically ill and institutionalized people, with death certificates listing strangely similar causes and places of death, raised suspicions. Eventually, word of the program leaked out and protest ensued.

Hitler ordered the "Euthanasia" Program officially disbanded in late August 1941, in light of mounting criticism from the German public, especially from members of the German Catholic clergy. However, this did not mean an end to the "euthanasia" killing operation, which was continued secretly. Victims were no longer murdered in centrally located gassing institutions. Instead, doctors administered lethal injections to those selected for "euthanasia" in clinics and hospitals throughout Germany. In this way, the "Euthanasia" Program continued and expanded until the end of the war.

During the initial phase of operations, from 1939 until 1941, about 70,000 people were killed under the "Euthanasia" Program. At the proceedings of the International Military Tribunal in Nuremberg (1945-1946), it was estimated that the total number of "euthanasia" victims was 275,000 people.

The "Euthanasia" Program instituted the use of gas chambers and crematoria for systematic murder. The experts who participated in the "Euthanasia" Program were instrumental in establishing and operating the killing centers later used to implement the "Final Solution."

THE HOLOCAUST IN EASTERN EUROPE

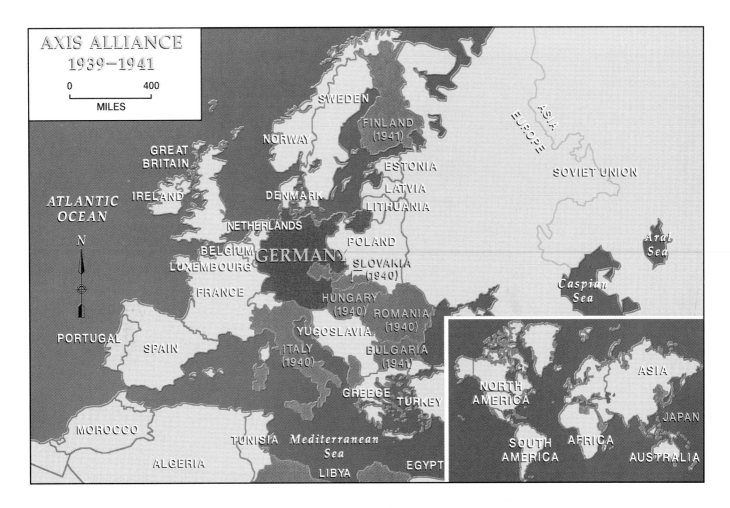

AXIS ALLIANCE
1939–1941

0   400
MILES

THE AXIS ALLIANCE IN WORLD WAR II

World War II, which involved most of the world's nations, was fought chiefly between two major alliances: the Axis and the Allies. The Tripartite Pact of September 27, 1940, allied Germany, Italy, and Japan and became known as the Berlin-Rome-Tokyo Axis, or Axis alliance. These three countries recognized German hegemony over most of continental Europe; Italian hegemony over the Mediterranean; and Japanese hegemony over East Asia.

During World War II, the Axis alliance came to include Slovakia (November 1940), Hungary (November 1940), Romania (November 1940), and Bulgaria (March 1941). Finland also fought with Germany against the Soviet Union but did not sign the Tripartite Pact and was not technically part of the Axis alliance. Yugoslavia joined the Axis alliance on March 25, 1941, but withdrew two days later after an anti-German coup. After Germany and its allies invaded and partitioned Yugoslavia, the newly established fascist satellite state of Croatia joined the Axis on June 15, 1941. Although an anti-democratic state sympathetic to the Axis, Spain refused either to join the Axis alliance or to enter the war with the Allies.

World War II began in Europe with the German invasion of Poland on September 1, 1939. In response, Great Britain and France, which had agreed to defend Poland in case of attack, declared war on Germany on September 3. Italy entered the war on June 10, 1940. Japan, at war in Asia since the 1930s, expanded the conflict with a surprise attack on the American fleet on December 7, 1941, at Pearl Harbor in Hawaii.

The Axis alliance was ultimately defeated. Italy signed an armistice with the Allies in September 1943. Germany surrendered unconditionally to the Allies in May 1945, as did Japan in September 1945.

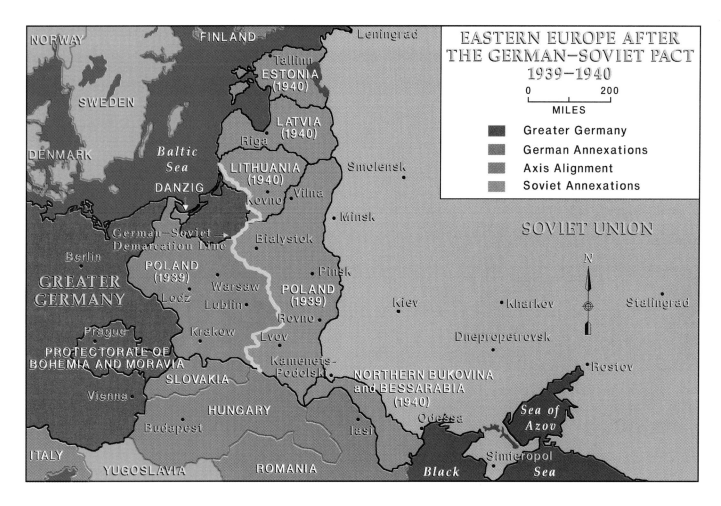

THE GERMAN-SOVIET PACT

The German-Soviet Pact, also known as the Ribbentrop-Molotov Pact after the two foreign ministers who negotiated the treaty, was a two-part agreement between the Soviet Union and Germany. It consisted of an economic agreement, signed on August 19, 1939, whereby Germany exchanged manufactured goods for Soviet raw materials, and a nonaggression pact, signed on August 23, 1939, whereby the signatories promised not to attack one another for 10 years.

The German-Soviet Pact enabled Germany to attack Poland, whose borders had been guaranteed by Britain and France, without fear of Soviet intervention, on September 1, 1939. Britain and France declared war on Germany on September 3, 1939.

The nonaggression pact included a secret protocol that divided Poland and the rest of eastern Europe into Soviet and German spheres of interest. The Soviet army moved into eastern Poland on September 17, 1939. In 1940, while Germany was preoccupied with the war against Britain and France, the Soviet Union also moved to secure its sphere of interest in eastern Europe, occupying the Baltic states, northern Bukovina, and Bessarabia. In the war (1939-1940) with Finland, the Soviet Union annexed large tracts of Finnish territory north of Leningrad.

After the French armistice in June 1940, Germany moved to secure its position in eastern Europe. Hungary, Romania, and Slovakia all joined the Axis in November 1940.

Hitler regarded the German-Soviet Pact as temporary. On December 18, 1940, he issued Directive 21 (code-named Operation Barbarossa), in which he ordered the German army to draft detailed plans for an attack on the Soviet Union. German forces invaded the Soviet Union on June 22, 1941, less than two years after the German-Soviet Pact had been signed.

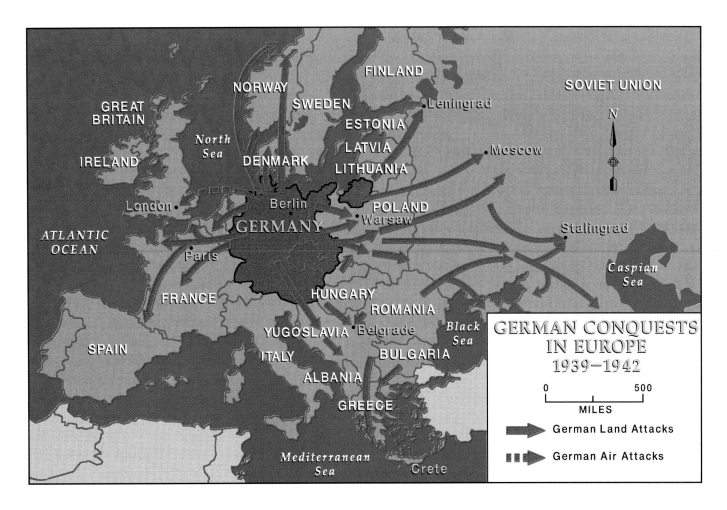

GERMAN CONQUESTS
IN EUROPE
1939-1942

0   500
MILES

→ German Land Attacks

▪▪▶ German Air Attacks

GERMAN CONQUESTS IN EUROPE 1939-1942

In the first phase of World War II in Europe, Germany sought to avoid a long war and defeat its opponents in a series of short campaigns. Germany quickly overran much of Europe and was victorious for more than two years by relying on a new military tactic called the "Blitzkrieg" (lightning war). Blitzkrieg tactics required the concentration of offensive weapons (such as tanks, planes, and artillery) along a narrow front. These forces would drive a breach in enemy defenses, permitting armored tank divisions to penetrate rapidly and roam freely behind enemy lines, causing shock and disorganization among the enemy defenses. German air power prevented the enemy from adequately resupplying or redeploying forces and from sending reinforcements to seal breaches in the front. German forces could then encircle opposing troops and force them to surrender.

Germany successfully used the Blitzkrieg tactic against Poland (attacked in September 1939), Denmark (April 1940), Norway (April 1940), Belgium (May 1940), the Netherlands (May 1940), Luxembourg (May 1940), France (May 1940), Yugoslavia (April 1941), and Greece (April 1941). Germany seemed invincible. Yet Germany did not defeat Great Britain, which was protected from German ground attack by the English Channel and the Royal Navy.

Despite the continuing war with Great Britain, German forces suddenly invaded the Soviet Union in June 1941. The German Blitzkrieg seemed at first to succeed. Soviet forces were either destroyed or driven back more than 600 miles to the gates of Moscow. In December 1941, Hitler unilaterally declared war on the United States, which consequently added its tremendous economic and military power to the coalition arrayed against him. A second German offensive in 1942 brought German forces in the east to the shores of the Volga River and the city of Stalingrad. But Germany proved unable to defeat the Soviet Union, which together with Great Britain and the United States seized the initiative from Germany. Germany became embroiled in a long war, leading ultimately to its defeat in May 1945.

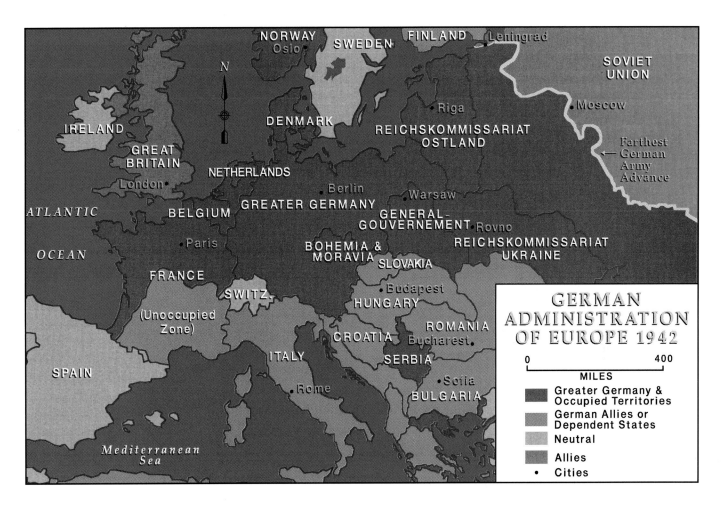

GERMAN ADMINISTRATION OF EUROPE

In 1942, Germany dominated most of Europe. Greater Germany was enlarged by the seizure of Austria and Luxembourg and territories from Czechoslovakia (the Protectorate of Bohemia and Moravia and the Sudetenland), Poland, France, Belgium, and the Baltic states. German military forces occupied Norway, Denmark, Belgium, northern France, Serbia, parts of northern Greece, and vast tracts of territory in eastern Europe. Italy, Hungary, Romania, Bulgaria, Slovakia, Finland, Croatia, and Vichy France were all either allied to Germany or subject to heavy German influence. German-occupied northern and western Europe had German military governors, as did the area immediately behind the front in eastern Europe. Between 1942 and 1944, German military forces extended the area under their occupation to southern France, central and northern Italy, Slovakia, and Hungary.

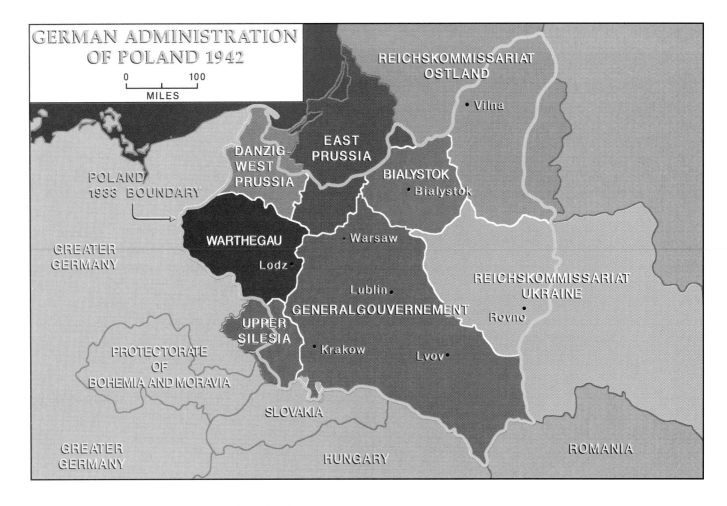

GERMAN ADMINISTRATION
OF POLAND 1942

0   100
MILES

GERMAN ADMINISTRATION OF POLAND

In October 1939, Germany annexed most of western Poland. The area around the city of Lodz became a new German province, the Warthegau. Northwestern Polish territory was incorporated into the German provinces of Danzig, West Prussia, and East Prussia. Eastern Upper Silesia, a small area of southwestern Poland, was incorporated into the German province of Upper Silesia. Central and southern Poland were organized into the Generalgouvernement (General Government) of Poland, which was established in October 1939. The full official German designation was the "General Government for the Occupied Areas of Poland" (Generalgouvernement fuer die besetzten polnischen Gebiete).

After the invasion of the Soviet Union in 1941, Germany also took over eastern Poland, which had been occupied—in accordance with the German-Soviet Pact—by the Soviet Union since 1939. The region around the city of Bialystok became a separate administrative district under German civilian control. Southeastern Poland, the region around Lvov,

was added to the Generalgouvernement, which then had a population of more than 12 million. East-central Poland became part of the German administration of the Ukraine, while northeastern Poland became part of the Reich Commissariat Ostland.

The German administrator of the Generalgouvernement was the Nazi lawyer Hans Frank, whose headquarters in Krakow became the Generalgouvernement's capital. German rule in the Generalgouvernement was extremely harsh. German authorities regarded the Polish population as a supply of forced laborers. A campaign of terror was directed against members of the Polish intelligentsia, many of whom were killed or sent to the camps. Polish teachers, priests, and cultural figures, who would form the core of the resistance movement, were especially targeted for persecution. The Germans destroyed Polish cultural and scientific institutions and plundered national treasures. Poles were supplied only with starvation rations, as the bulk of the country's food was confiscated by the Germans for their home front.

GERMAN
ADMINISTRATION OF
EASTERN EUROPE 1942

GERMAN ADMINISTRATION OF THE OCCUPIED EASTERN TERRITORIES

The German administration of the rest of the occupied east included both military and civilian governments. The areas immediately behind the front remained under German military authority. Territories conquered in the initial German attack were transferred to civilian administration. The Germans established a Ministry for the Occupied Eastern Territories (Reichsministerium fuer die besetzten Ostgebiete) under Alfred Rosenberg, responsible for administering territories under civilian authority. The eastern occupied territories were divided into two commissariats: the Reich Commissariat Ostland (Reichskommissariat Ostland) and the Reich Commissariat for the Ukraine (Reichskommissariat Ukraine).

The Reich Commissariat Ostland included Lithuania, Latvia, Estonia, most of Belorussia, and part of northeastern Poland. Hinrich Lohse was assigned to head Ostland, and established his office in Riga, the capital. The Reich Commissariat for the Ukraine was headed by Erich Koch, the district leader of the Nazi party in East Prussia, with Rovno as the capital. The Reich Commissariat for the Ukraine included part of eastern Poland and most of the Ukrainian SSR, as far east as the area around the cities of Kiev and Dnepropetrovsk.

Germany planned to annex most of the conquered eastern territories after they had been Germanized. Some areas were to serve as reservations for forced laborers, supplying German construction needs, but most of the conquered eastern territories would be resettled by German colonists. Most German plans for resettlement were postponed until the end of the war. Meanwhile, the regions were exploited ruthlessly for the German war effort: foodstuffs, raw materials, and war stocks were confiscated. Members of the local population were drafted for forced labor in war industries or military construction projects. Millions more were deported to Germany to be used as forced laborers in German war industries or agriculture.

GHETTOS IN
OCCUPIED POLAND
1939-1941

0   100
MILES

* Select Ghettos
Poland 1939 Boundary

GHETTOS IN POLAND

The term "ghetto" originated in Italy from the name of the Jewish quarter in Venice, which was established in the sixteenth century. The term described an area or street where Jews were required to live. During World War II, ghettoization of the Jewish people occurred primarily in eastern Europe between 1939 and 1942. The ghettos were enclosed districts of a city in which the Germans forced the Jewish population to live under miserable conditions. Ghettos isolated Jews by separating Jewish communities both from the population as a whole and from neighboring Jewish communities. The ghettos were overcrowded and dirty. Starvation, chronic shortages, and the curtailing of most urban services led to repeated outbreaks of epidemics and to a high death rate.

Under the provisions of the 1939 German-Soviet Pact, Germany occupied and annexed most of western Poland. Eastern Poland was not occupied by German forces until June 1941. In south-central Poland the Germans set up the Generalgouvernement (General Government), where most of the early ghettos were established. The first ghetto was established there in October 1939, in the town of Piotrkow Trybunalski. The first large ghetto was in the city of Lodz (February 1940), in the area of western Poland that had been annexed by Germany. The Warsaw ghetto, established on October 12, 1940, was the largest ghetto in the Generalgouvernement, in both area and population. There, more than 350,000 Jews—about 30 percent of the city's population—were eventually confined in about 2.4 percent of the city's total area. Other major ghettos in Poland at this time included Krakow (Cracow) and Tarnow.

The Nazis regarded the establishment of Jewish ghettos in Poland as a provisional measure to control, isolate, and segregate Jews. Beginning in 1942, after the decision had been made to kill the Jews, the Germans systematically destroyed the ghettos of Poland, deporting the Jews to extermination camps where they were killed. By the fall of 1944, none of the Polish ghettos remained and almost all Polish Jews had been killed.

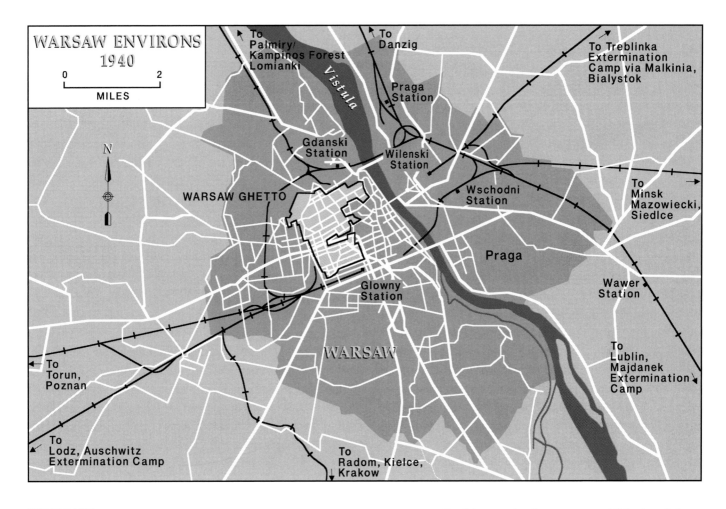

WARSAW ENVIRONS 1940

WARSAW

The city of Warsaw, capital of Poland, flanks both banks of the Vistula River; two-thirds of the city is located on the west bank and one-third is on the east bank. Before World War II, Warsaw was the center of Jewish life and culture in Poland. Warsaw's prewar Jewish population of more than 350,000 constituted about 30 percent of the city's total population. The Warsaw Jewish community was the largest in both Poland and Europe, and was the second largest in the world, behind that of New York City.

Following the outbreak of World War II with the German invasion of Poland on September 1, 1939, Warsaw suffered heavy air attacks and artillery bombardment. The city surrendered on September 28. German troops entered Warsaw on September 29.

For the first several weeks of the German occupation, Warsaw was under German military command. Civil administration of Warsaw began in late October, after the establishment of the Generalgouvernement. Warsaw was a regional center in the Generalgouvernement. The headquarters of the German civil administration in Warsaw were located in the Bruehl Palace.

Prewar Jewish organizations were prohibited and Jews were allowed to participate only in welfare or self-help organizations. The only Jewish representation was the Nazi-established Jewish council (Judenrat).

WARSAW GHETTO

On October 12, 1940, the Germans announced a decree ordering the establishment of a ghetto in Warsaw. All Jewish residents of Warsaw were ordered into the designated area, which was sealed off from the rest of the city in November 1940. The ghetto was enclosed by a wall that was over 10 feet high, topped with barbed wire, and closely guarded to prevent movement between the ghetto and the rest of Warsaw.

The Jewish council offices were located on Grzybowska Street in the southern part of the ghetto. Jewish organizations tried to meet the needs of the ghetto residents, who were constantly struggling for survival. Among the welfare organizations active in the ghetto were the Jewish Mutual Aid Society, the Federation of Associations in Poland for the Care of Orphans, and the Organization for Rehabilitation through Training (O.R.T.).

Emanuel Ringelblum, a historian prominent in Jewish

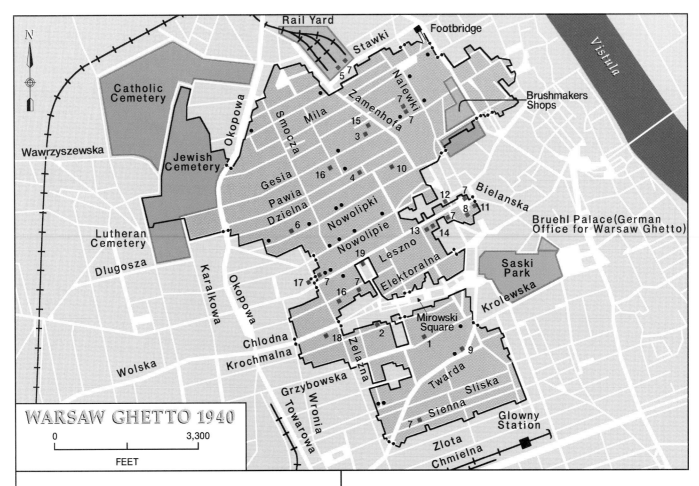

WARSAW GHETTO 1940

0   3,300

FEET

LEGEND

—— Ghetto Boundary November 15, 1940
       Wall with Barbed Wire on Top.
•• Entrances, Gates to Ghetto
• Selected Ghetto Factories
■ Selected Features
1. Jewish Council (Judenrat)
2. Jewish Police
3. Gesiowka Prison
4. Pawiak Prison
5. Umschlagplatz
6. Hiding Place of Ringelblum Archive
7. Hospitals
8. The Great Synagogue
9. Nozjik Synagogue
10. Moriah Synagogue
11. Z.T.O.S. (Jewish Mutual Aid Society)
12. C.E.N.T.O.S. (Federation of
     Associations in Poland for
     the Care of Orphans)
13. Office for Combatting Usury
     and Profiteering
14. O.R.T. (Organization for
     Rehabilitation through Training)
15. Post Office
16. Center for Vocational Training
17. Labor Bureau (Arbeitsamt)
18. Korczak Orphanage
19. Courthouse (Tribunals)

self-aid efforts, also founded a clandestine organization that aimed to provide an accurate record to future historians of events taking place in Warsaw and the Generalgouvernement throughout the ghetto's existence. This record came to be known as the "Oneg Shabbat" ("In Celebration of Sabbath," also known as the Ringelblum Archive). Only partly recovered after the war, the Ringelblum Archive proved an invaluable source of information about life in the ghetto and German policy toward the Jews of Poland.

Beginning in the spring of 1941, German manufacturers established workshops or factories in the ghetto to utilize Jewish forced labor. Such workshops were created in part to supply the German army. Among the firms active in the Warsaw ghetto were Toebbens, Schultz, Roehrich, Hoffmann, and Schilling, producers of textiles, armaments, and other manufactured goods. The "Brushmakers" area of the ghetto was a major center of brush manufacture.

The Germans controlled the movement of goods into and out of the Warsaw ghetto through the Transfer Office (Transferstelle), situated at the Umschlagplatz (transfer point and major rail yard). Located near the northern boundary of the ghetto, the Umschlagplatz functioned as the official

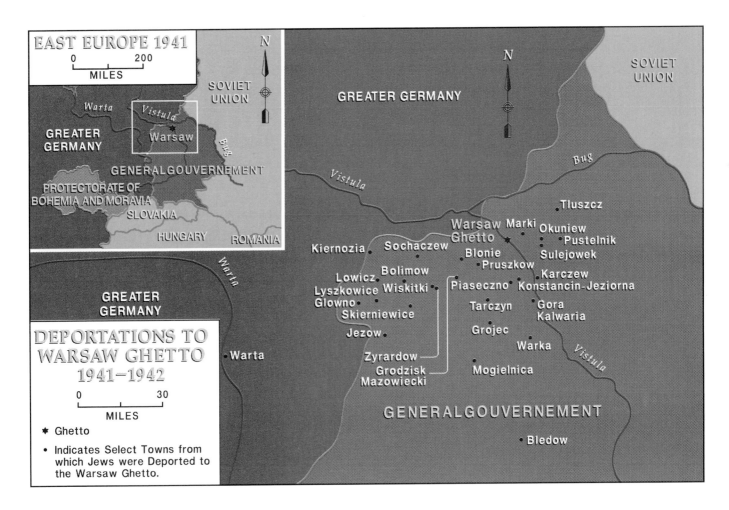

EAST EUROPE 1941
0   200
MILES

SOVIET UNION

Warta

Vistula
Warsaw

GREATER GERMANY

GENERALGOUVERNEMENT

PROTECTORATE OF BOHEMIA AND MORAVIA

SLOVAKIA

HUNGARY   ROMANIA

Bug

GREATER GERMANY

Warta

DEPORTATIONS TO WARSAW GHETTO 1941–1942

0   30
MILES

★ Ghetto

• Indicates Select Towns from which Jews were Deported to the Warsaw Ghetto.

GREATER GERMANY

SOVIET UNION

Vistula

Bug

Tluszcz

Warsaw Marki Okuniew
Ghetto   Pustelnik
Blonie   Sulejowek
Pruszkow
Karczew
Piaseczno Konstancin-Jeziorna

Kiernozia   Sochaczew

Bolimow
Lowicz
Lyszkowice Wiskitki
Glowno
Skierniewice

Jezow

Zyrardow
Grodzisk
Mazowiecki

Tarczyn   Gora Kalwaria

Grojec

Warka

Mogielnica

Vistula

GENERALGOUVERNEMENT

Bledow

transit point until the summer of 1942, when it became an assembly area for deportations from the ghetto.

In addition to the official movement of goods, smuggling took place at other parts of the ghetto boundary. Jews caught outside the ghetto faced imprisonment in Pawiak Prison or immediate execution. Pawiak Prison was the main facility used by the German Security Police and Security Service in the Warsaw district. It held mainly Polish political prisoners and some Jews. Between 1939 and 1944, the Germans imprisoned about 99,000 people at Pawiak: one-third of them were killed there and the rest were deported from Warsaw. The Jewish council in Warsaw ran the Gesiowka Prison, which was within the ghetto boundary and was mainly for Jewish prisoners. In 1943, after the destruction of the Warsaw ghetto, Pawiak became a forced-labor camp.

DEPORTATIONS TO THE WARSAW GHETTO

Between January and March 1941, Jews from smaller communities to the west of Warsaw were deported to the Warsaw ghetto. Between April and July 1942, Jews from the nearby towns east of Warsaw, from Germany, and from German-occupied areas were deported there. Several hundred

Roma (Gypsies) were also deported to the ghetto.

At its height, the total population of the Warsaw ghetto reached more than 400,000 people. Conditions in the ghetto worsened over time. In 1941, one year before the mass deportations, over 43,000 people died, more than one in every ten ghetto residents.

DEPORTATIONS FROM THE WARSAW GHETTO

Between July and mid-September 1942, over 300,000 people were deported from the Warsaw ghetto; more than 250,000 of them were deported to the Treblinka killing center. Deportees were forced to the Umschlagplatz (deportation point), which was connected to the Warsaw-Malkinia rail line. They were crowded into freight cars and most were deported, via Malkinia, to Treblinka.

The Germans demanded that the Jewish council organize the deportations, but Adam Czerniakow, who headed the Jewish council in Warsaw, refused to cooperate. Although Czerniakow did not call for resistance to the Germans, he did not sign the deportation order and committed suicide, swallowing a cyanide capsule on July 23, 1942.

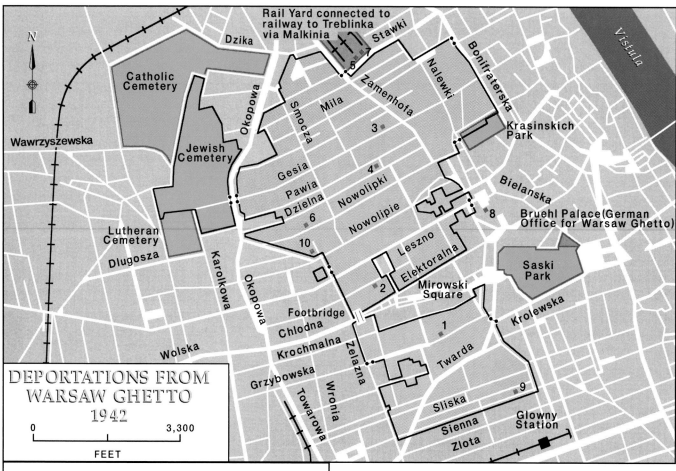

DEPORTATIONS FROM
WARSAW GHETTO
1942

0   3,300

FEET

LEGEND

—   Ghetto Boundary July 22, 1942, Wall with Barbed Wire on Top.

••   Entrances, Gates to Ghetto

▪   Selected Features

1. Jewish Council (Judenrat)
2. Jewish Police
3. Gesiowka Prison
4. Pawiak Prison
5. Umschlagplatz
6. Hiding Place of Ringelblum Archive
7. Czyste Hospital
8. The Great Synagogue
9. Korczak Orphanage
10. Deportation Office (Befehlsstelle)

The Germans developed various methods to trap Jews for deportations. Sometimes whole buildings were surrounded by police and SS units and those inside forced to the Umschlagplatz. Late in the deportation process, the Germans promised food to any Jews who went voluntarily to the assembly point. Starving and unaware that they would be transported to their deaths, some Jews reported and they too were deported to Treblinka. Children from Janusz Korczak's Sliska Street orphanage were rounded up and marched to the Umschlagplatz. Despite offers of rescue, Korczak and his assistants refused to leave the children and were deported along with them.

During the deportations, the Czyste Hospital in the ghetto served as a roundup center, where Jews were assembled before their transfer to the Umschlagplatz. The Deportation Office (Befehlsstelle), at the corner of Nowolipie and Zelazna streets, directed the entire process. Jewish police forces were at first employed in the deportations. Later, German forces and their Latvian and Ukrainian auxiliaries took charge of roundups. Toward the end of the deportations, German forces and collaborators searched streets and residences and imposed a daily quota on Jewish policemen as it became increasingly difficult to conduct large-scale roundups.

In September, at the end of the 1942 mass deportation, only about 55,000 Jews remained in the ghetto. The SS established a special section (the Werterfassung) to collect and sort the belongings of the victims for shipment to Germany. Following the mass deportation, the ghetto area was reduced in size and divided into three separate sections.

WARSAW GHETTO UPRISING

During the mass deportation from the Warsaw ghetto in

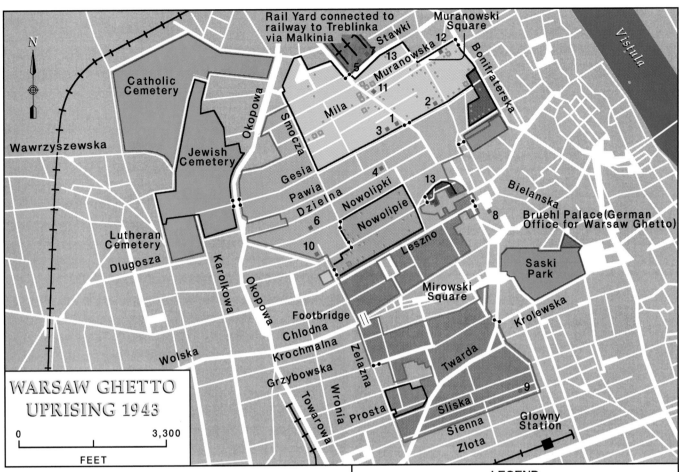

Rail Yard connected to railway to Treblinka via Malkinia

Muranowski Square

Vistula

Catholic Cemetery

Stawki

Muranowska

12

73

5

Bonifraterska

Okopowa

Smocza

Mila

11

2

N

Wawrzyszewska

Jewish Cemetery

Gesia

3

7

1

Pawia

4

Bielanska

Dzielna

Nowolipki

13

Bruehl Palace (German Office for Warsaw Ghetto)

8

Lutheran Cemetery

6

Nowolipie

Dlugosza

10

Leszno

Saski Park

Karolkowa

Okopowa

Mirowski Square

Footbridge

Chlodna

Krochmalna

Zelazna

Krolewska

Wolska

Grzybowska

Twarda

9

Prosta

Sliska

Glowny Station

Towarowa

Wronia

Sienna

Zlota

WARSAW GHETTO UPRISING 1943

0   3,300

FEET

1942, several Jewish underground organizations created an armed self-defense organization known as the Jewish Fighting Organization (Zydowska Organizacja Bojowa; ZOB). The Revisionist party (right-wing Zionists) formed another resistance organization, the Jewish Fighting Union (Zydowski Zwiazek Wojskowy; ZZW). Although initially there was tension between the ZOB and the ZZW, both groups decided to work together to oppose German attempts to destroy the ghetto.

The Germans tried to resume mass deportations of Jews from Warsaw in January 1943. A group of Jewish fighters infiltrated a column of Jews on its way to the Umschlagplatz and, at a prearranged signal, broke ranks and fought their German escorts. After seizing 5,000-6,500 ghetto residents to be deported, the Germans suspended further deportations. Encouraged by the apparent success of the resistance, which they believed may have halted deportations, the ghetto population began to construct subterranean bunkers and shelters in preparation for an uprising should the Germans begin the final deportation of all remaining Jews in the reduced ghetto.

The Germans renewed deportations from the Warsaw ghetto in April 1943, thereby beginning the final destruction

LEGEND

― Ghetto Boundary July 22, 1942
▬ Reduced Ghetto
▢ Main Ghetto
▢ Ghetto Factory Area: Toebbens, F.E. Schultz, K.G. Schultz, Roehrich, Hoffmann, Schilling
▢ Central Ghetto Factory Area, Toebbens
▢ Brushmakers Shops
▢ Area Resettled by Poles
▢ Area Unoccupied, Jews in Hiding
▫ January 1943 Revolt
• Bunkers & Fighting Points April-May 1943 Revolt
•• Entrances, Gates to Ghetto
▪ Selected Features (Ghetto Public Institutions)

1. Jewish Council (Judenrat)
2. Jewish Police
3. Gesiowka Prison
4. Pawiak Prison
5. Umschlagplatz (Assembly Point and Transfer Office)
6. Hiding Place of Ringelblum Archive
7. Czyste Hospital, Deportation Center
8. The Great Synagogue
9. Korczak Orphanage
10. Deportation Office (Befehlsstelle)
11. ZOB Headquarters
12. ZZW Headquarters
13. SS Werterfassung

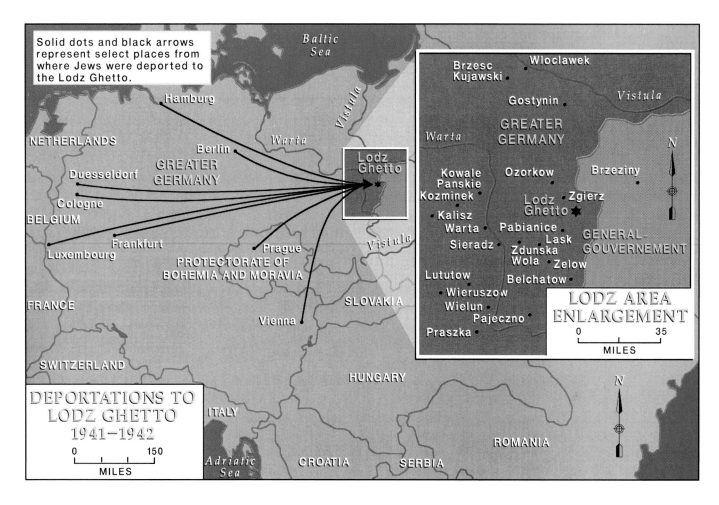

Solid dots and black arrows represent select places from where Jews were deported to the Lodz Ghetto.

DEPORTATIONS TO LODZ GHETTO 1941–1942

0   150
MILES

LODZ AREA ENLARGEMENT

0   35
MILES

of the ghetto. The renewal of deportations was the signal for an armed uprising within the ghetto. The Warsaw ghetto uprising lasted about one month, from April 19 until May 16, 1943, and was the largest, most important Jewish uprising, and the first urban uprising, in German-occupied Europe.

When the destruction of the Warsaw ghetto began on April 19, most of the ghetto population refused to report to assembly points for deportation. Many hid from the Germans in the previously prepared bunkers and shelters.

ZOB commander Mordecai Anielewicz led resistance forces in the Warsaw ghetto uprising. In the first days of fighting, Anielewicz commanded the Jewish fighters in street battles with the Germans. The ZOB also blew up a workshop in the "Brushmakers" area. When street fighting shifted to fighting from concealed bunkers, Anielewicz and a large group of fighters retreated to the ZOB headquarters' bunker on Mila Street. The ZZW headquarters' bunker was on Muranowski Square.

On the third day of the uprising, forces under German commander SS General Juergen Stroop began burning the ghetto, building by building, to force the remaining Jews out of hiding. Jewish resistance fighters made sporadic raids from their bunkers, but the Germans systematically reduced the ghetto to rubble. Anielewicz and those with him were killed in an attack on his command bunker on Mila Street, which fell to German forces on May 8.

On May 16, 1943, Stroop ordered the Great Synagogue on Tlomackie Street destroyed to symbolize German victory. The ghetto itself was in ruins. Although only about 50,000 Jews remained in the ghetto after the January 1943 deportations, Stroop reported to Berlin that he had captured 56,065 Jews and destroyed 631 bunkers. He estimated that 5,000 to 6,000 Jews had been killed in the bombardment and fires. Stroop also reported that he had shot more than 7,000 and captured and deported almost 7,000 Jews to Treblinka, where they were killed. Most of the remaining Jews were deported to the Poniatowa and Trawniki forced-labor camps and to the Majdanek extermination camp.

LODZ

The city of Lodz is located about 75 miles southwest of Warsaw, Poland. The Jews of Lodz formed, after Warsaw, the second largest Jewish community in prewar Poland. One week after German forces attacked Poland on September 1, 1939,

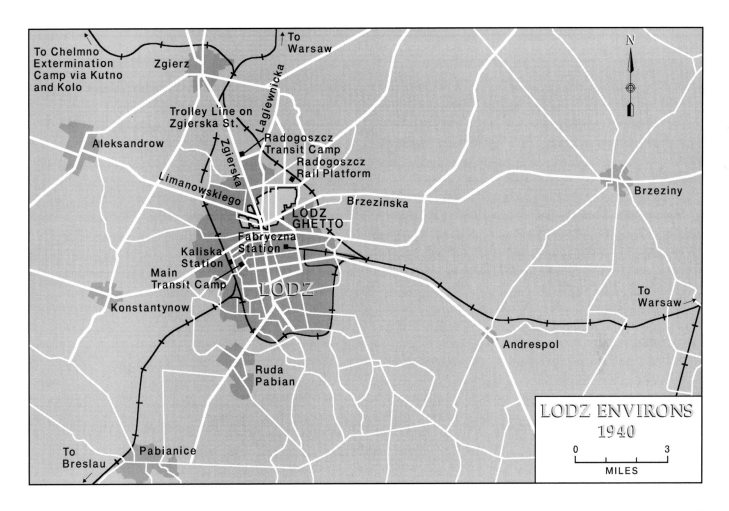

To Chelmno Extermination Camp via Kutno and Kolo

Zgierz

To Warsaw

Trolley Line on Zgierska St.

Lagiewnicka

Aleksandrow

Zgierska

Radogoszcz Transit Camp

Radogoszcz Rail Platform

Limanowskiego

Brzezinska

LODZ GHETTO

Fabryczna Station

Kaliska Station

Main Transit Camp

LODZ

Konstantynow

Ruda Pabian

Brzeziny

To Warsaw

Andrespol

LODZ ENVIRONS 1940

0   3
MILES

To Breslau

Pabianice

Lodz was occupied by the German army and annexed to Germany as part of the Warthegau district. The Germans renamed the city Litzmannstadt, after a German general, Karl Litzmann, who had captured that city during World War I.

In early February 1940, the Germans ordered the establishment of a ghetto in the northeastern section of Lodz. Over 150,000 Jews, more than a third of the entire population of Lodz, were forced into a small area of the city.

In 1941 and 1942, almost 40,000 Jews were deported to the Lodz ghetto: 20,000 from Germany, Austria, the Protectorate of Bohemia and Moravia, and Luxembourg, and almost 20,000 more Jews from the smaller provincial towns in the Lodz region. Further, about 5,000 Roma (Gypsies) from Austria were deported to the Lodz ghetto, where they were confined in a segregated block of buildings.

The Lodz ghetto was isolated from the rest of the city by barbed-wire fencing. Special SS units guarded the ghetto perimeter. Internal order in the ghetto was the responsibility of Jewish ghetto police. The ghetto area was divided into three parts by the intersection of two major roads, which were excluded from the ghetto. The three segments of the ghetto were accessible to each other via bridges constructed over the two thoroughfares. Streetcars for the non-Jewish population of Lodz traversed the ghetto but were not permitted to stop within it.

Lodz had been a key industrial center in prewar Poland, and thus the Lodz ghetto became a major production center under the German occupation. As early as May 1940, the Germans began to establish factories in the ghetto and to utilize Jewish residents for forced labor. By August 1942, there were almost 100 factories within the ghetto. The major factories produced textiles, especially uniforms, for the German army. Mordechai Chaim Rumkowski, chairman of the Jewish council in the Lodz ghetto, hoped to prevent the destruction of the ghetto by making it as productive as possible. He gambled that making Jewish labor essential to German factories would spare Jews from eventual deportation and preserve the Lodz ghetto until the end of the war.

Living conditions in the ghetto were horrendous. Most of the area did not have running water or a sewer system. Hard labor, overcrowding, and starvation were the dominant features of life. The overwhelming majority of ghetto residents worked in German factories, receiving only meager food rations from their employers. More than 20 percent of

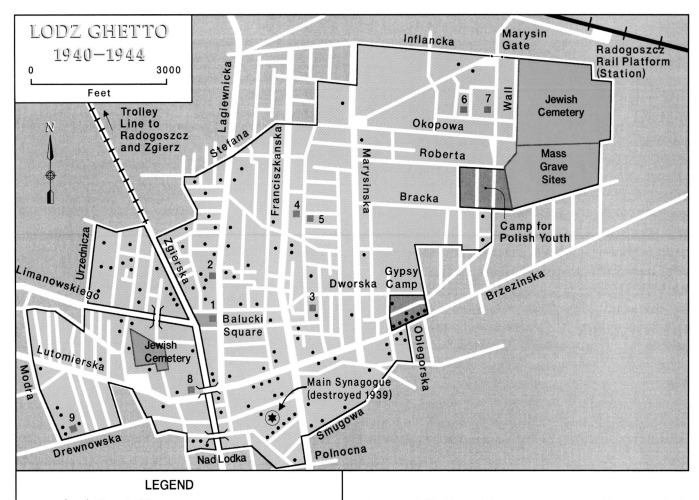

LEGEND

⎯⎯ Footbridges
⎯⎯ Ghetto Fence; Barbed Wire
• Ghetto Factories
■ Select Features
1. German & Jewish Administration
2. Hospital No.1
3. House of Culture; Assembly Point
4. Central Prison
5. Assembly Point
6. School; Assembly Point
7. Orphanage
8. Jewish Police Headquarters
9. Hospital; Assembly Point

the ghetto's population died as a result of the harsh living conditions.

DEPORTATIONS FROM THE LODZ GHETTO

In January 1942, deportations from Lodz to the Chelmno killing center began. By September 1942, over 70,000 Jews and about 5,000 Roma had been deported to Chelmno, where they were killed in mobile gas vans (trucks with a hermetically sealed compartment that served as a gas chamber). Jews were rounded up in assembly points before deportation. The Germans at first required the Jewish council to prepare lists of deportees, but soon switched to direct roundups organized by the German police. Hundreds of Jews, mainly children, the elderly, and the sick, were killed on the spot while the deportation was in progress.

Between September 1942 and May 1944, there were no major deportations from Lodz to extermination camps, and the ghetto resembled a forced-labor camp. In the spring of 1944, the Nazis decided to destroy the Lodz ghetto. By then, Lodz was the last remaining ghetto in Poland, with a population of about 75,000 Jews. In June and July 1944 the Germans resumed deportations from Lodz, and about 3,000 Jews were deported to Chelmno. The ghetto residents were informed by Rumkowski that they were being transferred to work camps in Germany. The deportations continued in August, but most of the remaining ghetto population was deported to the Auschwitz-Birkenau extermination camp.

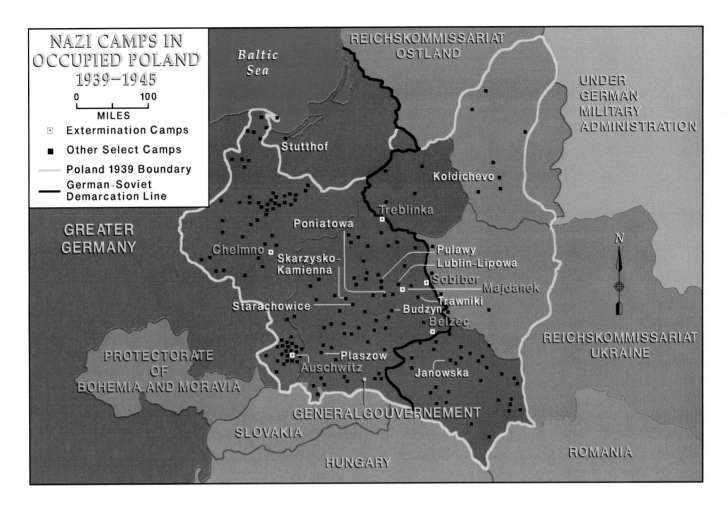

NAZI CAMPS IN POLAND

Tens of thousands of non-Jewish Poles were imprisoned in Nazi concentration and forced-labor camps. As throughout occupied Europe, the Germans used terror and the extensive camp system to instill fear in people and to wreak destruction upon institutions and culture. Poles were prisoners in nearly every camp, but especially in the Auschwitz and Stutthof camp systems. Both camps had an extensive system of subcamps or forced-labor camps: Auschwitz in the southwest and Stutthof in north-central Poland. Conditions in the camps were intolerable. Prisoners were provided with little food, inadequate housing and sanitary facilities, and virtually no medical care. Epidemics and disease were common. Prisoners were literally worked to death.

Polish Jews were the primary targets of Nazi policy in Poland, as were Jews throughout German-occupied Europe. Immediately following the German occupation of Poland in September 1939, Jews were drafted for forced labor, mainly clearing rubble and debris in Polish cities damaged by the invasion. Jews continued to be used for forced labor after they were concentrated in ghettos. Eventually, the Nazis established hundreds of forced-labor camps, where tens of thousands of Jews were forced to work in construction, military, and agricultural projects.

The Germans established six extermination camps on former Polish soil—Chelmno, Belzec, Sobibor, Treblinka, Auschwitz-Birkenau, and Majdanek. Extermination camps were killing centers designed and built for the sole purpose of efficiently killing millions of people. Auschwitz and Majdanek functioned as penal camps and labor camps as well as killing centers. Chelmno, Belzec, Sobibor, and Treblinka served only as killing centers, mainly for Polish Jews, as well as Jews and Roma (Gypsies) from other parts of Europe. These four camps were dismantled in 1943, since most of the Jews in Poland had already been killed. Chelmno was reopened in 1944, to kill the Jews remaining in the Lodz ghetto. An estimated 3.5 million Jews were killed in the killing centers as part of the "Final Solution."

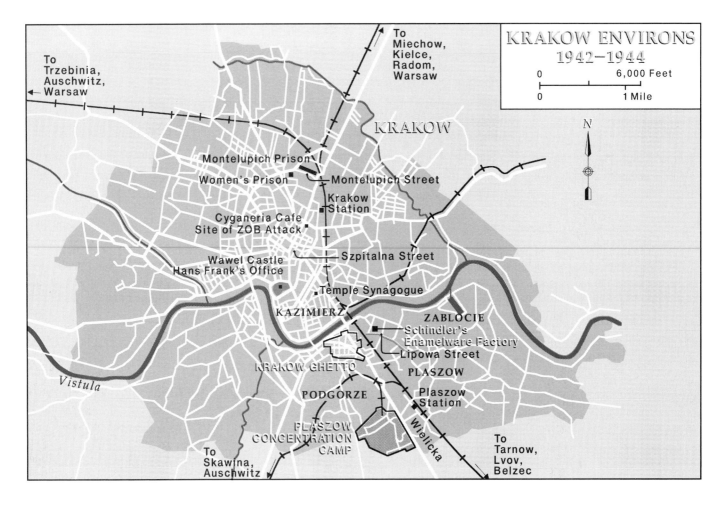

KRAKOW

The city of Krakow (Cracow) is in southern Poland. In 1939 there were 60,000 Jews residing in Krakow, almost one-quarter of its total population of about 250,000.

The German army occupied Krakow in the first week of September 1939. Persecution of the Jews began immediately and intensified after the Germans declared Krakow the capital of the Generalgouvernement territory in the interior of occupied Poland. Wawel Castle became the residence of the Nazi lawyer Hans Frank, who had been appointed administrator of the Generalgouvernement. Montelupich Prison became a Gestapo prison. In 1942, the Plaszow camp was established in the south of the city as a forced-labor camp for the Jews of Krakow. In 1944, Plaszow became a concentration camp.

In May 1940, the Germans began to expel Jews from Krakow to neighboring towns. By March 1941, the majority of Jews had been evicted and only about 15,000 remained in Krakow. In early March 1941, the Germans ordered the establishment of a ghetto, to be situated in Podgorze in the south of Krakow rather than in Kazimierz, the traditionally Jewish quarter of the city. The Germans concentrated Krakow Jews and those from surrounding towns and villages in the ghetto.

Almost 20,000 Jews were confined in the ghetto, which was enclosed by barbed-wire fences and, in places, by a stone wall. Streetcars traveled through the ghetto but made no stops within its boundary.

The Germans established several factories inside the ghetto, among them the Optima and the Madritsch factories, where Jews were used for forced labor. Several hundred Jews were also employed in factories and forced-labor projects outside the ghetto.

In March 1942, the Germans arrested about 50 intellectuals in the ghetto and deported them to the Auschwitz-Birkenau extermination camp. In the second half of 1942, the Germans deported about 13,000 people from the ghetto. During the deportations, Plac Zgody and the Optima factory were the major assembly points. Most of the deportees were sent to the Belzec extermination camp; some were sent to Auschwitz, which was only 40 miles from Krakow. Hundreds of people were shot in the ghetto during the deportations.

In March 1943, the Germans destroyed the Krakow ghetto. More than 2,000 people were deported to Auschwitz-Birkenau and killed. The remainder of the ghetto population was deported to the nearby Plaszow camp.

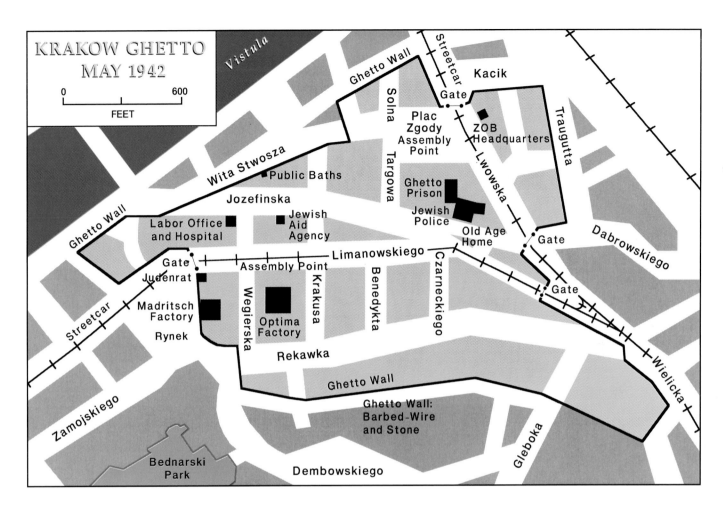

KRAKOW GHETTO MAY 1942

0 — 600

FEET

Vistula

Ghetto Wall

Streetcar

Kacik

Solna

Gate

Plac Zgody Assembly Point

ZOB Headquarters

Targowa

Lwowska

Traugutta

Wita Stwosza

Public Baths

Jozefinska

Ghetto Prison

Jewish Police

Ghetto Wall

Labor Office and Hospital

Jewish Aid Agency

Dabrowskiego

Old Age Home

Gate

Limanowskiego

Czarneckiego

Gate

Gate

Assembly Point

Judenrat

Benedykta

Krakusa

Wegierska

Madritsch Factory

Optima Factory

Streetcar

Rynek

Rekawka

Wielicka

Zamojskiego

Ghetto Wall

Gleboka

Ghetto Wall: Barbed-Wire and Stone

Bednarski Park

Dembowskiego

RESISTANCE IN THE KRAKOW GHETTO

A Jewish resistance movement existed in the Krakow ghetto from the ghetto's establishment. Underground operations initially focused on supporting education and welfare organizations. In October 1942, however, the Jewish Fighting Organization (Zydowska Organizacja Bojowa; ZOB), an underground organization independent of the Warsaw ZOB, prepared to fight the Germans. The ZOB decided not to fight within the limited confines of the ghetto, but instead to use the ghetto as a base from which to attack targets throughout the city of Krakow. The most important ZOB attack took place in the center of Krakow at the Cyganeria cafe, which was frequented by German officers.

Krakow ghetto fighters also attempted to join partisan groups active in the Krakow region. In successive skirmishes with the Germans, the Jewish underground fighters suffered heavy losses. In the fall of 1944 the remnants of the resistance escaped from Poland, crossing into neighboring Slovakia and then into Hungary, where they joined with Jewish resistance groups in Budapest.

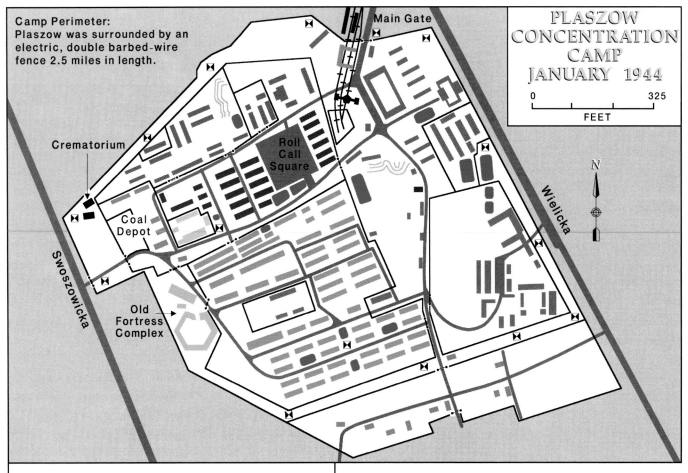

Camp Perimeter:
Plaszow was surrounded by an electric, double barbed-wire fence 2.5 miles in length.

Main Gate

Crematorium

Coal Depot

Old Fortress Complex

Roll Call Square

Swoszowicka

Wielicka

PLASZOW CONCENTRATION CAMP JANUARY 1944

0 — 325
FEET

N

LEGEND

- Roads
- Gates
- Barbed-Wire Fence
- Watchtowers
- Ponds
- Railroad Tracks
- Gravel Pits

- Barracks for SS and Ukrainian Guards
- Camp Administration
- Camp Commandant's House
- Factory Area
- Hospital Camp
- Housing for German Civilians
- Kitchen
- Men's Camp
- Polish Reeducation Work Camp
- Stables and Garage
- Warehouses
- Women's Camp

PLASZOW CONCENTRATION CAMP

The Plaszow camp was originally a forced-labor camp established in 1942 in the south of Krakow. The original site of the camp included two Jewish cemeteries. From time to time the camp was enlarged, and it reached its maximum size in 1944, the same year that it became a concentration camp. The Plaszow camp was surrounded by an electrified barbed-wired fence and was divided into several sections. The camp had barracks for German personnel, factories, warehouses, a men's camp and a women's camp, and a reeducation camp for Polish workers. Poles and Jews were segregated within the camp. The largest number of people confined in Plaszow at any one time was more than 20,000. Thousands were killed there.

The German industrialist Oskar Schindler established an enamelware factory in Krakow, adjacent to the Plaszow camp. He attempted to protect his Jewish workers, some 900 people, from abuse in the Plaszow camp and from deportation to extermination camps. When he moved the factory and his Jewish work force to the Sudetenland (an area formerly in Czechoslovakia) in 1944, he was able to rescue more than 1,000 Jews.

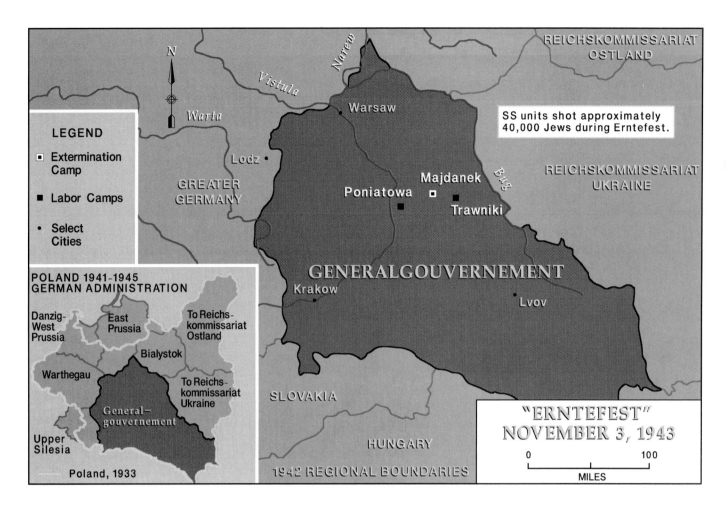

LEGEND

- ▫ Extermination Camp
- ■ Labor Camps
- • Select Cities

POLAND 1941-1945
GERMAN ADMINISTRATION

Danzig-West Prussia

East Prussia

To Reichs-kommissariat Ostland

Bialystok

Warthegau

To Reichs-kommissariat Ukraine

General-gouvernement

Upper Silesia

— Poland, 1933

REICHSKOMMISSARIAT OSTLAND

Warsaw

SS units shot approximately 40,000 Jews during Erntefest.

Lodz

GREATER GERMANY

REICHSKOMMISSARIAT UKRAINE

Majdanek

Poniatowa

Trawniki

GENERALGOUVERNEMENT

Krakow

Lvov

SLOVAKIA

HUNGARY

1942 REGIONAL BOUNDARIES

"ERNTEFEST" NOVEMBER 3, 1943

0   100

MILES

In the summer of 1944, as the Soviet army approached, the Germans prepared to dismantle the Plaszow camp. Prisoners were transferred to other camps closer to Germany or deported to the Auschwitz-Birkenau extermination camp and killed there. The Germans also attempted to remove all traces of the crimes that had been committed in the camp. They ordered that the mass graves at Plaszow be opened and the bodies exhumed and burned. In January 1945, the last prisoners from Plaszow were sent to Auschwitz.

"ERNTEFEST"

Translated from the German, "Erntefest" means "Harvest Festival." The word "Erntefest" was the code name for the German operation to kill all Jews remaining in the Generalgouvernement in the fall of 1943. The timing of the operation was apparently in response to the uprising and attempted mass escape of Jews at the Sobibor extermination camp in October 1943. The SS believed that additional Jewish-led revolts were possible in the Generalgouvernement; to prevent further resistance, the SS decided to kill most of the remaining Jews who were employed in forced-labor projects and were concentrated in the Trawniki, Poniatowa, and Majdanek camps.

"Erntefest" began at dawn on November 3, 1943. The Trawniki and Poniatowa labor camps were surrounded by SS and police units. Jews were then taken out of the camps in groups and shot in nearby pits, which had been dug for this purpose. At Majdanek, Jews were first separated from the other prisoners, and then taken in groups to nearby trenches and shot. Jews from other labor camps in the Lublin area were also taken to Majdanek and shot. Music was played through loudspeakers at both Majdanek and Trawniki to drown out the noise of the mass shooting. The extermination operation was completed in a single day. Approximately 40,000 Jews were killed during "Erntefest," almost half of them at Majdanek.

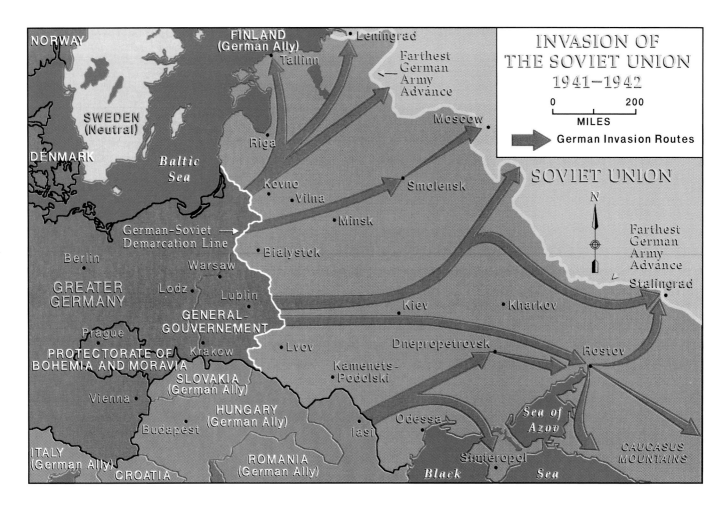

INVASION OF
THE SOVIET UNION
1941–1942

0   200
MILES
➡ German Invasion Routes

GERMAN INVASION OF THE SOVIET UNION

The German invasion of the Soviet Union, code-named Operation Barbarossa, began on June 22, 1941. It was the largest German military operation of World War II. More than three million German soldiers, reinforced by half a million auxiliaries from Germany's allies (Finnish, Romanian, Hungarian, Italian, Slovakian, and Croatian troops, and a contingent from Spain), attacked the Soviet Union across a broad front, from the Baltic Sea in the north to the Black Sea in the south. Three German army groups advanced deep into Soviet territory. The Soviet leadership had refused to heed warnings of the impending German attack, so Germany achieved tactical surprise and the Soviet army was initially overwhelmed. Millions of Soviet soldiers were encircled, cut off from supplies and reinforcements, and forced to surrender.

By early September 1941, German forces were at the gates of Leningrad in the north, Smolensk in the center, and Dnepropetrovsk in the south. German troops continued to advance to the outskirts of Moscow. Yet after months of campaigning, the German army was exhausted. Its supply lines were hampered by the great distances involved (Moscow is almost 1,000 miles east of Berlin). German forces were also unprepared for winter fighting, having expected the Blitzkrieg tactic to result in the swift surrender of the Soviet Union. Winter conditions hampered major military operations and took a significant toll on German soldiers.

In December 1941, the Soviet Union launched a counteroffensive which was initially successful in forcing a German retreat from the outskirts of Moscow. But by April 1942, German forces were able to stabilize the front east of Smolensk. Germany resumed the offensive in the spring of 1942 with a massive attack in the south toward the city of Stalingrad on the Volga River and the oil fields of the Caucasus. By August 1942, German forces neared the city. With the battle for Stalingrad, German domination of Europe was at its height.

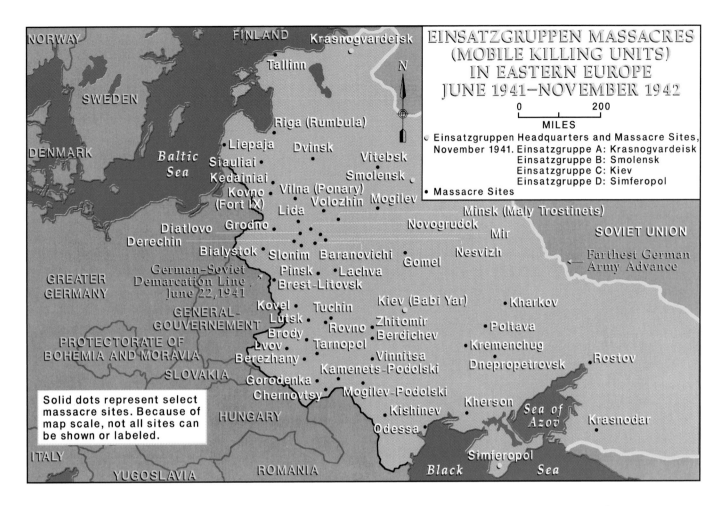

EINSATZGRUPPEN MASSACRES
(MOBILE KILLING UNITS)
IN EASTERN EUROPE
JUNE 1941–NOVEMBER 1942

0   200
MILES

○ Einsatzgruppen Headquarters and Massacre Sites,
November 1941. Einsatzgruppe A: Krasnogvardeisk
Einsatzgruppe B: Smolensk
Einsatzgruppe C: Kiev
Einsatzgruppe D: Simferopol
● Massacre Sites

Solid dots represent select massacre sites. Because of map scale, not all sites can be shown or labeled.

EINSATZGRUPPEN

Einsatzgruppen (mobile killing units) were German special duty squads, composed primarily of SS and police personnel, assigned to kill Jews as part of the Nazi program to murder the Jews of Europe. The Einsatzgruppen also killed Roma (Gypsies), Soviet political commissars, and others whom the Nazis deemed racially or politically unacceptable. Einsatzgruppen operated behind the front lines in German-occupied territories in eastern Europe. During the invasion of the Soviet Union in June 1941, the Einsatzgruppen followed the German army as it advanced deep into Soviet territory, and carried out mass-murder operations. The German army was responsible for logistical support for the Einsatzgruppen, providing supplies, transportation, and housing. At first the Einsatzgruppen shot primarily Jewish men. Soon, wherever the Einsatzgruppen went they shot all Jewish men, women, and children, without regard for age or gender.

The Einsatzgruppen following the German army into the Soviet Union were composed of four battalion-sized operational groups. Einsatzgruppe A fanned out from East Prussia across Lithuania, Latvia, and Estonia toward Leningrad. It massacred Jews in Kovno, Riga, and Vilna. Einsatzgruppe B started from Warsaw in occupied Poland, and fanned out across Belorussia toward Smolensk. It massacred Jews in Grodno, Minsk, Brest-Litovsk, Slonim, Gomel, and Mogilev, among other places. Einsatzgruppe C began operations from the western Generalgouvernement and fanned out across the Ukraine toward Kharkov and Rostov-on-Don. It committed massacres in Lvov, Tarnopol, Zolochev, Kremenets, Kharkov, Kiev, and elsewhere. Of the four units, Einsatzgruppe D operated farthest south. It carried out massacres in the southern Ukraine and the Crimea, especially in Nikolayev, Kherson, Simferopol, Sevastopol, and Feodosiya.

By the spring of 1943, the Einsatzgruppen had killed more than a million Jews and tens of thousands of Soviet political commissars, partisans, and Roma.

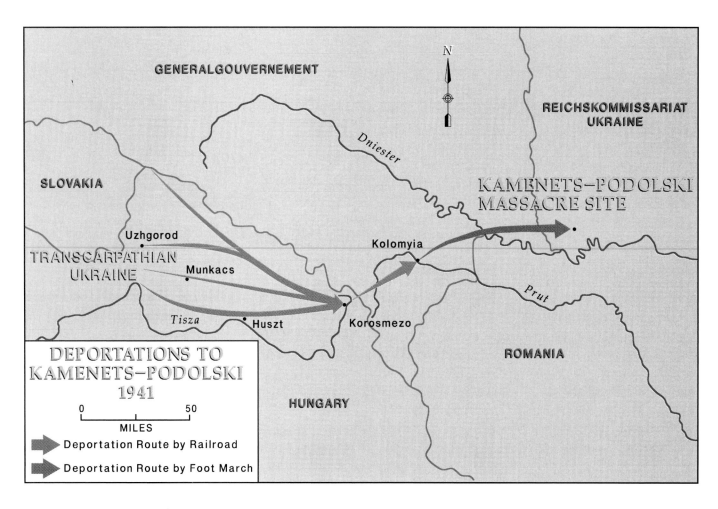

KAMENETS-PODOLSKI

The city of Kamenets-Podolski is in the western Ukraine. It was occupied by German forces during the invasion of the Soviet Union in June 1941. After the invasion, officials in Hungary (Germany's ally) decided to deport foreign Jews (mostly Polish and Russian Jews) living in Hungary to German-occupied eastern Europe. As elsewhere in Europe, Jews who could not establish citizenship were especially vulnerable to deportation; many Hungarian Jews who could not document their citizenship were thus also deported. Many Jewish communities, especially in the Transcarpathian Ukraine, were deported in their entirety. Jews were loaded into freight cars and taken to Korosmezo, near the prewar Hungarian-Polish border, and were handed over to the Germans. By the end of August 1941, almost 20,000 Jews had been deported from Hungary. Once in German hands, the Jews, still often in family units, were forced to march from Kolomyia to Kamenets-Podolski. Einsatzgruppen detachments in Kamenets-Podolski and troops under the command of the Higher SS and Police Leader for the southern region carried out mass killings of the Jewish deportees. These Jews were massacred together with the local Jewish population of the city.

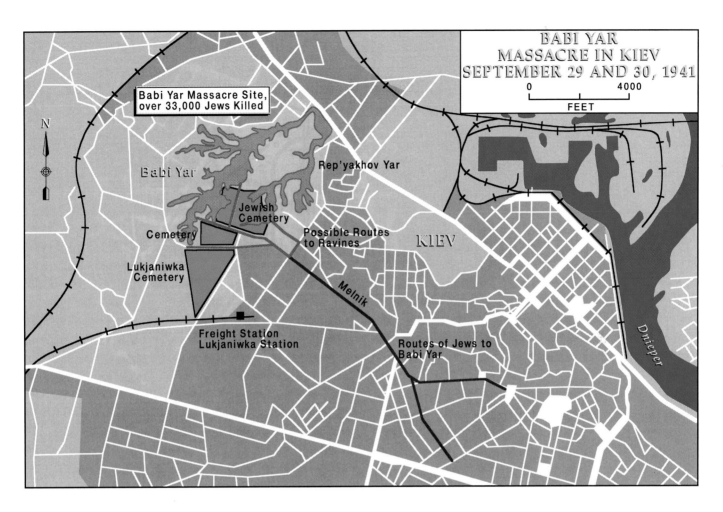

BABI YAR

One of the largest massacres perpetrated by members of the Einsatzgruppen took place just outside the Ukrainian capital city of Kiev. Tens of thousands of Jews were systematically massacred at Babi Yar, a ravine to the northwest of the city.

German forces entered Kiev in September 1941. During the first days of the occupation, several buildings used by the German army were blown up, apparently by the Soviet security police (the NKVD). The Germans blamed the Jews for the explosion and, ostensibly in retaliation, decided to kill the Jews of Kiev. At that time, there were about 60,000 Jews in the city. Detachments of the Einsatzgruppen, together with Ukrainian auxiliary units, were assigned to carry out the massacre.

In late September, the Germans posted notices requiring all Jews to report for resettlement outside the city of Kiev. Failure to report was made a capital offense. Masses of Jews reported and were directed to proceed along Melnik Street toward the Jewish cemetery and Babi Yar. Under guard, the Jews were directed to hand over all their valuables and to disrobe. As the victims moved into the ravine, they were shot in small groups by Einsatzgruppen detachments. The massacre continued for two days. It is estimated that over 33,000 Jews were killed in this operation. In the months that followed the massacre, thousands more Jews were shot at Babi Yar. Many non-Jews, including Roma (Gypsies) and Soviet prisoners of war, were also killed at Babi Yar.

In July 1943, as Soviet forces appeared likely to recapture Kiev, the Germans attempted to destroy any traces of the crimes committed at Babi Yar. As part of Aktion 1005, which aimed to obliterate the evidence of mass murder all over Europe, the Germans forced prisoners to reopen the mass graves and cremate the bodies. Once this was done, the Germans killed the remaining prisoners. The Soviet army liberated Kiev in November 1943.

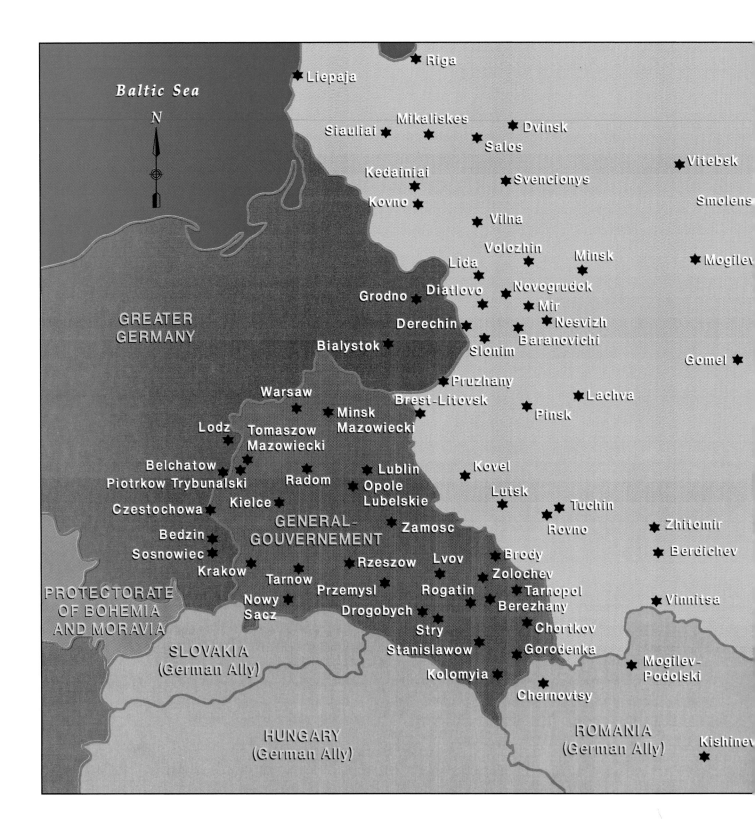

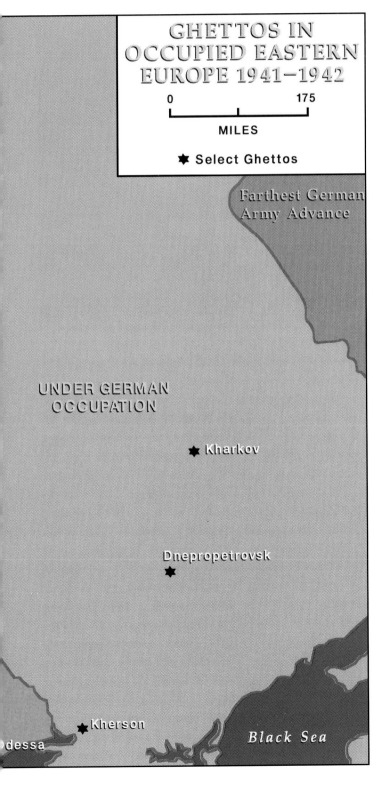

GHETTOS IN OCCUPIED EASTERN EUROPE 1941–1942

0   175

MILES

★ Select Ghettos

Farthest German Army Advance

UNDER GERMAN OCCUPATION

★ Kharkov

Dnepropetrovsk
★

★ Kherson

Odessa

Black Sea

GHETTOS IN EASTERN EUROPE

Ghettoization of Jews, which isolated Jewish communities from the population as a whole and from one another, occurred primarily in eastern Europe (Poland, the Baltic states, and occupied areas of the Soviet Union) between 1939 and 1942 and in Hungary after the 1944 German occupation.

The Nazis regarded the establishment of Jewish ghettos in Poland, begun in the fall of 1939, as a provisional measure. In western Poland, ghettoization preceded the massacre of Jews. The destruction of the ghettos began in late 1941, and attained full measure in the summer of 1942 with the deportation of Polish Jews to the extermination camps.

The occupation of eastern Poland, the Baltic states, Belorussia, and most of the Ukraine took place following the German invasion of the Soviet Union in June 1941. In these areas, Einsatzgruppen massacres preceded ghettoization. Relatively few ghettos were established and of these, most were in larger cities because Einsatzgruppen detachments killed Jews in smaller communities outright. Ghettos were established in Bialystok, Lvov, Rovno, and elsewhere in eastern Poland. In the Baltic states, ghettos were established in Riga, Kovno, and Vilna (Vilna was then part of Lithuania), among other cities. The Minsk ghetto was the largest in the Soviet Union, with a population of about 80,000.

Einsatzgruppen massacres continually reduced the Jewish population of these ghettos. By the end of 1943, most of the ghettos of eastern Europe were destroyed. Most Jews were killed, either by Einsatzgruppen detachments or after their deportation to the killing centers in occupied Poland. The others were deported to forced-labor camps in the Baltic states and eastern Poland.

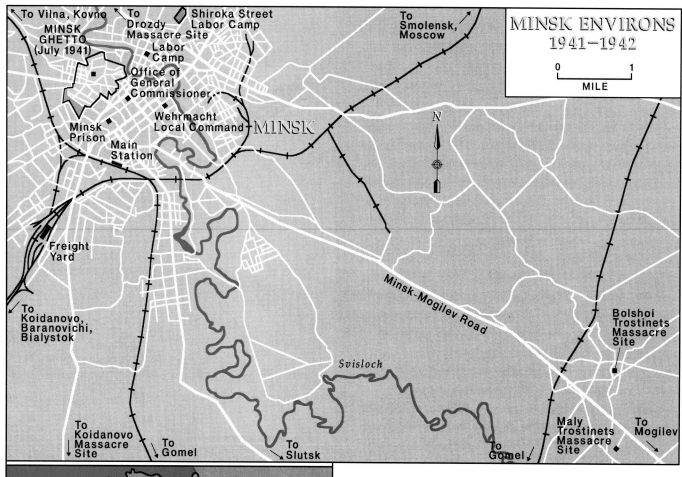

MINSK

German forces occupied Minsk, capital of the Belorussian Soviet Socialist Republic (SSR) in the Soviet Union, shortly after beginning the invasion of the Soviet Union on June 22, 1941. During the German occupation, the Belorussian SSR became part of the Reich Commissariat Ostland (Reichskommissariat Ostland). Within this German civilian administration, Minsk became a district capital. Wilhelm Kube, the German general commissioner of Belorussia, governed from Minsk.

In late July 1941, the Germans ordered the establishment of a ghetto in a small section of the northwestern part of Minsk. About 80,000 people, including Jews from nearby towns, were crowded into the Minsk ghetto.

Between November 1941 and October 1942, over 20,000 Jews from Germany and the Protectorate of Bohemia and Moravia were deported to Minsk. Many were killed upon arrival in Maly Trostinets, a small village about eight miles to the east. Others were housed in a separate ghetto in Minsk that segregated German Jews from local Belorussian Jews. Little contact was permitted between residents of the two ghettos.

Jews were forced to work on labor projects in factories

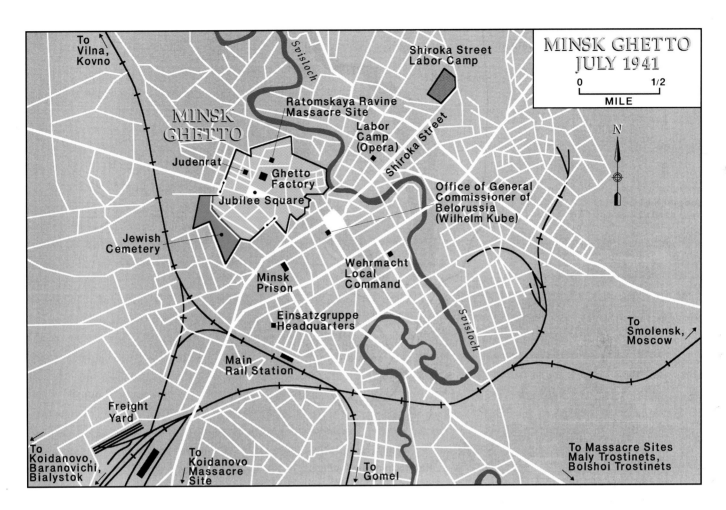

inside the ghetto. They were also used for forced labor outside the ghetto, especially in the Shiroka Street labor camp and the opera house (where Jewish private property was sorted and stored).

Detachments of the Einsatzgruppen began massacres in Minsk in July 1941, even before the establishment of the ghetto. Shootings of Jews occurred almost daily. By January 1942, Einsatzgruppen reports indicated that only 25,000 Jews remained in the ghetto. The rest had been killed by members of the Einsatzgruppen and by Lithuanian police auxiliaries. In July 1942, the Einsatzgruppen killed more than 10,000 Jews from both ghettos. Several thousand Jews were killed in Koidanovo, a small town southwest of Minsk. Thousands more were killed in Tuchinka, and many died inside the

ghetto. Both the Shiroka Street camp and Jubilee Square in the ghetto were assembly points for Jews rounded up by the Germans for immediate execution.

In August 1941, an anti-German underground was established in the Minsk ghetto. Members of the underground organized escapes from the ghetto and formed partisan units in the forests to the southeast and northwest of Minsk. Jews from Minsk established seven different partisan units. In all, about 10,000 Jews fled to the forests; most of them were killed during the war.

The Minsk ghetto was destroyed by the Germans in the fall of 1943. Some Jews were deported to the Sobibor extermination camp. About 4,000 Jews were killed at Maly Trostinets.

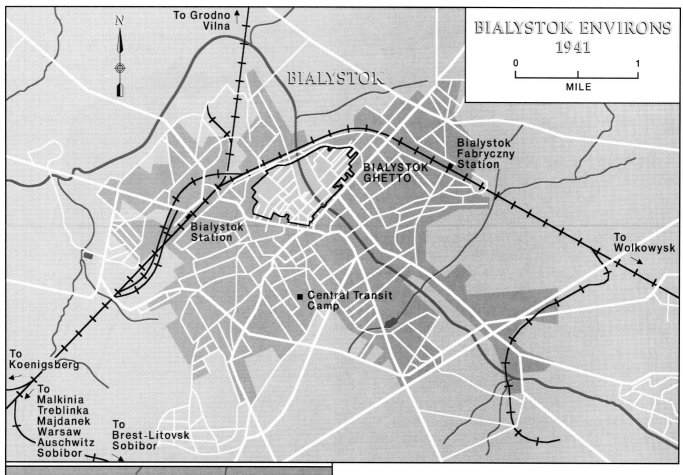

BIALYSTOK ENVIRONS
1941

0   1
MILE

To Grodno
Vilna

BIALYSTOK

Bialystok
Fabryczny
Station

BIALYSTOK
GHETTO

Bialystok
Station

To
Wolkowysk

■ Central Transit
Camp

To
Koenigsberg

To
Malkinia
Treblinka
Majdanek
Warsaw
Auschwitz
Sobibor

To
Brest-Litovsk
Sobibor

GREATER
GERMANY
N

REICHSKOMMISSARIAT
OSTLAND

• Augustow

Grodno

BIALYSTOK DISTRICT

Neman

• Kolno   Knyszyn   • Sokolka

Narew   • Krynki

Bialystok

Lomza   • Grodek

Lapy   Narew

Narew

• Bielsk
Podlaski

Bransk

Pruzhany

Bug   • Siemiatycze

REICHSKOMMISSARIAT
UKRAINE

GENERALGOUVERNEMENT

BIALYSTOK

According to the terms of the German-Soviet Pact of 1939, Bialystok, a city in northeastern Poland, was assigned to the Soviet zone of occupation. Soviet forces entered the city in September 1939, and held it until the German army occupied Bialystok in June 1941. In the early days of the German occupation, Einsatzgruppen detachments rounded up and killed thousands of Jews in Bialystok.

In August 1941, the Germans ordered the establishment of a ghetto in Bialystok. About 50,000 Jews from the city and the surrounding region were confined in a small area of Bialystok city. The ghetto had two sections, divided by the Biala River. Most Jews in the Bialystok ghetto worked in forced-labor projects, primarily in large textile factories located within the ghetto boundaries. The Germans also sometimes used Jews in forced-labor projects outside the ghetto.

In early 1943, thousands of Bialystok Jews were deported to the Treblinka extermination camp. During the deportations, hundreds of Jews, mainly those deemed too weak or sick to travel, were killed at Prage's Garden and at the Jewish cemetery.

In August 1943, the Germans began the final destruction of

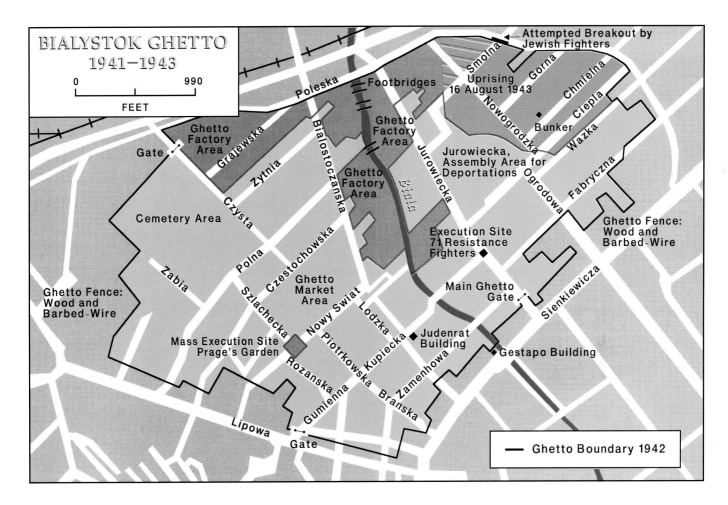

the Bialystok ghetto. German forces and Ukrainian auxiliaries surrounded the ghetto and began systematically rounding up Jews for deportation to Treblinka. Over 10,000 Jews were held in a central transit camp in the city before their deportation to Treblinka. Others were sent to the Majdanek extermination camp. From Majdanek, those deportees whom the Germans considered fit for forced labor were transported to the Poniatowa, Blizyn, or Auschwitz camps; the rest were killed at Majdanek. More than 1,000 Jewish children were sent first to the Theresienstadt ghetto in Bohemia, and then to Auschwitz-Birkenau, where they were killed.

During the August 1943 deportations, when all hope for survival within the ghetto was abandoned, the Bialystok ghetto underground staged an uprising against the Germans. In an unsuccessful attempt to break out of the ghetto and join partisans in the nearby forests, armed Jews attacked German forces near the ghetto fence along Smolna Street. The fighting in the northeastern section of the ghetto lasted for five days; hundreds of Jews died in this battle. Seventy-one Jewish fighters were killed after being discovered in a bunker and captured by the Germans. More than a hundred Jews managed to escape from the ghetto and join partisan groups in the Bialystok area.

The Soviet army liberated Bialystok in August 1944.

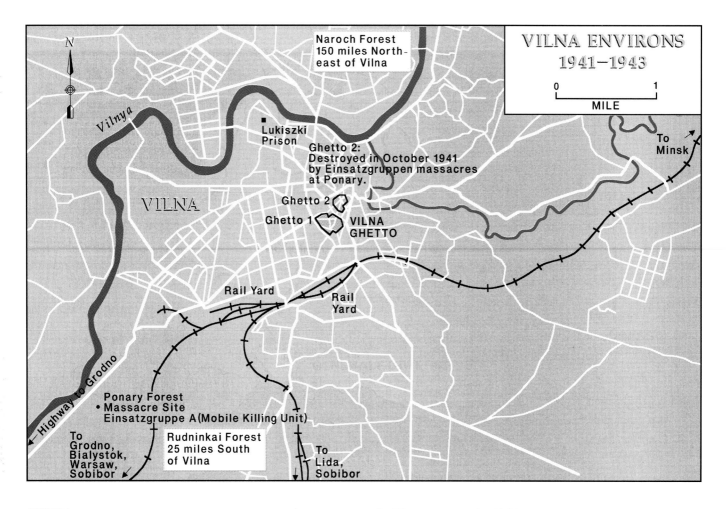

VILNA

Poland and Lithuania both claimed Vilna (Vilnius) after World War I. Polish forces occupied Vilna in 1920, and before the outbreak of World War II, the city of Vilna was part of northeastern Poland. Under the terms of the German-Soviet Pact, Vilna, along with the rest of eastern Poland, was occupied by Soviet forces in late September 1939. In October 1939, the Soviet Union transferred the Vilna region to Lithuania. However, Soviet forces occupied Lithuania in June 1940 and in August 1940 incorporated Vilna, along with the rest of Lithuania, into the Soviet Union. On June 22, 1941, Germany attacked Soviet forces in eastern Europe. The German army occupied Vilna on June 24, 1941, the third day after the invasion.

The Germans established two ghettos—ghetto #1 and ghetto #2—in Vilna in early September 1941. Jews considered incapable of work were concentrated in ghetto #2. In October 1941, German Einsatzgruppen detachments and Lithuanian auxiliaries destroyed ghetto #2, killing the ghetto population in Ponary, a wooded area about eight miles southwest of Vilna. Lukiszki Prison served as a collection center for Jews who were to be taken to Ponary and shot. By the end of 1941,

the Einsatzgruppen had killed about 40,000 Jews in Ponary.

The Jews in ghetto #1 were forced to work in factories or in construction projects outside the ghetto. Some Jews were sent to labor camps in the Vilna region. In periodic killing operations, most of the ghetto's inhabitants were massacred at Ponary. From the spring of 1942 until the spring of 1943, there were no mass killing operations in Vilna. The Germans renewed the killings during the final liquidation of ghetto #1 in late September 1943. Children, the elderly, and the sick were sent to the Sobibor extermination camp or were shot at Ponary. The surviving men were sent to labor camps in Estonia, while the women were sent to labor camps in Latvia.

The Vilna ghetto had a significant Jewish resistance movement. A group of Jewish partisans known as the United Partisan Organization (Fareynegte Partizaner Organizatsye; FPO) was formed in 1942 and operated within the ghetto. The resistance created hiding places for weapons and prepared to fight the Germans. In early September 1943, realizing that the Germans intended the final destruction of the ghetto, resistance members skirmished with the Germans, who had entered the ghetto to begin the deportations. The Jewish council, however, agreed to cooperate in the deportations of

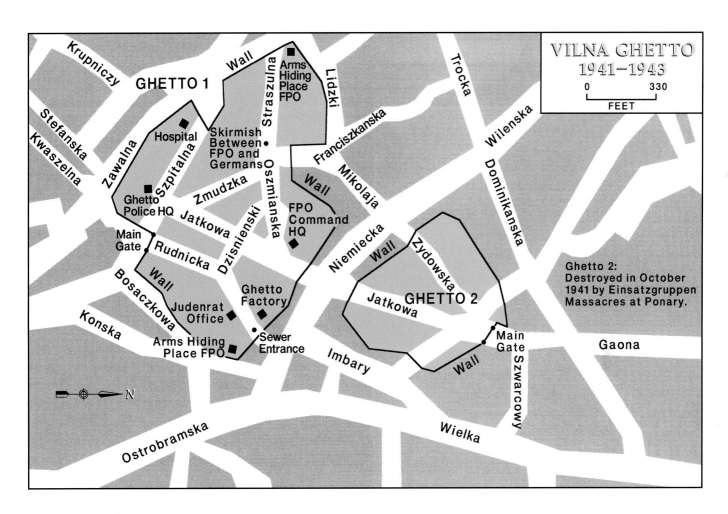

VILNA GHETTO
1941–1943

0   330
FEET

Ghetto 2:
Destroyed in October
1941 by Einsatzgruppen
Massacres at Ponary.

Jews from the ghetto, hoping to minimize bloodshed. Consequently, the FPO decided to flee to the nearby forests to fight the Germans. Some ghetto fighters escaped the final destruction of the ghetto, leaving through the sewers to join partisans in the Rudninkai and Naroch forests outside the city.

In September 1943, in an attempt to destroy the evidence of the killing of Jews at Ponary, the Germans forced detachments of Jewish laborers to open the mass graves and burn the corpses. Jews from nearby labor camps continued to be killed at Ponary. During the German occupation, tens of thousands of Jews from Vilna and the surrounding area, as well as Soviet prisoners of war and others suspected of opposing the Germans, were massacred at Ponary.

The Soviet army liberated Vilna in July 1944.

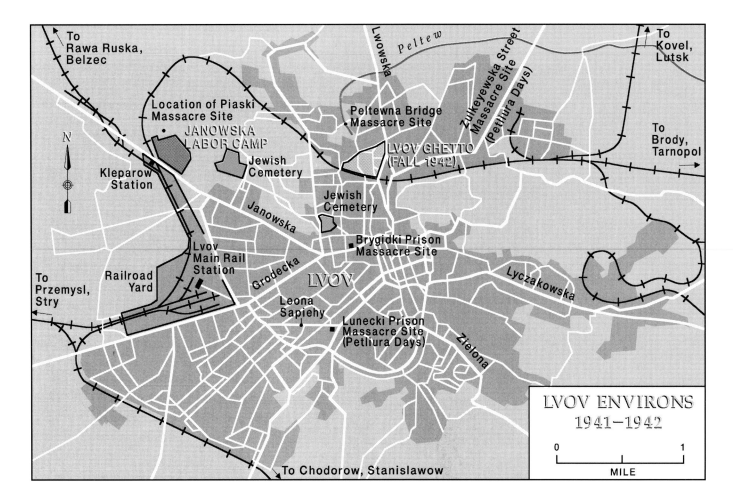

LVOV ENVIRONS
1941–1942

0   1
MILE

LVOV

The city of Lvov (Lviv) in southeastern Poland was occupied by the Soviet Union in 1939, under the terms of the German-Soviet Pact. Lvov was subsequently occupied by Germany after the invasion of the Soviet Union in June 1941.

Encouraged by German forces, Ukrainian nationalists staged a violent pogrom against the Jews in early July 1941, killing about 4,000 Jews. Another pogrom, known as the Petliura Days, was organized in late July. This pogrom was named for Simon Petliura, who had organized anti-Jewish pogroms in the Ukraine after World War I. For three days, Ukrainian militants went on a rampage through the Jewish districts of Lvov. They took groups of Jews to the Jewish cemetery and to Lunecki Prison and shot them. More than 2,000 Jews were killed and thousands more were injured.

In early November 1941, the Germans established a ghetto in the north of Lvov. Thousands of elderly and sick Jews were killed as they crossed the bridge on Peltewna Street on their way to the ghetto. In March 1942, the Germans began deporting Jews from the ghetto to the Belzec killing center. By August 1942, more than 65,000 Jews had been deported from the Lvov ghetto and killed. Thousands of Jews were sent for forced labor to the nearby Janowska camp. The ghetto was finally destroyed in early June 1943. The remaining ghetto residents were sent to the Janowska labor camp or deported to Belzec. Thousands of Jews were killed in the ghetto during this liquidation.

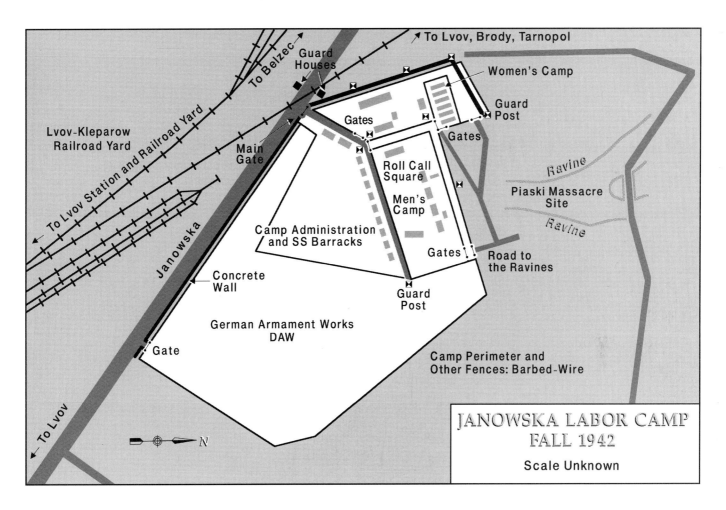

To Lvov, Brody, Tarnopol

To Belzec

Guard Houses

Women's Camp

Guard Post

Lvov-Kleparow Railroad Yard

To Lvov Station and Railroad Yard

Gates

Main Gate

Gates

Roll Call Square

Men's Camp

Ravine

Piaski Massacre Site

Ravine

Janowska

Camp Administration and SS Barracks

Gates

Road to the Ravines

Concrete Wall

Gates

Guard Post

German Armament Works DAW

To Lvov

Gate

Camp Perimeter and Other Fences: Barbed-Wire

N

JANOWSKA LABOR CAMP
FALL 1942
Scale Unknown

JANOWSKA CAMP

In September 1941, the Germans set up a factory in the northeastern suburbs of Lvov, on Janowska Street. It became part of a network of factories owned and operated by the SS called the German Armament Works (Deutsche Ausruestungswerke; DAW). Jews were used as forced laborers, mainly in carpentry and metalwork. The Germans established a camp housing them adjacent to the factory in October 1941.

In addition to being a forced-labor camp for Jews, Janowska was also a transit camp during the mass deportations of Polish Jews to the killing centers in 1942. Jews underwent a selection process in Janowska similar to that used at Auschwitz-Birkenau and Majdanek. Those classified as fit to work remained at Janowska for forced labor. The majority, rejected as unfit for work, were deported to Belzec and killed or were shot at the Piaski ravine, just north of the camp. In the summer and fall of 1942, thousands of Jews (mainly from the Lvov ghetto) were deported to Janowska and killed.

The evacuation of the Janowska camp began in November 1943. Prisoners were forced to open the mass graves and burn the bodies, as the Germans attempted to destroy the traces of mass murder (Aktion 1005). On November 19, 1943, these prisoners staged an uprising and a mass escape attempt. A few succeeded in escaping, but most were recaptured and killed.

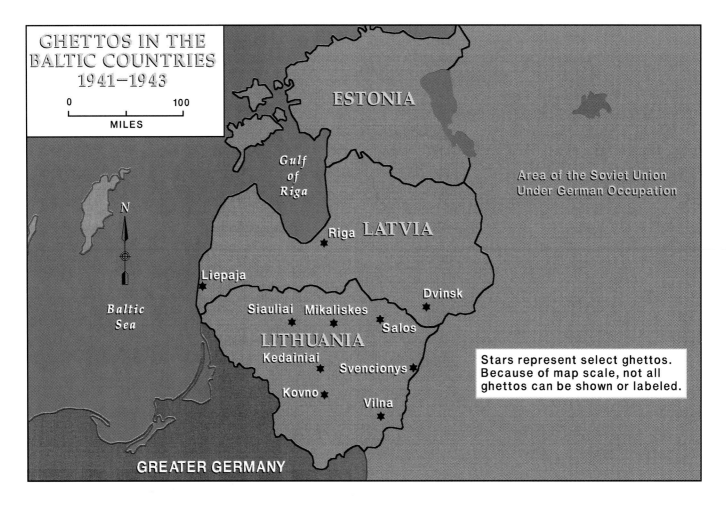

GHETTOS IN THE
BALTIC COUNTRIES
1941–1943

0   100
MILES

ESTONIA

Gulf
of
Riga

Area of the Soviet Union
Under German Occupation

N

Riga   LATVIA

Liepaja

Baltic
Sea

Dvinsk

Siauliai   Mikaliskes

Salos

LITHUANIA

Kedainiai

Svencionys

Stars represent select ghettos.
Because of map scale, not all
ghettos can be shown or labeled.

Kovno

Vilna

GREATER GERMANY

THE BALTIC COUNTRIES 1940-1945

Between the two world wars, the Baltic states (Estonia, Lithuania, and Latvia) were independent republics. The Vilna region, which had been part of Poland, was transferred to Lithuania through a Soviet-Lithuanian treaty of October 1939. The Soviet Union occupied the Baltic states in June 1940 and annexed them in August 1940. In June and July 1941, following the German invasion of the Soviet Union, the Germans occupied the Baltic states. During the German occupation, the Baltic states were included in the Reich Commissariat Ostland (Reichskommissariat Ostland), a German civilian administration.

The pre-1941 Jewish population of Lithuania, swelled by the influx of refugees from German-occupied Poland, was about 250,000. The Lithuanians carried out pogroms against the Jews both shortly before and immediately after the arrival of German forces. In June and July 1941, German Einsatzgruppen detachments, together with Lithuanian auxiliaries, began killing the Jews of Lithuania. By the end of August 1941, most of the Jews in rural Lithuania had been killed. By November 1941, most of the Jews who had been concentrated in ghettos in the larger cities had also been killed.

The surviving 40,000 Jews were concentrated in the Vilna, Kovno, Siauliai, and Svencionys ghettos, and in various labor camps in Lithuania.

In 1943, the Vilna and Svencionys ghettos were destroyed, and those of Kovno and Siauliai were converted into concentration camps. Some 15,000 Lithuanian Jews were deported to labor camps in Latvia and Estonia. About 5,000 Jews were deported to the killing centers in Poland. Shortly before withdrawing from Lithuania in the fall of 1944, the Germans deported about 10,000 Jews from Kovno and Siauliai to camps in Germany.

Before the war, about 94,000 Jews lived in Latvia. Detachments of German Einsatzgruppen, together with Latvian, Lithuanian, and Ukrainian auxiliaries, massacred most of the Latvian Jews. Ghettos were established in the larger cities of Riga, Dvinsk, and Liepaja. Thousands of German and Austrian Jews were deported to the Riga ghetto in 1941 and early 1942. Einsatzgruppen killed most of them, along with most Latvian Jews. By the beginning of 1943 only about 5,000 Jews remained in Latvia. They were concentrated in the Riga, Dvinsk, and Liepaja ghettos and in a few labor camps, the largest of which was Kaiserwald in Riga.

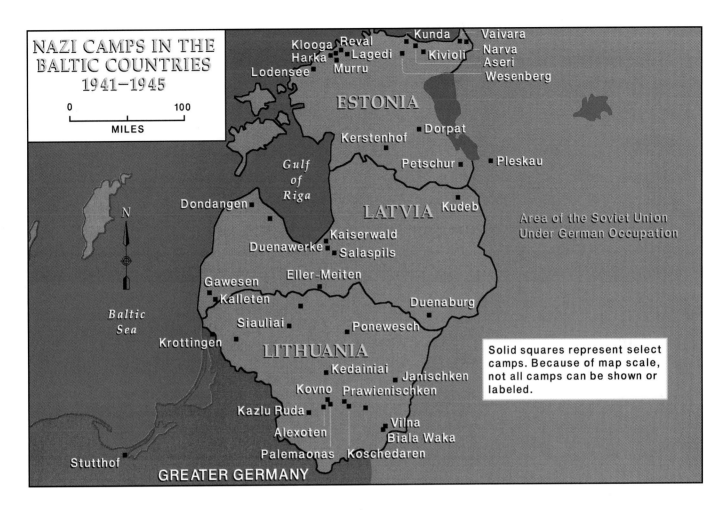

NAZI CAMPS IN THE BALTIC COUNTRIES 1941–1945

0   100
MILES

Kunda   Vaivara
Klooga Reval   Narva
Harka   Lagedi   Kivioli   Aseri
Lodensee   Murru   Wesenberg

ESTONIA

Kerstenhof   Dorpat

Gulf of Riga   Petschur   Pleskau

Dondangen   LATVIA   Kudeb

Area of the Soviet Union Under German Occupation

Kaiserwald
Duenawerke   Salaspils

Eller-Meiten

Gawesen   Duenaburg
Kalleten

Baltic Sea   Siauliai   Ponewesch

Krottingen   LITHUANIA

Solid squares represent select camps. Because of map scale, not all camps can be shown or labeled.

Kedainiai
Kovno   Janischken
Prawienischken
Kazlu Ruda
Alexoten   Vilna
Palemaonas   Koschedaren   Biala Waka
Stutthof
GREATER GERMANY

No ghettos were created in Estonia, the northernmost and smallest of the Baltic states. In 1939, the Jewish population of Estonia numbered about 4,500. Almost half of the Estonian Jews lived in Tallinn, the capital city. The rest lived in other towns, such as Tartu, Valga, Parnu, Narva, Viljandi, Rakvere, Voru, and Nomme. German Einsatzgruppen, together with Estonian auxiliaries, had massacred the Jews of Estonia by the end of 1941.

After the fall of 1942, tens of thousands of Jews from other European countries were sent to forced-labor camps inside Estonia. The main camp was Vaivara. Jewish forced laborers built military defenses for the German army and mined shale oil. With the advance of the Soviet army in the fall of 1944, the Estonian camps were evacuated, as were other camps throughout the Baltic. The Jews were transferred by sea to the Stutthof concentration camp near Danzig.

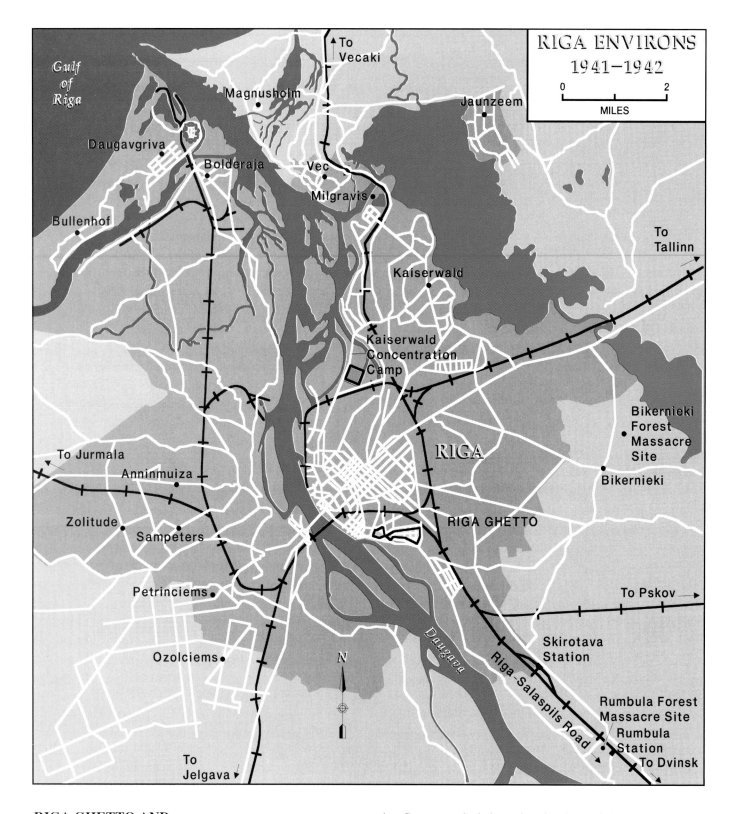

RIGA ENVIRONS
1941–1942

RIGA GHETTO AND
KAISERWALD LABOR CAMP

From 1918 to 1940, Riga was the capital of independent Latvia. In August 1940, the Soviet Union annexed Latvia and Riga became the capital of the Latvian SSR. German forces occupied Riga in early July 1941. Riga became the capital of the German administration in the Reich Commissariat Ostland.

Before World War II, about 40,000 Jews lived in Riga, representing slightly more than 10 percent of the city's population. German Einsatzgruppen detachments, together with Latvian auxiliaries, killed several thousand Jews shortly

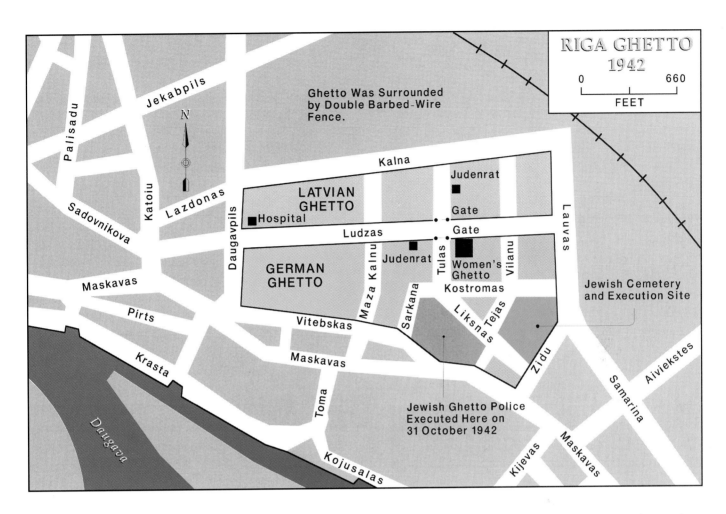

after German forces entered the city. In mid-August, the Germans ordered the establishment of a ghetto in the southeastern area of the city. In late November and early December of 1941, the Germans began to move about 28,000 Jews to a fenced-in area of the ghetto; they were then killed in the Rumbula Forest, near the Rumbula railway station, five miles southeast of Riga along the Riga-Dvinsk railway and the Riga-Salaspils road.

The surviving Jews were fenced into what became known as the "small" or "Latvian" ghetto. The Germans deported more than 15,000 Jews from Germany, Austria, and the Protectorate of Bohemia and Moravia to Riga. They were concentrated in the residences of those Jews killed at Rumbula in November 1941. This ghetto was called the "big" or "German" ghetto. Most of the German Jews deported to Riga were also later killed in the Rumbula Forest.

Several hundred Jews in the Riga ghetto organized resistance against the Germans. Small groups sought to escape from the ghetto and join partisans in the surrounding forests. In October 1942, one small group was discovered outside the

ghetto by the Germans and killed. In reprisal for partisan activities, the Germans seized and killed more than 100 people from the ghetto, and executed almost all Jewish policemen for participating in resistance activities.

In the summer of 1943, the Germans deported some of the ghetto inhabitants to the Kaiserwald concentration camp, which had been established in March in the north of the city. Others were deported to Kaiserwald subcamps in Latvia. The ghetto was finally destroyed in December 1943, and the last Jews were deported to Kaiserwald. The surviving Jews in Latvia, from the destroyed ghettos of Riga, Liepaja, and Dvinsk, were concentrated in Kaiserwald and its subcamps.

In 1944, in an attempt to destroy evidence of mass murder, the Germans forced prisoners to reopen mass graves in Rumbula and burn the bodies as part of Aktion 1005. Once their work was completed, these prisoners were also killed. In the summer of 1944, the Germans killed thousands of Jewish prisoners in Kaiserwald and its subcamps. Those remaining were later deported to the Stutthof concentration camp.

On October 13, 1944, the Soviet army liberated Riga.

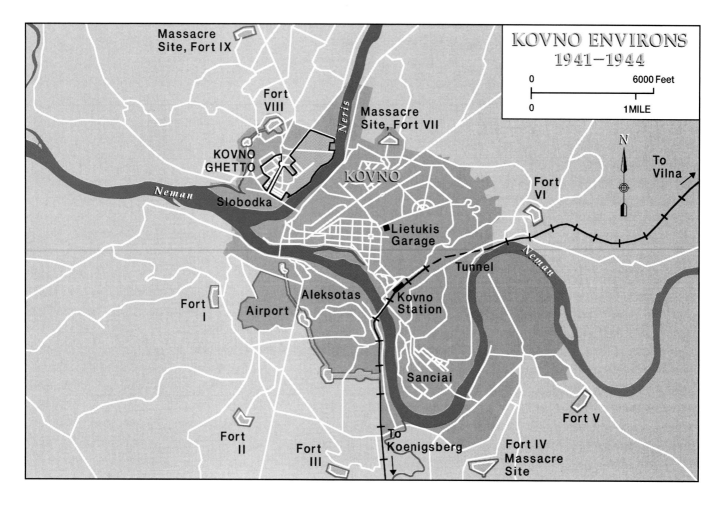

KOVNO GHETTO

Before World War II, Kovno (Kaunas) was the capital of and largest city in Lithuania. It had a Jewish population of 40,000, about one-quarter of the city's total population. The Soviet Union occupied Kovno in 1940. Immediately before and following the German occupation of the city on June 24, 1941, rampaging Lithuanian mobs began to attack Jews in Kovno, especially along Jurbarko and Krisciukaicio streets. Hundreds of Jews were killed during this period. Dozens more were taken to the Lietukis Garage and killed there.

In early July 1941, German Einsatzgruppen detachments and their Lithuanian auxiliaries began systematic massacres of Jews in several of the forts around Kovno. These forts had been constructed by the Russian tsars in the nineteenth century for the defense of the city. Einsatzgruppen detachments and Lithuanian auxiliaries shot thousands of Jewish men, women, and children, primarily in Fort Nine, but also in Forts Four and Seven.

In August 1941, the Germans concentrated the remaining Jews in a ghetto established in the Slobodka suburb of Kovno. The ghetto had two parts, the small ghetto and the large ghetto, separated by Paneriu Street. Each ghetto was enclosed by barbed wire and guarded by Lithuanian auxiliaries and German police. The Jews were employed primarily as forced laborers at various sites outside the ghetto.

On October 4, 1941, the small ghetto was liquidated. Those Jews deemed fit for work were transferred to the large ghetto; the rest were shot at Fort Nine. On October 28, 1941, about 10,000 Jews from the large ghetto were killed. In the fall of 1943, the large ghetto was liquidated. Thousands of Jews were deported to forced-labor camps in Estonia, and the Kovno ghetto was converted into a concentration camp. In July 1944, the Germans evacuated the camp, deporting the remaining Jews to the Dachau concentration camp in Germany or to the Stutthof camp, near Danzig, on the Baltic coast.

The Kovno ghetto had an extensive Jewish resistance movement. The resistance acquired arms, developed secret training areas in the ghetto, and established contact with Soviet partisans in the forests around Kovno. In 1943, the General Jewish Fighting Organization (Yidishe Algemeyne Kamfs Organizatsye) was established, uniting the major resistance groups in the ghetto. Under this organization's direction, hundreds of ghetto fighters escaped the Kovno

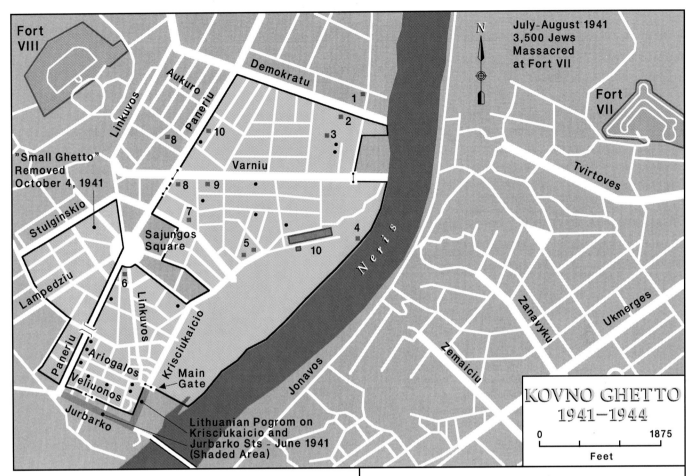

**KOVNO GHETTO
1941–1944**

0   1875

Feet

ghetto to join partisan groups. Very few fighters survived the war.

The Jewish council in Kovno and its chairman, Dr. Elchanan Elkes, actively supported the ghetto underground. Moreover, a number of Jewish policemen participated in resistance activities. The Germans shot about 40 members of the Jewish police for such activities.

The Soviet army liberated Kovno in August 1944.

LEGEND

⧓ **Footbridge**
— **Ghetto Surrounded with Barbed-Wire Fence**
• **Underground Hiding Places**
↦ **Gates**
▪ **Select Features**

1. **Hiding Place for Books**
2. **Clandestine Arms Training**
3. **Ammunition Hiding Place**
4. **Clandestine Meeting Place**
5. **Clandestine School and Arms Training**
6. **Young Zionists**
7. **Pharmacy (Clandestine Radio)**
8. **Safe House**
9. **Jewish Council Building (Judenrat)**
10. **Workshop**

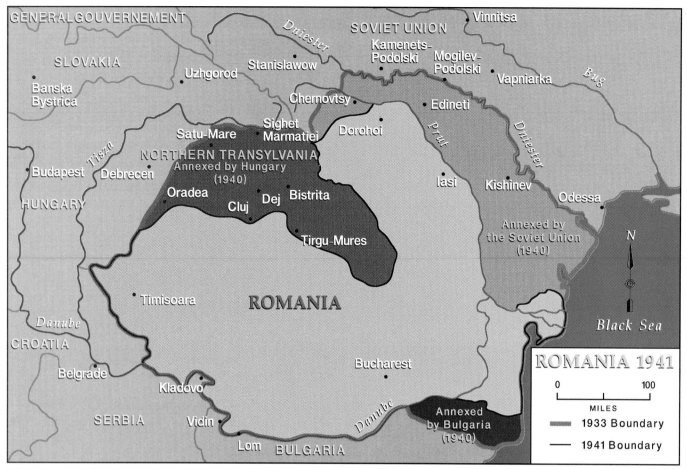

ROMANIA 1941

0   100

MILES

1933 Boundary
1941 Boundary

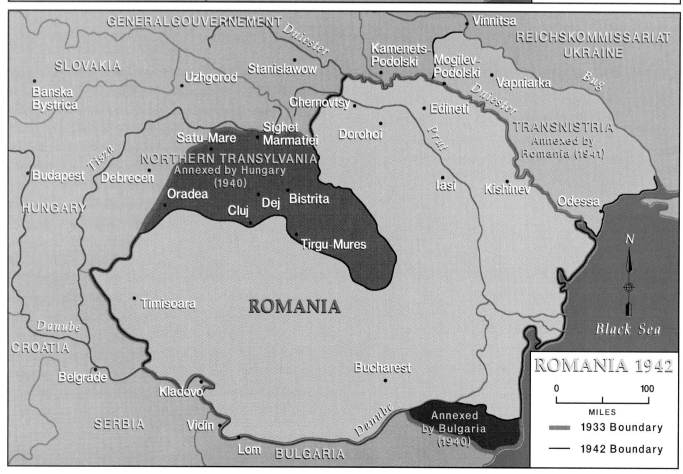

ROMANIA 1942

0   100

MILES

1933 Boundary
1942 Boundary

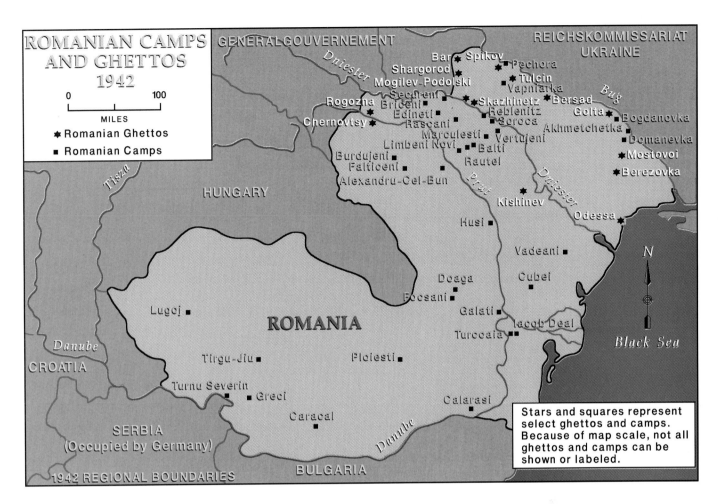

ROMANIAN CAMPS AND GHETTOS 1942

0 — 100
MILES

★ Romanian Ghettos
■ Romanian Camps

GENERALGOUVERNEMENT

REICHSKOMMISSARIAT UKRAINE

Dniester

Bar ★ Spikov
Shargorod ■ Pechora
Mogilev-Podolski ■ Tulcin
Secireni ■ Vapniarka
Rogozna ★ Skazhinetz ■ Bersad
Briceni ■ Reblenitz
Edineti ★ Golta
Chernovtsy ★ Raşcani ■ Soroca Akhmetchetka ■ Bogdanovka
Vertujeni ■ Domanevka
Limbeni Novi ■ Balti
Burdujeni ■ Rautel ★ Mostovoi
Falticeni ■ ★ Berezovka
Alexandru-Cel-Bun
Prut
Kishinev
Husi Odessa ■
Vadeani ■
Doaga Cubei ■
Focsani ■
Galati ■
Iacob Deal
Turcoaia ■■

Bug

Dniester

N

Black Sea

HUNGARY

Tisza

ROMANIA

Lugoj ■

Danube

Tirgu-Jiu ■

Ploiesti ■

CROATIA

Turnu Severin ■
■ Greci

Caracal

Calarasi ■

SERBIA
(Occupied by Germany)

Danube

BULGARIA

1942 REGIONAL BOUNDARIES

Stars and squares represent select ghettos and camps. Because of map scale, not all ghettos and camps can be shown or labeled.

THE HOLOCAUST OF ROMANIAN JEWRY

Romania had a prewar Jewish population of about 750,000, the third largest Jewish community in Europe, after the Soviet Union and Poland. Romania was stripped of territory in the summer and fall of 1940. On June 28, 1940, the Soviet Union occupied Romanian territory, seizing Bessarabia, located between the Prut and Dniester rivers, and northern Bukovina, along the Carpathian Mountains in the northeast (Romania reoccupied these territories in June and July 1941). Hungarian and Bulgarian demands on Romanian territory were settled in the 1940 Vienna Arbitration Awards, sponsored by Germany and Italy. Romania was forced to cede northern Transylvania to Hungary on August 30, 1940, and southern Dobruja to Bulgaria on September 7, 1940. After the German occupation of Hungary in 1944, the Jews of northern Transylvania were included in the deportation of Hungarian Jews to Auschwitz. Bulgaria did not deport the Jews of southern Dobruja. The remaining Jews in Romania were subject to Romanian rule.

As Romania came under German influence and with the rise of the Romanian fascist organization, the Iron Guard, Romanian authorities introduced increasingly harsh measures against Jews. Romania generally did not deport Jews to the extermination camps in German-occupied Poland, ultimately rejecting German plans to send 200,000 Romanian Jews to the Belzec extermination camp. However, Romanian forces, in cooperation with Einsatzgruppen detachments, brutally killed hundreds of thousands of Jews, mainly residents of Bessarabia, northern Bukovina, and Transnistria (the area of the Ukraine transferred to Romanian rule in 1941).

Romania joined Germany and Italy in the Axis alliance on November 20, 1940, and participated in the invasion of the Soviet Union on June 22, 1941. Within days of the invasion, Romanian authorities staged a pogrom in the city of Iasi, the regional capital of northeastern Romania and a center of Iron Guard activity. At least 8,000 Jews, nearly a fifth of the city's Jewish population, were killed, thousands in their homes and in the streets of the city. Thousands more were arrested and shot in the courtyard of the Iasi police headquarters. Over 4,000 Jews, survivors of the pogrom, were deported in sealed trains to Calarasi and Podul Iloaei. More than half of those deported died, deprived of food and water during days of travel in the heat of summer.

Einsatzgruppen detachments and Romanian units roamed

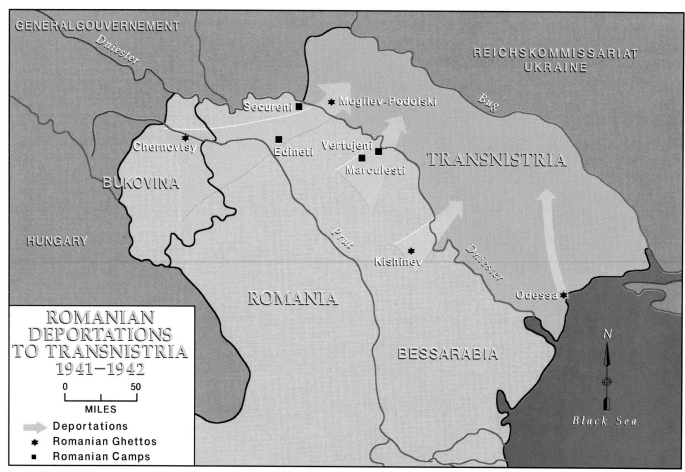

ROMANIAN DEPORTATIONS TO TRANSNISTRIA 1941–1942

0   50
MILES

➤ Deportations
★ Romanian Ghettos
■ Romanian Camps

GENERALGOUVERNEMENT

Dniester

REICHSKOMMISSARIAT UKRAINE

Secureni ■   ★ Mogilev-Podolski

Chernovtsy ★

Edineti ■   Vertujeni ■

BUKOVINA   Marculesti

TRANSNISTRIA

Bug

HUNGARY

Prut

ROMANIA

Kishinev ★   *Dniester*

Odessa ★

BESSARABIA

N

Black Sea

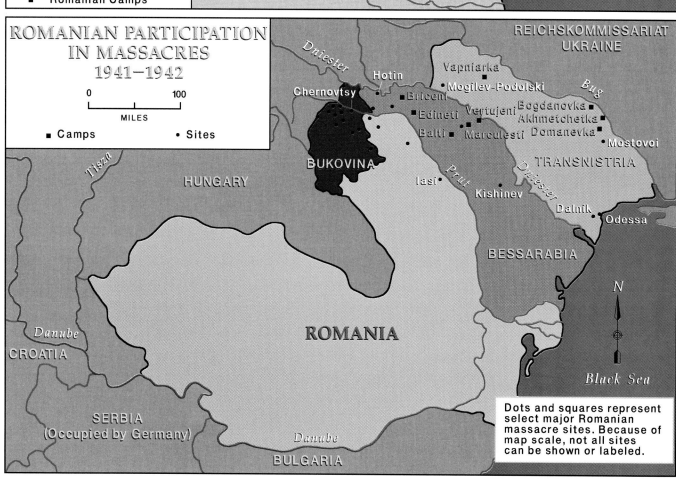

ROMANIAN PARTICIPATION IN MASSACRES 1941–1942

0   100
MILES

■ Camps   • Sites

REICHSKOMMISSARIAT UKRAINE

Dniester

Hotin •

Chernovtsy   Vapniarka ■

• Mogilev-Podolski

Briceni •   *Bug*

Edineti •   Vertujeni ■   Bogdanovka ■

BUKOVINA   Balti •   Marculesti ■   Akhmetchetka ■

Domanevka ■

Mostovoi •

TRANSNISTRIA

Tisza

HUNGARY

Iasi •   *Prut*

Kishinev •   *Dniester*

Dalnik •

Odessa •

BESSARABIA

N

Danube

CROATIA

ROMANIA

SERBIA
(Occupied by Germany)   *Danube*

BULGARIA

Black Sea

Dots and squares represent select major Romanian massacre sites. Because of map scale, not all sites can be shown or labeled.

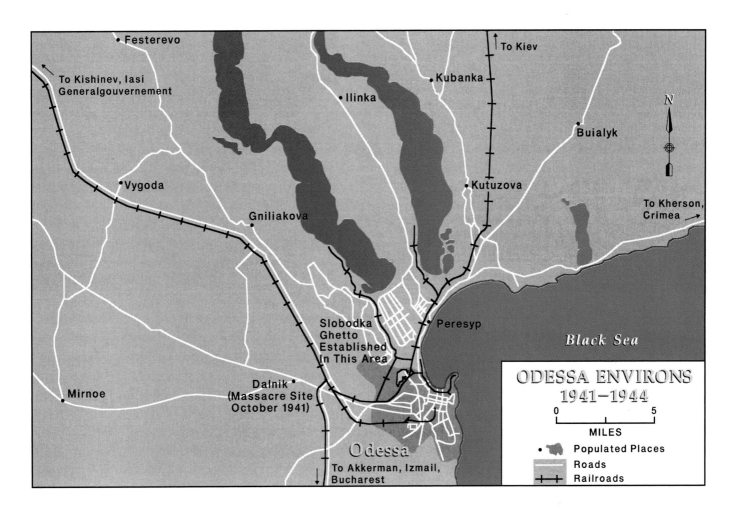

ODESSA ENVIRONS
1941–1944

0 ——— 5
MILES

• Populated Places
▬ Roads
┼┼ Railroads

through Bessarabia, northern Bukovina, and the southern Ukraine, massacring large numbers of Jews. When Romanian and German units entered Kishinev, the capital of Bessarabia, they began slaughtering the Jewish residents. In July the surviving Jews, about 11,000 people, were concentrated in a ghetto and drafted for forced labor. Many were killed. In October, the remaining Jews in the Kishinev ghetto were deported by the Romanians to camps and ghettos in Transnistria, as were most of the surviving Jews of Bessarabia and northern Bukovina. Many Jews were killed while being forced to cross the Dniester River, the border line between Bessarabia and Transnistria. Some died on the way to Transnistria, and about two-thirds died after arrival, mostly from starvation or during epidemics.

Thousands more were massacred by the Romanians in Transnistria. Over 50,000 Jews were interned in Bogdanovka, a Romanian camp along the Bug River in Transnistria. In December 1941, Romanian troops, together with Ukrainian auxiliaries, massacred almost all the Jews in that camp; shootings continued for more than a week. The Romanians also massacred Jews in the Domanevka and Akhmetchetka camps.

By the fall of 1944, when Romania left the Axis alliance, more than 350,000 Romanian Jews had been killed.

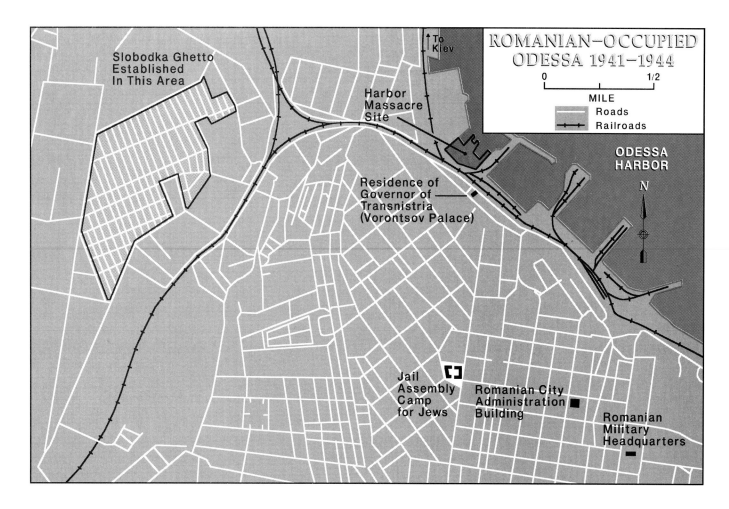

THE MASSACRE OF THE JEWS OF ODESSA

Before World War II, 180,000 Jews lived in Odessa, a Black Sea port city in the Ukraine. On October 16, 1941, after a long siege, Romanian and German forces occupied Odessa. At least half of the city's Jewish population had already fled. The remaining Jewish population of Odessa under occupation was between 80,000 and 90,000 people.

Odessa became the capital of Transnistria. On October 22, 1941, Romanian military headquarters in Odessa were blown up. The blast killed more than 60 officers, including the military governor of the city. In reprisal, Romanian army units assembled 19,000 Jews in a public square in the harbor area, shot them, doused the bodies with gasoline, and burned them. Another 20,000 Jews were assembled at the local jail and then taken to the village of Dalnik, where the Romanians shot some of the Jews and locked others into warehouses that were then set ablaze and sprayed with machine-gun fire. After the massacre, some Jews in Odessa were deported to Romanian camps in Bogdanovka, Domanevka, and Akhmetchetka.

At the end of December 1941, the remaining 35,000 to 40,000 Jews in Odessa were ordered into a ghetto established in Slobodka. They were left there without shelter for over a week. Many died of exposure in harsh winter conditions. By the end of February 1942, most of the surviving Jews in the Slobodka ghetto were killed or deported to the Berezovka region of Transnistria, where the majority were included in the massacre of local Jews by ethnic Germans living in the region. Others died of starvation, disease, and exposure.

The Soviet army liberated Odessa in April 1944.

NAZI EXTERMINATION CAMPS

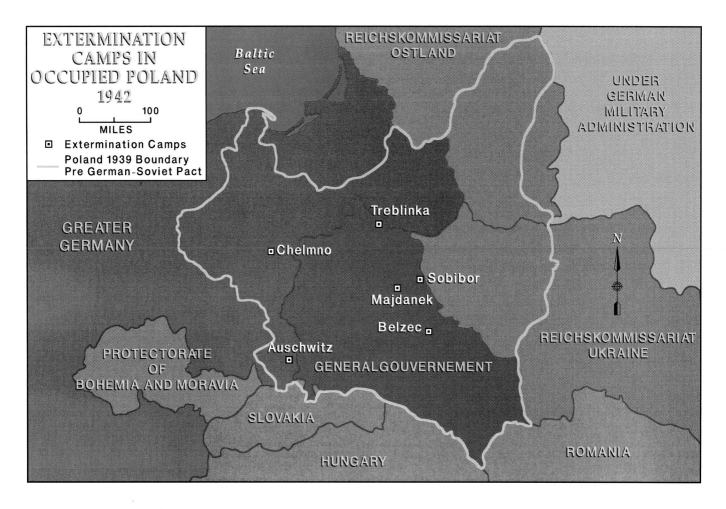

EXTERMINATION CAMPS IN OCCUPIED POLAND 1942

0   100 MILES

☐ Extermination Camps
Poland 1939 Boundary
Pre German-Soviet Pact

EXTERMINATION CAMPS

Extermination camps were killing centers designed to carry out genocide. The Nazis established six extermination camps in former Polish territory—Chelmno, Belzec, Sobibor, Treblinka, Auschwitz-Birkenau (part of the Auschwitz complex), and Majdanek. Both Auschwitz and Majdanek functioned as concentration and forced-labor camps as well as killing centers. The overwhelming majority of the victims of the extermination camps were Jews.

The first extermination camp was established at Chelmno in the Warthegau, an area annexed to Germany. Gassing operations began there in December 1941. Victims at Chelmno were killed in gas vans (hermetically sealed trucks with engine exhaust diverted to the interior compartment). Chelmno operated without interruption until March 1943 and was reopened during the final liquidation of the Lodz ghetto in 1944. The victims of Chelmno were primarily Jews from the Warthegau region, especially from the Lodz ghetto. Those deported from Lodz included some Jews previously sent there from Germany, Austria, Bohemia and Moravia, and Luxembourg, and about 5,000 Roma (Gypsies). Other victims of the Chelmno extermination camp included several hundred

Poles and Soviet prisoners of war.

The Belzec, Sobibor, and Treblinka extermination camps were established as part of Aktion Reinhard (Operation Reinhard), the Nazi plan to kill the Jews of southern and central Poland. During the German occupation of Poland in World War II, this territory was known as the Generalgouvernement. All three camps used carbon monoxide generated by stationary engines attached to gas chambers to kill the victims. Belzec operated from March to December 1942. Sobibor operated from April 1942 to October 1943. Treblinka operated from July 1942 to the fall of 1943.

The overwhelming majority of victims of the Operation Reinhard camps were Polish Jews. At Belzec they were primarily from the ghettos of southern Poland. Jews were deported to Sobibor mostly from the ghettos of eastern Poland, especially from the Lublin area. Transports to Treblinka arrived mainly from the Jewish ghettos of central Poland, above all from the Warsaw ghetto. Additional transports of Jews arrived from western and central Europe as well as from the Balkans. More than 1.7 million Jews and several thousand Roma were murdered as part of Operation Reinhard.

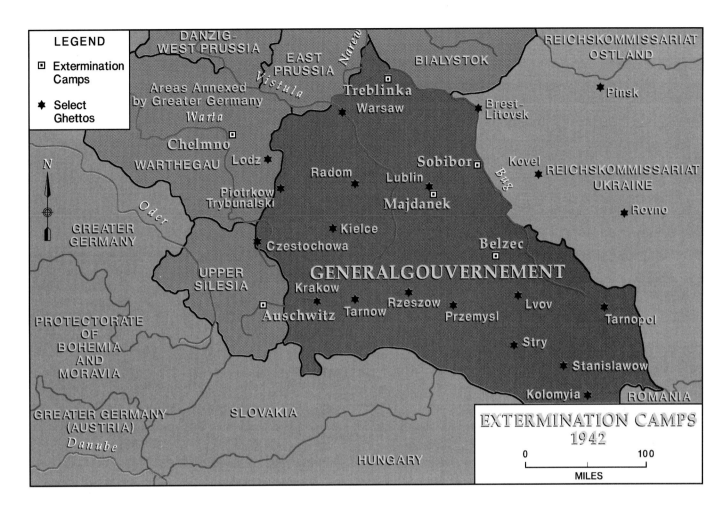

LEGEND

▣ Extermination Camps

★ Select Ghettos

DANZIG-WEST PRUSSIA

EAST PRUSSIA

Vistula

Narew

BIALYSTOK

REICHSKOMMISSARIAT OSTLAND

★ Pinsk

Areas Annexed by Greater Germany

Warta

Treblinka

Warsaw

Brest-Litovsk

N

Chelmno

WARTHEGAU

Lodz ★

Radom

Sobibor ▣

Kovel

REICHSKOMMISSARIAT UKRAINE

Oder

Lublin

Piotrkow Trybunalski

Majdanek ▣

★ Rovno

GREATER GERMANY

★ Kielce

Czestochowa

Belzec ▣

GENERALGOUVERNEMENT

UPPER SILESIA

Krakow

Tarnow

Rzeszow

Lvov

PROTECTORATE OF BOHEMIA AND MORAVIA

Auschwitz ▣

Przemysl

Tarnopol

★ Stry

★ Stanislawow

GREATER GERMANY (AUSTRIA)

Danube

SLOVAKIA

Kolomyia ★

ROMANIA

HUNGARY

EXTERMINATION CAMPS 1942

0   100

MILES

Auschwitz was a concentration, forced-labor, and extermination camp. It was located near the prewar German-Polish border in Eastern Upper Silesia, an area annexed to Germany after the 1939 invasion of Poland. Auschwitz-Birkenau began operating as an extermination camp in March 1942. New arrivals underwent selection on arrival. Those deemed fit for forced labor were removed from incoming transports, while the overwhelming majority of deportees were sent directly to gas chambers. At the height of gassing operations in Auschwitz there were four gas chambers using Zyklon B (crystalline hydrogen cyanide) as the killing agent. Gassing operations in Auschwitz continued until November 1944.

Trains brought Jews almost daily to Auschwitz-Birkenau from virtually every German-occupied country. The victims at Auschwitz numbered more than 1.1 million Jews from all over Europe, between 70,000 and 75,000 Poles, about 21,000 Roma, and 15,000 Soviet prisoners of war.

Majdanek was located near Lublin in the Generalgouvernement. Like Auschwitz, it functioned as a concentration, forced-labor, and extermination camp. Prisoners sent to Majdanek underwent selection on arrival. Those considered unable to work were sent directly to the gas chambers; the remainder were used for forced labor. Gassing operations began at Majdanek in October 1942 and continued until the fall of 1943. The gas chambers used both carbon monoxide and Zyklon B. The victims at Majdanek included Jews from central Poland, especially Lublin, Warsaw, and Bialystok; Jews from western Europe; more than 100,000 non-Jewish Poles; tens of thousands of Soviet prisoners of war; and some Roma. Non-Jews were usually not victims of gassing operations at Majdanek, but died as a result of the terrible conditions in the camp.

An estimated 3.5 million Jews were killed in these six extermination camps as part of the "Final Solution."

EUROPEAN RAIL
SYSTEM 1939

0   200
MILES

● Cities with a 1939 Jewish
   Population of 40,000 or Greater

□ Extermination Camps 1942

Major Railroads

Riga

Vilna

London ●

● Amsterdam

Berlin ●

Warsaw ● Treblinka □

Chelmno □

Lodz ●

Sobibor □

Majdanek □

Belzec □

Auschwitz □ ● Krakow

Lvo

Paris ●

Vienna ●

● Budapest

Salonika ●

DEPORTATIONS

The Wannsee Conference was held on January 20, 1942, in Berlin, to discuss and coordinate the implementation of the "Final Solution," which was already under way. At Wannsee, the SS estimated that the "Final Solution" would involve 11 million European Jews, including those from non-occupied countries such as Ireland, Sweden, Turkey, and Great Britain.

The European rail network played a crucial role in the implementation of the "Final Solution." Jews from Germany and German-occupied Europe were deported by rail to the extermination camps in occupied Poland, where they were killed. The Germans attempted to disguise their intentions, referring to deportations as "resettlement to the east." The victims were told they were to be taken to labor camps, but in reality, from 1942 onward, deportation meant transit to killing centers for most Jews.

Deportations on this scale required the coordination of numerous German government ministries, including the Central Office for Reich Security (Reichssicherheitshauptamt; RSHA), the Transport Ministry, and the Foreign Office. The RSHA coordinated and directed the deportations; the Transport Ministry organized train schedules; and the Foreign Office negotiated with German-allied states to hand over their Jews.

Both freight and passenger cars were used for the deportations. The deportees were usually not provided with food or water for the journey, even when they had to wait days on railroad spurs for other trains to pass. The people being deported in sealed freight cars suffered from intense heat during summer and freezing temperatures during winter, and also from the stench of urine and excrement. Aside from a bucket, there was no provision for sanitary requirements. Without food or water, many deportees died before the trains reached their destination. Armed guards shot anyone trying to escape. Between the fall of 1941 and the fall of 1944, the German railways transported millions of people to their deaths in the killing centers in occupied Poland.

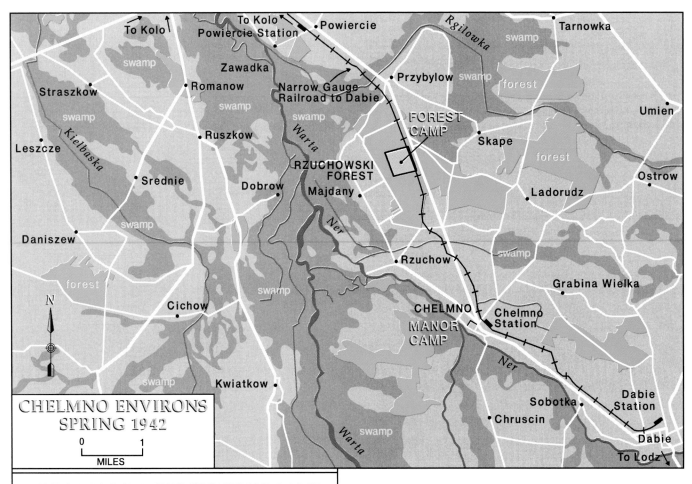

CHELMNO ENVIRONS
SPRING 1942

0   1
MILES

CHELMNO EXTERMINATION CAMP

0   100
MILES

☐ Extermination Camp

Poland 1939 Boundary
Pre German-Soviet Pact

CHELMNO EXTERMINATION CAMP

The village of Chelmno is located about 45 miles west of Lodz in western Poland, which under German occupation in World War II was in the Warthegau. The German name for the village was Kulmhof. The Chelmno killing center was established to kill Jews from the nearby Lodz ghetto and in the Warthegau. It was the first Nazi camp where poison gas was used for mass murder.

The Chelmno camp was operated by the Chelmno Special Commando, made up of both security police and regular uniformed policemen. The camp was situated close to the Powiercie railway station and had two sites, located 2.5 miles apart: the Schlosslager (manor-house camp) and the Waldlager (forest camp). The Schlosslager was an old manor house inside the village of Chelmno. It held the reception and extermination center, and residences for the camp staff. The manor-house area was surrounded by a high wooden fence. The Waldlager, in the nearby Rzuchowski Forest, included mass graves and crematory ovens.

Victims transported to Chelmno by freight train were transferred at the Kolo junction to a train running on a narrow-gauge track, which took them to the Powiercie

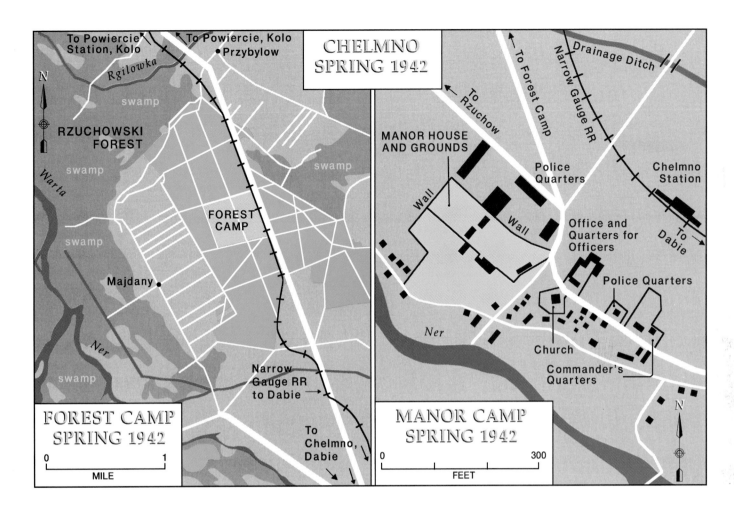

CHELMNO
SPRING 1942

FOREST CAMP
SPRING 1942

0   1
MILE

MANOR CAMP
SPRING 1942

0   300
FEET

station. Deportees were transported in trucks from the station to the manor-house camp. Upon entering the camp, they were concentrated in the courtyard, told that they would be sent to a labor camp, and instructed to wash. Groups of 50 at a time were ordered to strip on the ground floor of the building. Men, women, and children were not put into separate groups. Valuables and possessions were confiscated at this point.

The victims were then taken past deceptive signs pointing "To the Washroom" to an enclosed ramp sloping downward to a gas van. Guards forced the deportees to run down the ramp into the van. A tube directed the van's exhaust into the hermetically sealed compartment, which held between 50 and 70 people. Once the carbon monoxide had killed all those locked inside, the van was driven to mass graves in the forest camp. There were three gas vans at Chelmno.

A few Jewish prisoners were selected from incoming transports for a forced-labor detachment (Sonderkommando) assigned to the killing area in the camp. These prisoners removed corpses from the gas vans and buried them in mass graves. From the summer of 1942, bodies were burned in crematoria or on pyres in the forest camp. The Sonderkommando also sorted victims' clothing and cleaned the vans. After a short time, members of the Sonderkommando would be killed and replaced with new arrivals.

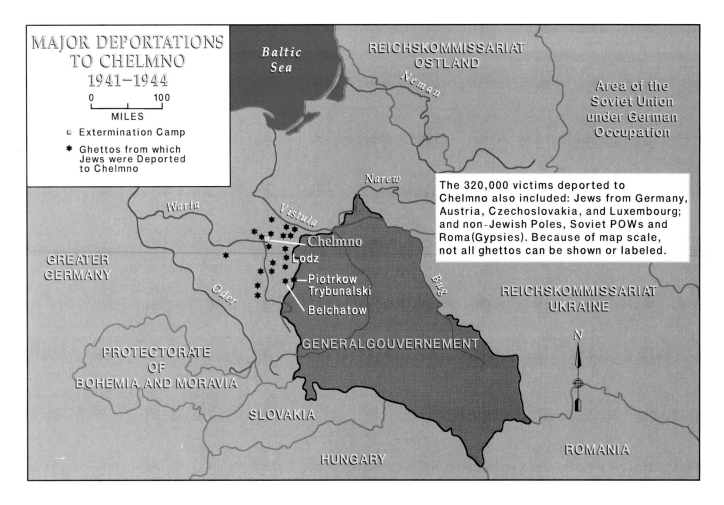

MAJOR DEPORTATIONS
TO CHELMNO
1941–1944

0   100
MILES

▢ Extermination Camp

✳ Ghettos from which
Jews were Deported
to Chelmno

The 320,000 victims deported to
Chelmno also included: Jews from Germany,
Austria, Czechoslovakia, and Luxembourg;
and non-Jewish Poles, Soviet POWs and
Roma(Gypsies). Because of map scale,
not all ghettos can be shown or labeled.

DEPORTATIONS TO CHELMNO

Gassing operations began in Chelmno on December 8, 1941, and lasted until March 1943. From early December 1941 until mid-January 1942, Jews from nearby towns and villages were deported by truck directly to Chelmno. The first transports included Jews from Kolo, Dabie, Sompolno, Klodowa, Babiak, and Kowale Panskie. Some 5,000 Roma (Gypsies) who had been deported from Austria and incarcerated in the Lodz ghetto were also among the camp's first victims.

From mid-January 1942, victims from the Lodz ghetto were deported to Chelmno in crowded freight trains. Transports from the Lodz ghetto also included Jews who had been deported from Germany, Austria, Bohemia and Moravia, and Luxembourg. Throughout 1942, Jews from the Warthegau region were murdered at Chelmno. Other victims of the Chelmno killing center included several hundred Poles and Soviet prisoners of war.

Transports to Chelmno ceased in March 1943 because most of the Jews in the Warthegau (except for the Lodz ghetto) had been killed. The camp was dismantled and the manor house demolished. The Germans renewed deportations to Chelmno in June 1944 to facilitate the liquidation of the Lodz ghetto. Killing operations took place until mid-July 1944 in the forest camp, where two reception huts and two crematoria were built. From mid-July, the remaining inhabitants of the ghetto were deported to Auschwitz-Birkenau.

Beginning in September 1944, a group of Jewish prisoners was forced to exhume and cremate corpses from the mass graves at Chelmno as part of the operation (Aktion 1005) to obliterate evidence of German mass murder. The Nazis executed most of the remaining prisoners and abandoned the Chelmno camp on the night of January 17, 1945, as the Soviet army approached. Approximately 320,000 people had been killed in Chelmno.

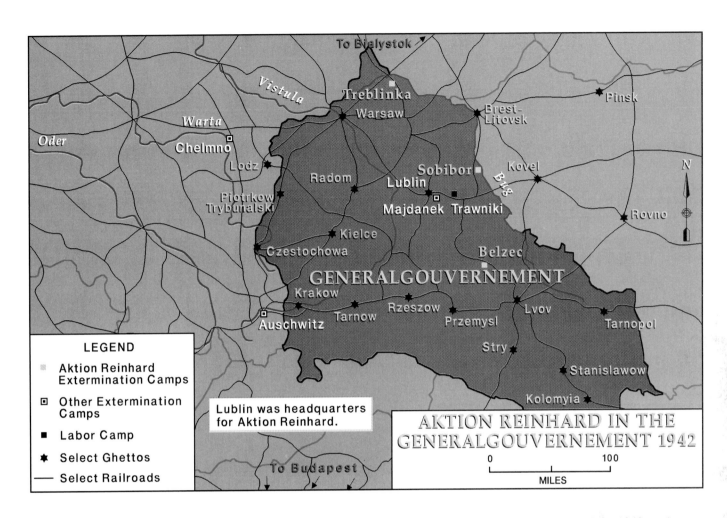

LEGEND

▪ Aktion Reinhard Extermination Camps

▫ Other Extermination Camps

■ Labor Camp

★ Select Ghettos

— Select Railroads

Lublin was headquarters for Aktion Reinhard.

AKTION REINHARD IN THE GENERALGOUVERNEMENT 1942

0 _____ 100

MILES

AKTION REINHARD

Aktion Reinhard (Operation Reinhard) was the code name for the German plan to kill the Jews of the Generalgouvernement. The operation was named for SS General Reinhard Heydrich, director of the Central Office for Reich Security (RSHA), who died in June 1942 as a result of injuries sustained during an assassination attempt by Czech partisans. The RSHA was the office responsible for coordinating deportations to the killing centers. SS officials directed Operation Reinhard from headquarters in Lublin. Lublin also served as a collection center to inventory the confiscated personal property of the victims prior to its shipment to Germany.

Three killing centers—Belzec, Sobibor, and Treblinka—were established as part of Operation Reinhard. The gas chambers in all three camps used carbon monoxide generated by stationary engines. Gassing operations took place in Belzec from March to December 1942; in Sobibor from April 1942 to October 1943; and in Treblinka from July 1942 to August 1943.

The overwhelming majority of victims in the Operation Reinhard camps were Jews deported from ghettos in Poland. Ghettoization was a transitional policy, designed to concentrate and control Jews living in the Generalgouvernement. Once the killing centers were operational, the ghettos were liquidated and Jews were deported by rail to the killing centers. The victims of Belzec were mainly Jews from the ghettos of southern Poland. Jews deported to Sobibor came mainly from the Lublin area and other ghettos of the eastern Generalgouvernement. Deportations to Treblinka originated mainly in central Poland, primarily in the Warsaw ghetto. In all, more than 1.7 million Jews were killed as part of Operation Reinhard. Additional transports of Jews arrived from western and central Europe and from the Balkans. The victims of the Operation Reinhard camps also included several thousand Roma (Gypsies).

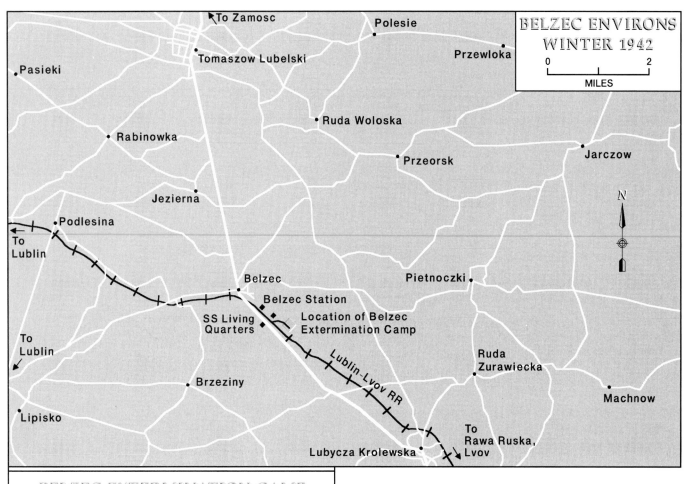

BELZEC EXTERMINATION CAMP

The small town of Belzec is located between the cities of Zamosc and Lvov in southeastern Poland. During the German occupation of Poland in World War II, this area was in the Generalgouvernement.

In early 1940, the Germans established a labor camp for Jews in Belzec, where Jews were forced to build fortifications and antitank ditches along the demarcation line between German- and Soviet-occupied Poland. This labor camp was liquidated in the fall of 1940.

Constructed as part of Operation Reinhard, the Nazi plan to kill all Jews in the Generalgouvernement, Belzec was the second Nazi killing center to begin operation, and the first of the Operation Reinhard camps.

The availability of good rail connections and Belzec's location in the center of the large Jewish populations of the Lvov, Krakow, and Lublin regions led to the construction of an extermination camp there in November 1941. Located along the Lublin-Lvov railway line, the extermination camp was 1,620 feet from the Belzec railway station. A siding connected the camp and the station. The SS guards assigned to the camp were housed in a separate compound near the Belzec station.

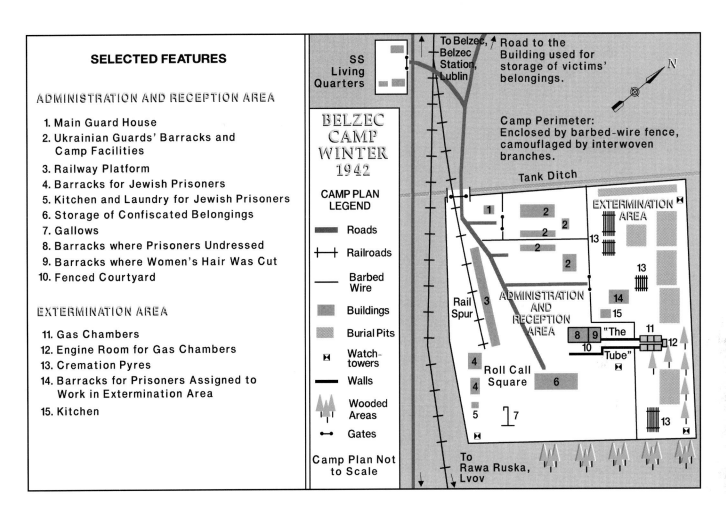

SELECTED FEATURES

ADMINISTRATION AND RECEPTION AREA

1. Main Guard House
2. Ukrainian Guards' Barracks and Camp Facilities
3. Railway Platform
4. Barracks for Jewish Prisoners
5. Kitchen and Laundry for Jewish Prisoners
6. Storage of Confiscated Belongings
7. Gallows
8. Barracks where Prisoners Undressed
9. Barracks where Women's Hair Was Cut
10. Fenced Courtyard

EXTERMINATION AREA

11. Gas Chambers
12. Engine Room for Gas Chambers
13. Cremation Pyres
14. Barracks for Prisoners Assigned to Work in Extermination Area
15. Kitchen

SS Living Quarters

BELZEC CAMP WINTER 1942

CAMP PLAN LEGEND

- Roads
+—+ Railroads
— Barbed Wire
▨ Buildings
▨ Burial Pits
⊠ Watch-towers
▬ Walls
🌲 Wooded Areas
•—• Gates

Camp Plan Not to Scale

To Belzec, Belzec Station, Lublin

Road to the Building used for storage of victims' belongings.

Camp Perimeter: Enclosed by barbed-wire fence, camouflaged by interwoven branches.

Tank Ditch

EXTERMINATION AREA

ADMINISTRATION AND RECEPTION AREA

Rail Spur

Roll Call Square

"The Tube"

To Rawa Ruska, Lvov

Belzec was divided into a combined administration-reception area and an extermination compound. A narrow enclosed path called the "tube" connected the two. The reception area held the railway siding and a ramp. The extermination area included the gas chambers and mass graves. Rail tracks ran from the gas chambers to the burial pits, but the exact configuration of these tracks is unknown. Each side of the camp measured 886 feet. Branches woven into the barbed-wire fence and trees planted around the perimeter served as camouflage.

Gassing operations began in mid-March 1942. Trains of 40 to 60 freight cars, with 80 to 100 people crowded into each car, arrived at the Belzec railway station. Twenty freight cars at a time were detached and brought from the station into the camp. The victims were then ordered to disembark at the platform of the reception area. German officers announced that the deportees had arrived at a transit camp and were to hand over all valuables in their possession.

Men were separated from women and children. All were forced to undress and run through the "tube," which led directly into gas chambers labeled as showers. Once the chamber doors were sealed, an engine, installed in an outside shed, was started. Carbon monoxide was funneled into the gas chamber, killing all those inside. The process was then repeated with the next 20 freight cars.

Members of the Sonderkommandos—groups of prisoners kept alive for forced labor in the killing area—removed bodies from the gas chambers and buried the victims. In addition, these prisoners sorted through the victims' possessions, prepared them for transportation to Germany, and cleaned the freight cars for the next deportation.

After deportations to Belzec ceased in December 1942, prisoner detachments exhumed bodies from burial pits and cremated them in an effort to obliterate all traces of mass murder (Aktion 1005).

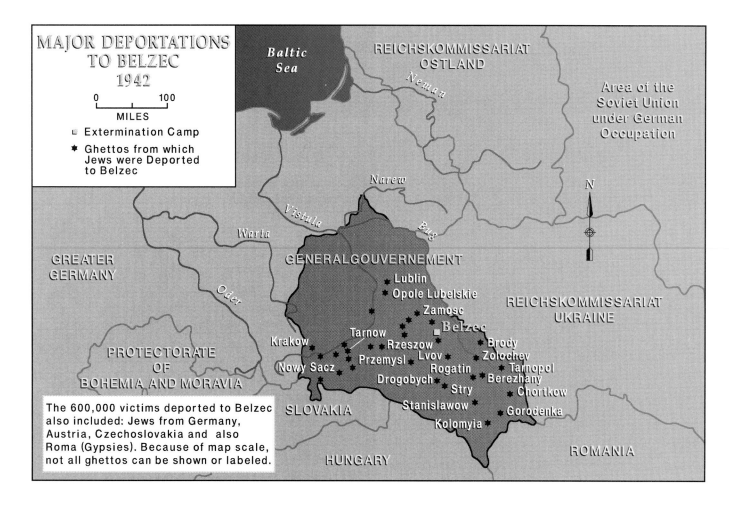

MAJOR DEPORTATIONS
TO BELZEC
1942

0   100
MILES

▫ Extermination Camp

✳ Ghettos from which
Jews were Deported
to Belzec

The 600,000 victims deported to Belzec
also included: Jews from Germany,
Austria, Czechoslovakia and also
Roma (Gypsies). Because of map scale,
not all ghettos can be shown or labeled.

DEPORTATIONS TO BELZEC

Between March and December 1942 at least 600,000 people were deported to Belzec and killed. Most of the victims were Jews from the ghettos of southern Poland. The Germans also deported Jews from Germany, Austria, and Bohemia and Moravia to Belzec. Further, several hundred Roma (Gypsies) were deported to the camp and murdered. The Belzec killing center was finally dismantled in July 1943.

The remaining prisoners, who had been assigned to the camp's work force, were deported to the Sobibor extermination camp and killed.

After Belzec was dismantled, the Germans established a farm at the site, planting trees and crops to disguise the area. A Ukrainian, a former guard at the camp, farmed the land. Soviet forces liberated the Belzec camp area in the summer of 1944.

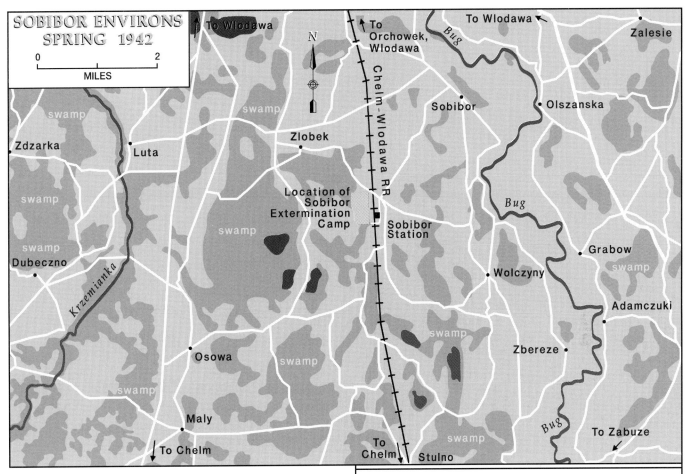

SOBIBOR ENVIRONS SPRING 1942

SOBIBOR EXTERMINATION CAMP

The small village of Sobibor is in central Poland, about three miles west of the Bug River and five miles south of Wlodawa. During the German occupation of Poland, this area was in the Generalgouvernement.

Sobibor was the second killing center constructed as part of Operation Reinhard. It was built along the Chelm-Wlodawa railway line, in a wooded, swampy, and thinly populated region. The camp covered a rectangular area of 1,312 by 1,969 feet. Branches woven into the barbed-wire fence and trees planted around the perimeter camouflaged the site. The entire camp was surrounded by a minefield 50 feet wide.

The Sobibor camp was divided into three parts: an administration area, a reception area, and an extermination area. The administration area included camp offices, housing for the German and Ukrainian guards assigned to the camp, and barracks for the prisoner labor force. The reception area held the railway siding, ramp, barracks where the victims disrobed, and warehouses for the victims' possessions. The extermination area included gas chambers, mass graves, and barracks for prisoners assigned to forced labor. A narrow

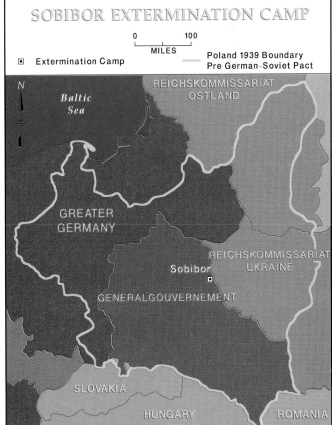

SOBIBOR EXTERMINATION CAMP

□ Extermination Camp

Poland 1939 Boundary
Pre German-Soviet Pact

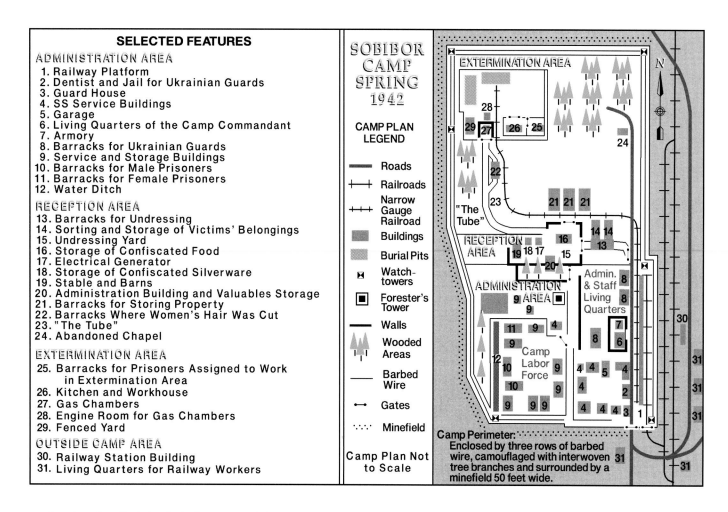

SELECTED FEATURES

ADMINISTRATION AREA
1. Railway Platform
2. Dentist and Jail for Ukrainian Guards
3. Guard House
4. SS Service Buildings
5. Garage
6. Living Quarters of the Camp Commandant
7. Armory
8. Barracks for Ukrainian Guards
9. Service and Storage Buildings
10. Barracks for Male Prisoners
11. Barracks for Female Prisoners
12. Water Ditch

RECEPTION AREA
13. Barracks for Undressing
14. Sorting and Storage of Victims' Belongings
15. Undressing Yard
16. Storage of Confiscated Food
17. Electrical Generator
18. Storage of Confiscated Silverware
19. Stable and Barns
20. Administration Building and Valuables Storage
21. Barracks for Storing Property
22. Barracks Where Women's Hair Was Cut
23. "The Tube"
24. Abandoned Chapel

EXTERMINATION AREA
25. Barracks for Prisoners Assigned to Work in Extermination Area
26. Kitchen and Workhouse
27. Gas Chambers
28. Engine Room for Gas Chambers
29. Fenced Yard

OUTSIDE CAMP AREA
30. Railway Station Building
31. Living Quarters for Railway Workers

SOBIBOR CAMP SPRING 1942

CAMP PLAN LEGEND

Roads
Railroads
Narrow Gauge Railroad
Buildings
Burial Pits
Watch-towers
Forester's Tower
Walls
Wooded Areas
Barbed Wire
Gates
Minefield

Camp Plan Not to Scale

EXTERMINATION AREA

"The Tube"

RECEPTION AREA

ADMINISTRATION AREA

Admin. & Staff Living Quarters

Camp Labor Force

N

Camp Perimeter: Enclosed by three rows of barbed wire, camouflaged with interwoven tree branches and surrounded by a minefield 50 feet wide.

enclosed path called the "tube" connected the reception and extermination areas.

Gassing operations began in April 1942. Trains of 40 to 60 freight cars would arrive at the Sobibor railway station. Twenty cars at a time entered the reception area, where victims were unloaded onto the platform. German officers announced that the deportees had arrived at a transit camp and were to hand over all valuables. They were ordered into the barracks and forced to undress and run through the "tube," which led directly into gas chambers labeled as showers. The womens' hair was shorn in a special barracks inside the "tube." Once the gas chamber doors were sealed,

an engine in an adjacent room was started and carbon monoxide gas was piped into the gas chambers, killing all those inside. The process was then repeated with the next freight cars.

Groups of prisoners kept alive for forced labor in Sobibor removed bodies from the chambers and buried them, sorted through confiscated possessions, and cleaned the freight cars in preparation for the next transport.

Even before gassing operations at Sobibor ceased in the fall of 1943, bodies were exhumed from the burial pits and cremated in an effort to obliterate all traces of mass murder (Aktion 1005).

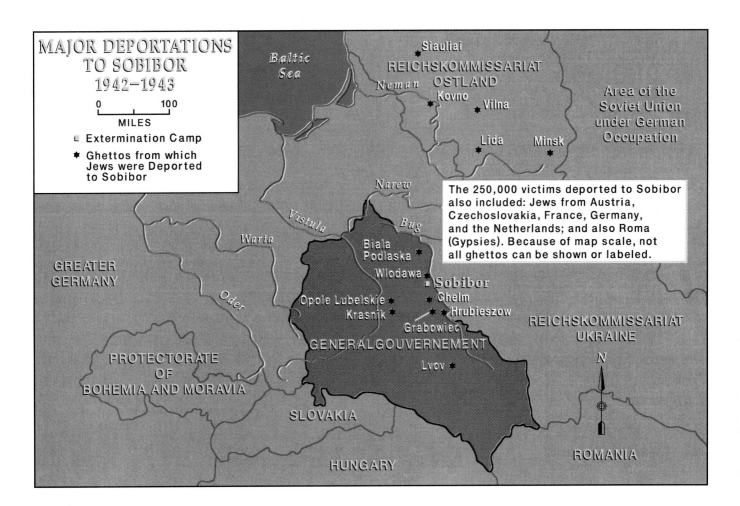

MAJOR DEPORTATIONS
TO SOBIBOR
1942–1943

0   100
MILES

▫ Extermination Camp

✳ Ghettos from which
Jews were Deported
to Sobibor

Baltic
Sea

Siauliai

REICHSKOMMISSARIAT
Neman   OSTLAND

Kovno
Vilna

Area of the
Soviet Union
under German
Occupation

Lida   Minsk

Narew

The 250,000 victims deported to Sobibor
also included: Jews from Austria,
Czechoslovakia, France, Germany,
and the Netherlands; and also Roma
(Gypsies). Because of map scale, not
all ghettos can be shown or labeled.

Vistula   Bug

Warta

Biala
Podlaska
Wlodawa

GREATER
GERMANY

Oder

Sobibor
Opole Lubelskie   Chelm
Krasnik   Hrubieszow

REICHSKOMMISSARIAT
UKRAINE

Grabowiec
GENERALGOUVERNEMENT

N

PROTECTORATE
OF
BOHEMIA AND MORAVIA

Lvov

SLOVAKIA

ROMANIA

HUNGARY

DEPORTATIONS TO SOBIBOR

Deportations to Sobibor took place between April 1942 and the fall of 1943, with one exception: at the end of July 1942, large-scale deportations were suspended for two months while repairs were made on the Chelm-Lublin railway.

Jews deported to Sobibor came mainly from the ghettos of eastern Poland, especially from the Lublin area. Jews were also deported to Sobibor from German-occupied Soviet territory, and from Bohemia and Moravia, Austria, the Netherlands, Belgium, and France. In all, about 250,000 people were killed at Sobibor.

Jewish prisoners attempted a revolt and mass escape from Sobibor in mid-October 1943. German and Ukrainian guards opened fire, preventing the prisoners from reaching the main exit and forcing them to attempt escape through the minefield. About 300 escaped; over 100 were recaptured and later shot. After the revolt, Sobibor was closed and the camp dismantled.

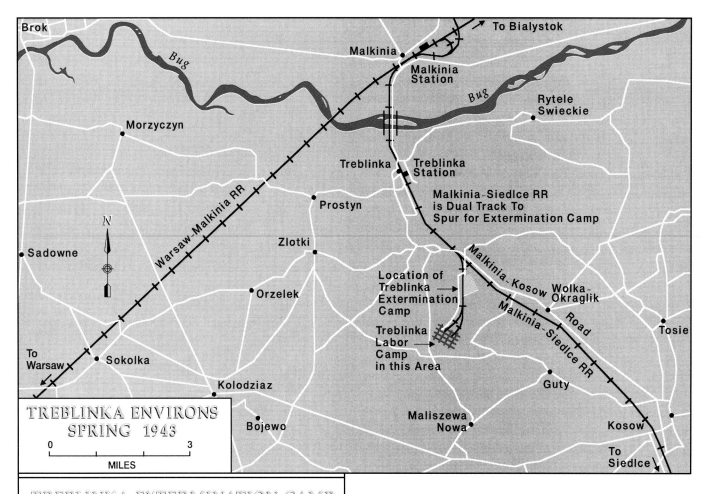

TREBLINKA ENVIRONS
SPRING 1943

0   3
MILES

TREBLINKA EXTERMINATION CAMP

0   100
MILES

▣ Extermination Camp

Poland 1939 Boundary
Pre German-Soviet Pact

TREBLINKA EXTERMINATION CAMP

The village of Treblinka, located about 50 miles northeast of Warsaw, was in the northern region of the Generalgouvernement. In June 1941, a labor camp known as Treblinka I was established near the village. The Poles and Jews imprisoned there were forced to work in quarries to extract materials for the construction of fortifications along the German-Soviet demarcation line in occupied Poland.

The Treblinka killing center was established as part of Operation Reinhard. Construction was completed in July 1942. Deportations to the two other Operation Reinhard camps, Belzec and Sobibor, had already begun.

The Treblinka killing center was located in a sparsely populated area near the Polish village of Wolka Okraglik along the Malkinia-Siedlce railway line. The camp was 2.5 miles southeast of the village and the railway station of Treblinka. A branch railway track was built leading from the labor camp, Treblinka I, to the extermination camp, Treblinka II, and continued to the nearby railway station in the village of Treblinka. The site was heavily wooded and hidden from view.

The camp was laid out in a trapezoid of 1,312 by 1,968

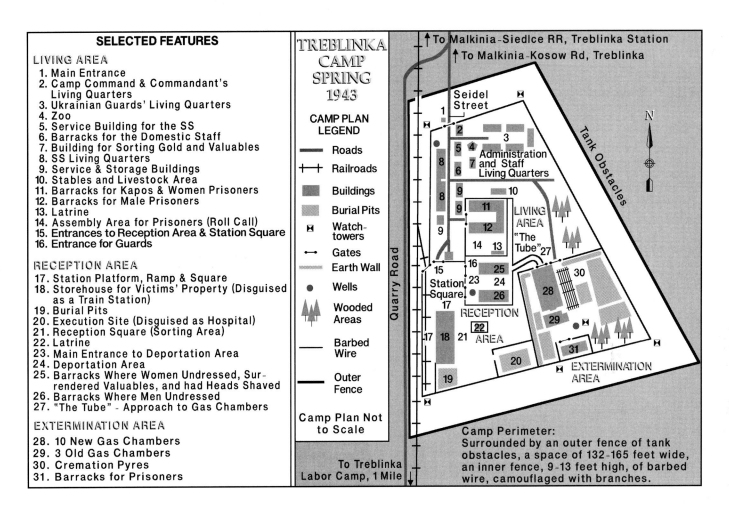

SELECTED FEATURES

LIVING AREA
1. Main Entrance
2. Camp Command & Commandant's Living Quarters
3. Ukrainian Guards' Living Quarters
4. Zoo
5. Service Building for the SS
6. Barracks for the Domestic Staff
7. Building for Sorting Gold and Valuables
8. SS Living Quarters
9. Service & Storage Buildings
10. Stables and Livestock Area
11. Barracks for Kapos & Women Prisoners
12. Barracks for Male Prisoners
13. Latrine
14. Assembly Area for Prisoners (Roll Call)
15. Entrances to Reception Area & Station Square
16. Entrance for Guards

RECEPTION AREA
17. Station Platform, Ramp & Square
18. Storehouse for Victims' Property (Disguised as a Train Station)
19. Burial Pits
20. Execution Site (Disguised as Hospital)
21. Reception Square (Sorting Area)
22. Latrine
23. Main Entrance to Deportation Area
24. Deportation Area
25. Barracks Where Women Undressed, Surrendered Valuables, and had Heads Shaved
26. Barracks Where Men Undressed
27. "The Tube" - Approach to Gas Chambers

EXTERMINATION AREA
28. 10 New Gas Chambers
29. 3 Old Gas Chambers
30. Cremation Pyres
31. Barracks for Prisoners

TREBLINKA CAMP SPRING 1943

CAMP PLAN LEGEND

- Roads
- Railroads
- Buildings
- Burial Pits
- Watch-towers
- Gates
- Earth Wall
- Wells
- Wooded Areas
- Barbed Wire
- Outer Fence

Camp Plan Not to Scale

To Treblinka Labor Camp, 1 Mile

To Malkinia-Siedlce RR, Treblinka Station
To Malkinia-Kosow Rd, Treblinka

Seidel Street

Administration and Staff Living Quarters

LIVING AREA "The Tube"

Station Square

RECEPTION AREA

EXTERMINATION AREA

Camp Perimeter: Surrounded by an outer fence of tank obstacles, a space of 132-165 feet wide, an inner fence, 9-13 feet high, of barbed wire, camouflaged with branches.

feet. Branches woven into the barbed-wire fence and trees planted around the perimeter served as camouflage, blocking any view into the camp from the outside. Watchtowers 26 feet high were placed along the fence and at each of the four corners.

The camp was divided into three parts: the reception area, the living area, and the extermination area. The living area contained housing for German and Ukrainian guards assigned to the camp, offices, a clinic, storerooms, and workshops. One section contained barracks that housed Jewish prisoners forced to work in the camp.

Incoming trains of about 50 or 60 cars first stopped at the Treblinka village railway station. Twenty cars at a time were detached from the train and brought into the camp. Victims were ordered to disembark in the reception area, which contained the railway siding and platform. German officers announced that the deportees had arrived at a transit camp and were to hand over all valuables. The reception

area also contained a fenced-in "deportation square" with two barracks in which deportees—men separated from women and children—had to undress, and two large storerooms where victims' possessions, confiscated upon arrival, were sorted for shipment back to Germany.

A camouflaged, fenced-in path, referred to as the "tube," led from the reception area to the extermination area. Victims were forced to run along this path to the gas chambers, labeled as showers. Once the chamber doors were sealed, an engine installed in a room attached to the gas chambers was started. Carbon monoxide was funneled into the gas chambers, killing those inside. The bodies of the gassing victims were interred in huge trenches. The process was then repeated.

Deportees who were too weak to reach the gas chambers on their own were told they would receive medical attention. They were instead taken to a camouflaged area, which was disguised with a Red Cross flag as a hospital, and shot.

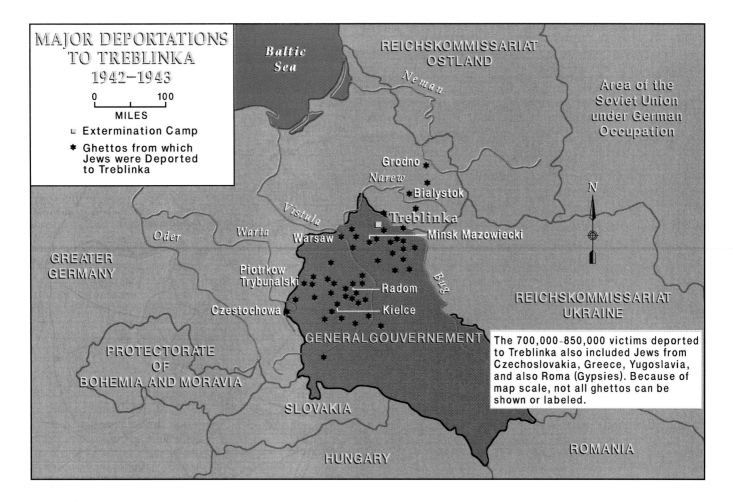

MAJOR DEPORTATIONS
TO TREBLINKA
1942–1943

0   100
MILES

▫ Extermination Camp

✱ Ghettos from which
  Jews were Deported
  to Treblinka

The 700,000–850,000 victims deported to Treblinka also included Jews from Czechoslovakia, Greece, Yugoslavia, and also Roma (Gypsies). Because of map scale, not all ghettos can be shown or labeled.

MAJOR DEPORTATIONS TO TREBLINKA

Deportations to Treblinka came mainly from the Jewish ghettos of central Poland. Between late July and September 1942, more than 250,000 Jews from Warsaw were deported to Treblinka. Although transports from Poland originated primarily in the Warsaw ghetto and ghettos near Warsaw, they also arrived from the areas of Radom, Lublin, and Bialystok.

Jews were also deported to Treblinka from the Theresienstadt ghetto in Bohemia, from Greece and Slovakia, and from the Bulgarian-occupied zones in Greece and Yugoslavia. Other transports came from Austria, Belgium, France, Germany, and the Soviet Union. About 2,000 Roma (Gypsies) were deported to Treblinka and killed.

Deportations to Treblinka continued until May 1943. A few isolated transports arrived after that date. In an effort to obliterate traces of mass killing (Aktion 1005), mass graves at Treblinka were opened and the corpses exhumed to be burned on huge pyres. The burning of corpses continued until the end of July 1943.

Jewish inmates organized a resistance group in Treblinka in early 1943. When Aktion 1005 neared completion in the camp, the prisoners feared they would be killed and the camp dismantled. The resistance leaders decided to revolt. On August 2, 1943, prisoners quietly seized weapons from the camp armory, but were discovered before they could take over the camp. Hundreds of prisoners stormed the main gate in an attempt to escape. Many were killed by machine-gun fire. More than 300 did escape, most only to be captured and killed by German police and troops. Most of the camp was burned down by the prisoners in the uprising. The surviving prisoners were forced to remove all remaining traces of the camp's existence. They too were then shot.

The camp was finally dismantled in the fall of 1943. Between 700,000 and 850,000 people had been killed there.

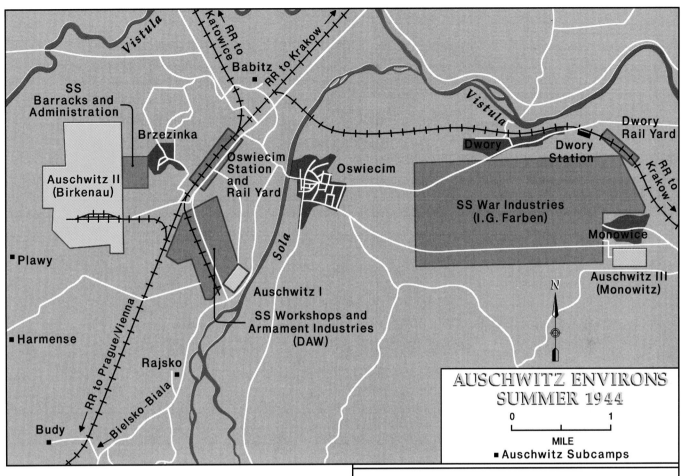

AUSCHWITZ ENVIRONS
SUMMER 1944

0   1
MILE

■ Auschwitz Subcamps

AUSCHWITZ

Auschwitz was the largest camp established by the Germans. It was a complex of camps, including a concentration, extermination, and forced-labor camp. It was located 37 miles west of Krakow, near the prewar German-Polish border in Eastern Upper Silesia, an area annexed to Germany in 1939. Three large camps established near the Polish town of Oswiecim constituted the Auschwitz camp complex: Auschwitz I, Auschwitz II (Birkenau), and Auschwitz III (Monowitz).

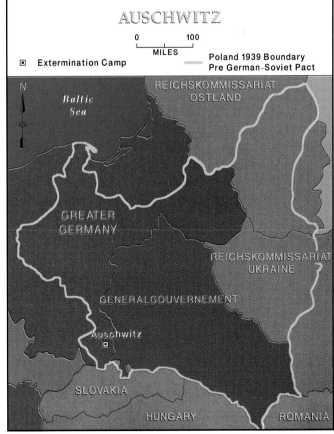

AUSCHWITZ

0   100
MILES

▣ Extermination Camp   Poland 1939 Boundary
Pre German-Soviet Pact

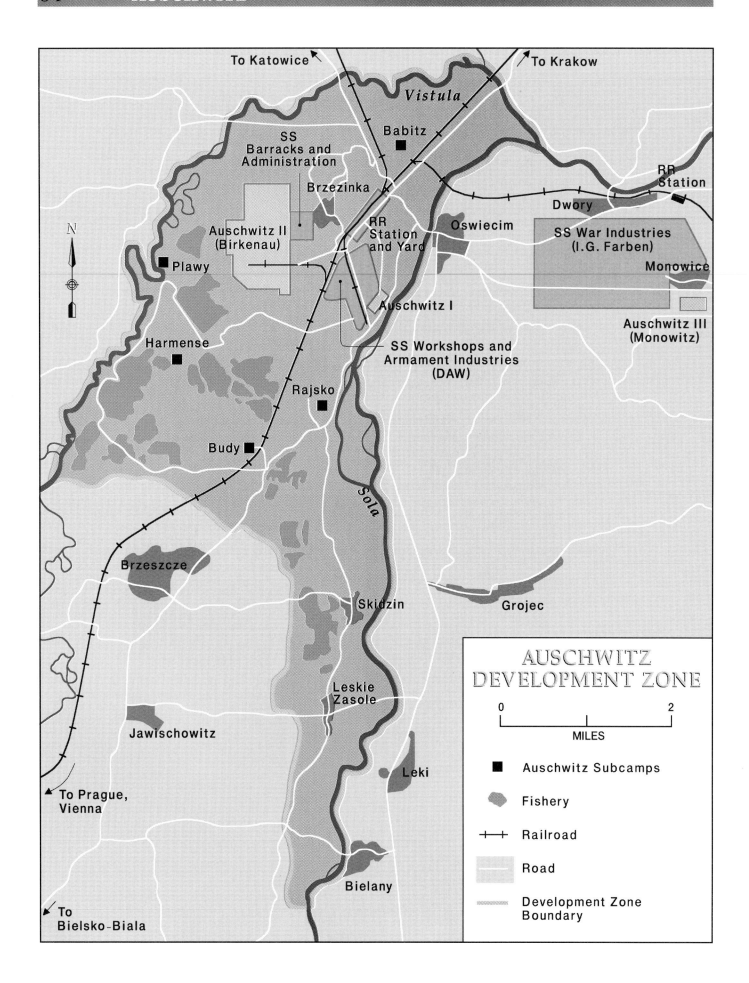

To Katowice

To Krakow

Vistula

Babitz

SS
Barracks and
Administration

Brzezinka

RR
Station

Dwory

RR
Station
and Yard

Auschwitz II
(Birkenau)

Oswiecim

SS War Industries
(I.G. Farben)

Monowice

Plawy

Auschwitz I

Auschwitz III
(Monowitz)

Harmense

SS Workshops and
Armament Industries
(DAW)

Rajsko

Budy

Sola

Brzeszcze

Skidzin

Grojec

Leskie
Zasole

Jawischowitz

Leki

To Prague,
Vienna

Bielany

To
Bielsko-Biala

AUSCHWITZ DEVELOPMENT ZONE

0 ———————— 2
MILES

■ Auschwitz Subcamps

   Fishery

+—+—+ Railroad

   Road

   Development Zone
   Boundary

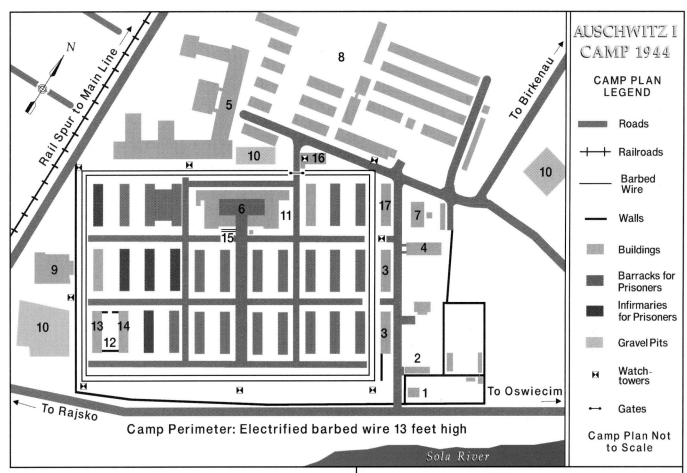

AUSCHWITZ I
CAMP 1944

CAMP PLAN
LEGEND

	Roads
	Railroads
	Barbed Wire
	Walls
	Buildings
	Barracks for Prisoners
	Infirmaries for Prisoners
	Gravel Pits
	Watch-towers
	Gates

Camp Plan Not to Scale

Camp Perimeter: Electrified barbed wire 13 feet high

AUSCHWITZ I

Auschwitz I, the main camp, was the first camp established near Oswiecim. Construction began in May 1940 in the Zasole suburb of Oswiecim, in artillery barracks formerly used by the Polish army. The camp was continuously expanded by forced labor. The first prisoners were Germans deported from the Sachsenhausen concentration camp in Germany and Polish political prisoners from Tarnow.

Although Auschwitz I was primarily a concentration camp, serving a penal function, it also had a gas chamber and crematorium. An improvised gas chamber was located in the basement of the prison, Block 11, and later a gas chamber was constructed in the crematorium.

SS physicians carried out so-called medical experiments in the hospital, Barrack (Block) 10. They conducted pseudo-scientific research on infants, twins, and dwarfs, and forced

SELECTED FEATURES

1. Camp Commandant's House
2. Main Guard House
3. Camp Administrative Offices
4. Gestapo
5. Reception Building/Prisoner Registration
6. Kitchen
7. Gas Chamber and Crematorium
8. Storage Buildings and Workshops
9. Storage of Confiscated Belongings
10. Gravel Pit: Execution Site
11. Camp Orchestra Site
12. "Black Wall," Execution Site
13. Block 11: Punishment Bunker
14. Block 10: Medical Experiments
15. Gallows
16. Block Commander's Barracks
17. SS Hospital

sterilizations, castrations, and hypothermia experiments.

Between the crematorium and the medical-experiments barrack stood the "Black Wall," where thousands of prisoners were executed.

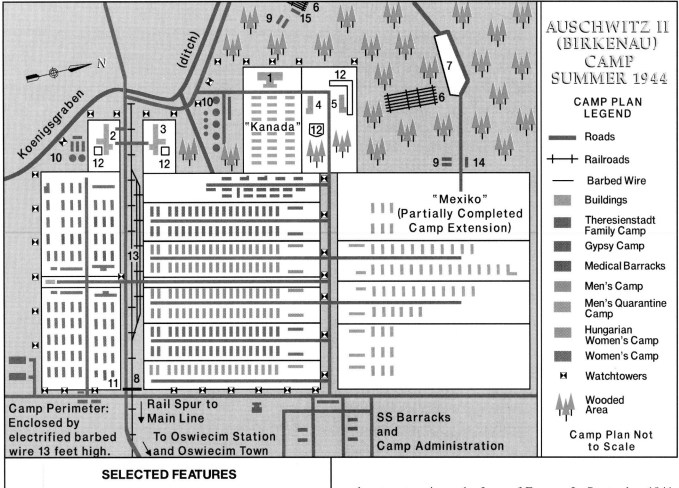

AUSCHWITZ II (BIRKENAU) CAMP SUMMER 1944

CAMP PLAN LEGEND

- Roads
- Railroads
- Barbed Wire
- Buildings
- Theresienstadt Family Camp
- Gypsy Camp
- Medical Barracks
- Men's Camp
- Men's Quarantine Camp
- Hungarian Women's Camp
- Women's Camp
- Watchtowers
- Wooded Area

Camp Plan Not to Scale

"Mexiko" (Partially Completed Camp Extension)

Camp Perimeter: Enclosed by electrified barbed wire 13 feet high.

Rail Spur to Main Line
To Oswiecim Station and Oswiecim Town

SS Barracks and Camp Administration

SELECTED FEATURES

1. "Sauna" (Disinfection)
2. Gas Chamber and Crematorium #2
3. Gas Chamber and Crematorium #3
4. Gas Chamber and Crematorium #4
5. Gas Chamber and Crematorium #5
6. Cremation Pyres
7. Mass Graves for Soviet POWs
8. Main Guard House
9. Barracks for Disrobing
10. Sewage Treatment Plants
11. Medical Experiments Barrack
12. Ash Pits
13. "Rampe" (Railroad Platform)
14. Provisional Gas Chambers #1
15. Provisional Gas Chambers #2

AUSCHWITZ II

Construction of Auschwitz II, or Auschwitz-Birkenau, began in Brzezinka in October 1941. Of the three camps established near Oswiecim, Auschwitz-Birkenau had the largest prisoner population. It was divided into nine sections separated by electrified barbed-wire fences and patrolled by SS guards and dogs. The camp included sections for women, men, Roma (Gypsies), and families deported from the Theresienstadt ghetto.

Auschwitz-Birkenau played a central role in the German plan to exterminate the Jews of Europe. In September 1941, the Germans tested Zyklon B gas as an instrument of genocide. The "success" of these experiments led to the adoption of Zyklon B at Auschwitz. At first, gassing occurred at two farmhouses converted into gas chambers. Provisional gas chamber I went into operation in January 1942 and was later dismantled. Provisional gas chamber II began operations in June 1942 and continued through the fall of 1944. These facilities were judged inadequate for the scale of gassing planned at Auschwitz-Birkenau. Four large crematoria buildings were constructed between March and June 1943. Each had three components: a disrobing area, a large gas chamber, and crematorium ovens. Gassing operations continued until November 1944.

Trains arrived at Auschwitz-Birkenau almost daily with transports of Jews from virtually every German-occupied country of Europe—from as far north as Norway to the island of Rhodes off the coast of Turkey and from western France to eastern Poland. The role of Auschwitz-Birkenau in the German plan to kill the Jews of Europe is symbolized by the deportations from Hungary. Between May and July 1944, nearly 440,000 Hungarian Jews were deported to

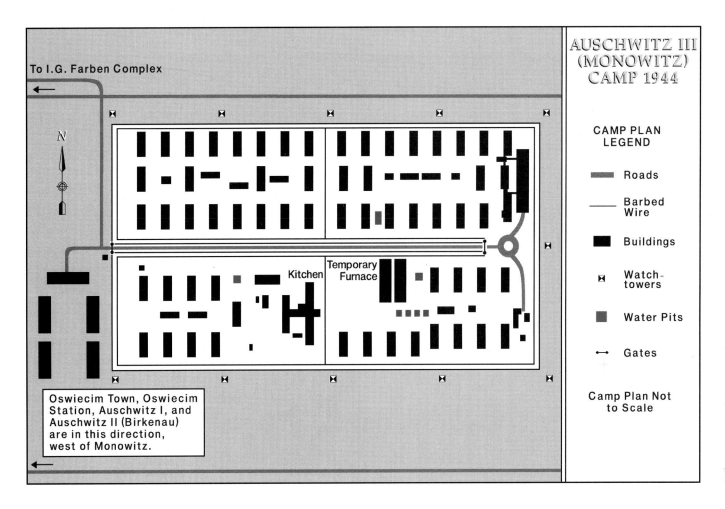

To I.G. Farben Complex

N

AUSCHWITZ III
(MONOWITZ)
CAMP 1944

CAMP PLAN
LEGEND

Roads

Barbed
Wire

Buildings

Watch-
towers

Water Pits

Gates

Camp Plan Not
to Scale

Kitchen

Temporary
Furnace

Oswiecim Town, Oswiecim
Station, Auschwitz I, and
Auschwitz II (Birkenau)
are in this direction,
west of Monowitz.

Auschwitz-Birkenau; most of them were sent directly to the gas chambers and killed.

New arrivals at Auschwitz-Birkenau underwent selection. The majority were found unfit for forced labor and were sent immediately to the gas chambers, which were disguised as shower installations to mislead the victims. The belongings of those gassed were confiscated and sorted in the "Kanada" (Canada) warehouse for shipment back to Germany.

At least 1.1 million Jews were killed in Auschwitz. Other victims included between 70,000 and 75,000 Poles, 21,000 Roma, and about 15,000 Soviet prisoners of war.

A prisoner forced-labor detachment (Sonderkommando) assigned to the extermination area of the camp staged an uprising and destroyed Crematorium IV in October 1944, blowing up one of the gas chambers in Auschwitz-Birkenau. Gassing operations continued, however, until November 1944. The SS destroyed the remaining installations as Soviet forces approached.

AUSCHWITZ III

Auschwitz III, also called Buna or Monowitz, was established in nearby Monowice to provide forced laborers for the Buna synthetic rubber works. The German conglomerate I.G. Farben established a factory at Dwory in order to take advantage of cheap concentration camp labor and the nearby Silesian coalfields. It invested more than 700 million Reichsmarks (about 1.4 million U.S. dollars in 1942) in Auschwitz III.

Prisoners selected for forced labor were registered and tattooed with identification numbers on their left arms in Auschwitz I. They were then assigned to forced labor in Auschwitz or in one of the many subcamps attached to Auschwitz III.

The Germans forcibly expelled the entire local population from Oswiecim and from an area of 40 square miles around the camp. This area became known as the camp's "development zone" and was reserved for the camp's exclusive use. Most of the Auschwitz subcamps were established within this officially designated area, including Althammer, Blechhammer, Budy, Fuerstengrube, Gleiwitz, Rajsko, and Tschechowitz. Auschwitz inmates were employed on huge farms, including the experimental agricultural station at Rajsko, in coal mines, in stone quarries, in

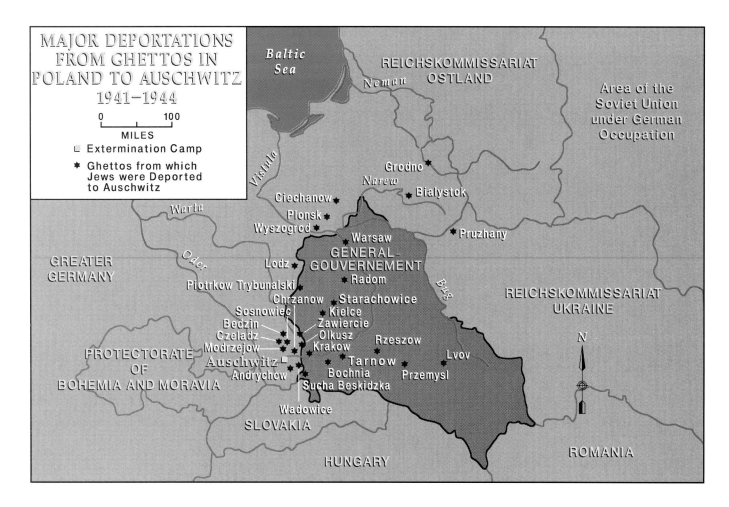

MAJOR DEPORTATIONS
FROM GHETTOS IN
POLAND TO AUSCHWITZ
1941–1944

fisheries, and especially in armaments industries such as the German Armament Works (DAW; established in 1941). Periodically, prisoners underwent selection. If they were judged too weak or sick to continue working, they were transported to Auschwitz-Birkenau and killed.

The SS began evacuating Auschwitz and its associated subcamps on January 18, 1945, as Soviet forces approached the area. Almost 60,000 prisoners, mostly Jews, were forced on a death march to Wodzislaw. Death marches were forced marches of concentration camp prisoners made over a long distance under heavy guard and extremely harsh conditions. During the forced evacuation of Auschwitz, prisoners were brutally mistreated and many were killed. SS guards shot anyone who fell behind.

Upon their arrival in Wodzislaw, the inmates were put on freight trains and transported to various concentration camps, especially Gross-Rosen, Buchenwald, Dachau, and Mauthausen. The journey lasted days; often the prisoners were provided with no food or water.

On January 27, 1945, the Soviet army entered Auschwitz and liberated those prisoners who had not been evacuated.

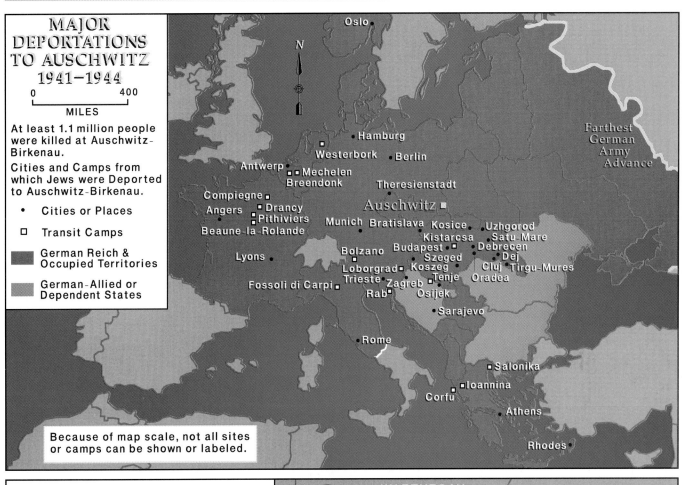

MAJOR DEPORTATIONS TO AUSCHWITZ 1941–1944

0 — 400
MILES

At least 1.1 million people were killed at Auschwitz-Birkenau.

Cities and Camps from which Jews were Deported to Auschwitz-Birkenau.

- • Cities or Places
- □ Transit Camps
- German Reich & Occupied Territories
- German-Allied or Dependent States

Because of map scale, not all sites or camps can be shown or labeled.

Oslo

Hamburg
Westerbork
Berlin
Antwerp
Mechelen
Breendonk
Theresienstadt
Compiegne
Angers
Drancy
Auschwitz
Pithiviers
Beaune-la-Rolande
Munich
Bratislava
Kosice
Uzhgorod
Kistarcsa
Satu-Mare
Lyons
Bolzano
Budapest
Debrecen
Dej
Szeged
Koszeg
Cluj
Tirgu-Mures
Loborgrad
Trieste
Zagreb
Tenje
Oradea
Fossoli di Carpi
Rab
Osijek
Sarajevo
Rome
Salonika
Ioannina
Corfu
Athens
Rhodes

Farthest German Army Advance

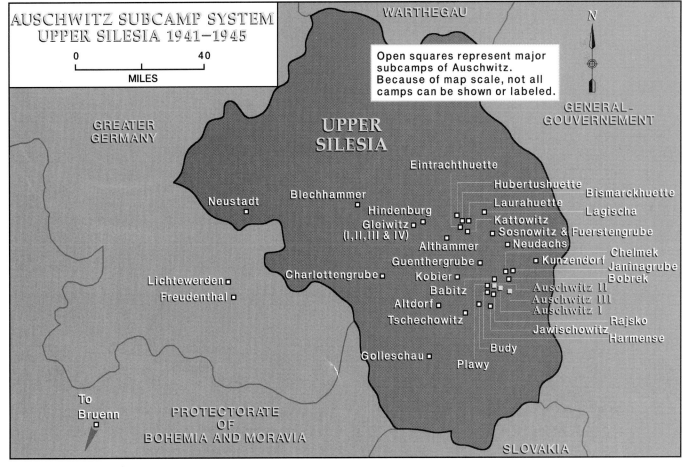

AUSCHWITZ SUBCAMP SYSTEM UPPER SILESIA 1941–1945

0 — 40
MILES

Open squares represent major subcamps of Auschwitz. Because of map scale, not all camps can be shown or labeled.

WARTHEGAU

GENERAL-GOUVERNEMENT

GREATER GERMANY

UPPER SILESIA

Eintrachthuette
Hubertushuette
Bismarckhuette
Neustadt
Blechhammer
Laurahuette
Lagischa
Hindenburg
Kattowitz
Gleiwitz
(I, II, III & IV)
Sosnowitz & Fuerstengrube
Neudachs
Althammer
Chelmek
Guenthergrube
Kunzendorf
Janinagrube
Charlottengrube
Kobier
Bobrek
Lichtewerden
Babitz
Auschwitz II
Freudenthal
Auschwitz III
Altdorf
Auschwitz I
Rajsko
Tschechowitz
Jawischowitz
Harmense
Budy
Golleschau
Plawy

To Bruenn

PROTECTORATE OF BOHEMIA AND MORAVIA

SLOVAKIA

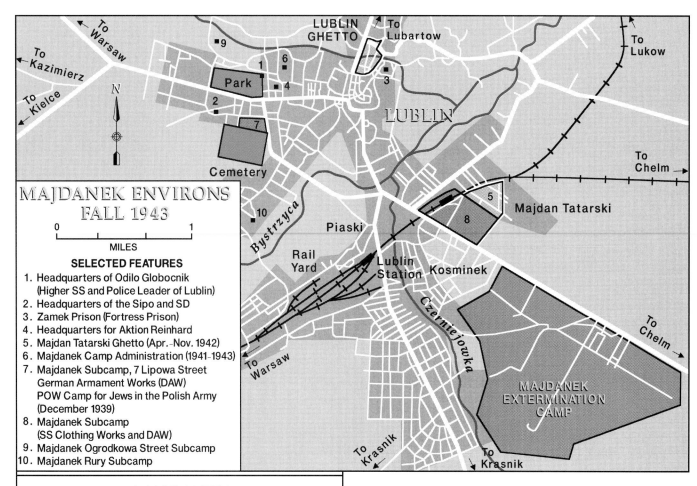

MAJDANEK ENVIRONS
FALL 1943

0   1
MILES

SELECTED FEATURES

1. Headquarters of Odilo Globocnik
   (Higher SS and Police Leader of Lublin)
2. Headquarters of the Sipo and SD
3. Zamek Prison (Fortress Prison)
4. Headquarters for Aktion Reinhard
5. Majdan Tatarski Ghetto (Apr.–Nov. 1942)
6. Majdanek Camp Administration (1941–1943)
7. Majdanek Subcamp, 7 Lipowa Street
   German Armament Works (DAW)
   POW Camp for Jews in the Polish Army
   (December 1939)
8. Majdanek Subcamp
   (SS Clothing Works and DAW)
9. Majdanek Ogrodkowa Street Subcamp
10. Majdanek Rury Subcamp

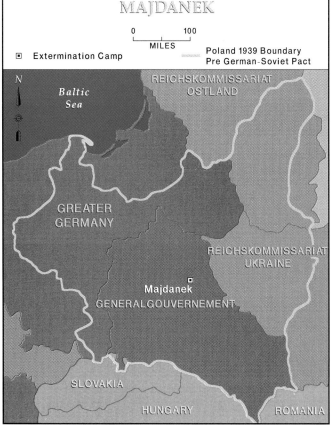

MAJDANEK

0   100
MILES

Poland 1939 Boundary
Pre German-Soviet Pact

▣ Extermination Camp

MAJDANEK AND LUBLIN

The Majdanek camp, also called Lublin-Majdanek, was situated along the Lublin-Zamosc-Chelm highway. Located adjacent to the Majdan Tatarski suburb of Lublin, Poland, the camp was in the Generalgouvernement. Majdanek had four subcamps in Lublin, where prisoners worked in German armaments industries or on other forced-labor projects. Majdanek also served as an execution place for hostages who were transported from the Zamek Prison in Lublin. Lublin itself served as headquarters for Operation Reinhard.

Two ghettos were established in Lublin. The Lublin ghetto was opened in March 1941 with a population of more than 30,000 Jews. By the end of March 1942, most were deported to the Belzec killing center. In April 1942, a new ghetto was established in Majdan Tatarski, near the Majdanek camp, for the remaining Jewish population of Lublin. Nearly 5,000 Jews lived in this ghetto. They were deported to Majdanek when the ghetto was liquidated in November 1942.

MAJDANEK EXTERMINATION CAMP

Like Auschwitz, Majdanek was a concentration, forced-labor, and extermination camp. Unlike the Operation Reinhard

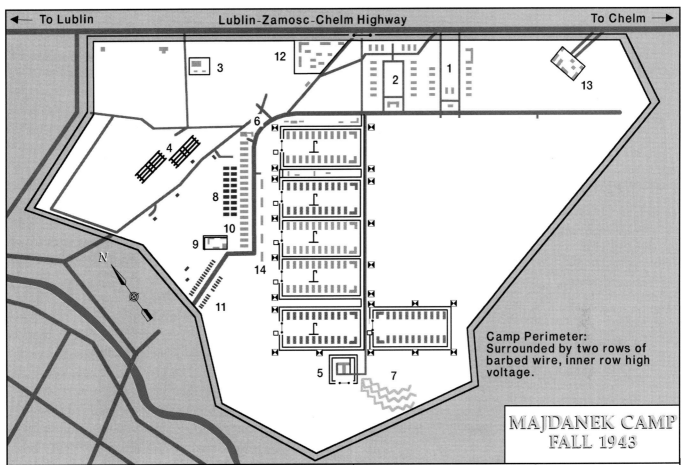

To Lublin ← | Lublin-Zamosc-Chelm Highway | To Chelm →

N

Camp Perimeter:
Surrounded by two rows of
barbed wire, inner row high
voltage.

MAJDANEK CAMP
FALL 1943

CAMP PLAN LEGEND

▬▬ Roads	▬ Buildings
⊷ Gates	▬ Compound I Women's Camp
┄ Barbed Wire	▬ Compound II, Field Hospital for Wehrmacht Auxiliary (Recruited from Soviet POWs)
⋈ Watch-towers	▬ Compound III Men's Camp
☐ Watch-posts	▬ Compound IV Male Hostages / POWs
■ Open Structures	▬ Compound V Men's Hospital Camp
Γ Gallows	▬ Compound VI Unoccupied

SELECTED FEATURES

1. Camp Administration
2. SS Barracks
3. Camp Commandant's House
4. Cremation Pyres
5. Crematorium
6. Gas Chambers
7. Mass Execution Ditches (November 3, 1943 "Harvest Festival")
8. Potato Bins
9. Dog Kennel
10. Warehouses
11. Compost Heaps
12. Warehouse Compound for Construction Materials
13. Camp Farm
14. Workshops

Camp Plan Not to Scale

camps, Majdanek was built adjacent to and within sight of a major city—Lublin. Construction of a large camp began in early October 1941. Until 1943 the camp was officially a prisoner-of-war camp run by the Waffen-SS. In mid-February 1943, Majdanek was reclassified a concentration camp.

The Majdanek camp was divided into six compounds. In the fall of 1943, Compound I was a women's camp; Compound II was a field hospital for Russian collaborators attached to the German army; Compound III was a men's camp mainly for Polish political prisoners and Jews from Warsaw and Bialystok; Compound IV was a camp for men, mainly Soviet prisoners of war, civilian hostages, and political prisoners; Compound V served as a men's hospital camp; and Compound VI was established but remained unoccupied.

Gassing operations at Majdanek began in October 1942 and continued until the fall of 1943. Majdanek had at least three gas chambers—which used both carbon monoxide and Zyklon B—and a large crematorium. Unlike the Operation Reinhard camps, which used stationary engines to generate carbon monoxide gas, the Majdanek camp was supplied with canisters of compressed gas.

On November 3, 1943, the Germans removed from the

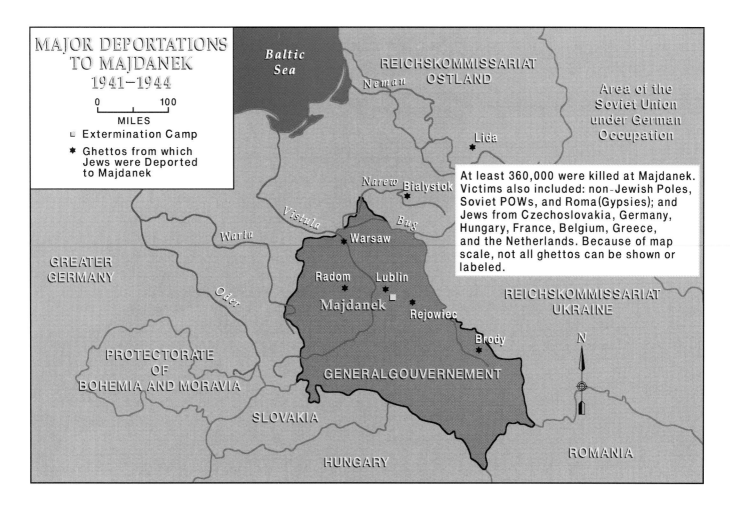

MAJOR DEPORTATIONS
TO MAJDANEK
1941–1944

0 ——— 100
MILES

▫ Extermination Camp

✳ Ghettos from which
Jews were Deported
to Majdanek

Baltic Sea

REICHSKOMMISSARIAT OSTLAND

Neman

Area of the Soviet Union under German Occupation

Lida

Narew   Bialystok

At least 360,000 were killed at Majdanek. Victims also included: non-Jewish Poles, Soviet POWs, and Roma(Gypsies); and Jews from Czechoslovakia, Germany, Hungary, France, Belgium, Greece, and the Netherlands. Because of map scale, not all ghettos can be shown or labeled.

Vistula

Bug

Warta

Warsaw

GREATER GERMANY

Oder

Radom   Lublin

Majdanek

Rejowiec

REICHSKOMMISSARIAT UKRAINE

Brody

N

PROTECTORATE OF BOHEMIA AND MORAVIA

GENERALGOUVERNEMENT

SLOVAKIA

HUNGARY

ROMANIA

camp all remaining Jewish prisoners—almost 18,000 people—and shot them in large prepared ditches near the crematorium parallel to Compound VI. This was part of Operation Harvest Festival (Aktion "Erntefest"), the code name for the execution of the remaining Jews of the Generalgouvernement.

The Germans hastily evacuated Majdanek as the Soviet army approached Lublin in July 1944. They did not have time to dismantle the camp entirely, although some of the remaining prisoners were transferred to Auschwitz. The Soviet army liberated Lublin on July 24, 1944. Majdanek was the first killing center liberated, and the only one captured virtually intact. The Germans dismantled or partially destroyed the other killing centers.

DEPORTATIONS TO MAJDANEK

The victims of Majdanek included Jews from central Poland, especially Lublin, Warsaw, and Bialystok; Jews from western Europe; more than 100,000 non-Jewish Poles; and tens of thousands of Soviet prisoners of war. As in Auschwitz-Birkenau, prisoners sent to Majdanek underwent selection on arrival. Those considered incapable of work were sent directly to the gas chambers. The remainder were employed for forced labor.

More than 360,000 people were killed at Majdanek. Most died from starvation, exhaustion, disease, and the harsh regimen imposed at the camp. The overwhelming majority of those killed in Majdanek's gas chambers were Jews.

THE HOLOCAUST IN WESTERN EUROPE

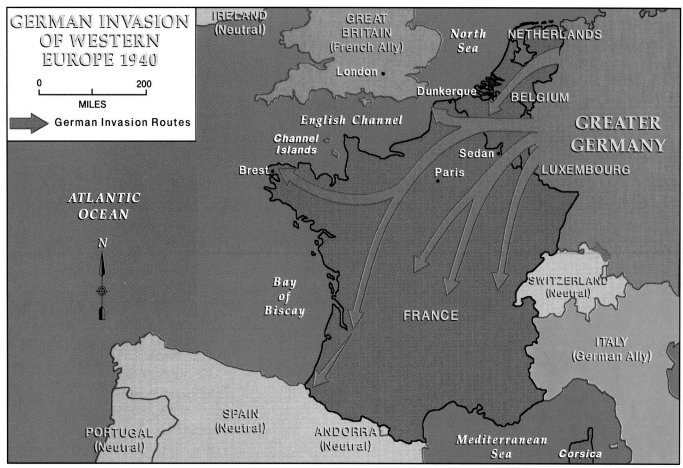

GERMAN INVASION OF WESTERN EUROPE 1940

0   200
MILES

→ German Invasion Routes

IRELAND (Neutral)

GREAT BRITAIN (French Ally)

London

North Sea

NETHERLANDS

Dunkerque

BELGIUM

English Channel

Channel Islands

Brest

ATLANTIC OCEAN

N

GREATER GERMANY

LUXEMBOURG

Sedan
Paris

SWITZERLAND (Neutral)

Bay of Biscay

FRANCE

ITALY (German Ally)

PORTUGAL (Neutral)

SPAIN (Neutral)

ANDORRA (Neutral)

Mediterranean Sea

Corsica

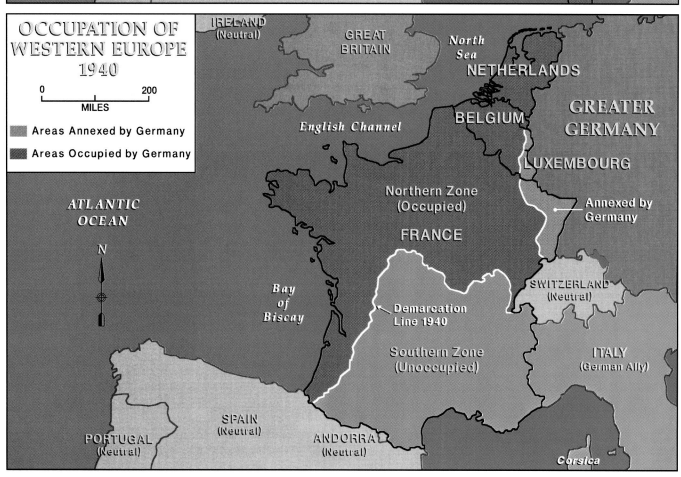

OCCUPATION OF WESTERN EUROPE 1940

0   200
MILES

▇ Areas Annexed by Germany
▇ Areas Occupied by Germany

IRELAND (Neutral)

GREAT BRITAIN

North Sea

NETHERLANDS

English Channel

BELGIUM

GREATER GERMANY

LUXEMBOURG

Annexed by Germany

ATLANTIC OCEAN

N

Northern Zone (Occupied)

FRANCE

SWITZERLAND (Neutral)

Bay of Biscay

Demarcation Line 1940

Southern Zone (Unoccupied)

ITALY (German Ally)

PORTUGAL (Neutral)

SPAIN (Neutral)

ANDORRA (Neutral)

Corsica

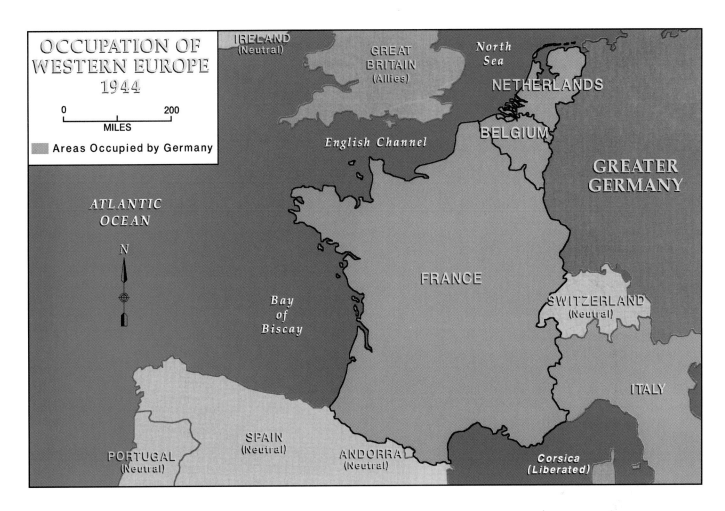

OCCUPATION OF
WESTERN EUROPE
1944

0   200
MILES

Areas Occupied by Germany

IRELAND
(Neutral)

GREAT
BRITAIN
(Allies)

North
Sea

NETHERLANDS

BELGIUM

GREATER
GERMANY

English Channel

ATLANTIC
OCEAN

N

FRANCE

SWITZERLAND
(Neutral)

Bay
of
Biscay

ITALY

SPAIN
(Neutral)

PORTUGAL
(Neutral)

ANDORRA
(Neutral)

Corsica
(Liberated)

THE INVASION OF FRANCE AND THE LOW COUNTRIES

The campaign against the Low Countries and France lasted less than six weeks. Germany attacked in the west on May 10, 1940. Initially, the Allies believed that Germany would attack through Belgium and the Netherlands and therefore rushed forces to meet the Germans there. The main German attack however, went through Luxembourg and the Ardennes Forest near the French city of Sedan. German tanks and infantry burst through the French defensive lines and advanced to the coast, trapping the British and French armies in the north. The Allies successfully evacuated over 300,000 troops from Dunkerque (Dunkirk) to Britain, but France was decisively defeated. Paris, the French capital, fell to the Germans on June 14, 1940. As part of the armistice agreement France signed with Germany on June 22, Germany occupied northern France while southern France remained unoccupied. A new French government was established in the town of Vichy, which was in the unoccupied southern part of France. The Vichy government declared neutrality in the war, but promised cooperation with Germany.

The Germans viewed the defeat of Britain's Royal Air Force (RAF) as a prerequisite for an invasion of Britain. When the German air force failed to win air superiority over southeastern England in 1940, Hitler decided to postpone indefinitely preparations for the invasion of the British Isles.

VICHY AND THE DEPORTATION OF THE JEWS IN FRANCE

During the 1930s, many German Jews and other refugees fled to France from Nazi Germany. By 1939, however, France imposed restrictions on Jewish immigration and set up internment camps for refugees. When Germany defeated France in June 1940, there were more than 300,000 Jews in France.

France signed an armistice with Germany in June 1940. Under the terms of the armistice, northern France remained under German occupation. Germany de facto annexed the French provinces of Alsace and Lorraine. Southern France remained unoccupied and governed by an exclusively French administration. Marshal Henri Philippe Petain became the head of state, with full power, of this French government, which had its seat in the town of Vichy. The Vichy regime declared neutrality in the war, but actually cooperated closely

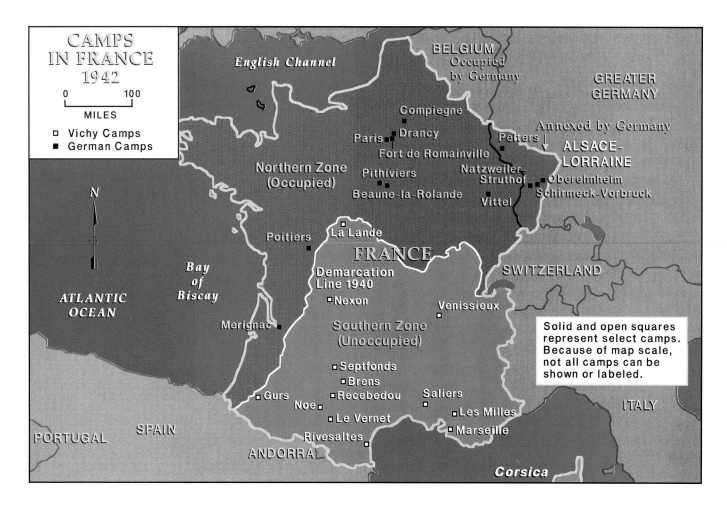

CAMPS
IN FRANCE
1942

0   100
MILES

□ Vichy Camps
■ German Camps

N

English Channel

BELGIUM
Occupied
by Germany

GREATER
GERMANY

Annexed by Germany

Compiegne

Paris ■ Drancy
Fort de Romainville

Peiters
ALSACE-
LORRAINE

Northern Zone
(Occupied)

Pithiviers
Beaune-la-Rolande

Natzweiler-
Struthof
Vittel

Oberehnheim
Schirmeck-Vorbruck

La Lande

Poitiers

FRANCE

SWITZERLAND

Bay
of
Biscay

Demarcation
Line 1940

ATLANTIC
OCEAN

□ Nexon

Venissieux

Solid and open squares
represent select camps.
Because of map scale,
not all camps can be
shown or labeled.

Merignac ■

Southern Zone
(Unoccupied)

□ Septfonds
□ Brens
□ Gurs   □ Recebedou   Saliers
Noe □   □
□ Le Vernet   □ Les Milles
Rivesaltes □   □ Marseille

ITALY

PORTUGAL   SPAIN

ANDORRA

Corsica

with Germany. Vichy passed antisemitic legislation and cooperated with Germany in the deportation of Jews from France.

Persecution of Jews began almost immediately after the defeat of France. The Vichy regime passed the comprehensive Statut des Juifs (Jewish Law), which consisted of two antisemitic laws, one passed in October 1940 and one in June 1941. The legislation provided the legal foundation for the persecution of Jews in France. It excluded Jews from public life, removing them from the civil service, the army, the professions, commerce, and industry. In July 1941, Vichy inaugurated an extensive program of "Aryanization," confiscating Jewish-owned property for the French state. Many Jews became destitute. Foreign Jews were particularly vulnerable and thousands were subsequently deported to camps. In November 1941, the Vichy government established the General Union of French Jews as a Jewish organization to run Jewish communal affairs.

Preparations for the inclusion of Jews in western Europe in the "Final Solution" began in early 1942. This meant, in part, the systematic roundup of Jews and their deportation to the killing centers in occupied Poland. Throughout the

summer and fall of 1942, French police rounded up Jews, mainly those without French citizenship, in both the occupied and unoccupied zones. In mid-July, nearly 13,000 Jews were seized in Paris and interned in a sports arena, the Velodrome d'Hiver, with little food or water, until their deportation to Auschwitz. Throughout France, Jews were assembled in camps and then loaded onto cattle cars. They were deported first to the Drancy transit camp (northeast of Paris), which became the main center for deportations from France. Over 60 transports left Drancy, mainly for the Auschwitz-Birkenau killing center. More than 40,000 Jews were deported in 1942.

German and Italian forces occupied the southern zone of France in November 1942, and the Germans began to seize Jews throughout German-occupied France. Having won the cooperation of Vichy authorities in the deportation of foreign and stateless Jews, German authorities then sought to deport Jews with French citizenship. By 1943, French police participated with the Germans in the roundup of Jews. Thousands of French Jews went into hiding, escaped to nearby neutral countries (such as Spain or Switzerland), or sought protection in the Italian occupation zone. Thousands joined partisan units to fight the Germans.

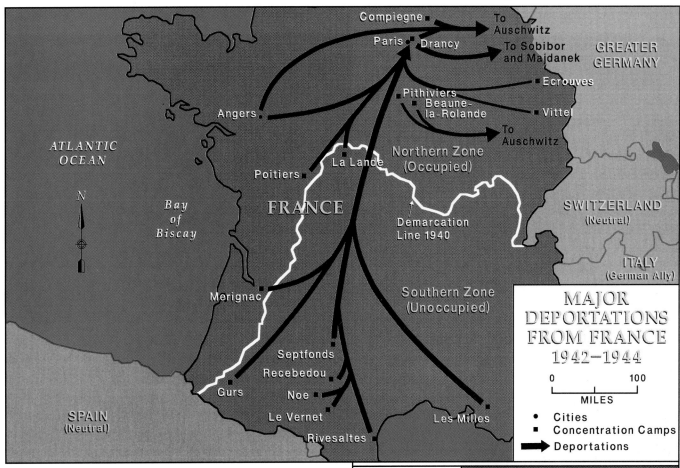

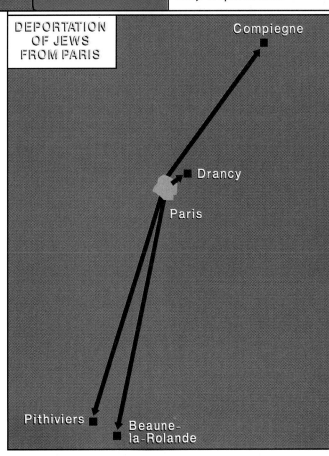

The last deportation from France to the killing centers in the east occurred in the summer of 1944. By then, about 75,000 Jews, mostly foreign, had been deported from France. Most had been killed. Almost all were deported to Auschwitz-Birkenau, but several transports were sent to Majdanek and Sobibor.

The Allied landing in Normandy, in northwestern France, on June 6, 1944, began the liberation of France from Vichy and German domination. By the end of 1944, Allied forces had liberated France. To avoid capture, many Vichy officials fled to Germany.

DEPORTATIONS FROM PARIS AND THE DRANCY TRANSIT CAMP

Paris

The Jewish community in Paris was the largest in France. In 1939, more than 200,000 Jews lived there. Most were eastern Europeans who had recently immigrated to France. The 11th, 18th, and 20th districts had the largest number of Jewish residents in Paris. About half of the Jewish population of Paris left the city after the Germans invaded France in May 1940.

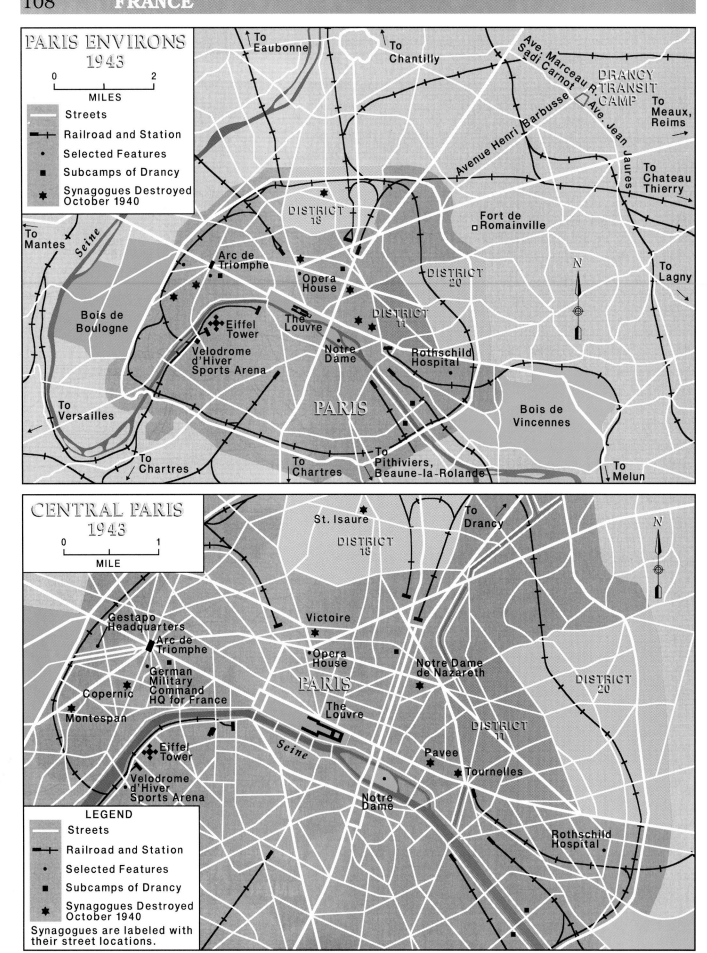

PARIS ENVIRONS 1943

0   2
MILES

— Streets
—+— Railroad and Station
• Selected Features
■ Subcamps of Drancy
★ Synagogues Destroyed October 1940

To Eaubonne
To Chantilly
Ave. Marceau R.
Sadi Carnot
Ave. Jean Jaures
DRANCY TRANSIT CAMP
To Meaux, Reims
To Chateau Thierry
Avenue Henri Barbusse
To Mantes
Seine
DISTRICT 18
Fort de Romainville
DISTRICT 20
To Lagny
N
Arc de Triomphe
Opera House
DISTRICT 11
Bois de Boulogne
Eiffel Tower
The Louvre
Velodrome d'Hiver Sports Arena
Notre Dame
Rothschild Hospital
To Versailles
PARIS
Bois de Vincennes
To Chartres
To Chartres
To Pithiviers, Beaune-la-Rolande
To Melun

CENTRAL PARIS 1943

0   1
MILE

St. Isaure
To Drancy
N
DISTRICT 18
Gestapo Headquarters
Arc de Triomphe
Victoire
Opera House
German Military Command HQ for France
Notre Dame de Nazareth
Copernic
PARIS
DISTRICT 20
Montespan
The Louvre
DISTRICT 11
Eiffel Tower
Seine
Velodrome d'Hiver Sports Arena
Pavee
Notre Dame
Tournelles
Rothschild Hospital

LEGEND
— Streets
—+— Railroad and Station
• Selected Features
■ Subcamps of Drancy
★ Synagogues Destroyed October 1940
Synagogues are labeled with their street locations.

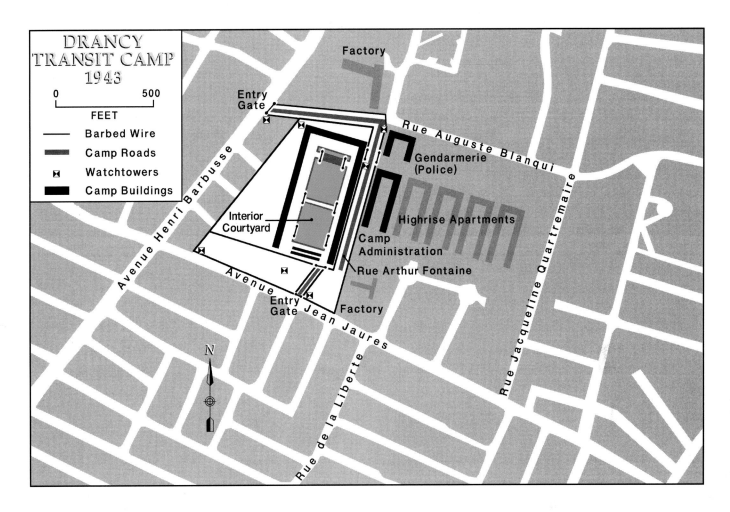

DRANCY
TRANSIT CAMP
1943

0 ———— 500
FEET

——— Barbed Wire
▬▬ Camp Roads
⊠ Watchtowers
■ Camp Buildings

Factory

Entry
Gate

Rue Auguste Blanqui

Gendarmerie
(Police)

Avenue Henri Barbusse

Interior
Courtyard

Highrise Apartments

Camp
Administration

Rue Arthur Fontaine

Rue Jacqueline Quartremaire

Avenue Jean Jaures

Entry
Gate

Factory

Rue de la Liberte

N

After the French armistice with Germany in June 1940, Paris, in the German-occupied zone, became the seat of the German military government and the Gestapo in France. French officials established a government in Vichy in the unoccupied zone, but Paris remained France's largest, most important city.

The persecution of the Jews in Paris began almost immediately after the German occupation. In October 1940, the Nazis exploded bombs in seven synagogues in central Paris, signifying their determination to take violent action against the Jews. The Central Consistory of French Jews, the Children's Aid Society, the Organization for Rehabilitation through Training (O.R.T.), and the Coordinating Committee of Jewish Welfare Societies all worked in Paris to alleviate the hardships caused by German and Vichy antisemitic legislation.

Between 1940 and 1941, the Germans arrested about 10,000 Jews in Paris. About the same number fled the city for the unoccupied zone in the south. In 1942, the Germans began systematic mass deportations of foreign and stateless Jews from Paris. Only Jews with French citizenship or a valid German work permit were exempted. French police assisted in the roundups for these deportations. The Jews were deported to the transit camps of Pithiviers, Beaune-la-Rolande, and above all Drancy, and from there to the killing centers in occupied Poland. In mid-July 1942, nearly 13,000 Jews, most of them foreign or stateless, were rounded up and interned in the Velodrome d'Hiver, a sports arena in south-central Paris that became a makeshift assembly center. They were then deported through Drancy to Auschwitz.

In 1942, nearly 30,000 Jews were deported from Paris. Meanwhile, thousands of Jews fled Paris or went into hiding. By mid-1943, 60,000 Jews remained in the city. The Germans began deporting Jewish inhabitants of children's homes, homes for the aged, and the Rothschild Hospital. Even Jews with valid German work permits faced deportation. Early in 1944, the Germans also began the systematic deportation to Auschwitz-Birkenau of Jews with French citizenship.

Allied forces liberated Paris on August 25, 1944. Tens of thousands of Jews had fled Paris during the occupation and

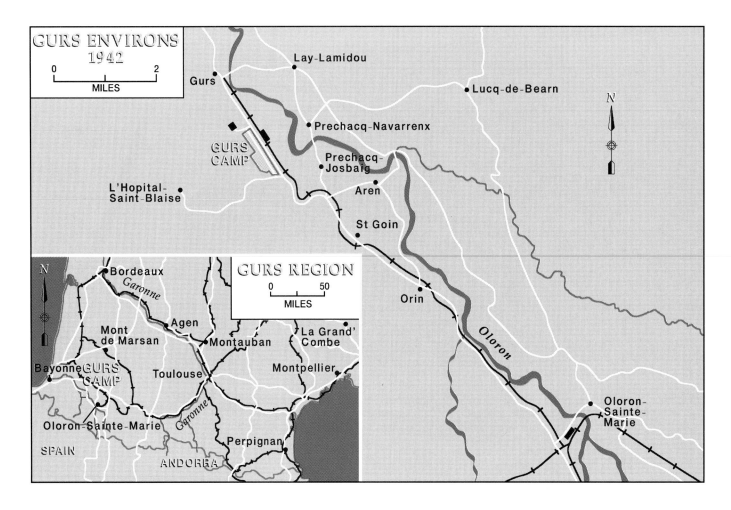

hidden in the provinces or escaped to neutral Spain, Portugal, or Switzerland. More than 20,000 Jews had remained in hiding in Paris itself. At least 50,000, mostly foreign or stateless Jews, had been deported from Paris and killed.

Drancy Transit Camp

In August 1941, a transit camp was established in the northeastern Parisian suburb of Drancy, from which the camp took its name. The Germans initially used Drancy as an internment camp; it then became the major transit camp for the deportations of Jews from France. The camp was a multistory U-shaped building that had served as a police barracks for the city of Paris before the war. The entire building and the courtyard it enclosed were surrounded by barbed wire and guarded by French police. Until 1943, when the Germans took direct control of the camp, French officials staffed the camp under German SS supervision.

The Drancy camp could hold about 5,000 prisoners. Approximately 70,000 prisoners passed through the camp between 1941 and 1944. Five subcamps of Drancy were established in Paris: at the Austerlitz train station, the Hotel de Cahen d'Anvers, the Levitan furniture warehouse, the wharf in Bercy, and the Rue de Faubourg. These were mostly warehouses for the storage of property confiscated from Jews before their deportation.

Systematic deportations from France began in March 1942, and ended in the summer of 1944; about 75,000 Jews were deported. The overwhelming majority of Jews deported from France were deported from the Drancy transit camp to the Auschwitz-Birkenau killing center. In 1942, other transports left from Compiegne, Pithiviers, Beaune-la-Rolande, and the provincial town of Angers. All deportations from France in 1942 went to Auschwitz-Birkenau. In 1943, 17 transports left Drancy. Two left for Sobibor, two for both Majdanek and Sobibor, and the remaining 13 transports for Auschwitz-Birkenau. In 1944, 14 transports left Drancy. Eleven went to Auschwitz, one transport each went to the Bergen-Belsen and Buchenwald concentration camps, and one went to Kovno. In all, more than 65,000 Jews were deported to their deaths from Drancy.

In early August 1944, Allied forces reached Paris. In mid-August, when the Germans transferred the administration of Drancy to the Swedish Red Cross, only about 1,500 prisoners were still there.

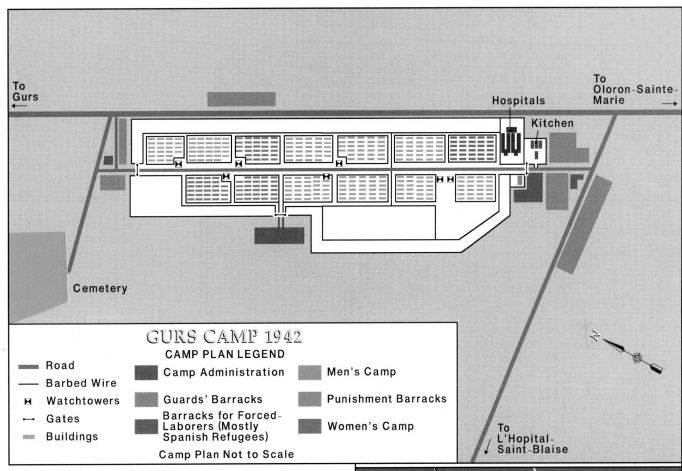

GURS CAMP 1942

CAMP PLAN LEGEND

- Road
- Barbed Wire
- Watchtowers
- Gates
- Buildings

Camp Administration
Guards' Barracks
Barracks for Forced-Laborers (Mostly Spanish Refugees)

Men's Camp
Punishment Barracks
Women's Camp

Camp Plan Not to Scale

GURS INTERNMENT AND TRANSIT CAMP

The Gurs camp was one of the first and largest camps established in prewar France. It was located in the Basque region of southwestern France, just south of the village of Gurs. About 50 miles from the Spanish border, the camp was situated in the foothills of the Pyrenees Mountains northwest of Oloron-Sainte-Marie, along the road to Navarrenx.

The French government established the Gurs camp in April 1939, before war with Germany and well before the occupation of France in June 1940. Originally, Gurs served as an internment camp for Republican refugees and members of the International Brigade fleeing Spain after the victory of the Spanish nationalists under General Francisco Franco. The French government interned these refugees in Gurs and in similar Mediterranean internment camps. In early 1940, the French government also interned about 4,000 German Jewish refugees and many French leftist political leaders who opposed the war with Germany. After the French armistice with Germany in June 1940, Gurs became a Vichy internment camp. Conditions in the camp were very primitive. It was crowded and there was a constant shortage of fresh water, food, and clothing.

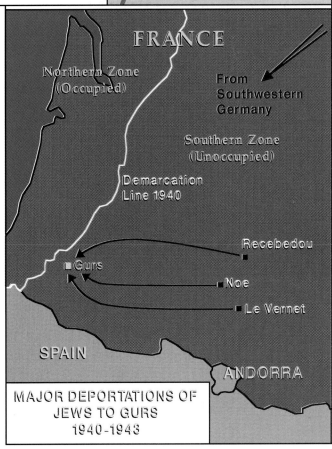

MAJOR DEPORTATIONS OF JEWS TO GURS 1940-1943

CAMPS IN FRANCE 1944

0 — 100
MILES

Solid squares represent select camps. Because of map scale, not all camps can be shown or labeled.

OCCUPATION OF SOUTHERN ZONE NOVEMBER 1942

0 — 200
MILES

In October 1940, German authorities deported about 7,500 Jews from southwestern Germany across the border into the unoccupied zone of France. Vichy officials then interned most of them in Gurs. Between August 1942 and November 1943, Vichy authorities deported approximately 6,000 Jewish prisoners from Gurs, the majority of them directly to the Drancy transit camp outside Paris in northern France. From Drancy, they were deported to the killing centers in occupied Poland. Allied forces liberated Gurs in the summer of 1944.

THE CAMP SYSTEM IN FRANCE 1944

By 1944, Germany had expanded the number of forced-labor camps in France. The Germans assigned Jews to build military fortifications at sites along France's Atlantic coastline in preparation for an expected Allied amphibious invasion. These sites included Calais, Samer, Arras, Berck Plage, Watten, Cambrai, Saleux, and Pihen-les-Guines. Further, many camps were established as subcamps of the Natzweiler-Struthof concentration camp in Alsace. Among these were Hayingen, Longwy-Thil, Deutschoth, Markirch, Schwindratzheim, Sennheim, and Wesserling. Subcamps of Natzweiler-Struthof were also established near Metz and Muehlhausen.

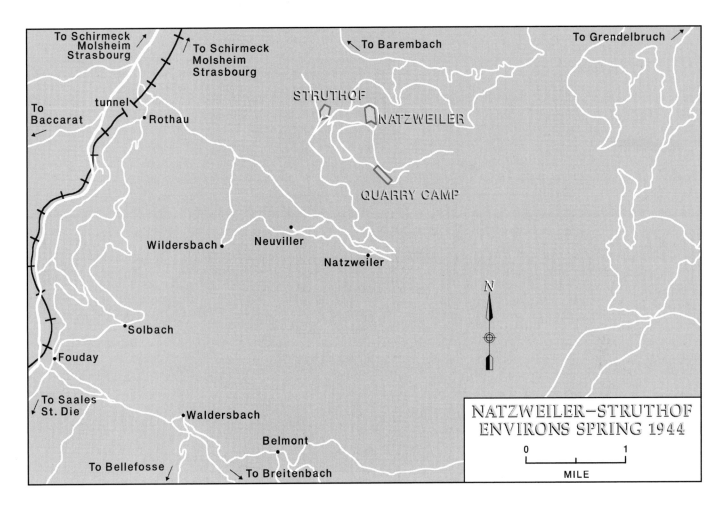

NATZWEILER-STRUTHOF
ENVIRONS SPRING 1944

0   1
MILE

NATZWEILER-STRUTHOF
CONCENTRATION CAMP

The Germans established the Natzweiler-Struthof concentration camp near Natzweiler, about 31 miles southwest of Strasbourg, the capital of Alsace (in eastern France). It was one of the smaller concentration camps built by the Germans. Until construction was completed in May 1941, prisoners were housed in the nearby Hotel Struthof, hence the name Natzweiler-Struthof. The camp was designed to hold about 1,500 prisoners. Prisoners worked in nearby granite quarries, in construction projects, and in the maintenance of the camp.

Beginning in the summer of 1943, the Germans detained many "Night and Fog" prisoners in Natzweiler-Struthof. "Night and Fog" (Nacht und Nebel) referred to the German attempt to subdue growing anti-German resistance in western Europe. Suspected resistance fighters were arrested and their families were not notified; the prisoners simply disappeared into the "Night and Fog." Many of the prisoners in the Natzweiler-Struthof camp were members of the French Resistance.

In August 1943, a gas chamber was constructed in Natzweiler-Struthof in one of the buildings that had formed part of the hotel compound. The bodies of more than 80 Jewish prisoners who were gassed at Natzweiler-Struthof were sent for study to the Strasbourg University Institute of Anatomy. The gas chamber was also used in pseudoscientific medical experiments involving poison gas. The victims of these experiments were primarily Roma (Gypsies) who had been transferred from Auschwitz. Prisoners were also used in experiments involving treatment for typhus and yellow fever.

In 1944, concentration camp prisoners became increasingly important in German armaments production. The Germans used prisoners throughout the Natzweiler-Struthof camp system as forced laborers for the production of arms and the construction of underground manufacturing facilities. Allied air raids on industrial complexes necessitated the construction of such facilities.

There were about 50 subcamps in the Natzweiler-Struthof camp system, located mostly in Alsace and Lorraine and in the adjacent German provinces of Baden and Wuerttemberg. By the fall of 1944, there were about 7,000 prisoners in the main camp and more than 20,000 in subcamps.

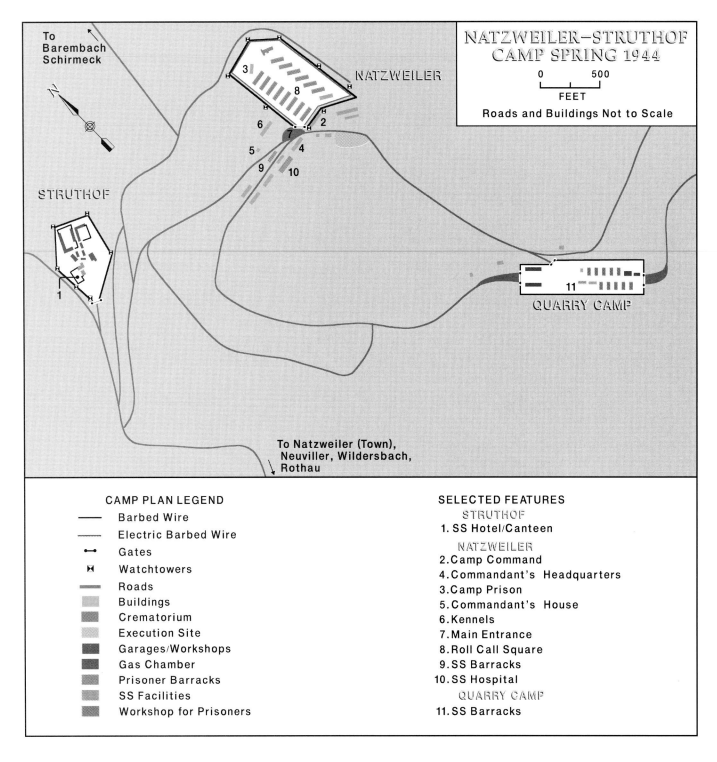

NATZWEILER–STRUTHOF
CAMP SPRING 1944

0   500
FEET

Roads and Buildings Not to Scale

To
Barembach
Schirmeck

NATZWEILER

STRUTHOF

To Natzweiler (Town),
Neuviller, Wildersbach,
Rothau

QUARRY CAMP

CAMP PLAN LEGEND

— Barbed Wire
— Electric Barbed Wire
↦ Gates
⋈ Watchtowers
— Roads
Buildings
Crematorium
Execution Site
Garages/Workshops
Gas Chamber
Prisoner Barracks
SS Facilities
Workshop for Prisoners

SELECTED FEATURES

STRUTHOF
1. SS Hotel/Canteen

NATZWEILER
2. Camp Command
4. Commandant's Headquarters
3. Camp Prison
5. Commandant's House
6. Kennels
7. Main Entrance
8. Roll Call Square
9. SS Barracks
10. SS Hospital

QUARRY CAMP
11. SS Barracks

With the approach of Allied forces in September 1944, the main camp at Natzweiler-Struthof was evacuated and the prisoners distributed among the subcamps. In March 1945, the Germans evacuated the subcamps and sent most of the prisoners on death marches—forced marches over long distances and under brutal conditions—toward the Dachau concentration camp in southern Germany. More than 17,000 people died in the Natzweiler-Struthof camp system.

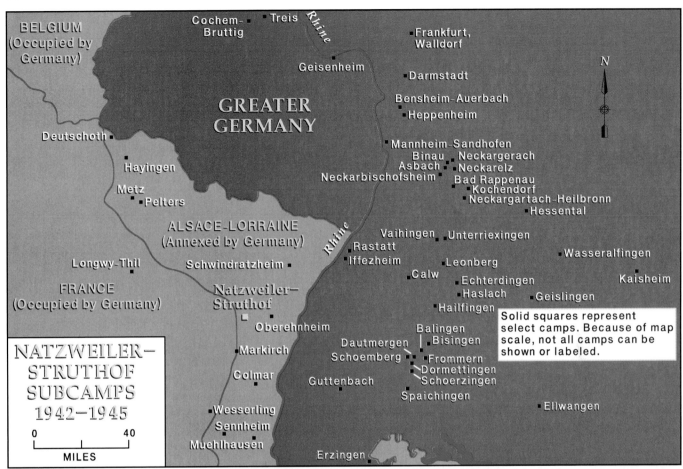

NATZWEILER–STRUTHOF SUBCAMPS 1942–1945

0 — 40
MILES

BELGIUM (Occupied by Germany)

Cochem-Bruttig

Treis

Rhine

Frankfurt, Walldorf

Geisenheim

Darmstadt

GREATER GERMANY

Bensheim-Auerbach

Heppenheim

Deutschoth

Mannheim-Sandhofen

Binau   Neckargerach

Asbach   Neckarelz

Neckarbischofsheim

Bad Rappenau

Kochendorf

Neckargartach-Heilbronn

Hessental

Hayingen

Metz

Pelters

ALSACE-LORRAINE (Annexed by Germany)

Rhine

Vaihingen   Unterriexingen

Rastatt

Iffezheim

Longwy-Thil

Schwindratzheim

FRANCE (Occupied by Germany)

Natzweiler–Struthof

Oberehnheim

Markirch

Colmar

Leonberg

Wasseralfingen

Calw

Echterdingen

Kaisheim

Haslach

Geislingen

Hailfingen

Balingen

Bisingen

Dautmergen

Schoemberg

Frommern

Dormettingen

Schoerzingen

Guttenbach

Spaichingen

Wesserling

Sennheim

Muehlhausen

Erzingen

Ellwangen

Solid squares represent select camps. Because of map scale, not all camps can be shown or labeled.

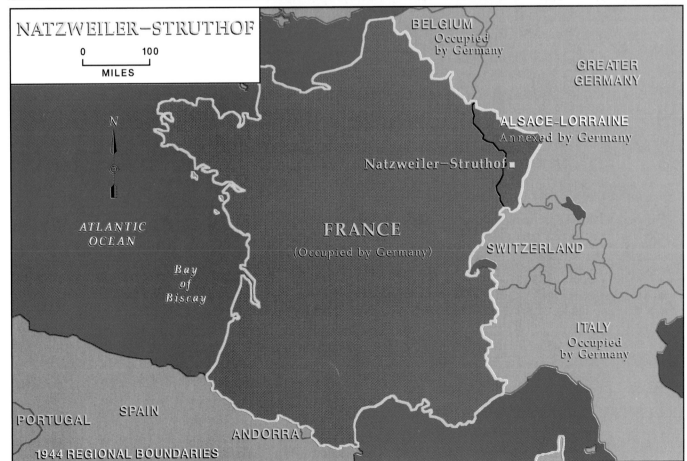

NATZWEILER–STRUTHOF

0 — 100
MILES

BELGIUM Occupied by Germany

GREATER GERMANY

ALSACE-LORRAINE Annexed by Germany

Natzweiler–Struthof

ATLANTIC OCEAN

Bay of Biscay

FRANCE (Occupied by Germany)

SWITZERLAND

ITALY Occupied by Germany

PORTUGAL

SPAIN

ANDORRA

1944 REGIONAL BOUNDARIES

THE LOW COUNTRIES 1939

0   100

MILES

North Sea

N

NETHERLANDS

Groningen

Leeuwarden

Assen

Alkmaar

Kampen

Ijsel

Haarlem

Amsterdam

Apeldoorn

Enschede

Utrecht

The Hague

Neder Rijn

Arnhem

Rotterdam

Waal

Maas

GREATER
GERMANY

's-Hertogenbosch

Breda

Eindhoven

Maas

Rhine

Turnhout

Brugge

Antwerp

Oostende

Ghent

Scheldc

Mechelen

Maastricht

Aalst

Leuven

Brussels

BELGIUM

Meuse

Liege

Mons

Malmedy

Sambre

Namur

Charleroi

Clervaux

Bastogne

Mosel

Diekirch

Wiltz

LUXEMBOURG

Luxembourg

FRANCE

Meuse

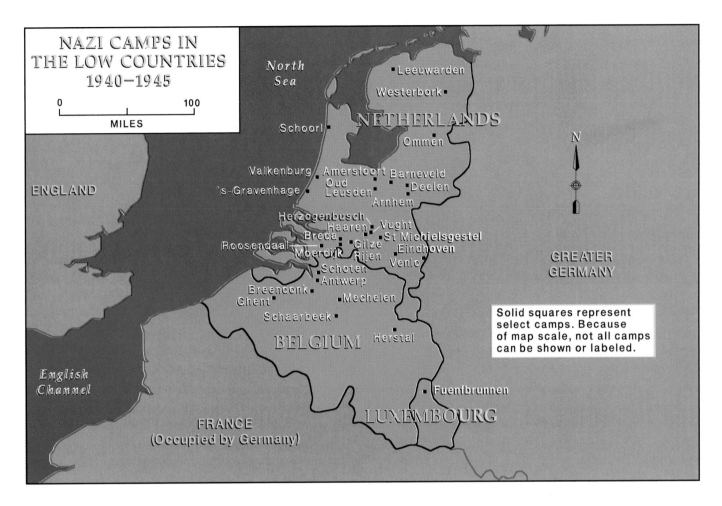

NAZI CAMPS IN
THE LOW COUNTRIES
1940–1945

0 100
MILES

North
Sea

• Leeuwarden

Westerbork •

NETHERLANDS

Schoorl •

• Ommen

ENGLAND

Valkenburg • Amersfoort • Barneveld
's-Gravenhage • Oud • Deelen
Leusden •
Arnhem
Herzogenbusch
Haaren • Vught
Breda • • St Michielsgestel
Roosendaal • Gilze • Eindhoven
Moerdijk • Rijen Venlo
Schoten •
• Antwerp

GREATER
GERMANY

Breendonk •
Ghent • • Mechelen
Schaarbeek •

BELGIUM Herstal •

Solid squares represent
select camps. Because
of map scale, not all camps
can be shown or labeled.

English
Channel

• Fuenfbrunnen

LUXEMBOURG

FRANCE
(Occupied by Germany)

THE DEPORTATION OF THE JEWS FROM THE LOW COUNTRIES

Germany invaded and occupied Luxembourg, Belgium, and the Netherlands—the Low Countries—in May 1940. In all three countries, the Germans instituted anti-Jewish laws and ordinances. They restricted the civil rights of Jews, confiscated their property and businesses, and banned them from certain professions. Jews were isolated from their fellow countrymen and forced to wear a yellow star on their clothing. Beginning in the summer of 1942, Jews in these countries faced deportation to the killing centers, mostly to Auschwitz-Birkenau.

LUXEMBOURG

After the German occupation in May 1940, the Grand Duchess of Luxembourg and her government fled to Great Britain. The Germans did not permit a native administration in Luxembourg and the country was instead administered directly by the German Reich. In August 1942, Germany formally annexed Luxembourg.

Before the war, more than 3,000 Jews lived in Luxembourg. More than 1,000 were foreign and stateless

Jews who had found refuge there after 1933. In 1941, Jews were interned in the Fuenfbrunnen camp near the city of Ulflingen in northern Luxembourg. This camp served as a transit camp for the deportation of the Jews. More than 1,000 Jews fled Luxembourg before the deportations began. Between 1941 and 1943, the remaining Jews were deported and Luxembourg was declared "free of Jews" (judenfrei). Some Jews survived, either in hiding or because they were married to non-Jews and exempted from the deportations. Almost 2,000 Jews from Luxembourg were killed in the camps.

BELGIUM

After the German invasion of Belgium in 1940, a Belgian government-in-exile that worked with the Allies was formed in London. King Leopold III, however, remained in Belgium during the German occupation. Thus, inside Belgium, a German military administration coexisted with a civilian Belgian administration.

Belgian Jews were rounded up, initially for forced labor. They worked primarily in the construction of military fortifications in northern France, and also in construction projects,

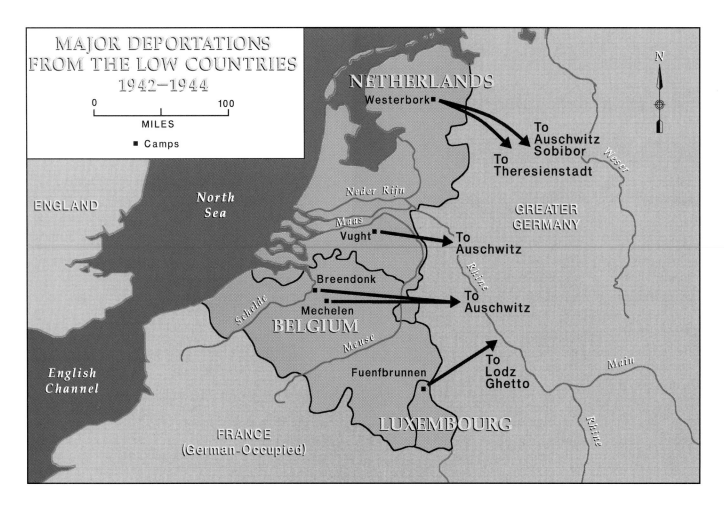

MAJOR DEPORTATIONS
FROM THE LOW COUNTRIES
1942–1944

clothing and armaments factories, and stone quarries in Belgium.

The German administration was responsible for the deportation of the Jews in Belgium. Upon the German occupation, more than 65,000 Jews lived in Belgium, primarily in Antwerp and Brussels. The overwhelming majority of them were foreign and stateless Jews who had found refuge in Belgium after World War I. In the summer of 1940, some German Jews and political refugees were deported to camps in southern France, such as Gurs and St. Cyprien.

There was wide support in Belgium for resistance to German occupation. About 25,000 Jews avoided deportation by hiding from the German authorities. The Belgian civilian administration refused to cooperate in the deportations. The German military police (Feldgendarmerie) carried out the deportations largely without assistance from the Belgians. Between 1942 and 1944, more than 25,000 Jews from Belgium were deported to Auschwitz and killed. The

Breendonk and Mechelen camps served as collection centers for the deportations.

THE NETHERLANDS

In the Netherlands, a Dutch civilian administration continued to function, under German supervision, during the German occupation. However, Queen Wilhelmina and her government fled to Great Britain. German policy in the Netherlands was determined by a Nazi commissioner, Arthur Seyss-Inquart, who insisted on strict compliance with anti-Jewish measures. In January 1941, the Germans ordered all Jews to report for registration. More than 140,000 responded. In early 1942, the Germans sent more than 3,000 Jews to forced-labor camps in the Netherlands.

Deportations from the Netherlands began in 1942. The Germans required all Dutch Jews to move to Amsterdam, the country's largest city. Stateless and foreign Jews who had entered the Netherlands during the 1930s were sent to the Westerbork transit camp. Some Jews from the provinces were

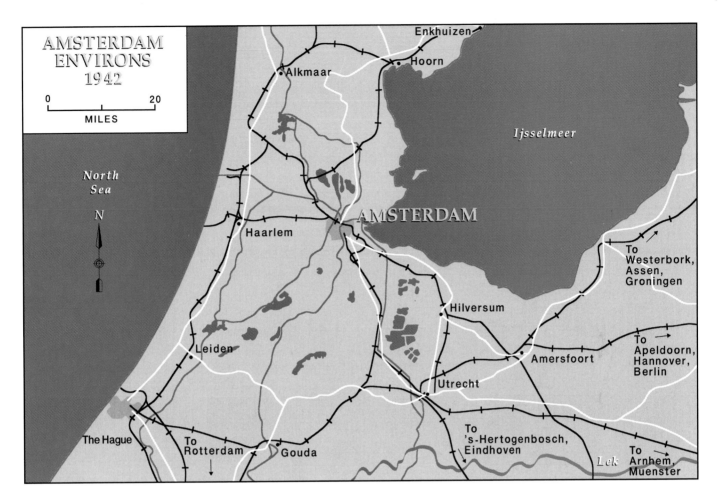

concentrated in the Vught camp. In late June 1942, the Germans announced that Jews would be deported to labor camps in Germany. In reality, they were deported to the Auschwitz-Birkenau and Sobibor killing centers in occupied Poland.

The Dutch churches protested to the German occupation authorities. Public protests had little effect, however, since the Dutch civilian administration cooperated with the Germans. The Dutch police, with few exceptions, participated in roundups. Jews were concentrated in Westerbork and then deported to Auschwitz and also to Sobibor. In little more than two years, more than 100,000 Jews were deported; most were killed. Less than 25 percent of Dutch Jewry survived the war.

AMSTERDAM, THE NETHERLANDS

When the Germans occupied the Netherlands in May 1940, Amsterdam, the country's largest city, had a Jewish population of about 75,000. Nearly 10,000 were foreign Jews who had found refuge in Amsterdam in the 1930s.

In February 1941, the Germans arrested several hundred Jews and deported them first to Buchenwald and then to Mauthausen. Almost all of them were killed. The arrests and the brutal treatment shocked the city. In response, Communist activists organized a general strike on February 25. Major factories, the transportation system, and most public services came to a standstill in Amsterdam. The Germans brutally suppressed the strike after three days, crippling Dutch resistance organizations in the process. They also hardened their policies toward the Jews in the Netherlands.

In January 1942, the Germans ordered all Dutch Jews to relocate to Amsterdam. Within Amsterdam, Jews were restricted to certain fenced-off sections of the city. Foreign and stateless Jews were sent directly to the Westerbork transit camp. In July 1942, the Germans began mass deportations of Jews to the killing centers in occupied Poland, primarily to Auschwitz but also to Sobibor. The city administration, the Dutch municipal police, and Dutch railway workers all cooperated in the deportations. Jews were arrested in the

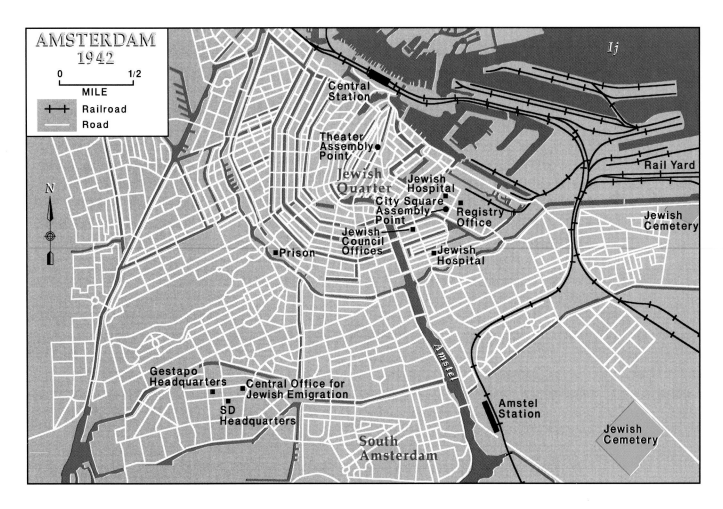

AMSTERDAM
1942

0   1/2
MILE

Railroad
Road

Central Station

Theater Assembly Point

Jewish Quarter

Jewish Hospital

City Square Assembly Point

Registry Office

Jewish Council Offices

Jewish Hospital

Prison

Rail Yard

Jewish Cemetery

Gestapo Headquarters

Central Office for Jewish Emigration

SD Headquarters

Amstel Station

Jewish Cemetery

South Amsterdam

Amstel

Ij

N

streets of Amsterdam and taken to the assembly point for deportations—the municipal theater building. When several hundred people were assembled in the building and in the back courtyard, they were transferred to Westerbork. In October 1942, the Germans transferred all Jews in forced-labor camps and their families to Westerbork. They were deported to Auschwitz-Birkenau within a few weeks.

In May 1943, 7,000 Jews, employees of the Jewish council in Amsterdam, were ordered to assemble in an Amsterdam city square for deportation. Only 500 people complied. The Germans responded by sealing the Jewish quarter and rounding up Jews. From May through September 1943, the Germans launched raids to seize Jews in the city.

The Germans confiscated the property left behind by deported Jews. In 1942 alone the contents of nearly 10,000 apartments in Amsterdam were expropriated by the Germans and shipped to Germany. Some 25,000 Jews, including at least 4,500 children, went into hiding to evade deportation. About one-third of those in hiding were discovered, arrested, and deported.

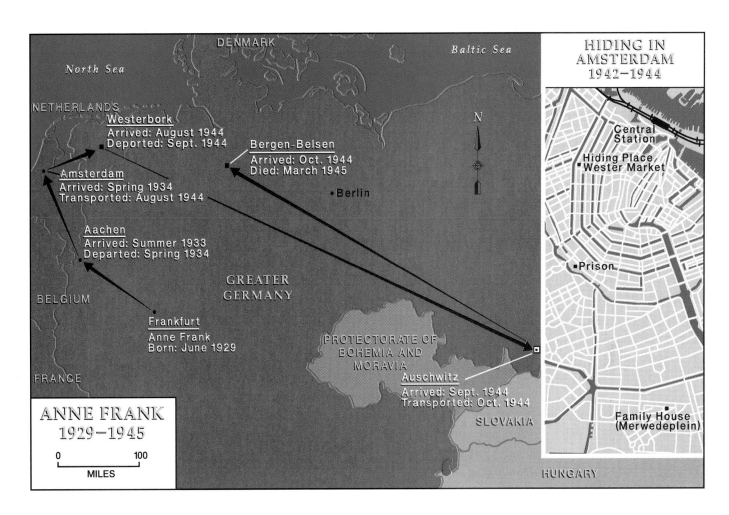

ANNE FRANK

Anne Frank was one of the hundreds of thousands of Jewish children who died in the Holocaust. Born in Germany in 1929, she fled with her family to the Netherlands after the Nazi takeover of power in 1933.

The Germans occupied Amsterdam in May 1940. In July 1942, when Germany began the deportation of Jews from the Netherlands to the Auschwitz-Birkenau and Sobibor killing centers in occupied Poland, Anne and her family went into hiding with four other people. For two years, they lived in a secret attic apartment, constructed behind the office of the family-owned business at 263 Prinsengracht. Friends smuggled food and clothing to them, at great risk to their own lives. On August 4, 1944, they were discovered by the Gestapo.

The Franks were arrested and sent to the Westerbork transit camp. They were deported to Auschwitz-Birkenau in September 1944. After a few weeks Anne and her sister, Margot, were transferred to the Bergen-Belsen concentration camp near Celle, in northern Germany. They died of typhus in March 1945, a month before the liberation of the camp. Anne's mother died in Auschwitz. Only Anne's father, Otto, survived the war. He was liberated at Auschwitz by Soviet forces in 1945.

While in hiding, Anne kept a diary in which she recorded her fears, hopes, and experiences. The diary was found in the secret apartment after the family was arrested and was kept for Anne by one of those who had helped hide the family. It was published after the war in many languages. Anne Frank has become a symbol for the lost promise of the children who died in the Holocaust.

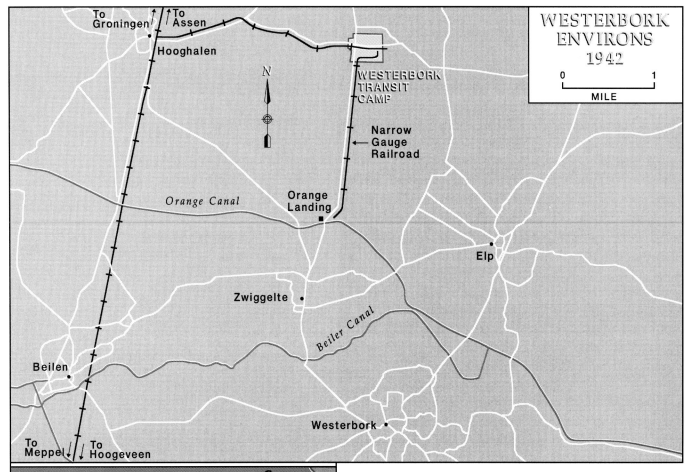

WESTERBORK TRANSIT CAMP, THE NETHERLANDS

The Westerbork camp was in the northeastern part of the Netherlands in the Dutch province of Drenthe, near the towns of Westerbork and Assen. The Dutch government established a camp at Westerbork in October 1939 to intern Jewish refugees who had entered the Netherlands illegally.

Germany invaded and occupied the Netherlands in May 1940. In early 1942, the German occupation authorities decided to enlarge Westerbork and convert it into a transit camp for Jews. The systematic concentration of Jews from the Netherlands in Westerbork began in July 1942. From Westerbork, they were deported to the killing centers in German-occupied Poland. The Germans deported more than 100,000 Jews from Westerbork: about 60,000 to Auschwitz, over 34,000 to Sobibor, almost 5,000 to the Theresienstadt ghetto, and nearly 4,000 to the Bergen-Belsen concentration camp. Most were killed.

The majority of Jews sent to Westerbork remained there only a short time before they were deported. However, Westerbork did have a resident population of Jews who worked in the camp and were thus exempt from deportation.

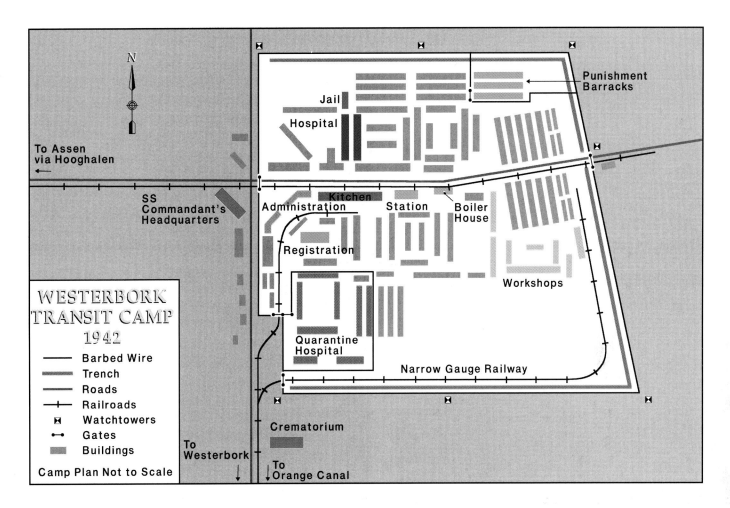

WESTERBORK TRANSIT CAMP 1942

Barbed Wire
Trench
Roads
Railroads
Watchtowers
Gates
Buildings

Camp Plan Not to Scale

Jail
Hospital
Punishment Barracks
To Assen via Hooghalen
SS Commandant's Headquarters
Kitchen
Administration
Station
Boiler House
Registration
Workshops
Quarantine Hospital
Narrow Gauge Railway
Crematorium
To Westerbork
To Orange Canal

Many worked in the camp hospital, which was exceptionally large. Others worked in the camp administration, in the camp's workshops, in the fields and gardens, and in construction projects around the camp.

Dutch police guarded the camp, where conditions were relatively good. The Dutch provided the camp with supplies, and the prisoners had adequate food, clothing, housing, and sanitary facilities.

In early April 1945, as Allied forces approached the camp, the Germans abandoned Westerbork. Fewer than 1,000 prisoners remained when Allied forces liberated the camp later that month.

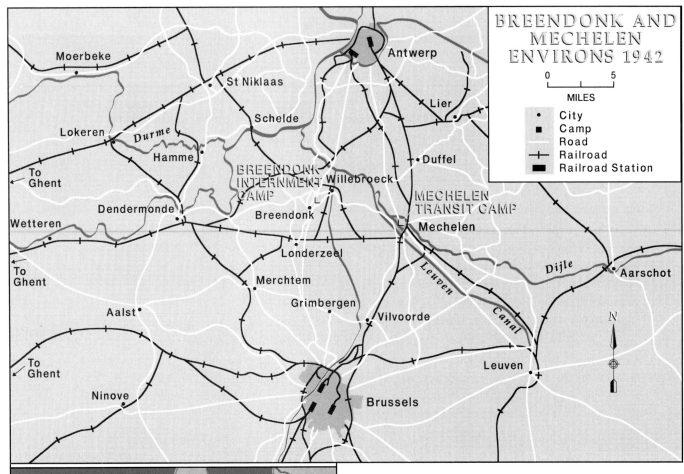

BREENDONK AND
MECHELEN
ENVIRONS 1942

0   5
MILES

- • City
- ■ Camp
- — Road
- —+— Railroad
- ■■ Railroad Station

MECHELEN TRANSIT CAMP, BELGIUM

In the summer of 1942, the Germans converted the Dossin military barracks in Mechelen (Malines), Belgium, into a transit camp in preparation for the deportation of Jews from Belgium. The Germans considered Mechelen an ideal location for a transit camp since it was situated about midway between the major Jewish population centers in Antwerp and Brussels and had good rail connections to the east. The camp was a single three-story building surrounded by barbed wire. It was located in a populated area of the town, near the Dijle River, and was connected to a rail line.

In late July 1942, the Germans ordered Jews to report to Mechelen, ostensibly to be sent to work camps in Germany. In reality they were to be deported to Auschwitz. Few Jews voluntarily reported to the camp. The Germans then began to arrest Jews throughout Belgium and intern them in Mechelen.

Between August and December 1942, two transports with about 1,000 Jews each left the camp every week for the Auschwitz-Birkenau killing center. Between August 1942 and July 1944, 28 trains carrying more than 25,000 Jews were deported from Belgium via Mechelen, mostly to Auschwitz. Several transports of Roma (Gypsies) were also

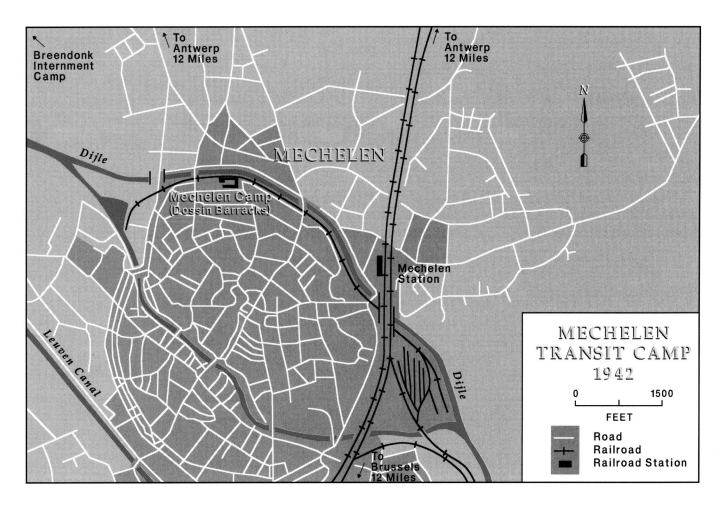

deported from Mechelen to Auschwitz.

The arrests of Jews and the beginning of deportations met with increasing resistance in Belgium. In 1942, the Jewish underground destroyed the registry of Belgian Jews, hindering their deportation. There were many escapes from the trains and in mid-April 1943, the Jewish underground, together with the Belgian resistance, derailed a train carrying Jews from the Mechelen camp to Auschwitz. Most of the Jews on that transport were later deported. Thousands of Jews went into hiding or fled Belgium to neutral Switzerland or to Spain and Portugal via the unoccupied zone in southern France.

As Allied forces approached in 1944, the Germans closed the Mechelen camp.

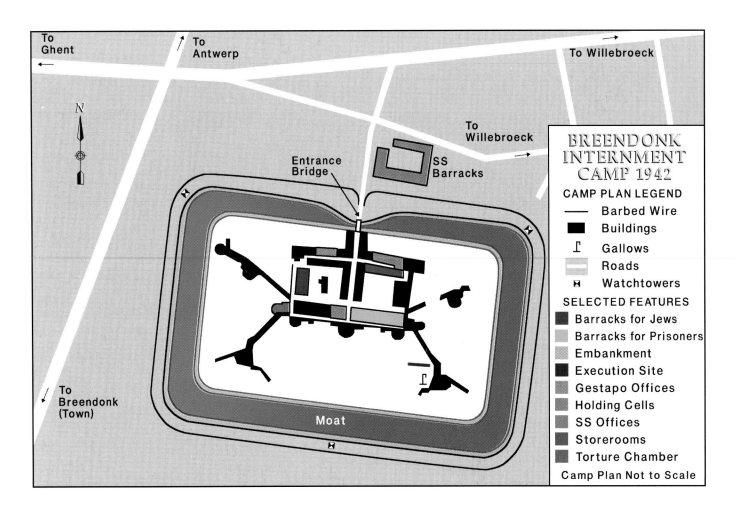

To Ghent

To Antwerp

To Willebroeck

N

To Willebroeck

Entrance Bridge

SS Barracks

To Breendonk (Town)

Moat

BREENDONK INTERNMENT CAMP 1942

CAMP PLAN LEGEND
—— Barbed Wire
■ Buildings
⌐ Gallows
▦ Roads
◪ Watchtowers

SELECTED FEATURES
Barracks for Jews
Barracks for Prisoners
Embankment
Execution Site
Gestapo Offices
Holding Cells
SS Offices
Storerooms
Torture Chamber

Camp Plan Not to Scale

BREENDONK INTERNMENT CAMP, BELGIUM

The Breendonk internment camp was originally a Belgian fortress built in the beginning of the twentieth century along the Antwerp-Brussels highway. It was one in a chain of fortresses constructed to defend Belgium against German attack. The fortress was near the town of the same name, about 12 miles southwest of Antwerp. It was surrounded by high walls and a water-filled moat, and measured 656 by 984 feet. In August 1940, the Germans, who had occupied Belgium in May 1940, turned the fortress into a detention camp.

Fewer than 4,000 prisoners were confined in Breendonk.

Most of the non-Jewish prisoners were members of the Belgian resistance or were held as hostages by the Germans. Approximately 800 people were killed in the camp.

Jewish prisoners in Breendonk were segregated from other prisoners until 1942. Thereafter, they were transferred to the Mechelen transit camp or deported to the Auschwitz-Birkenau killing center.

With Allied forces approaching the camp, the Germans evacuated Breendonk in August 1944. The remaining prisoners were transferred to the Mechelen camp and then to camps in Germany.

THE HOLOCAUST IN CENTRAL EUROPE

DEPORTATIONS OF JEWS FROM GERMANY
1941–1944

0   150
MILES

Baltic Sea

Danzig

Hamburg

NETHERLANDS

Hannover

Berlin

GREATER
GERMANY

Duesseldorf

Lodz

Cologne

Leipzig

BELGIUM

Breslau

Frankfurt

Theresienstadt

Krako

Auschwitz

PROTECTORATE OF
BOHEMIA AND
MORAVIA

FRANCE

Stuttgart

SLOVAKIA

To Gurs
Transit
Camp

Arrows represent select deportations
of Jews to destinations in eastern
Europe. Because of map scale, not all
deportations or destinations can be
shown or labeled.

Munich

Vienna

N

HUNGARY

ITALY

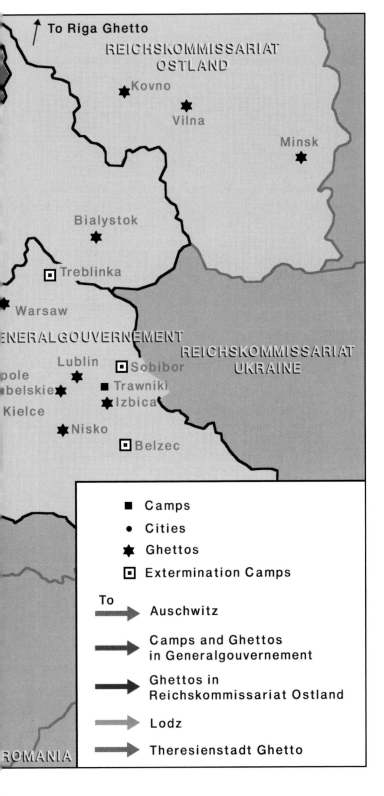

To Riga Ghetto

REICHSKOMMISSARIAT
OSTLAND

Kovno

Vilna

Minsk

Bialystok

Treblinka

Warsaw

ENERALGOUVERNEMENT

REICHSKOMMISSARIAT
UKRAINE

Lublin   Sobibor
pole
belskie   Trawniki
Kielce   Izbica

Nisko

Belzec

- ■ Camps
- ● Cities
- ★ Ghettos
- ▣ Extermination Camps

To → Auschwitz

→ Camps and Ghettos
  in Generalgouvernement

→ Ghettos in
  Reichskommissariat Ostland

→ Lodz

→ Theresienstadt Ghetto

ROMANIA

DEPORTATION OF JEWS FROM GERMANY

According to the *American Jewish Yearbook*, approximately 432,000 Jews emigrated from Greater Germany (Germany, Austria, and the Sudetenland) between 1933 and 1940. Still, over 200,000 Jews remained in Germany at the start of World War II. During the war, Jews in Germany, as in all areas of German-occupied Europe, were deported and killed as part of the "Final Solution."

In the early years of the war, new legislative restrictions were imposed on those Jews remaining in Germany. Jews became subject to a strict curfew and were excluded from certain areas of the cities in which they lived. Once food rationing was instituted, Jews received reduced rations and were forbidden to buy certain foods. Jews were ordered to turn in to the police their radios, electrical appliances, bicycles, and cars. As of September 1941, Jews were forbidden to use public transportation and all Jews over the age of six were ordered to wear yellow stars. While ghettos were generally not established in Germany, strict residence ordinances forced Jews into certain areas of German cities, concentrating them in "Jewish buildings."

The first deportations of Jews from Germany took place in February 1940 as part of the Nisko and Lublin Plan, which called for a Jewish reservation in the Lublin region of the Generalgouvernement. This plan failed since the town of Nisko was not fully equipped for a camp and German officials in the Generalgouvernement complained that there were so many Jews in Poland that it was impossible to absorb still more from Germany. In October 1940, local German officials in southwestern Germany deported 7,500 Jews to France. Most were interned in the Gurs camp.

Systematic deportations of Jews from Germany began in late September 1941, even before the killing centers were established in occupied Poland. Between October and December 1941, nearly 50,000 Jews were deported from Germany, mostly to the Lodz and Warsaw ghettos (Poland), the Minsk ghetto (Belorussia), the Kovno ghetto (Lithuania), and the Riga ghetto (Latvia). German Jews sent to Lodz and Warsaw were later deported along with Polish Jews to the extermination camps at Chelmno and Treblinka.

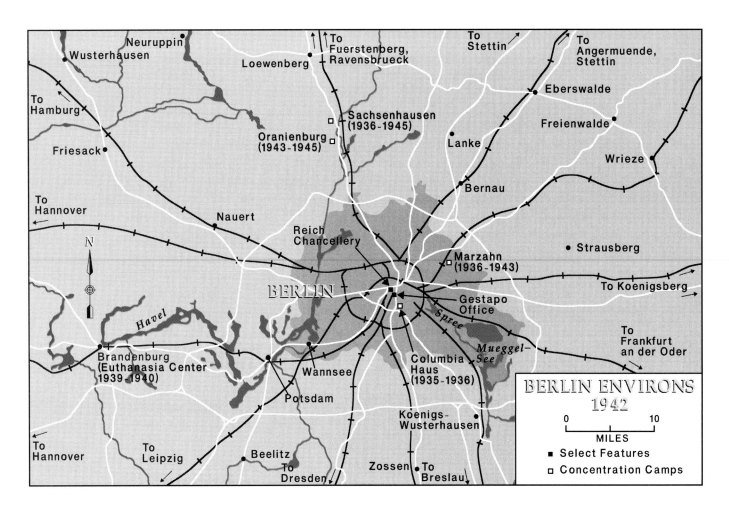

Some Jews deported from Germany to ghettos in the Baltic states and Belorussia were shot, shortly after arrival, by Einsatzgruppen. Jews surviving the initial slaughter were enclosed in special "German sections" of eastern ghettos, where they were segregated from local Jews. Such sections were established, for example, in Riga and Minsk. Most of the Jews from Germany were killed during the destruction of these ghettos. In 1942 and 1943, most of the Jews remaining in Germany were deported directly to the extermination camps, mainly Auschwitz-Birkenau.

Elderly or prominent Jews from Germany, Austria, and western Europe, as well as Jews from the Protectorate of Bohemia and Moravia, were deported to the Theresienstadt ghetto. For most Jews, deportation to Theresienstadt preceded deportation to the east. Jews were routinely deported from Theresienstadt to ghettos in Poland and the Baltic states, and also directly to the killing centers in occupied Poland. Tens of thousands also died in the Theresienstadt ghetto itself, mostly from starvation or during epidemics.

Only about 15,000 Jews remained in Germany and about 7,000 in Austria after the mass deportations ended in early 1943. Almost all the Jews deported from Germany were killed. Most of the remaining Jews were married to non-Jews or were classified as part Jews and were thus exempt from deportation until 1944-1945. Thousands of Jews remained in hiding.

THE DEPORTATIONS OF JEWS FROM BERLIN

According to the census of June 16, 1933, the Jewish population of Berlin, Germany's capital city, was about 160,000. Berlin's Jewish community was the largest in Germany, comprising more than 32 percent of all Jews in the country. In the face of Nazi persecution, many Jews emigrated from Berlin. Berlin's Jewish population fell to about 80,000 people as a result of emigration from Nazi Germany between 1933 and 1939, despite the movement of other German Jews to Berlin.

Like the Jews of Germany as a whole, the Jews of Berlin faced persecution and discrimination after 1933. In April 1933, Jewish stores and businesses were boycotted and most Jewish civil servants and professionals were summarily fired or pensioned. In May 1933, "un-German" books—those written by Jews, liberals, and leftists, among others—were publicly burned in front of the opera house.

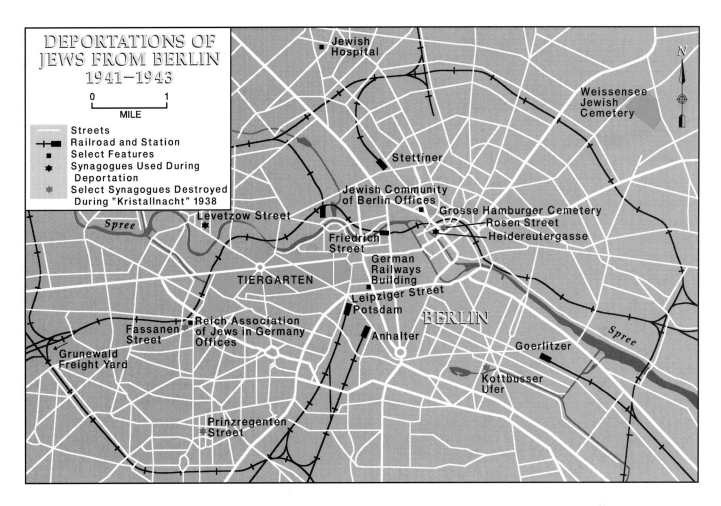

DEPORTATIONS OF
JEWS FROM BERLIN
1941–1943

0   1
MILE

Streets
Railroad and Station
Select Features
Synagogues Used During
  Deportation
Select Synagogues Destroyed
  During "Kristallnacht" 1938

Jewish
Hospital

N

Weissensee
Jewish
Cemetery

Stettiner

Jewish Community
of Berlin Offices

Grosse Hamburger Cemetery
Rosen Street
Heidereutergasse

Levetzow Street

Spree

Friedrich
Street

German
Railways
Building

TIERGARTEN

Leipziger Street

Potsdam

BERLIN

Spree

Anhalter

Goerlitzer

Reich Association
of Jews in Germany
Offices

Fassanen
Street

Kottbusser
Ufer

Grunewald
Freight Yard

Prinzregenten
Street

During "Kristallnacht," the "Night of Broken Glass" pogrom on November 9-10, 1938, most of Berlin's synagogues were burned down and Jewish-owned stores and homes were looted and vandalized. The shattering of shop windows, especially along Leipziger Street, gave the pogrom its name. Dozens of Jews were killed and thousands were arrested and taken to concentration camps, particularly to Sachsenhausen.

Deportations of Jews from Berlin to ghettos and extermination camps in eastern Europe took place between October 1941 and April 1943. Assembly points for the deportations were established at synagogues on Levetzow Street and Heidereutergasse, at the Jewish cemetery on Grosse Hamburger Street, and on Rosen Street. Later, even the Jewish home for the aged, the community office building, and the Jewish hospital were used as assembly centers. After enough Jews for an entire transport (usually 1,000 people) had been assembled in these makeshift centers, they were taken to the rail station—usually the freight yards at Grunewald, sometimes the Anhalter or Putlitz Street train stations. They were then loaded onto passenger rail cars, or sometimes onto freight cars.

The first deportation of Jews from Berlin occurred in October 1941, when 1,000 Jews were transported to the Lodz ghetto in Poland. By January 1942, about 10,000 Jews had been deported from Berlin to ghettos in eastern Europe, mainly Lodz, Riga, Minsk, and Kovno. Elderly Jews from Berlin were deported to Theresienstadt in 1942 and 1943. Beginning in 1942, Jews were also deported from Berlin directly to the killing centers, primarily to Auschwitz-Birkenau. In 1943, most of the staff of the Reich Association of Jews in Germany, the central Jewish representative organization, was deported to Theresienstadt. All Jewish organizations and offices were disbanded. The majority of the remaining Jews in Berlin were deported by the end of April 1943.

More than 60,000 Jews were deported from Berlin: more than 10,000 to the ghettos in eastern Europe, about 15,000 to Theresienstadt, and more than 35,000 to the killing centers in occupied Poland. Hundreds of Jews committed suicide rather than submit to the deportations. Thousands of Jews remained in Berlin, mostly those who had gone into hiding and also part-Jews and Jews with a non-Jewish spouse, who were initially excluded from deportation.

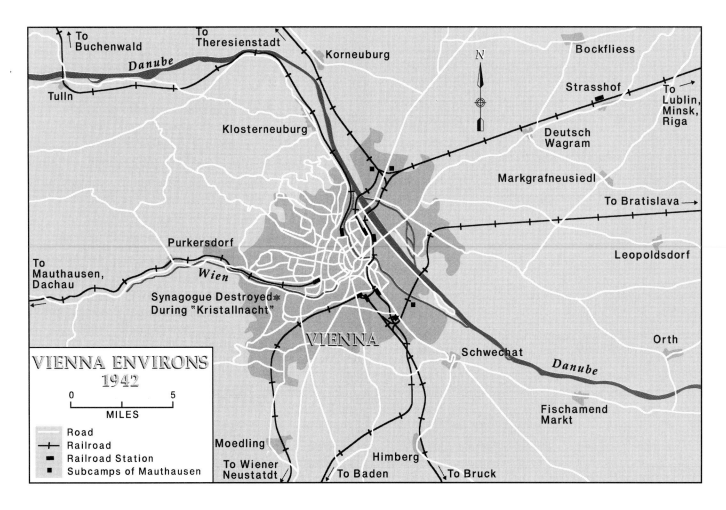

VIENNA ENVIRONS 1942

0 — 5
MILES

- Road
- —+— Railroad
- ■ Railroad Station
- ■ Subcamps of Mauthausen

Almost all of those deported were killed.

A center of Jewish life in Germany, Berlin was, as the capital of the Reich, also the center for the planning of the "Final Solution," the Nazi plan to kill the Jews of Europe. The Wannsee Conference, named for the resort district in southwest Berlin where it was held, took place in January 1942. Officials from the Nazi party, the SS, and the German state met to coordinate and finalize the "solution to the Jewish problem." At the conference, these officials were informed that the SS would be responsible for carrying out the "Final Solution," and that the Jews of Europe would be deported to occupied Poland and killed.

The city of Berlin surrendered to Soviet forces in early May 1945. Germany surrendered unconditionally to Allied forces on May 7, ending the "thousand-year Reich" after 12 bloody years.

THE DEPORTATION OF THE JEWS OF VIENNA

In 1936, the Jewish population of Vienna, the capital of Austria, was about 175,000, or about 9 percent of the city's population. Vienna had by far the largest Jewish community in Austria and was an important center of Zionism, Jewish

culture, and education. Jews also played an important role in the economic and cultural life of Austria.

Following the German incorporation of Austria (the "Anschluss") in March 1938, the Germans quickly extended Nazi anti-Jewish legislation to Austria. They expelled Jews from the country's economic, cultural, and social life. The Jewish community offices were closed and its board members sent to the Dachau concentration camp. By the summer of 1939, the Property Transfer Office had overseen the closure or confiscation of hundreds of Jewish-owned factories and thousands of businesses.

Over a hundred thousand Jews fled Austria after its incorporation and Vienna became a focal point of Jewish emigration from Austria. Those seeking exit visas and other documentation necessary for emigration were required to stand in long lines, night and day, in front of municipal, police, and passport offices. All emigrants were forced to pay an exit fee and their property was confiscated. The Central Office for Jewish Emigration, headed by the SS officer Adolf Eichmann, was established to accelerate Jewish emigration.

The November 1938 "Kristallnacht" pogrom was particularly brutal in Vienna. Most of the city's synagogues and

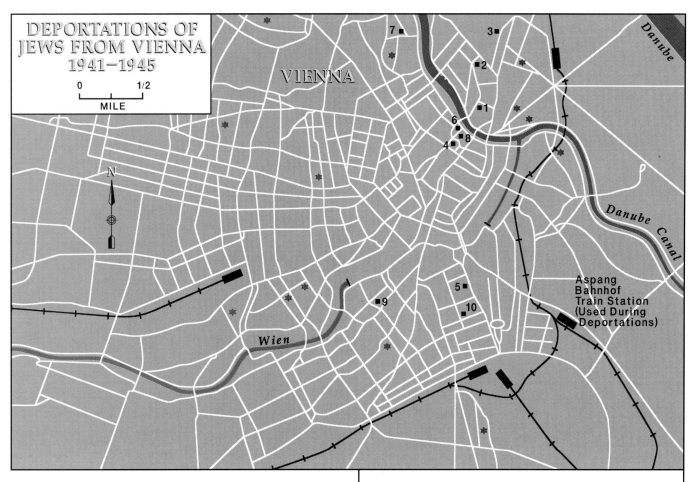

DEPORTATIONS OF
JEWS FROM VIENNA
1941–1945

0   1/2
MILE

VIENNA

N

Wien

Danube

Danube Canal

Aspang
Bahnhof
Train Station
(Used During
Deportations)

small prayerhouses were destroyed, burned out in full view of the fire departments and the public. Thousands of Jews were arrested and deported to the Dachau or Buchenwald concentration camps. Eichmann permitted their release only if they were able to produce documentation of their imminent emigration.

During the war, German policy regarding the Jewish population shifted from one of expropriation and Jewish emigration to forced deportation. Systematic mass deportations from Vienna began in October 1941. The Nazis established centers where Jews were to be assembled before their deportation. About 35,000 Jews were deported from Vienna to ghettos in eastern Europe, mostly to Minsk, Riga, Izbica, and Lodz, and to ghettos in the Lublin region of Poland. Most Jews sent to Minsk and Riga were shot by Einsatzgruppen detachments shortly after their arrival. Over 15,000 Viennese Jews were deported to Theresienstadt. Thousands of Jews were also sent to concentration camps in Germany. By November 1942 only about 7,000 Jews remained in Austria, most of whom were married to non-Jews. Some Jews remained in hiding.

In July 1944, more than 10,000 Hungarian Jews were

LEGEND

⎯⎯ Roads

⊢⊢ Railroads

▬ Railroad Station

■ Select Features

✶ Select Synagogues Destroyed
During "Kristallnacht"

Assembly Points

1. Collection Center for Jews
2. Collection Point for Sick Jews
3. Collection Camp for Jews

Select Features

4. Administration for Confiscated Jewish
   Property
5. Central Office for Jewish Emigration
6. Gestapo Headquarters
7. Jewish Council
8. Jewish Community of Vienna Offices
9. Passport Office for Jewish Emigrants
10. Sipo and SD Headquarters

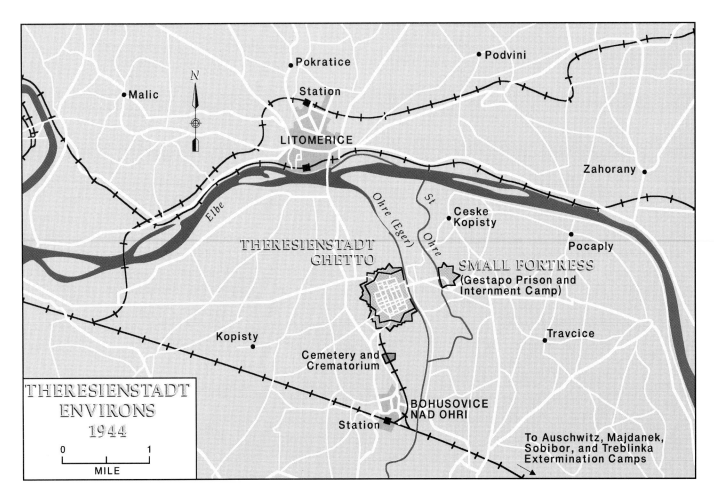

THERESIENSTADT ENVIRONS 1944

0 — 1 MILE

deported to Vienna. They arrived at the Strasshof railway station and were incarcerated in a nearby camp, where they were used for forced labor. Several of the forced-labor camps in Vienna were under the administration of the Mauthausen concentration camp.

Soviet forces liberated Vienna on April 13, 1945.

THERESIENSTADT

The fortress town of Terezin, located northwest of Prague, was established in the late eighteenth century by Joseph II, emperor of the Austrian empire. He named the town for his mother, the empress Maria Theresa. The town was built in the shape of a star and was surrounded with high walls. It consisted mainly of barracks, armories, and subterranean storerooms. After World War I, the Austrian empire was dissolved and several independent states formed, including Austria, Hungary, and Czechoslovakia. Terezin became part of Czechoslovakia. Following the 1939 partition of Czechoslovakia, the town was in the German Protectorate of Bohemia and Moravia.

In November 1941, the Germans established the Theresienstadt ghetto in the old fortress town. The "small

fortress" located to the northeast of the town served as an internment camp and Gestapo prison for political prisoners, members of the resistance, and some Jews from the ghetto. The ghetto was administered by the Germans and guarded by Czech police. Tens of thousands of Jews from the Protectorate of Bohemia and Moravia were deported there. The majority of the Jews came from Prague as well as from Brno, Moravska Ostrava, Olomouc, and other towns of the Protectorate. In addition, tens of thousands of Jews from Germany and Austria—mostly elderly Jews and Jewish veterans of World War I—as well as Jews from Denmark, the Netherlands, Hungary, Slovakia, and Poland, were deported there.

Theresienstadt served an important propaganda function for the Germans. The publicly stated purpose for the deportation of the Jews from Germany was their "resettlement to the east," where they would be employed in forced-labor projects. Since it would not seem plausible that elderly Jews were to be used for forced labor, the Nazis used the Theresienstadt ghetto to hide the nature of the deportations. In Nazi propaganda, Theresienstadt was a "retirement" ghetto where elderly German Jews could "retire" in safety. The deportations to Theresienstadt were, however, a cover

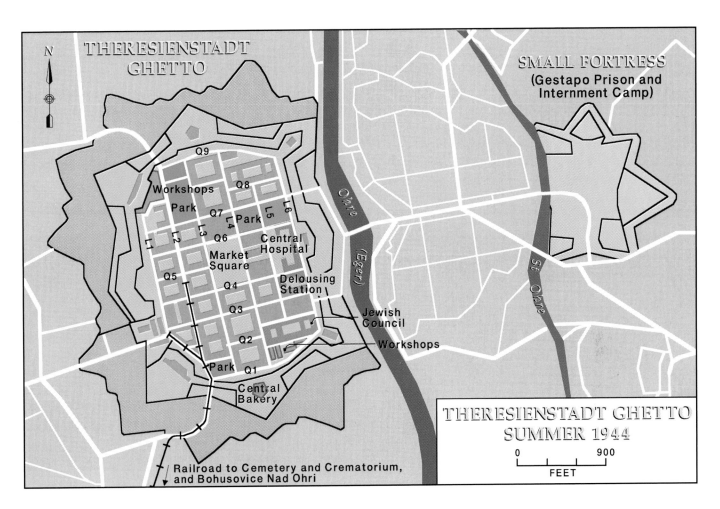

THERESIENSTADT GHETTO
SUMMER 1944

0   900
FEET

Railroad to Cemetery and Crematorium, and Bohusovice Nad Ohri

and the ghetto was in reality a collection center for deportations to locations further east.

Beginning in 1942, Jews from Theresienstadt were deported to the ghettos and killing centers in eastern Europe. Upon their arrival in the ghettos of Riga, Warsaw, Lodz, Minsk, and Bialystok, they were either massacred by German security police or deported along with other Jews to the extermination camps. Transports also left Theresienstadt directly for the Auschwitz, Treblinka, and Majdanek camps. In the ghetto itself, tens of thousands of people died, mostly from disease or starvation. In 1942, the death rate was so high that a crematorium capable of handling almost 200 bodies a day was built south of the ghetto.

As part of the attempt to use the Theresienstadt ghetto as a model ghetto for propaganda purposes, and to mask German killing operations in the occupied eastern territories, the Germans permitted a visit by the International Red Cross in June 1944. But it was all an elaborate hoax. The Germans intensified deportations from the ghetto shortly before the visit, and the ghetto itself was spruced up. Gardens were planted, houses painted, and new barracks built. Social and cultural events were staged for the visiting dignitaries. Once the visit was over, the deportations resumed.

Toward the end of the war, thousands of concentration camp prisoners were evacuated to Theresienstadt as the Germans attempted to keep large numbers of camp inmates out of Allied hands.

In early May 1945, the Nazis turned the administration of the ghetto over to the International Red Cross. On May 8, 1945, Soviet forces entered Theresienstadt.

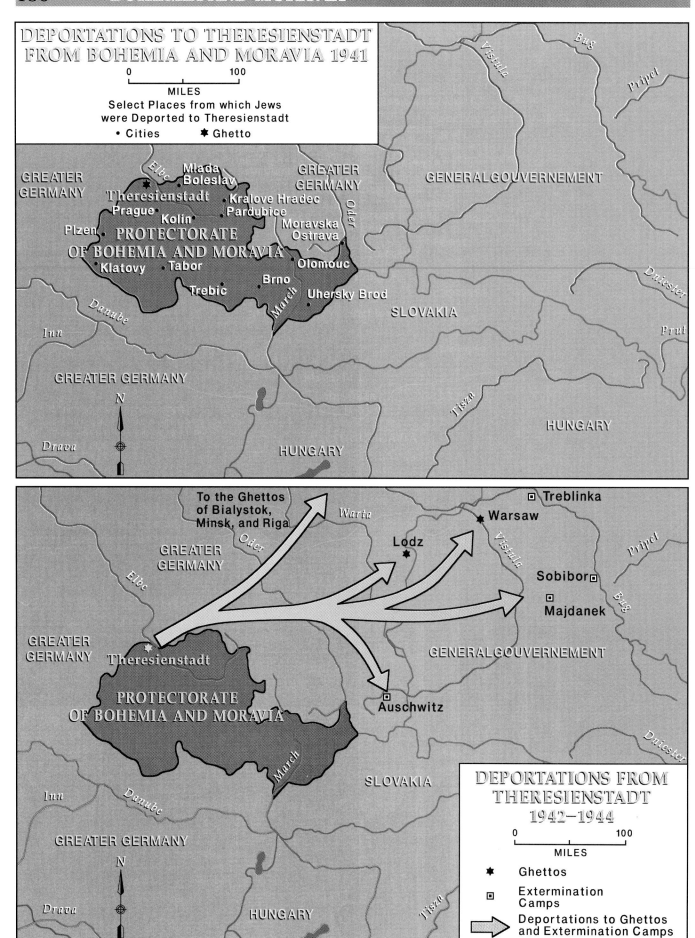

DEPORTATIONS TO THERESIENSTADT FROM BOHEMIA AND MORAVIA 1941

0 — 100
MILES

Select Places from which Jews
were Deported to Theresienstadt
• Cities ★ Ghetto

GREATER GERMANY

GREATER GERMANY

GENERALGOUVERNEMENT

Mlada Boleslav

Theresienstadt
Prague
Kolin
Kralove Hradec
Pardubice

Plzen

PROTECTORATE OF BOHEMIA AND MORAVIA

Moravska Ostrava

Klatovy
Tabor
Olomouc

Trebic
Brno
Uhersky Brod

SLOVAKIA

GREATER GERMANY

Danube

HUNGARY

HUNGARY

N

Drava

DEPORTATIONS FROM THERESIENSTADT 1942–1944

To the Ghettos of Bialystok, Minsk, and Riga

Treblinka

Warsaw

GREATER GERMANY

Lodz

Sobibor

Majdanek

GREATER GERMANY

Theresienstadt

GENERALGOUVERNEMENT

PROTECTORATE OF BOHEMIA AND MORAVIA

Auschwitz

SLOVAKIA

0 — 100
MILES

★ Ghettos

▣ Extermination Camps

⇨ Deportations to Ghettos and Extermination Camps

Inn

Danube

N

Drava

HUNGARY

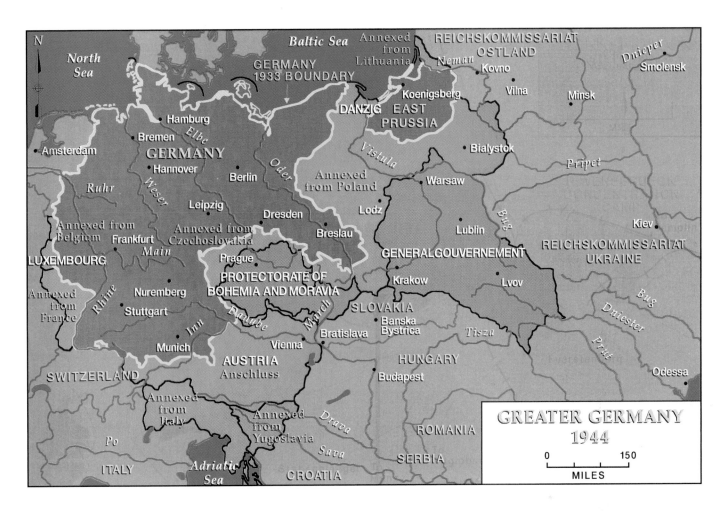

GREATER GERMANY 1944

Between 1938 and 1944, Germany annexed or incorporated vast tracts of territory from its neighbors. Before the war, Germany incorporated Austria, the Sudetenland (from Czechoslovakia), and the Memel territory (from Lithuania), and established a Protectorate over the Czech provinces of Bohemia and Moravia.

During the war, the expansion of German territory increased dramatically, keeping pace with German military victories. After the defeat of Poland in the fall of 1939, Germany annexed most of western Poland and the Danzig district. Central and southern Poland were organized into the Generalgouvernement (General Government) of Poland. After the invasion of the Soviet Union in 1941, the region around the city of Bialystok became a separate district under German civilian administration.

Germany defeated France in June 1940, occupying the Low Countries and most of northern France. Further, Germany seized the provinces of Alsace and Lorraine from France, and Eupen and Malmedy from Belgium, incorporating them under a German civilian administration. In 1942, Germany officially annexed Luxembourg, despite that country's vigorous resistance.

Following the German invasion and the partition of Yugoslavia in the spring of 1941, Germany annexed part of northern Slovenia. After the Italian armistice with the Allies in 1943 and the subsequent German occupation of Italian-held areas, Germany incorporated southern Slovenia and a strip of territory along the Dalmatian coast. German forces also moved into northern Italy, engaging Allied forces south of Rome. The Tyrol and Trieste areas of northern Italy were also incorporated into Germany.

In early 1944, Greater Germany was at its largest. However, Allied military victory would soon reverse these gains. With the unconditional surrender of Germany in early May 1945, the Allies nullified all German territorial annexations. The Allies reduced, occupied, and partitioned Germany in 1945.

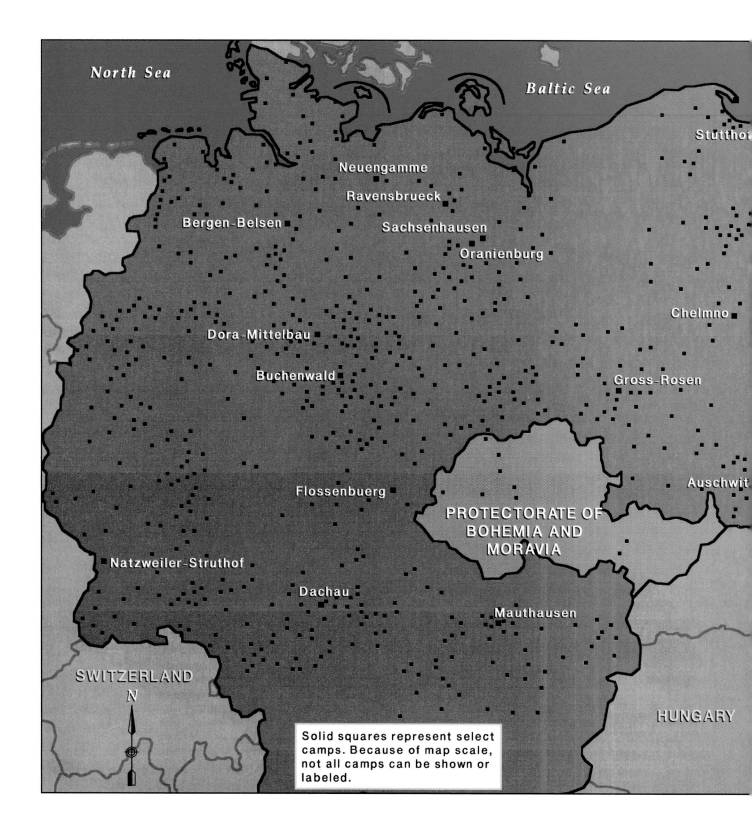

North Sea

Baltic Sea

Stuttho

Neuengamme

Ravensbrueck

Bergen-Belsen

Sachsenhausen

Oranienburg

Chelmno

Dora-Mittelbau

Buchenwald

Gross-Rosen

Auschwit

Flossenbuerg

PROTECTORATE OF
BOHEMIA AND
MORAVIA

Natzweiler-Struthof

Dachau

Mauthausen

SWITZERLAND
N

HUNGARY

Solid squares represent select
camps. Because of map scale,
not all camps can be shown or
labeled.

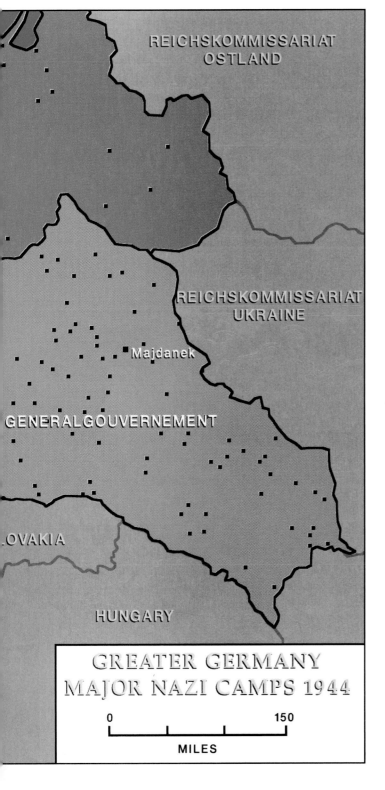

GREATER GERMANY
MAJOR NAZI CAMPS 1944

0   150

MILES

CONCENTRATION CAMP SYSTEM 1939-1945

The Third Reich was a police state characterized by arbitrary arrests, the incarceration of people in concentration camps, and, during the war, systematic genocide. The Germans imprisoned people in concentration camps without regard for the accepted norms of legal procedure. They killed others outright, according to criteria established by Nazi racial and ideological doctrine.

The Nazi camp system began as one of repression against political adversaries of the Nazi state. In the early years of the Third Reich, the Nazis imprisoned primarily Communists and Socialists in concentration camps. In about 1935, the regime also began to imprison those whom it designated as racially or biologically inferior, especially Jews. During the war, the organization and scale of the Nazi camp system expanded rapidly and the purpose of the camps evolved beyond incarceration toward forced labor and outright murder.

Throughout German-occupied Europe, the Germans arrested those who resisted their domination and those they judged to be racially inferior or politically unacceptable. People arrested for resisting German rule were mostly sent to forced-labor or concentration camps. The war brought unprecedented growth in both the number of camps and the number of prisoners incarcerated in such camps. New concentration camps were established, including Stutthof, Auschwitz, Gross-Rosen, Plaszow, Dora-Mittelbau, Neuengamme, and Natzweiler-Struthof. Within three years the number of prisoners quadrupled, from about 25,000 before the war to about 100,000 in March 1942. The camp population came to include prisoners from almost every European nation.

The Germans deported Jews from all over occupied Europe to extermination camps in Poland, where they were systematically killed, and also to concentration camps, where they were drafted for forced labor—"extermination through work." Several hundred thousand Roma (Gypsies) and Soviet prisoners of war were also systematically murdered. Chelmno, constructed in December 1941, was the first killing center established. The Belzec, Sobibor, Treblinka, Auschwitz-Birkenau, and Majdanek camps were later added to the system

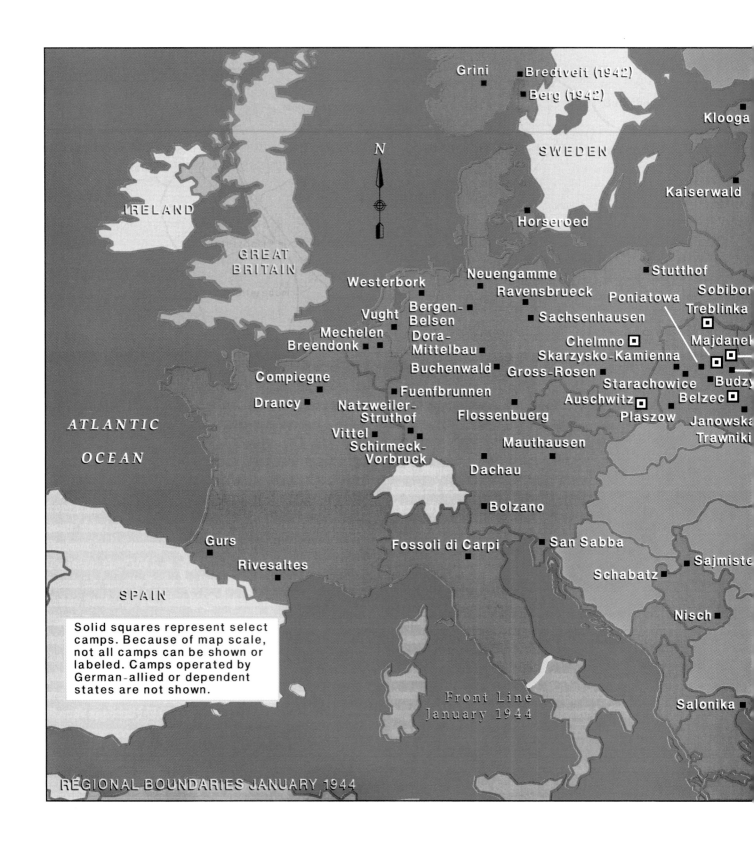

Grini   ■ Bredtveit (1942)

■ Berg (1942)

■ Klooga

SWEDEN

■ Kaiserwald

■ Stutthof

Neuengamme

Westerbork   Ravensbrueck   Poniatowa   Sobibor

Vught   Bergen-   ■ Sachsenhausen   Treblinka ▣
Belsen

Mechelen   Dora-   Chelmno ▣   Majdanek
Breendonk ■ ■   Mittelbau   Skarzysko-Kamienna   ▣ ▣

Buchenwald ■   Gross-Rosen ■   Budzy

Compiegne   Fuenfbrunnen   Starachowice   Belzec ▣

Drancy ■   Natzweiler-   ■   Auschwitz ▢   Janowska
     Struthof   Flossenbuerg   Plaszow   Trawniki

ATLANTIC   Vittel ■   Mauthausen
    Schirmeck-
OCEAN   Vorbruck   Dachau

■ Bolzano

Gurs   Fossoli di Carpi   ■ San Sabba

Rivesaltes   ■ Sajmiste

Schabatz ■

SPAIN

■ Nisch

Solid squares represent select
camps. Because of map scale,
not all camps can be shown or
labeled. Camps operated by
German-allied or dependent
states are not shown.

Front Line
January 1944   ■ Salonika

IRELAND

GREAT
BRITAIN

Horseroed

REGIONAL BOUNDARIES JANUARY 1944

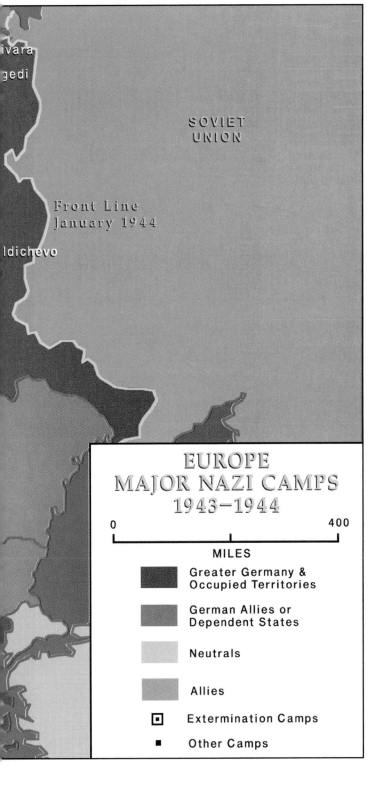

ivara
gedi

SOVIET
UNION

Front Line
January 1944

ldichevo

EUROPE
MAJOR NAZI CAMPS
1943-1944

0   400

MILES

Greater Germany &
Occupied Territories

German Allies or
Dependent States

Neutrals

Allies

Extermination Camps

Other Camps

of mass murder. Transit camps such as Westerbork, Gurs, Mechelen, and Drancy in western Europe and concentration camps like Bolzano and Fossoli di Carpi in Italy were used as collection centers for Jews, who were then deported by rail to the extermination camps.

Labor shortages in the German war economy became critical after German defeat in the battle of Stalingrad in 1942-1943. This led to the increased use of concentration camp prisoners as forced laborers in German armaments industries. Especially in 1943 and 1944, hundreds of subcamps were established in or near industrial plants. Subcamps were administered by the major camps, which supplied them with the required number of prisoners. Camps such as Auschwitz in Poland, Buchenwald in central Germany, Gross-Rosen in eastern Germany, Natzweiler-Struthof in eastern France, Ravensbrueck near Berlin, and Stutthof near Danzig on the Baltic coast became administrative centers of huge networks of subsidiary forced-labor camps. In addition to SS-owned enterprises (the German Armament Works, for example), private German firms—such as Messerschmidt, Junkers, Siemens, and I.G. Farben—increasingly relied on forced laborers to boost war production. Many of their factories became subcamps of the major concentration camps. One of the most infamous of these was Auschwitz III, or Monowitz, which supplied forced laborers to a synthetic rubber plant owned by I.G. Farben. Prisoners in all the concentration camps were literally worked to death.

According to SS reports, there were more than 700,000 prisoners registered in the concentration camps in January 1945.

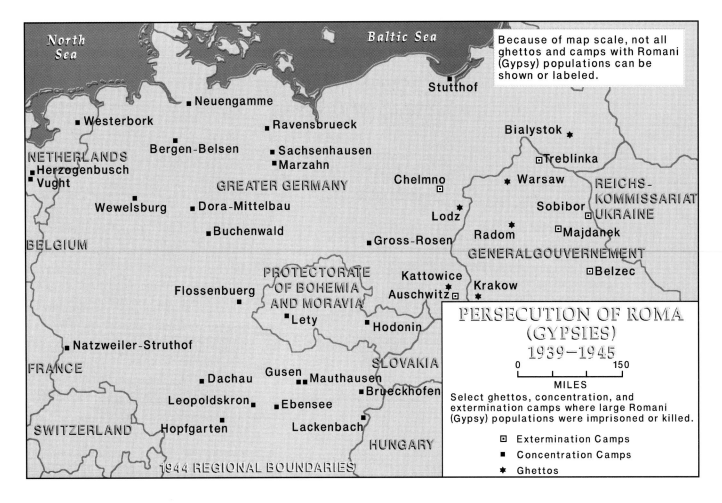

Because of map scale, not all ghettos and camps with Romani (Gypsy) populations can be shown or labeled.

PERSECUTION OF ROMA (GYPSIES) 1939–1945

0   150
MILES

Select ghettos, concentration, and extermination camps where large Romani (Gypsy) populations were imprisoned or killed.

☐ Extermination Camps
■ Concentration Camps
★ Ghettos

ROMA (GYPSIES)

Roma (Gypsies) were among the groups singled out on racial grounds for persecution by the Nazi regime and most of its allies. Judged to be "racially inferior," Roma were subjected to internment, deportation, and forced labor, and were sent to extermination camps. The fate of the Roma closely paralleled that of the Jews. The Nazis incarcerated thousands of Roma in the Bergen-Belsen, Sachsenhausen, Buchenwald, Dachau, Mauthausen, and Ravensbrueck concentration camps in Germany. Many Roma were interned and killed by the Ustasa (Croatian fascists) at the Jasenovac concentration camp in Croatia.

Between 1940 and 1945, when the camp was liberated, at least 23,000 Roma were registered as inmates of Auschwitz-Birkenau. A special compound was built there to house Romani (Gypsy) prisoners, who continued to live together as families. In the summer of 1944, the Germans closed the "Gypsy family camp" in Auschwitz-Birkenau. About 3,000 Roma were selected for forced labor. The remaining Romani prisoners—about 3,000—were sent to the gas chambers.

Some 5,000 Roma were deported from the Lodz ghetto to the Chelmno extermination camp, where they were killed in gas vans. Thousands of others were gassed in the extermination camps of Belzec, Sobibor, and Treblinka. Einsatzgruppen also killed tens of thousands of Roma in the German-occupied eastern territories.

Nazi physicians used Romani prisoners in medical experiments at Auschwitz, Ravensbrueck, Natzweiler-Struthof, and Sachsenhausen. It is not known precisely how many Roma were killed in the Holocaust. It is estimated that of the approximately one million Roma living in Europe before the war, between 250,000 and 500,000 were killed.

Solid squares represent camps in which medical experiments took place. At least 7,000 people were victims of Nazi medical experiments.

North Sea

N

Baltic Sea

REICHS-KOMMISSARIAT OSTLAND

■Neuengamme

■Ravensbrueck

■Sachsenhausen

GREATER GERMANY

REICHS-KOMMISSARIAT UKRAINE

Buchenwald ■

GENERALGOUVERNEMENT

PROTECTORATE OF BOHEMIA AND MORAVIA

Auschwitz
■

Natzweiler-
■Struthof

■Dachau

Mauthausen
■

SLOVAKIA

HUNGARY

NAZI MEDICAL EXPERIMENTS
1942–1945

SWITZERLAND

1944 REGIONAL BOUNDARIES

0   150
MILES

NAZI MEDICAL EXPERIMENTS

During World War II, some German physicians conducted pseudoscientific medical experiments in many different categories, utilizing thousands of concentration camp prisoners without their consent.

At Buchenwald, medical experiments involving typhus and other contagious diseases were carried out on prisoners. Hundreds died as a result. Also in Buchenwald, homosexual prisoners were used in artificial hormone and castration experiments. In Auschwitz I, SS physicians conducted pseudoscientific research on infants, twins, and dwarfs, forced sterilizations, castrations, and hypothermia experiments. In Mauthausen, prisoners were used in experiments involving testosterone, lice infestation, tuberculosis, and surgical procedures. More than 80 prisoners, mostly Jews, were gassed in Natzweiler-Struthof and their bodies sent to the Strasbourg University Institute of Anatomy for study. Poison gas and typhus experiments were also conducted at Natzweiler-Struthof.

In Ravensbrueck, medical experiments involved sterilization, the treatment of wounds with various substances (such as sulfanilamide) to prevent infections, and methods for treating broken bones in the arms and legs. In Dachau, SS doctors conducted experiments involving high altitudes (by using a decompression chamber), malaria, tuberculosis, and hypothermia. They also tested pharmaceutical products. Further, Dachau prisoners were used to test various methods of making seawater potable and methods of halting excess bleeding.

SS doctors carried out sterilization experiments on men, women, and children to discover a quick method by which to sterilize large numbers of people as part of Germany's population policy, and to facilitate the sterilization of part-Jews as proposed at the Wannsee Conference. Thousands of people, mainly women, were used in the experiments. Most were Jewish; the remainder were Roma (Gypsies). Thousands of prisoners died or were permanently crippled as a result of medical experiments.

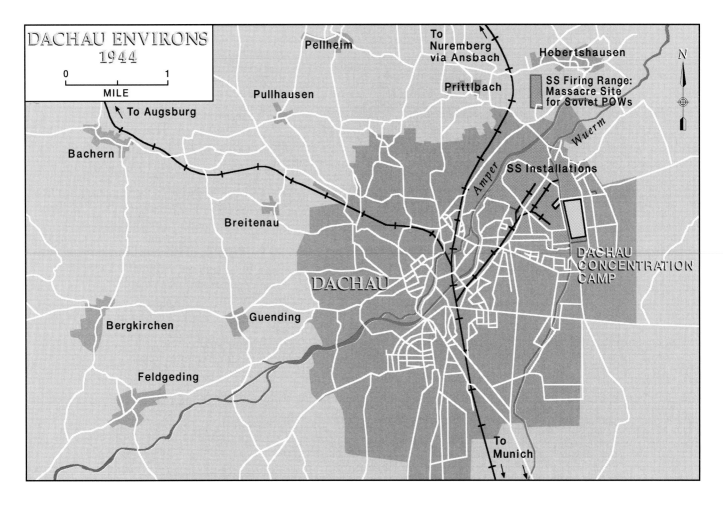

DACHAU CONCENTRATION CAMP

Established in March 1933, the Dachau concentration camp was the first regular concentration camp established by the Nazis. At first, the camp was located in an ammunition factory in the northeastern part of the town of Dachau, about 10 miles northwest of Munich in southern Germany. Later that year, an expanded camp was constructed at Dachau using prisoner labor, replacing the makeshift camp. This new camp became one of the main training centers for SS concentration camp guards, and the camp's organization and routine became the model for all Nazi concentration camps. Dachau remained in operation until April 1945, thus existing for the entire period of the Third Reich.

The Dachau camp was divided by the Wuerm River into two sections—the camp area and the crematoria area. The camp area consisted of 32 barracks, including one for clergy imprisoned for opposing the Nazi regime and one reserved for medical experiments. The camp administration was located in the gatehouse at the main entrance. The camp area had so-called farm buildings, containing the kitchen, herbiary, workshops, and a camp prison (Bunker). The courtyard between the prison and the central kitchen was an execution

site where prisoners were summarily shot. An electrified barbed-wire fence, a ditch, and a wall with seven guard towers surrounded the camp.

In 1942, the crematorium area was constructed next to the main camp. It included the old crematoria and the new crematorium (Barrack X) with a gas chamber. There is little evidence that the gas chamber in Barrack X was used. Instead, prisoners underwent selection; those who were judged too sick or weak to continue working were sent to the Hartheim "euthanasia" center near Linz, Austria. Several thousand Dachau prisoners were killed at Hartheim. Further, the SS used the firing range and the gallows tree in the crematoria area as execution sites for prisoners.

In Dachau, as in other Nazi camps, medical experiments were performed on prisoners. High-altitude experiments using a decompression chamber, malaria and tuberculosis experiments, hypothermia experiments, and experiments testing new medications were conducted. Prisoners were used to test methods of making seawater potable and of halting excessive bleeding. Hundreds of prisoners died or were permanently crippled as a result of these experiments.

Dachau prisoners were used as forced laborers. At first,

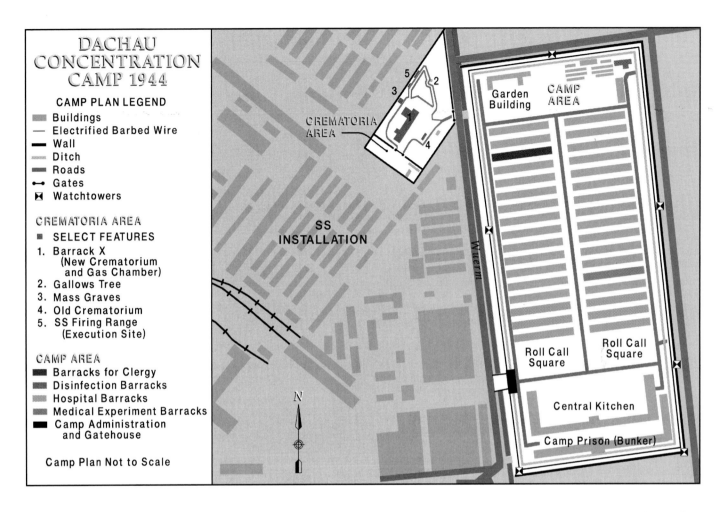

DACHAU CONCENTRATION CAMP 1944

CAMP PLAN LEGEND

- Buildings
- — Electrified Barbed Wire
- Wall
- Ditch
- Roads
- Gates
- Watchtowers

CREMATORIA AREA

- SELECT FEATURES
1. Barrack X
   (New Crematorium
   and Gas Chamber)
2. Gallows Tree
3. Mass Graves
4. Old Crematorium
5. SS Firing Range
   (Execution Site)

CAMP AREA

- Barracks for Clergy
- Disinfection Barracks
- Hospital Barracks
- Medical Experiment Barracks
- Camp Administration
  and Gatehouse

Camp Plan Not to Scale

CREMATORIA AREA

SS INSTALLATION

Waern

Garden Building   CAMP AREA

Roll Call Square   Roll Call Square

Central Kitchen

Camp Prison (Bunker)

N

---

they were employed in the operation of the camp, in various construction projects, and in small handicraft industries established in the camp. Prisoners built roads, worked in gravel pits, and drained marshes. During the war, forced labor utilizing concentration camp prisoners became increasingly important to German armaments production. In the summer and fall of 1944, to increase war production, satellite camps under the administration of Dachau were established near armaments factories throughout southern Germany. Dachau alone had more than 30 large subcamps in which over 30,000 prisoners worked almost exclusively on armaments. Thousands of prisoners were worked to death.

As Allied forces advanced toward Germany, the Germans began to evacuate concentration camps near the front to prevent the liberation of large numbers of prisoners. Transports from the evacuated camps arrived continuously at Dachau, resulting in a dramatic deterioration of conditions. After days of travel, with little or no food or water, the prisoners arrived weak and exhausted, near death. Typhus epidemics became a serious problem due to overcrowding, poor sanitary conditions, and the weakened state of the prisoners.

In April 1945, as American forces approached the Dachau camp, the Germans forced more than 7,000 prisoners, mostly Jews, on a death march from Dachau to Tegernsee far to the south. During the death march, the Germans shot anyone who could no longer continue; many also died of hunger, cold, or exhaustion. On April 29, 1945, American forces liberated Dachau. As they neared the camp, they found more than 30 coal cars filled with bodies brought to Dachau, all in an advanced state of decomposition. In early May 1945, American forces liberated the prisoners who had been sent on the death march. Approximately 30,000 prisoners were liberated when the American army entered Dachau. It is unlikely that the total number of victims who died in Dachau will ever be known.

DACHAU SUBCAMPS
1938–1945

0   50
MILES
Scale Approximate

N

GREATER GERMANY

Nuremberg

Neumarkt

PROTECTORATE OF
BOHEMIA AND
MORAVIA

Heidenheim
Baeumenheim
Ampermoching
Markt Schwaben
Thalheim

Stuttgart
Lauingen
Gablingen
Landshut
Neustift

Ulm
Burgau
Freising
Passau

Augsburg
Zangberg

Augsburg-Pfersee
Dachau

Schwabing
Muehldorf

Kaufering
Karlsfeld
Gendorf

Landsberg
Allach
Munich
Ampfing

Radofzell
Ueberlingen
Weilheim
Stephanskirchen

Schlachters
Kaufbeuren
Bad Toelz
Trostberg

Kempten
Feldafing
Rosenheim

Friedrichshafen
Gmund
Traunstein

Blaichach
Kottern
Tutzing
Thansau
Salzburg

Lochau
Bad
Oberdorf

Fischen
Fischbachau
Hallein
St. Gilgen

Oberstdorf-Birgsau
Plansee
Bayrischzell
Obersalzberg
St. Wolfgang

Garmisch-
Partenkirchen
Innsbruck
Bad Ischl

Weiss-See

SWITZERLAND
Fischhorn

Solid squares represent
select camps. Because of
map scale, not all camps
can be shown or labeled.

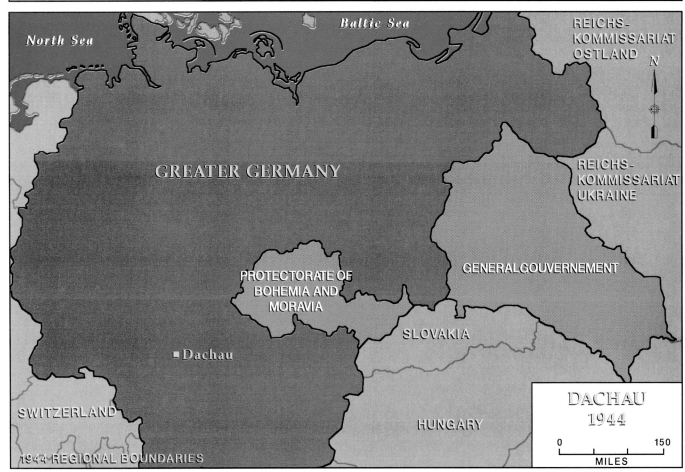

North Sea
Baltic Sea
REICHS-
KOMMISSARIAT
OSTLAND

N

GREATER GERMANY

REICHS-
KOMMISSARIAT
UKRAINE

PROTECTORATE OF
BOHEMIA AND
MORAVIA
GENERALGOUVERNEMENT

SLOVAKIA

Dachau

SWITZERLAND
HUNGARY

DACHAU
1944

0   150
MILES

1944 REGIONAL BOUNDARIES

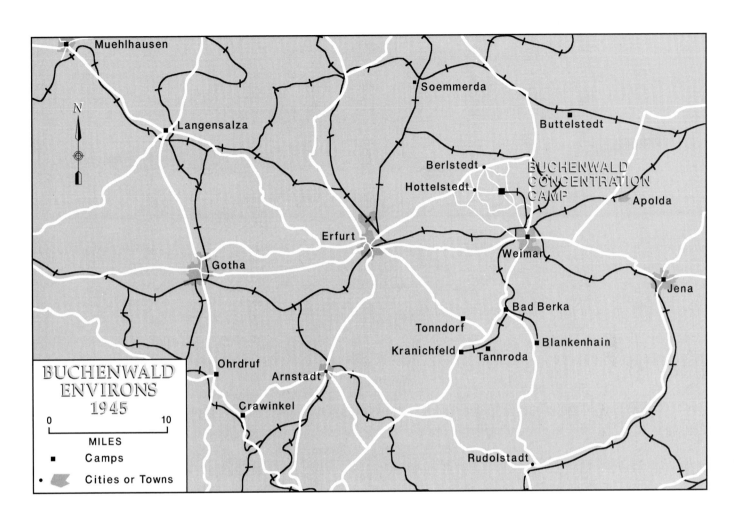

Muehlhausen

N

Langensalza

Soemmerda

Buttelstedt

Berlstedt

Hottelstedt

BUCHENWALD
CONCENTRATION
CAMP

Apolda

Erfurt

Weimar

Gotha

Jena

Bad Berka

Tonndorf

Kranichfeld   Tannroda   Blankenhain

Ohrdruf

Arnstadt

Crawinkel

Rudolstadt

BUCHENWALD
ENVIRONS
1945

0   10

MILES

■   Camps

•   Cities or Towns

BUCHENWALD CONCENTRATION CAMP

Buchenwald was one of the largest concentration camps established by the Nazis. The camp was constructed in 1937 in a wooded area on the northern slopes of the Ettersberg, about five miles northwest of Weimar in east-central Germany. Ironically, Weimar was known before the Nazi takeover of power as the home of Johann Wolfgang von Goethe, who embodied the German enlightenment of the eighteenth century, and as the birthplace of German constitutional democracy in 1919. During the Nazi regime, "Weimar" became associated with the Buchenwald concentration camp.

Buchenwald prisoners were confined in the northern part of the camp in an area called the main camp, while SS guard barracks and the camp administration compound were located in the southern part. The main camp was surrounded by an electrified barbed-wire fence, watchtowers, and a chain of posts outfitted with automatically activated machine guns. The jail, also known as the Bunker, was located at the entrance to the main camp. Shootings took place in the crematorium and in the stables.

Most of the early inmates at Buchenwald were political prisoners. However, in 1938, in the aftermath of

"Kristallnacht," almost 10,000 Jews were sent to Buchenwald, where they were subjected to extraordinarily cruel treatment.

During World War II, the Buchenwald camp system became an important source of forced labor; the prisoner population expanded rapidly, reaching more than 80,000 by 1945. Buchenwald prisoners were used in the German Armament Works (DAW), an enterprise owned and operated by the SS; in camp workshops; and in the camp's stone quarry. In March 1943 the Gustloff armament works, a large factory producing aircraft parts, was constructed in the western part of the camp. A rail siding completed in 1943 connected the camp with the freight yards in Weimar, facilitating the shipment of war supplies.

Buchenwald administered more than 100 subcamps located across central Germany, from Duesseldorf in the Rhineland to the border with the Protectorate of Bohemia and Moravia in the east. Prisoners in the satellite camps were put to work mostly in armaments factories, in stone quarries, and on construction projects. Periodically, prisoners throughout the Buchenwald camp system underwent selection. Those too weak or crippled to continue working were either sent to the Bernburg or Sonnenstein "euthanasia" centers and killed, or

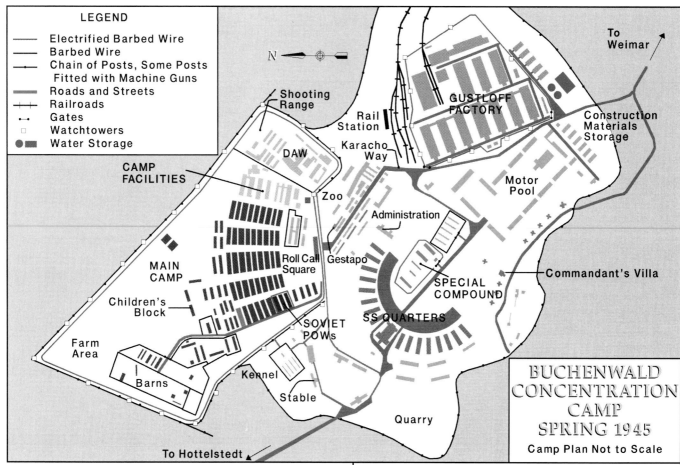

LEGEND

⎯ Electrified Barbed Wire
━ Barbed Wire
┼ Chain of Posts, Some Posts Fitted with Machine Guns
▬ Roads and Streets
┼┼┼ Railroads
⊷ Gates
□ Watchtowers
● ▬ Water Storage

BUCHENWALD CONCENTRATION CAMP SPRING 1945
Camp Plan Not to Scale

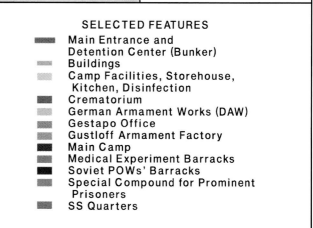

SELECTED FEATURES

▬ Main Entrance and Detention Center (Bunker)
Buildings
Camp Facilities, Storehouse, Kitchen, Disinfection
Crematorium
German Armament Works (DAW)
Gestapo Office
Gustloff Armament Factory
Main Camp
Medical Experiment Barracks
Soviet POWs' Barracks
Special Compound for Prominent Prisoners
SS Quarters

were killed by phenol injections administered by the camp doctor.

Beginning in 1941, a broad program of involuntary medical experiments on prisoners was conducted at Buchenwald, in special barracks in the northern part of the main camp. Medical experiments involving viruses and contagious diseases such as typhus resulted in hundreds of deaths.

In 1944, a "special compound" for prominent German political prisoners was established near the camp administration building in Buchenwald. Ernst Thaelmann, chairman of the Communist Party of Germany before Hitler's rise to power in 1933, was brought there and executed in August 1944.

In January 1945, as Soviet forces swept through Poland, the Germans evacuated thousands of concentration camp prisoners from western Poland to Buchenwald. After long, brutal death marches, prisoners arrived at Buchenwald in a state of exhaustion. Among these prisoners were several hundred children and young people from Auschwitz. They were housed in a special block for children in the north of the camp.

In early April 1945, as American forces approached the camp, the Germans began to evacuate almost 30,000 prisoners, mostly Jews, from Buchenwald. During the evacuation, about 8,000 prisoners died. Many lives were saved by the Buchenwald resistance, whose members held key administrative posts in the camp. They obstructed Nazi orders, delaying the evacuation. On April 11, 1945, starved and emaciated prisoners stormed the watchtowers, seizing control of the camp. Later that afternoon, American forces entered Buchenwald. They found more than 20,000 people in the camp.

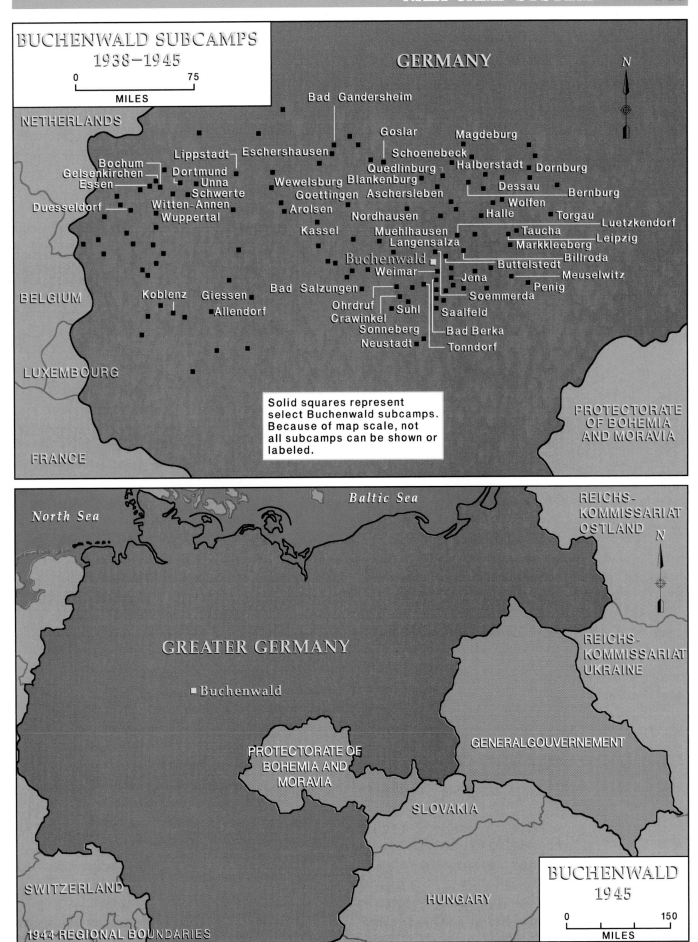

BUCHENWALD SUBCAMPS
1938–1945

0   75
MILES

GERMANY

N

NETHERLANDS

Bad Gandersheim

Goslar   Magdeburg
Schoenebeck
Lippstadt   Eschershausen   Quedlinburg   Halberstadt   Dornburg
Bochum   Blankenburg   Dessau
Gelsenkirchen   Dortmund   Bernburg
Essen   Unna   Wewelsburg   Wolfen
        Schwerte   Goettingen   Aschersleben   Halle
Duesseldorf   Witten-Annen   Arolsen   Torgau
        Wuppertal   Nordhausen   Luetzkendorf
                Kassel   Muehlhausen   Taucha   Leipzig
                        Langensalza   Markkleeberg
                    Buchenwald   Billroda
                    Weimar   Buttelstedt   Meuselwitz
Koblenz   Giessen   Jena   Penig
                    Bad Salzungen   Soemmerda
        Allendorf   Ohrdruf   Suhl   Saalfeld
BELGIUM   Crawinkel
                    Sonneberg   Bad Berka
LUXEMBOURG   Neustadt   Tonndorf

FRANCE

Solid squares represent
select Buchenwald subcamps.
Because of map scale, not
all subcamps can be shown or
labeled.

PROTECTORATE
OF BOHEMIA
AND MORAVIA

North Sea   Baltic Sea   REICHS-
                    KOMMISSARIAT
                    OSTLAND

                    N

GREATER GERMANY

                    REICHS-
                    KOMMISSARIAT
                    UKRAINE

■ Buchenwald

                GENERALGOUVERNEMENT

        PROTECTORATE OF
        BOHEMIA AND
        MORAVIA

            SLOVAKIA

SWITZERLAND   BUCHENWALD
                    1945

        HUNGARY   0   150
                    MILES
1944 REGIONAL BOUNDARIES

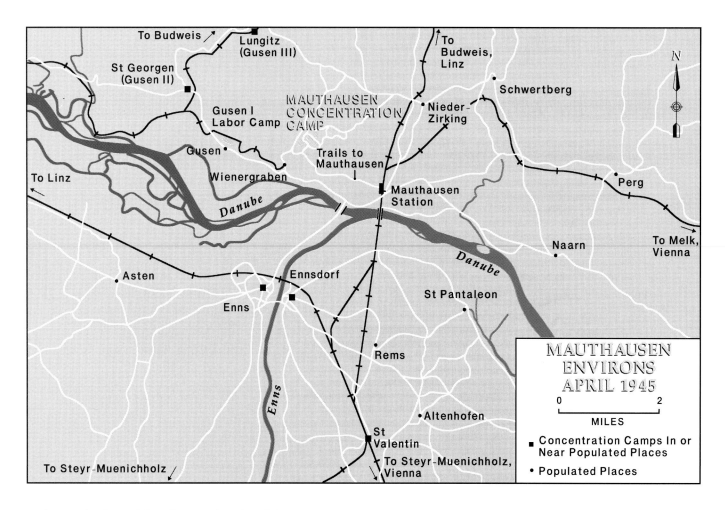

MAUTHAUSEN CONCENTRATION CAMP

The Mauthausen concentration camp, the main camp for Austria, was established shortly after Germany incorporated Austria in March 1938. It was built near an abandoned stone quarry, along the Danube River, about three miles from the town of Mauthausen in Upper Austria, 12.5 miles southeast of Linz.

The Germans designated the Mauthausen concentration camp a category III camp, indicating that it was a special penal camp with a harsh regimen. Inmates in the punishment detail were forced to carry heavy stone blocks up 186 steps from the camp quarry. The steps became known as the "Stairway of Death."

The main camp at Mauthausen had three main sections: Camp I, the residential prison camp; Camp II, the camp workshop area, where the prisoners were forced to work in SS enterprises; and Camp III, a quarantine camp built in the spring of 1944 to separate incoming prisoners from the main camp population.

Along the outer wall, opposite the roll call square (Appellplatz), were several stone buildings for camp services (kitchen, showers, and laundry). The camp prison (Bunker)

and gas chamber were also in these buildings. The crematorium was near the prison. In an area near the crematorium, prisoners selected for immediate execution were shot in the neck.

South of the main camp, off the entrance road to the camp, was the hospital camp, which was called the "Russian camp" since it was originally constructed for Russian prisoners of war. From the spring of 1943, ill or weak prisoners were kept in the hospital camp until they died.

As late as April 1945, a tent camp was set up outside the northern perimeter of the main camp to handle the influx of large numbers of prisoners, primarily Hungarian Jews, evacuated from camps along the Hungarian border with Austria.

The various camps were surrounded by a wall and/or an electrified wire. Watchtowers and SS guards surrounded the entire complex. The SS administration and barracks were located in the western area of the camp.

Mauthausen prisoners were used extensively as forced laborers. At first, prisoners were employed in the construction of the camp and in the neighboring quarry. During the war, forced labor utilizing concentration camp prisoners became

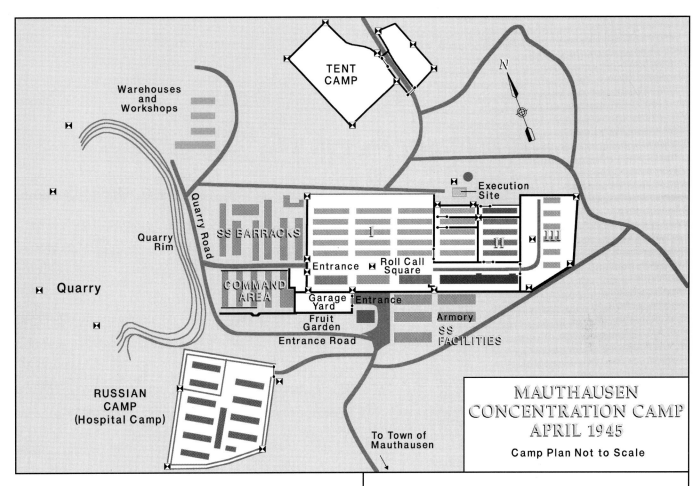

Warehouses
and
Workshops

TENT
CAMP

N

Quarry Road

Quarry
Rim

SS BARRACKS

Execution
Site

I

II

III

Quarry

COMMAND
AREA

Entrance

Roll Call
Square

Garage Yard

Entrance

Fruit
Garden

Armory

SS
FACILITIES

Entrance Road

RUSSIAN
CAMP
(Hospital Camp)

To Town of
Mauthausen

**MAUTHAUSEN
CONCENTRATION CAMP
APRIL 1945**
Camp Plan Not to Scale

CAMP PLAN LEGEND

— Electrified Barbed Wire
— Barbed Wire
— Wall
— Roads and Streets
↔ Gates
▢ Buildings
⊠ Watchtowers
▨ Bunker: Execution Site, Crematorium, and Gas Chamber
▨ Camp I
▨ Camp II
▨ Camp III
▨ Death Barracks
▨ Hospital
▨ Kitchen
▨ Laundry
▨ Russian Camp
▨ SS Buildings
▨ Water Storage

increasingly important to German armaments production. In the summer and fall of 1944, subcamps under the administration of Mauthausen were established near armaments factories throughout northern Austria. Mauthausen administered more than 60 subcamps, including Gusen, Gunskirchen, Melk, Ebensee, and Amstetten. Thousands of prisoners were worked to death.

Periodically, prisoners in the Mauthausen camp system underwent selection. Those the Nazis deemed too weak or sick to work were separated from the other prisoners and killed either in Mauthausen's own gas chamber, in mobile gas vans, or at the nearby Hartheim "euthanasia" killing center. Camp doctors in the infirmary used phenol injections to kill patients too weak to move. Nazi doctors also used Mauthausen prisoners in pseudoscientific medical experiments involving testosterone, lice infestation, tuberculosis, and surgical procedures.

As Allied forces advanced toward the interior of Germany, the Nazis began to evacuate concentration camps near the front lines in order to prevent the liberation of large numbers of prisoners. Transports from the evacuated camps, especially from Auschwitz, Sachsenhausen, and Gross-Rosen, began

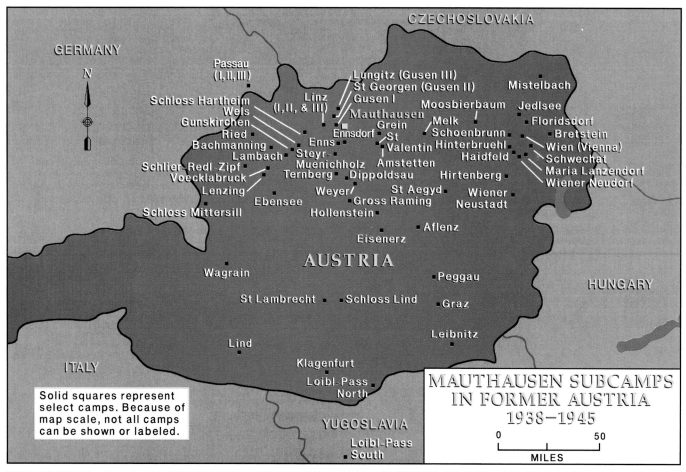

GERMANY

N

CZECHOSLOVAKIA

Passau
(I, II, III)

Lungitz (Gusen III)
St Georgen (Gusen II)   Mistelbach
Gusen I

Schloss Hartheim   Linz   Moosbierbaum   Jedlsee
Wels   (I, II, & III)   Mauthausen   Melk   Floridsdorf
Gunskirchen   Grein   Schoenbrunn   Bretstein
Ried   Ennsdorf   St   Hinterbruehl   Wien (Vienna)
Bachmanning   Enns   Valentin   Haidfeld   Schwechat
Lambach   Steyr   Amstetten   Maria Lanzendorf
Schlier-Redl-Zipf   Muenichholz   Hirtenberg   Wiener Neudorf
Voecklabruck   Ternberg   Dippoldsau
Lenzing   Weyer   St Aegyd   Wiener
Ebensee   Gross Raming   Neustadt
Schloss Mittersill   Hollenstein

Aflenz

Eisenerz

AUSTRIA

Wagrain

Peggau   HUNGARY

St Lambrecht   Schloss Lind

Graz

Leibnitz

Lind

ITALY

Klagenfurt

Loibl-Pass
North

Solid squares represent
select camps. Because of
map scale, not all camps
can be shown or labeled.

YUGOSLAVIA

Loibl-Pass
South

MAUTHAUSEN SUBCAMPS
IN FORMER AUSTRIA
1938–1945

0   50

MILES

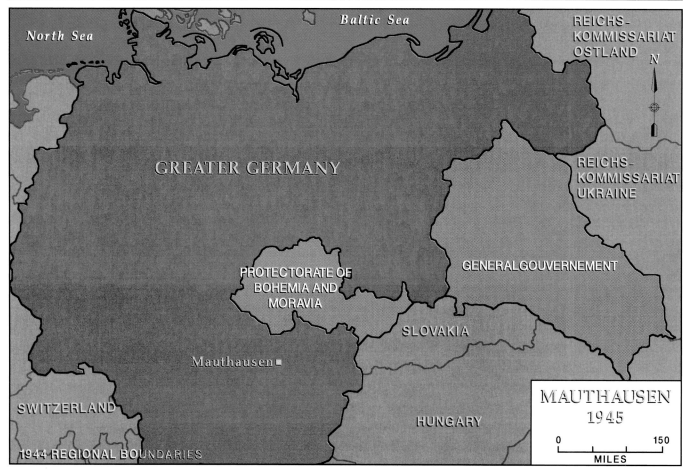

North Sea   *Baltic Sea*   REICHS-
KOMMISSARIAT
OSTLAND

N

GREATER GERMANY

REICHS-
KOMMISSARIAT
UKRAINE

PROTECTORATE OF
BOHEMIA AND
MORAVIA

GENERALGOUVERNEMENT

SLOVAKIA

Mauthausen

MAUTHAUSEN
1945

SWITZERLAND

HUNGARY

0   150

MILES

1944 REGIONAL BOUNDARIES

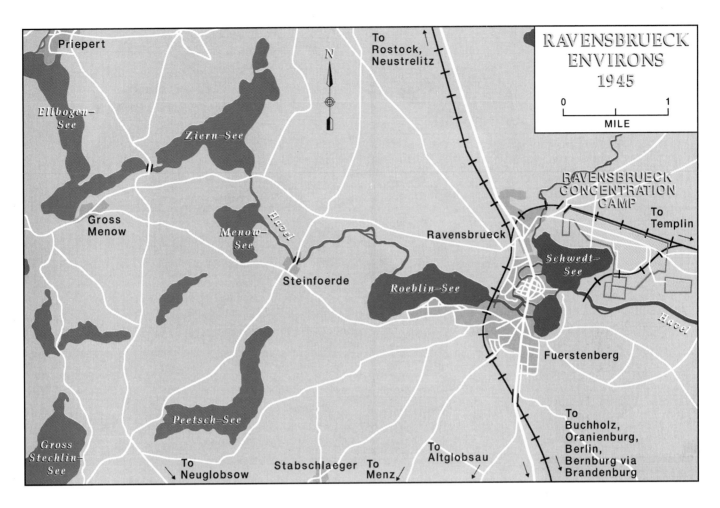

arriving at Mauthausen in 1945. The camp became increasingly overcrowded, resulting in the serious deterioration of already difficult conditions. Many prisoners died from starvation or disease. Typhus epidemics further reduced the camp's population.

Toward the end of the war, the number of prisoners in the Mauthausen camp system grew to more than 80,000. Camp records indicated at least 70,000 deaths among registered prisoners between 1938 and 1945.

American forces liberated Mauthausen in early May 1945.

RAVENSBRUECK CONCENTRATION CAMP

The Ravensbrueck concentration camp was the largest concentration camp for women established by the Nazis. Construction of the camp began in November 1938, near the small village of Ravensbrueck in northern Germany. The village was just north of Fuerstenberg, about 56 miles north of Berlin. It was situated on the banks of the Schwedt-See. A small men's camp was joined to the women's camp in 1941. Located east of the women's camp, the men's camp was situated along the railway to Templin.

The first prisoners at Ravensbrueck were about 1,000 women, transferred from the Lichtenburg camp in Saxony in May 1939. By the end of 1942, the female inmate population of Ravensbrueck had grown to about 10,000. In January 1945 the camp had more than 45,000 prisoners, mostly women. In addition to the male Nazi administrators, the camp staff included more than 150 female SS guards assigned to oversee the prisoners. Ravensbrueck served as one of the main training camps for female SS guards. SS personnel lived in special housing to the west of the camp.

Prisoners were required to perform forced labor. Women in the camp worked in agricultural projects, farming, and local industry. In 1944, forced labor became increasingly important to Germany's armaments production efforts. Ravensbrueck became the administrative center of a system of more than 40 subcamps with more than 70,000 prisoners, predominantly women. These subcamps, most of which were established adjacent to armaments factories, were located throughout Greater Germany, from Austria in the south to the Baltic Sea in the north. Several camps provided labor for construction projects or for clearing rubble in cities damaged by Allied air attacks. The SS also built an armaments factory near Ravensbrueck. Further,

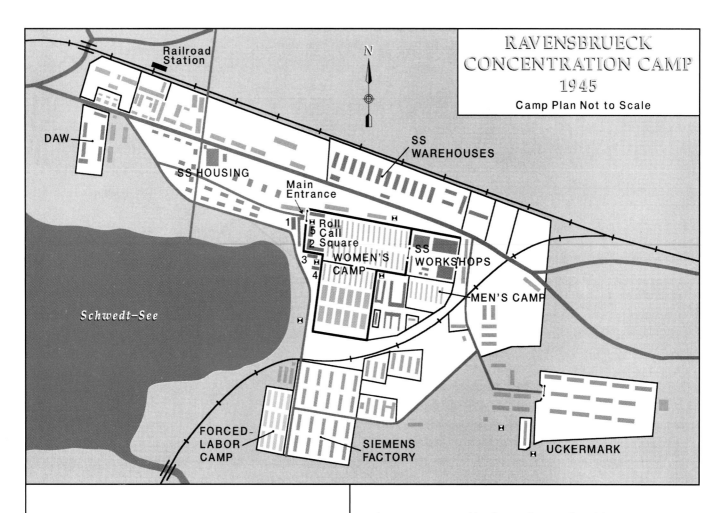

CAMP PLAN LEGEND
— Barbed Wire
+++ Railroads
— Roads
— Wall
↔ Gates
⋈ Watchtowers
▩ Buildings
▩ German Armament Works (DAW)
▩ Forced-Labor Camp
▩ Men's Camp
▩ Siemens Factory
▩ Uckermark (Former Youth Camp)
▩ Women's Camp
SS FACILITIES
▩ SS Housing
▩ SS Warehouses
▩ SS Workshops
▩ Command Area
  1. Commandant
  2. Prison Cells
  3. Crematorium
  4. Gas Chamber
  5. Administration

there were textile factories and a Siemens plant at Ravensbrueck.

Periodically, prisoners in the camp underwent selection. The Germans removed those prisoners considered too weak or injured to work. At first, selected prisoners were shot. Beginning in 1942, they were transferred to "euthanasia" killing centers (particularly to the center in nearby Bernburg) or to Auschwitz. Some prisoners were also killed in the camp infirmary with lethal injections. The bodies of those killed in the camp were cremated in the Fuerstenberg crematorium until 1943, when a crematorium was built at a site near the camp prison, just west of the women's camp. In 1944/1945, a gas chamber was constructed near the crematorium. Several thousand prisoners were gassed before the camp's liberation in April 1945.

Beginning in the summer of 1942, Ravensbrueck concentration camp prisoners were used in pseudoscientific medical experiments. Experiments included the treatment of wounds with various substances (such as sulfanilamide) to prevent infections. Various methods of setting and transplanting bones were tested; such experiments included amputations. Close to

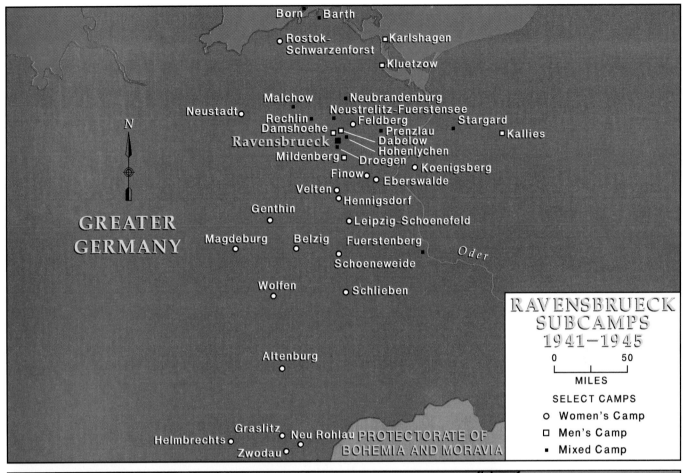

Born • Barth
• Rostok-
Schwarzenforst
• Karlshagen
• Kluetzow
Malchow
Neustadt •
Rechlin
Damshoehe
Ravensbrueck
Mildenberg
Neubrandenburg
Neustrelitz-Fuerstensee
Feldberg • Stargard
Prenzlau
Dabelow
Hohenlychen
Droegen
• Kallies
• Koenigsberg
Finow
• Eberswalde
Velten
Hennigsdorf
Genthin
Leipzig-Schoenefeld
Magdeburg Belzig Fuerstenberg
Schoeneweide
Wolfen • Schlieben
Altenburg

GREATER
GERMANY

Oder

N

Graslitz
Helmbrechts • Neu Rohlau PROTECTORATE OF
Zwodau BOHEMIA AND MORAVIA

RAVENSBRUECK
SUBCAMPS
1941–1945

0   50
MILES

SELECT CAMPS
○ Women's Camp
□ Men's Camp
■ Mixed Camp

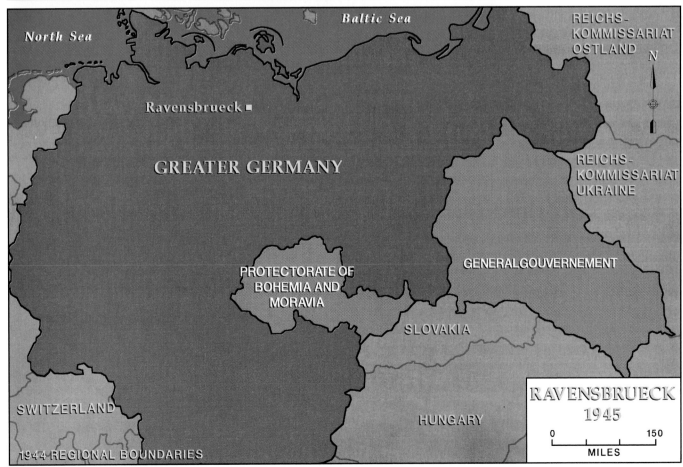

North Sea
Baltic Sea
REICHS-
KOMMISSARIAT
OSTLAND

N

Ravensbrueck ■

GREATER GERMANY

REICHS-
KOMMISSARIAT
UKRAINE

GENERALGOUVERNEMENT

PROTECTORATE OF
BOHEMIA AND
MORAVIA

SLOVAKIA

SWITZERLAND

HUNGARY

1944 REGIONAL BOUNDARIES

RAVENSBRUECK
1945

0   150
MILES

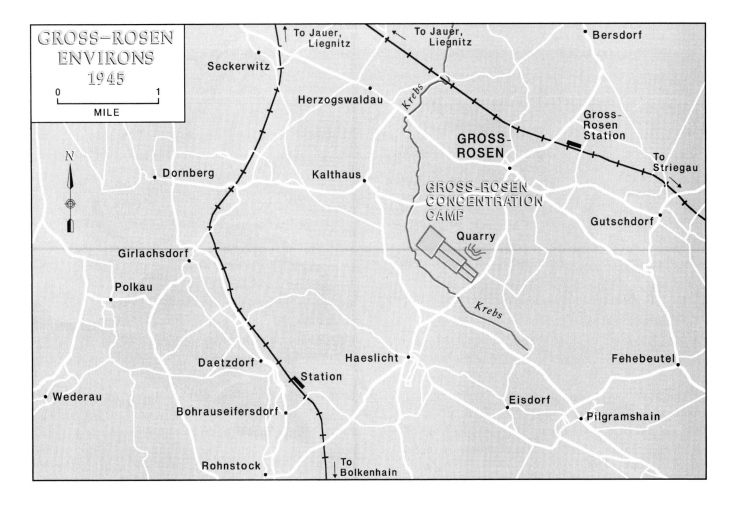

100 women, mostly Polish, were used in these experiments and most died as a result. The few surviving prisoners were crippled for the rest of their lives. SS doctors also carried out sterilization experiments on women and children, mostly Roma, in an attempt to discover a quick method of sterilizing large numbers of people as part of Germany's population policy.

In late March 1945, over 20,000 prisoners were forced on a death march toward Mecklenburg. Advancing Soviet forces liberated them during this march. Shortly before the camp's liberation, the Germans handed over several hundred female prisoners, mostly French, to the Swedish and Danish Red Cross. Soviet forces liberated Ravensbrueck on April 29-30, 1945. Only about 3,500 sick and weak female prisoners remained in the camp.

Between 1939 and 1945, more than 100,000 female prisoners passed through the Ravensbrueck camp system. They were deported to the camp from all over German-occupied Europe, especially from eastern Europe. Nearly 40 percent of the prisoners came from Poland and the German-occupied eastern territories. Almost 15 percent of the prisoners were Jews and almost 5 percent were Roma.

GROSS-ROSEN CONCENTRATION CAMP

The Gross-Rosen concentration camp was originally a labor camp, a subcamp of the Sachsenhausen concentration camp. In 1941, it was designated an autonomous concentration camp. The camp was built near the city of Striegau, just south of the town of Gross-Rosen (Rogoznica) in eastern Germany.

At first, the prisoners were employed primarily as forced laborers in the construction of the camp and in the SS-owned granite quarry nearby. The increasing emphasis on the use of concentration camp prisoners in armaments production led to the expansion of the Gross-Rosen camp, which became the center of an industrial complex and the administrative hub of a vast network of over 60 subcamps. The main camp held as many as 10,000 prisoners, and the subcamp system, spread across eastern Germany, as many as 80,000 prisoners, more than a third of them female. Gross-Rosen had an extremely high mortality rate. It is estimated that of the 120,000 prisoners who passed through the Gross-Rosen system, about 40,000 died.

Beginning in 1943, as many as 60,000 Jewish prisoners

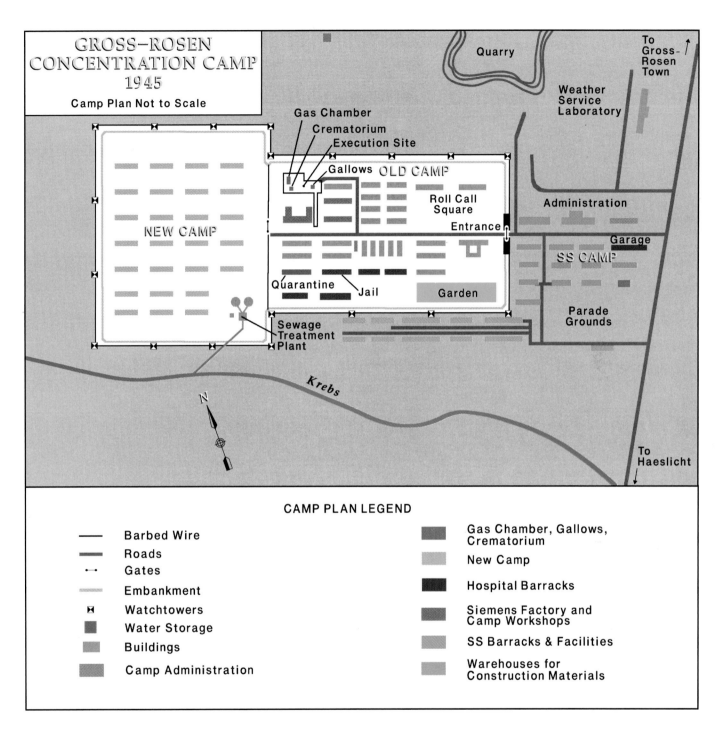

GROSS–ROSEN
CONCENTRATION CAMP
1945

Camp Plan Not to Scale

Quarry

To Gross-Rosen Town

Weather Service Laboratory

Gas Chamber
Crematorium
Execution Site
Gallows   OLD CAMP

Administration

Roll Call Square

Entrance

Garage

SS CAMP

NEW CAMP

Quarantine   Jail

Garden

Parade Grounds

Sewage Treatment Plant

Krebs

N

To Haeslicht

CAMP PLAN LEGEND

— Barbed Wire
— Roads
‹–› Gates
Embankment
⋈ Watchtowers
Water Storage
Buildings
Camp Administration

Gas Chamber, Gallows, Crematorium
New Camp
Hospital Barracks
Siemens Factory and Camp Workshops
SS Barracks & Facilities
Warehouses for Construction Materials

were deported to Gross-Rosen. Most came from Poland and, after March 1944, from Hungary; some came from western and southern Europe. Incoming prisoners were distributed within the Gross-Rosen camp system. Some were used as forced laborers in the Krupp and I.G. Farben works. Two networks of forced-labor camps for Jews were attached to Gross-Rosen. The first included more than 20 Jewish forced-labor camps, which had been part of the Organisation Schmelt system in Silesia. The second was a series of subcamps holding more than 10,000 Hungarian Jews assigned to build

an underground stronghold for Hitler.

As Soviet forces approached the camps in January 1945, the Germans began to evacuate the Gross-Rosen complex. The subcamps on the eastern bank of the Oder River were dissolved. In early February 1945, the main camp was evacuated, followed by the remaining subcamps. About 40,000 prisoners, half of whom were Jews, were forced on death marches and then transported by rail to the Bergen-Belsen, Buchenwald, Dachau, Flossenburg, Mauthausen, Dora-Mittelbau, and Neuengamme concentration camps

GROSS–ROSEN
SUBCAMPS
1940–1945

0   50

MILES

GREATER GERMANY

N

Guben

Gruenberg

Gassen   Neusalz
                Christianstadt

Buchwald-
Hohenwiese   Weisswasser   Halbau
Brandhofen   Merzdorf   Neuhammer   Hartmannsdorf
              Rauscha   Kittlitztreben
Klein Radisch   Niesky   Wiesau   Tannhausen
Kaltwasser   Bunzlau   Aslau   Dyhernfurth   Bunzlau II
Goerlitz   GROSS–ROSEN   Bad Salzbrunn
                        Bolkenhain   Graeben   Breslau   Namslau
Niederoderwitz   Hirschberg   Puerschkau
Zittau   Bad   Koenigszelt   Freiburg
Kratzau   Warmbrunn   Schweidnitz   Brieg
Morchenstern   Liebau   Hausdorf
Gablonz   Schatzlar   Nimptsch
Ober Hohenelbe   Peterswaldau
        Bernsdorf   Langenbielau
Weisswasser-   Gabersdorf   Kamenz
Hohenstatdt   Ober Altstadt   Neisse
              Parschnitz   Mittelsteine
              Landeshut
              Waldenburg   Falkenberg
              Friedland
              Halbstadt   Grulich
        Oberwuestegiersdorf   Geppersdorf
        Wuestewaltersdorf
              Ludwigsdorf

Solid squares represent
select camps. Because of
map scale, not all camps
can be shown or labeled.

PROTECTORATE OF
BOHEMIA AND MORAVIA   Bruennlitz

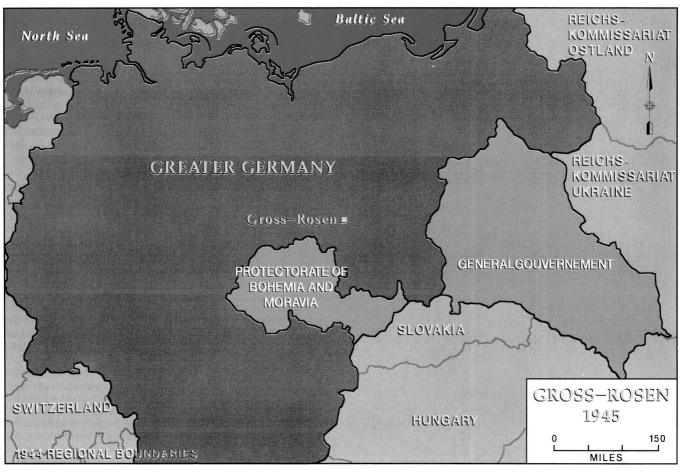

North Sea   Baltic Sea   REICHS-
                                    KOMMISSARIAT
                                    OSTLAND   N

GREATER GERMANY   REICHS-
                                    KOMMISSARIAT
                                    UKRAINE

              Gross–Rosen

        PROTECTORATE OF   GENERALGOUVERNEMENT
        BOHEMIA AND
        MORAVIA
                    SLOVAKIA

SWITZERLAND   GROSS–ROSEN
                                        1945
            HUNGARY
1944 REGIONAL BOUNDARIES   0   150
                                         MILES

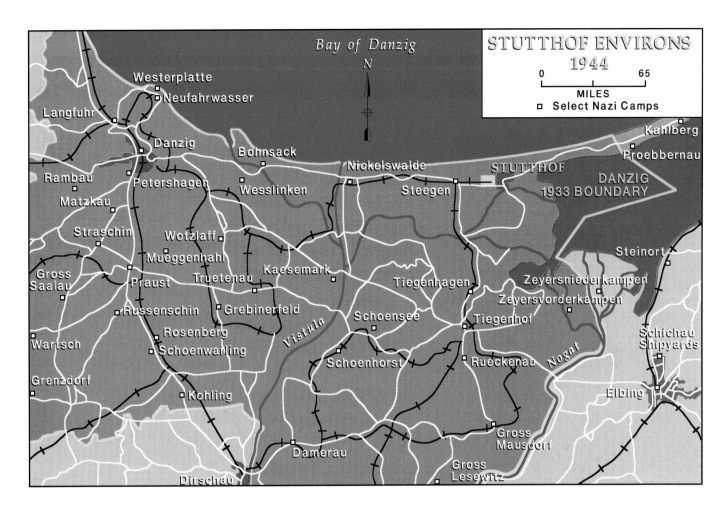

inside Germany. Many prisoners died during the evacuations due to the lack of food and water. SS guards killed prisoners who became too weak to continue.

Soviet forces liberated the Gross-Rosen camp area in February 1945.

STUTTHOF CONCENTRATION CAMP

In September 1939, the Germans constructed the Stutthof camp in a wooded area west of Stutthof (Sztutowo), a town about 22 miles east of Danzig (Gdansk). The area was secluded: to the north was the Bay of Danzig, to the east the Vistula Bay, and to the west the Vistula River. The land was very wet, almost at sea level. The camp was situated along the Danzig-Elbing highway on the way to the popular Baltic Sea resort town of Krynica Morska.

Originally, Stutthof was a civilian internment camp under the Danzig police chief. In November 1941, it was designated a special SS camp. Finally, in January 1942, Stutthof became a regular concentration camp.

The original camp (known as the old camp) was surrounded by barbed-wire fences. In 1943, the camp was enlarged and a new camp was constructed alongside the

earlier one. It was surrounded by electrified barbed-wire fences. The camp staff consisted of SS men and Ukrainian auxiliaries.

Tens of thousands of people, perhaps as many as 100,000, were deported to the Stutthof camp. The prisoners were mainly non-Jewish Poles. There were also Polish Jews from Warsaw and Bialystok, as well as from forced-labor camps in the Baltic states, which were evacuated in 1944 as Soviet forces approached.

Conditions in the camp were brutal. Many prisoners died in typhus epidemics that swept the camp in the winter of 1942 and again in 1944. Those whom the SS guards judged too weak or sick to work were gassed in the camp's small gas chamber. Gassing with Zyklon B gas began in June 1944. Camp doctors also killed sick or injured prisoners in the infirmary with lethal injections. More than 60,000 people died in the camp.

The Germans used Stutthof prisoners as forced laborers. Some prisoners worked in SS-owned businesses such as the German Armament Works (DAW), located near the camp. Others labored in local brickyards, in private industrial enterprises, in agriculture, or in the camp's own workshops. In

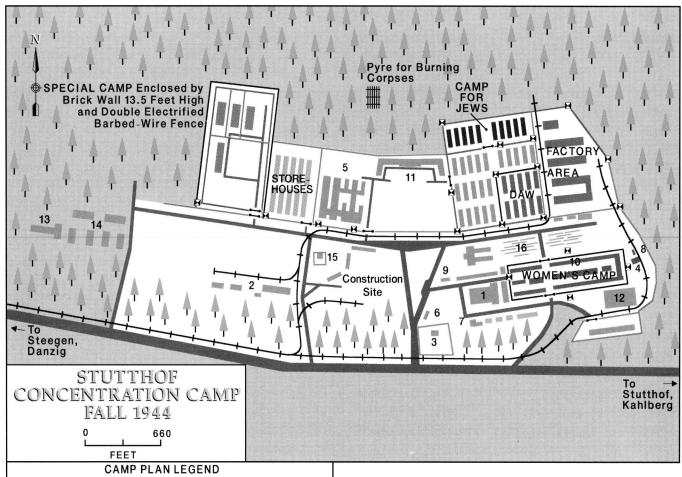

STUTTHOF CONCENTRATION CAMP FALL 1944

0 — 660
FEET

To Steegen, Danzig

To Stutthof, Kahlberg

SPECIAL CAMP Enclosed by Brick Wall 13.5 Feet High and Double Electrified Barbed-Wire Fence

Pyre for Burning Corpses

CAMP FOR JEWS

FACTORY AREA

DAW

STORE-HOUSES

Construction Site

WOMEN'S CAMP

N

CAMP PLAN LEGEND

- Roads
- Narrow Gauge Railroad
- Buildings
- Watchtowers
- Gates
- Electrified Barbed Wire
- Barbed Wire
- Forested Area, Trees
- Camp for Special Prisoners, Mainly German Political Prisoners
- Camp for Jews
- German Armament Works (DAW)
- Factory Area
- Storehouses
- Women's Camp

SELECTED FEATURES

1. Camp Administration Building
2. Civilian Workers' Barracks
3. Commandant's Villa
4. Crematoria
5. Disinfection and Laundry
6. Dog Kennel
7. Garage
8. Gas Chamber
9. Guard House
10. Hospital
11. New Kitchen (Never Completed)
12. Rabbit Hutches
13. School for Ukrainian Policemen
14. SS Barracks
15. SS Clubhouse
16. Vegetable Garden

1944, as forced labor by concentration camp prisoners became increasingly important in armaments production, a Focke-Wulff airplane factory was constructed at Stutthof. Eventually, the Stutthof camp system became a vast network of forced-labor camps. More than 100 Stutthof subcamps were established throughout northern and central Poland. The major subcamps were Thorn and Elbing.

In late 1944 and early 1945, nearly 50,000 Stutthof prisoners were forced on death marches and evacuations by both land and sea. They were transferred to camps in the interior of the Third Reich, mainly to Dachau, Buchenwald, Neuengamme, and Flossenbuerg. Marching in dreadful winter conditions, over 25,000 prisoners died.

Soviet forces reached the main camp at Stutthof in early May 1945 and liberated about 100 prisoners who had managed to hide during the final evacuation of the camp.

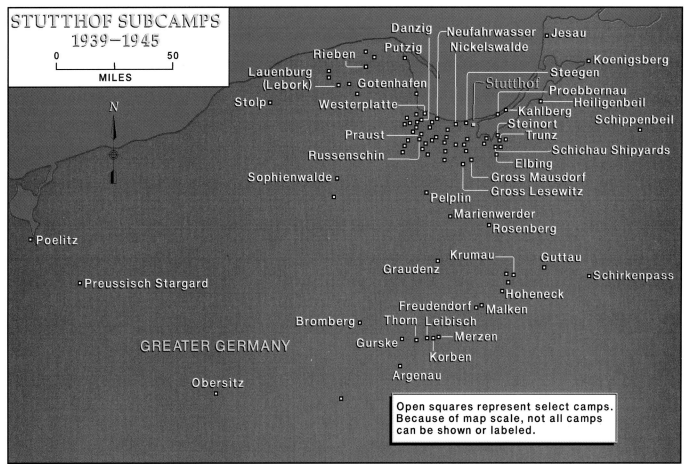

STUTTHOF SUBCAMPS
1939–1945

0   50
MILES

N

Danzig
Rieben
Putzig
Neufahrwasser   Jesau
Nickelswalde
Lauenburg
(Lebork)   Gotenhafen   Koenigsberg
Stolp   Steegen
Westerplatte   Stutthof
                                      Proebbernau
                                      Heiligenbeil
                   Kahlberg
Praust   Steinort   Schippenbeil
Russenschin   Trunz
                   Schichau Shipyards
Sophienwalde   Elbing
                   Gross Mausdorf
Pelplin   Gross Lesewitz
Marienwerder
Rosenberg

Poelitz

Preussisch Stargard   Krumau   Guttau
                Graudenz   Schirkenpass
                         Hoheneck
                Freudendorf Malken
Bromberg   Thorn Leibisch
GREATER GERMANY   Merzen
            Gurske
Obersitz   Korben
            Argenau

Open squares represent select camps.
Because of map scale, not all camps
can be shown or labeled.

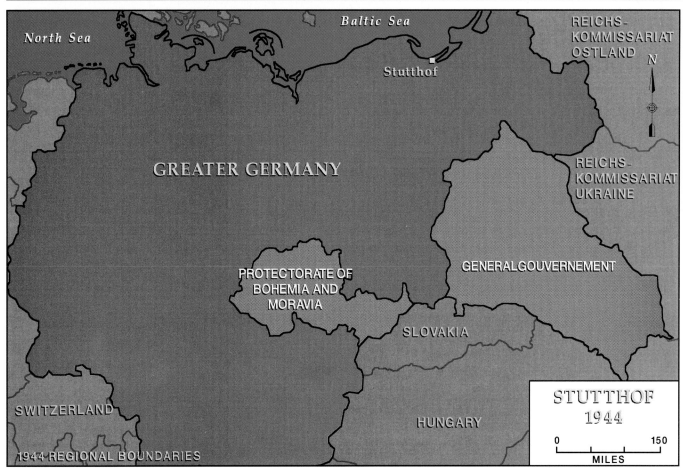

North Sea   Baltic Sea   REICHS-
                                      KOMMISSARIAT
                                      OSTLAND
                                      N
                   Stutthof
GREATER GERMANY
                                      REICHS-
                                      KOMMISSARIAT
                                      UKRAINE

                   GENERALGOUVERNEMENT

PROTECTORATE OF
BOHEMIA AND
MORAVIA
            SLOVAKIA

SWITZERLAND   STUTTHOF
                                      1944
            HUNGARY
1944 REGIONAL BOUNDARIES   0   150
                                      MILES

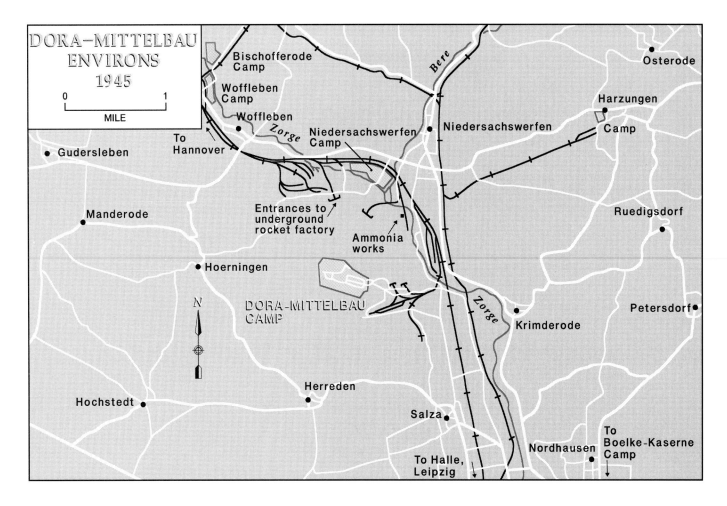

DORA-MITTELBAU ENVIRONS 1945

DORA-MITTELBAU CONCENTRATION CAMP

The Dora-Mittelbau (also known as Dora-Nordhausen or Nordhausen) camp was established in central Germany near the southern Harz Mountains, north of the town of Nordhausen. Dora-Mittelbau was originally a subcamp of Buchenwald. Prisoners from Buchenwald were sent to the area in 1943 to begin construction of a large industrial complex. In October 1944, the SS elevated Dora-Mittelbau to an independent concentration camp with more than 30 subcamps of its own.

Allied air raids on industrial complexes in Germany necessitated the construction of underground production facilities. Concentration camp prisoners dug huge tunnels into the surrounding mountains to house the production and storage areas. In 1943, prisoners at Dora-Mittelbau began construction of huge underground factories and development facilities for the V-2 missile program and other experimental weapons. These so-called Vengeance Weapons (Vergeltungswaffen), as the Germans called them, were constructed and stored in the underground facilities and bomb-proof shafts.

Until the spring of 1944, prisoners were kept mostly underground, deprived of daylight and fresh air, and enclosed in unstable tunnels. The mortality rate was higher than at most other concentration camps. Prisoners too weak or ill to work were sent to Auschwitz-Birkenau or Mauthausen to be killed. In 1944, a compound to house forced laborers was built above ground level south of the main factory area. Once full production of the missiles began in the fall of 1944, Dora-Mittelbau had a standing prisoner population of at least 12,000.

The Dora-Mittelbau camp was enclosed by an electrified barbed-wire fence, with the main entrance located in the east of the camp. To the west of the main entrance was the roll call area, where prisoners were assembled before they were marched off to forced labor. To the east, beyond the entrance, was the SS camp. The crematoria were in the north of the camp. The camp prison was in the south of the camp.

Dora-Mittelbau was the center of a vast network of forced-labor camps constructed in 1944-1945 throughout the Harz Mountain region, including those located in nearby Niedersachswerfen, Nordhausen, and Neusollstedt. Prisoners in the Dora-Mittelbau camp system quarried stone and worked in construction projects, munitions factories, the nearby

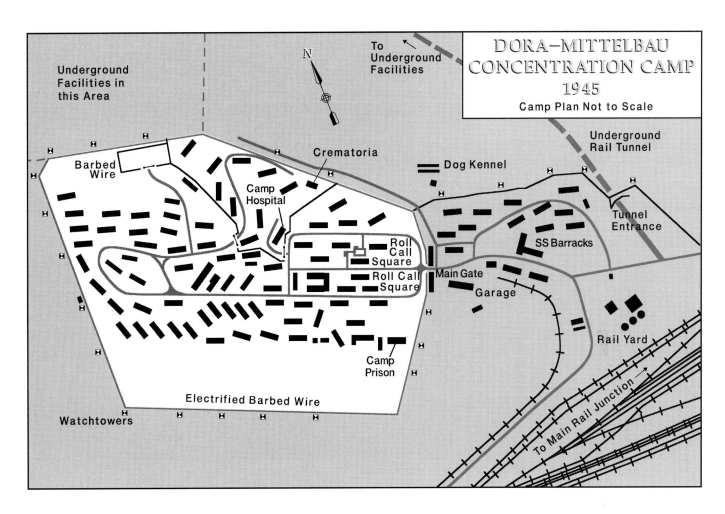

ammonia works, and other projects related to weapons development and production.

Dora-Mittelbau had a prisoner resistance organization, which sought mainly to delay production of the Vengeance Weapons and to sabotage the rockets that were produced. Prisoners suspected of sabotage were usually killed; more than 200 were publicly hanged for sabotaging production.

In early April 1945, the Nazis began to evacuate the prisoners from Dora-Mittelbau. Within days, most of the remaining prisoners were sent to Bergen-Belsen in northern Germany. Thousands were killed during death marches under horrendous conditions. When American forces liberated Dora-Mittelbau in April 1945, only a few prisoners were still in the camp.

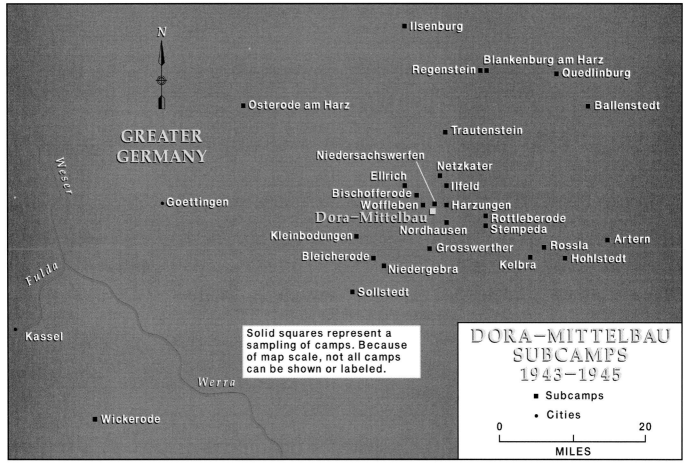

Ilsenburg

Blankenburg am Harz

Regenstein
Quedlinburg

Ballenstedt

Osterode am Harz

GREATER
GERMANY

Trautenstein

Niedersachswerfen
Netzkater

Ellrich
Ilfeld

Bischofferode

Goettingen
Woffleben
Harzungen

Dora–Mittelbau

Rottleberode
Kleinbodungen
Nordhausen
Stempeda

Grosswerther
Rossla
Artern

Bleicherode
Kelbra
Hohlstedt

Niedergebra

Sollstedt

Kassel

Solid squares represent a
sampling of camps. Because
of map scale, not all camps
can be shown or labeled.

DORA–MITTELBAU
SUBCAMPS
1943–1945

Werra

■ Subcamps
• Cities

Wickerode

0   20
MILES

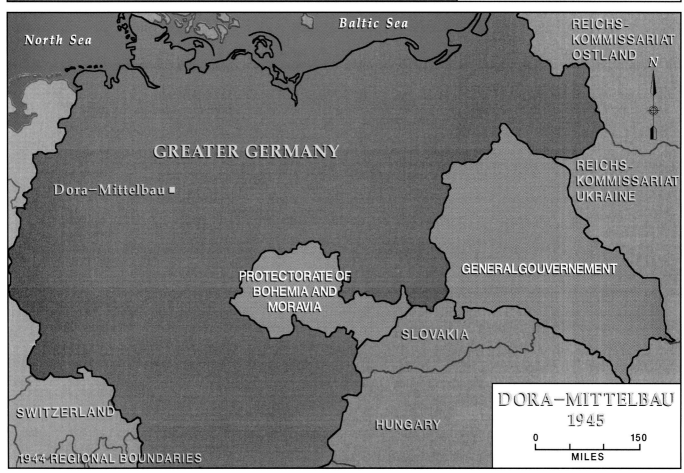

North Sea

Baltic Sea

REICHS-
KOMMISSARIAT
OSTLAND

GREATER GERMANY

N

Dora–Mittelbau ■

REICHS-
KOMMISSARIAT
UKRAINE

PROTECTORATE OF
BOHEMIA AND
MORAVIA

GENERALGOUVERNEMENT

SLOVAKIA

DORA–MITTELBAU
1945

SWITZERLAND

HUNGARY

0   150
MILES

1944 REGIONAL BOUNDARIES

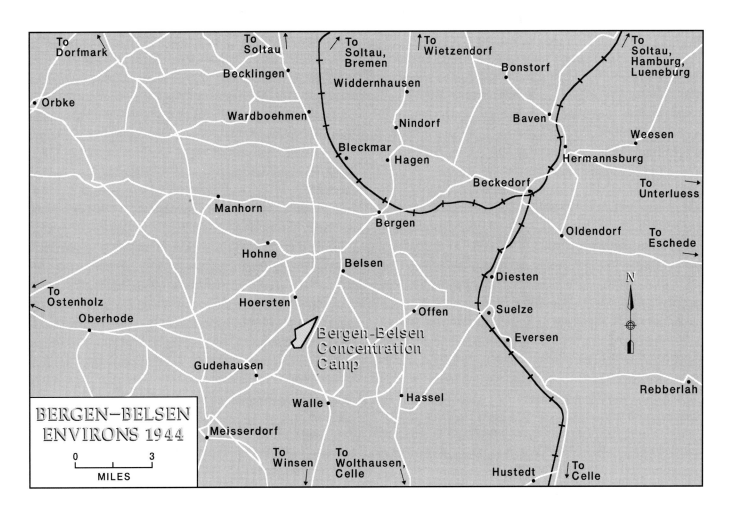

BERGEN–BELSEN
ENVIRONS 1944

0   3
MILES

BERGEN-BELSEN CONCENTRATION CAMP

The Bergen-Belsen concentration camp was established south of the small towns of Bergen and Belsen, about 11 miles north of Celle, Germany. Until 1943 Bergen-Belsen was a prisoner-of-war camp holding mostly Soviet POWs, many of whom were killed by starvation or disease. It was also an internment camp, housing several thousand Jewish prisoners who were to be exchanged for German nationals held by the Allies. Few of the Jewish detainees were ever actually exchanged. In 1944, the Germans permitted some 200 prisoners to leave for Palestine in exchange for German citizens, and more than 1,500 Hungarian Jews were permitted to enter Switzerland in return for payment. The Germans hoped that such exchanges would facilitate negotiations with American officials.

At first, prisoners in Bergen-Belsen were exempted from work. Beginning in 1944, they were subjected to forced labor, usually unloading trains, and excavation or construction projects. In December 1944, the Bergen-Belsen camp was redesignated a concentration camp.

The camp expanded to include eight sections: a detention camp, two camps for women, a special camp, neutrals camp, "star camp," Hungarian camp, and a tent camp. The detention camp housed those Jewish prisoners brought in from the Buchenwald and Natzweiler-Struthof concentration camps to construct the camp. The special camp housed Jews from Poland who held papers (passports, entrance visas, and the like) issued by foreign countries. The neutrals camp was reserved for several hundred Jews who were citizens of neutral countries. The "star camp" was reserved for about 4,000 Jewish prisoners, mostly from the Netherlands, who were to be exchanged for German nationals interned by the Allies. Prisoners in the "star camp" were not required to wear camp uniforms, but had the Star of David sewn onto their clothing, thus giving the camp its name. The Hungarian camp housed more than 1,600 Jews from Hungary.

Bergen-Belsen served as a collection camp for sick and injured prisoners who were sent there from other concentration camps. They were housed in a separate section, the hospital camp. After the hospital camp became overcrowded, sick female prisoners, among them Anne Frank, were held in the tent camp. Many seriously ill prisoners were killed with lethal injections in the camp infirmary.

As Allied forces advanced in late 1944 and early 1945,

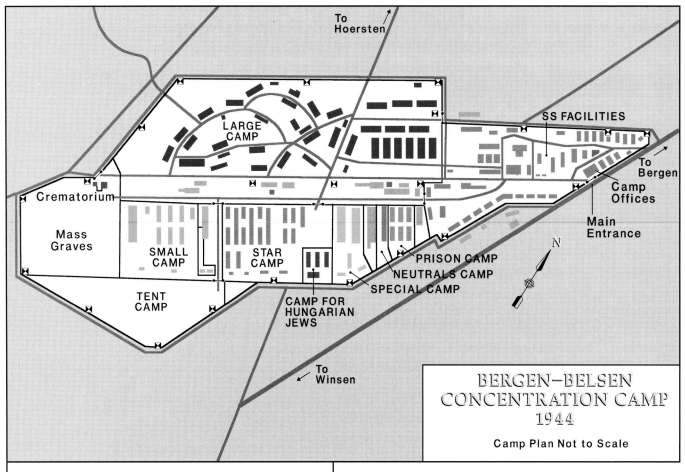

To
Hoersten

LARGE
CAMP

SS FACILITIES

To
Bergen

Crematorium

Camp
Offices

Mass
Graves

Main
Entrance

SMALL
CAMP

STAR
CAMP

N

PRISON CAMP
NEUTRALS CAMP
SPECIAL CAMP

TENT
CAMP

CAMP FOR
HUNGARIAN
JEWS

To
Winsen

BERGEN–BELSEN
CONCENTRATION CAMP
1944

Camp Plan Not to Scale

CAMP PLAN LEGEND

— Barbed-Wire and Other Fences

— Roads

↔ Gates

▭ Buildings

▨ Watchtowers

▪ Water Reservoir

▨ Camp Administration and
SS Compound

▨ Prison Camp

■ Camp for Hungarian Jews

■ Large Camp for Women

▨ Neutrals Camp

▨ Small Camp for Women

▨ Special Camp

▨ Star Camp

Bergen-Belsen became a collection camp for thousands of Jewish prisoners evacuated from camps closer to the front. The arrival of thousands of new prisoners, many of them survivors of death marches, overcrowded the camp. Overcrowding, poor sanitary conditions, and the lack of adequate food and shelter led to a typhus epidemic. In the first few months of 1945, tens of thousands of prisoners, perhaps as many as 35,000 people, died.

On April 15, 1945, British forces liberated Bergen-Belsen. Sixty thousand prisoners, most of them seriously ill, were found in the camp. Thousands of corpses lay unburied on the camp grounds. More than 10,000 former prisoners, too ill to recover, died after liberation. British forces burned down the whole camp to prevent the spread of typhus. Later, a displaced persons' camp was established in the German military school barracks near the original concentration camp.

THE HOLOCAUST IN SOUTHERN EUROPE AND HUNGARY

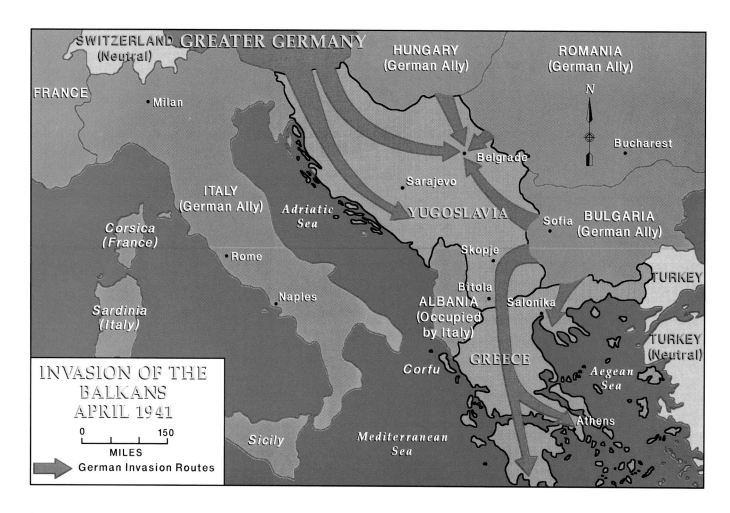

INVASION OF THE
BALKANS
APRIL 1941

0   150
MILES
German Invasion Routes

THE INVASION OF YUGOSLAVIA AND GREECE

Although Yugoslavia joined the Axis alliance with Germany, the Yugoslav government was toppled by an anti-German military coup in late March 1941. Further, an Italian attack on Greece was turned back and a Greek counterattack threatened Italian positions in the Balkans. Germany decided to intervene, securing the southern flank for the impending military operations against the Soviet Union.

Germany invaded Yugoslavia and Greece in early April 1941. Supported by contingents from Germany's allies (Italy, Bulgaria, Hungary, and Romania), German forces quickly subdued the Balkans. Once again a Blitzkrieg succeeded. British forces, sent to aid the Greeks, were forced to withdraw to the island of Crete. In mid-May, German paratroopers landed on Crete and, after heavy fighting, defeated the British.

Yugoslavia and Greece were partitioned among the victors. Germany occupied northwestern Yugoslavia, Serbia, and the region around Salonika in northern Greece. Germany also established the pro-German, fascist state of Croatia in northern Yugoslavia. Hungary received Backa, the region around Subotica in northern Yugoslavia. Bulgaria annexed Yugoslavian Macedonia (the area between the cities of Skopje and Bitola in southern Yugoslavia) and most of Thrace, in northern Greece. Germany occupied a small area of Thrace bordering neutral Turkey. Italy occupied the coastal areas of Yugoslavia and most of the rest of Greece. Germany and Italy jointly occupied Athens, the Greek capital.

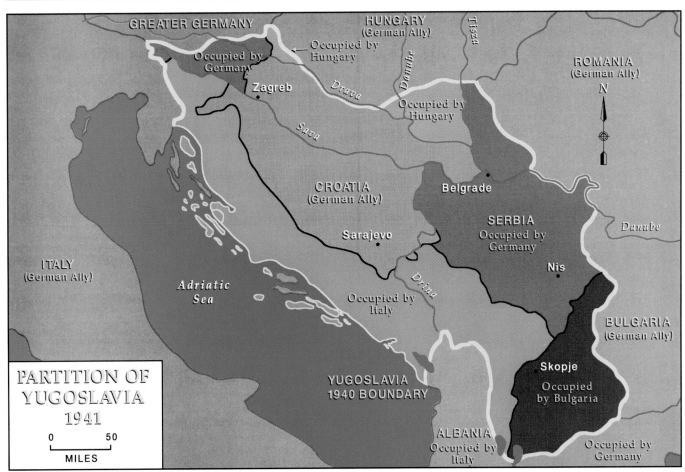

GREATER GERMANY

HUNGARY
(German Ally)

Occupied by
Germany

Occupied by
Hungary

Zagreb

Drava

Danube

Tisza

ROMANIA
(German Ally)

N

Occupied by
Hungary

Sava

CROATIA
(German Ally)

Belgrade

SERBIA
Occupied by
Germany

Danube

ITALY
(German Ally)

Adriatic
Sea

Sarajevo

Drina

Occupied by
Italy

Nis

BULGARIA
(German Ally)

Skopje

Occupied
by Bulgaria

PARTITION OF
YUGOSLAVIA
1941

0   50
MILES

YUGOSLAVIA
1940 BOUNDARY

ALBANIA
Occupied by
Italy

Occupied by
Germany

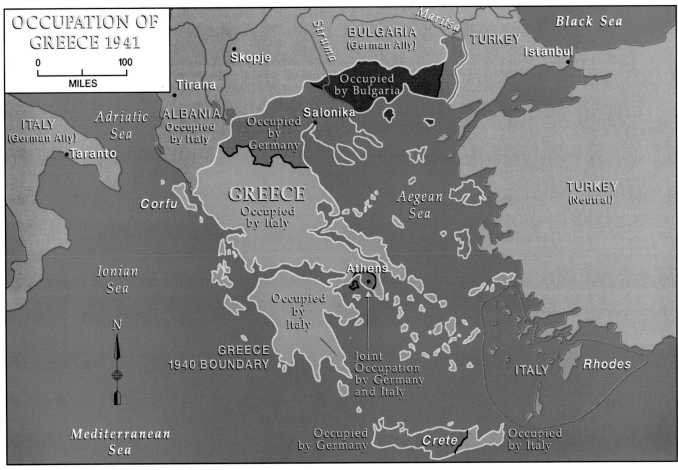

OCCUPATION OF
GREECE 1941

0   100
MILES

Struma

BULGARIA
(German Ally)

Maritsa

Black Sea

TURKEY

Skopje

Occupied
by Bulgaria

Istanbul

Tirana

ALBANIA
Occupied
by Italy

Salonika

Occupied
by
Germany

ITALY
(German Ally)

Adriatic
Sea

Taranto

Corfu

GREECE
Occupied
by Italy

Aegean
Sea

TURKEY
(Neutral)

Ionian
Sea

N

Occupied
by
Italy

Athens

Joint
Occupation
by Germany
and Italy

ITALY

Rhodes

GREECE
1940 BOUNDARY

Mediterranean
Sea

Occupied
by Germany

Crete

Occupied
by Italy

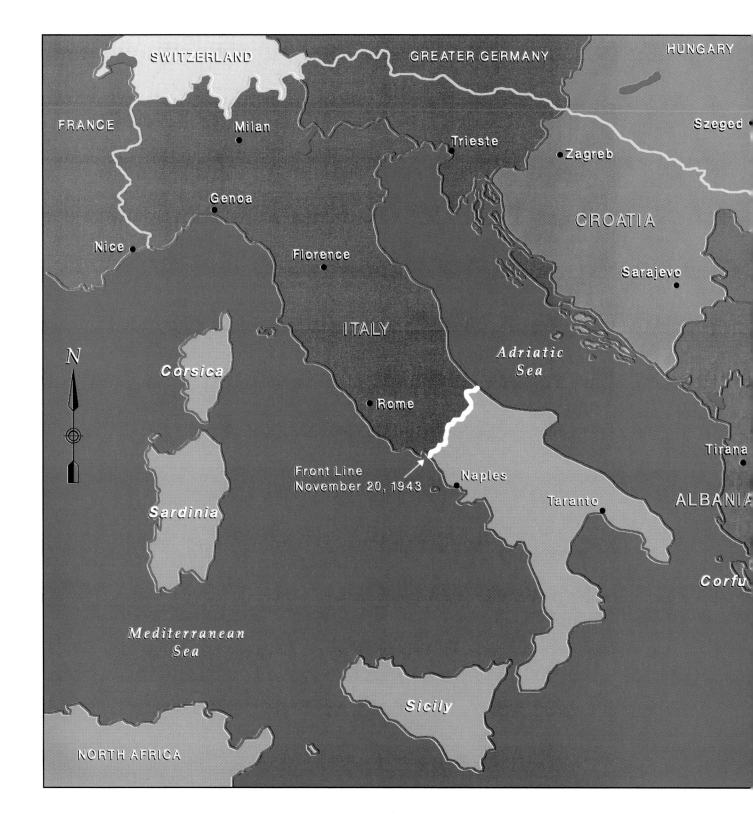

SWITZERLAND

GREATER GERMANY

HUNGARY

FRANCE

Milan

Trieste

Zagreb

Szeged

CROATIA

Genoa

Sarajevo

Nice

Florence

N

ITALY

Adriatic
Sea

Corsica

Rome

Front Line
November 20, 1943

Naples

Tirana

Sardinia

Taranto

ALBANIA

Mediterranean
Sea

Corfu

Sicily

NORTH AFRICA

THE HOLOCAUST IN YUGOSLAVIA AND GREECE

At the time of the Axis occupation in 1941, about 80,000 Jews lived in Yugoslavia, including about 4,000 foreign or stateless Jews who had found refuge in the country in the 1930s. Half of all the Jews lived in the province of Croatia (including Bosnia-Herzegovina), 16,000 in Serbia, 16,000 in the Backa region, and 8,000 in Macedonia. The largest Jewish population centers were in Sarajevo (Bosnia-Herzegovina), with 10,000, and Belgrade (Serbia) and Zagreb (Croatia), with 11,000 each. Approximately 100,000 Jews lived in Greece, almost half of them in Salonika in northern Greece. The fate of the Jews in Yugoslavia and Greece was influenced by the conflicting policies of Germany and its allies toward Jews.

Despite its alliance with Germany, Italy was not enthusiastic about the "Final Solution." Many Italians, including military officers and officials, protected Jews in the Italian occupation zones. Thousands of Jews seeking protection fled to Italian-controlled territory. It was not until the Italian armistice with the Allies in 1943—and the subsequent German occupation of northern Italy and the Italian occupation zones in Yugoslavia and Greece—that Jews there were included in the "Final Solution."

Initially, fascist Hungary, an ally of Germany, did not deport Jews from territory it occupied in Yugoslavia. But Hungarian army and police units went on a rampage and killed several thousand Jews and Serbs in the Yugoslav city of Novi Sad in January 1942. The deportation of most of the Jews from Hungarian-occupied territory began shortly after the Germans occupied Hungary in March 1944. The Germans concentrated the Jews of the Backa region (formerly part of Yugoslavia) in the Backa-Topolya, Baja, and Bacsalmas camps. From these camps they were deported to Auschwitz-Birkenau, where most were killed.

Bulgaria did not deport Bulgarian Jews, but did deport non-Bulgarian Jews from the territories it had annexed from Yugoslavia and Greece. In March 1943, Bulgaria arrested all the Jews in Macedonia, formerly part of Yugoslavia, and in Thrace, formerly part of Greece. In Macedonia, about 7,000 Jews were interned in a transit camp in Skopje. In Thrace, about 4,000 Jews were deported to Bulgarian assembly points at Gorna Dzhumaya and Dupnitsa, and handed over to the Germans. In all, Bulgaria deported more than 11,000 Jews to German-held territory, and by the end of the month, most of them had been deported to the Treblinka killing center.

Germany occupied Serbia (formerly part of Yugoslavia) and instituted a military government in 1941. Most of the Jews were interned in concentration camps—especially in Topovske Supe, Sajmiste, Schabatz, and Nisch. In August 1941, most of the interned male Jews were shot. In 1942, the SS brought a gas van—a truck with a hermetically sealed compartment that served as a gas chamber—to the Sajmiste camp, where most of the Jewish women and children

(continued on page 175)

GERMAN ADMINISTRATION OF SOUTHERN EUROPE 1943

0   150

MILES

- German Ally
- German-Occupied
- Liberated
- Neutral
- Boundary of Southern Europe

ROMANIA
Timisoara
Belgrade
SERBIA
Sofia
Skopje
BULGARIA
Salonika
TURKEY
GREECE
Aegean Sea
Athens

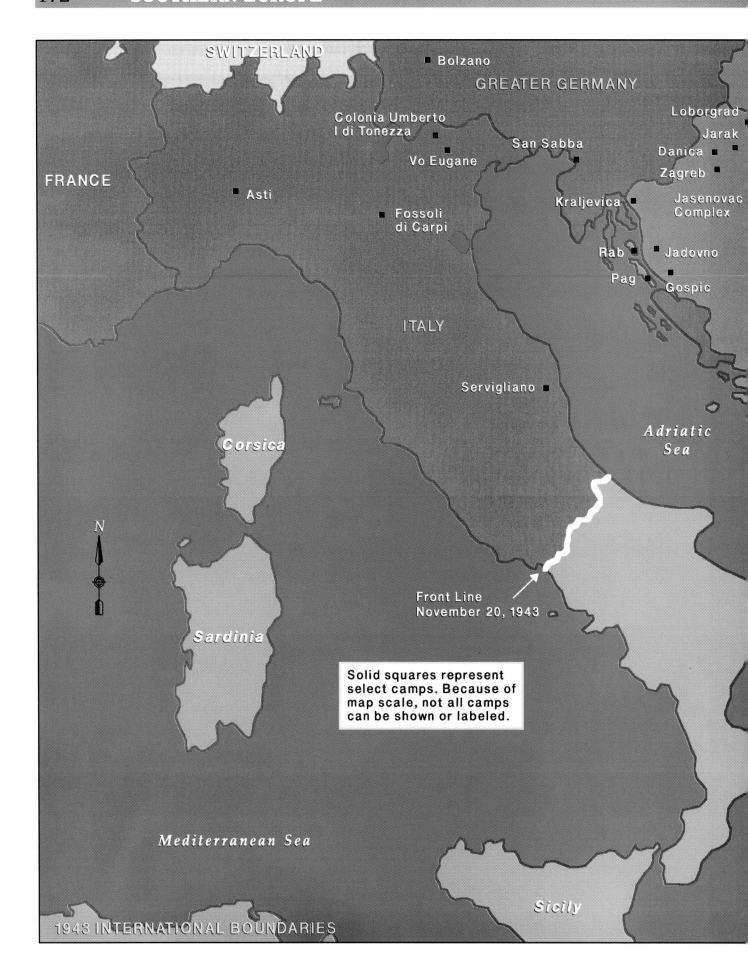

SWITZERLAND

■ Bolzano

GREATER GERMANY

Loborgrad

Colonia Umberto
I di Tonezza   ■
Jarak

San Sabba   ■   Danica ■   ■

Vo Eugane   Zagreb   ■

FRANCE   Jasenovac
Complex

Asti   Kraljevica ■

Fossoli
di Carpi   ■

Rab ■   ■ Jadovno

Pag ■

ITALY   Gospic

Servigliano ■

Adriatic
Sea

Corsica

N

Front Line
November 20, 1943

Sardinia

Solid squares represent
select camps. Because of
map scale, not all camps
can be shown or labeled.

Mediterranean Sea

Sicily

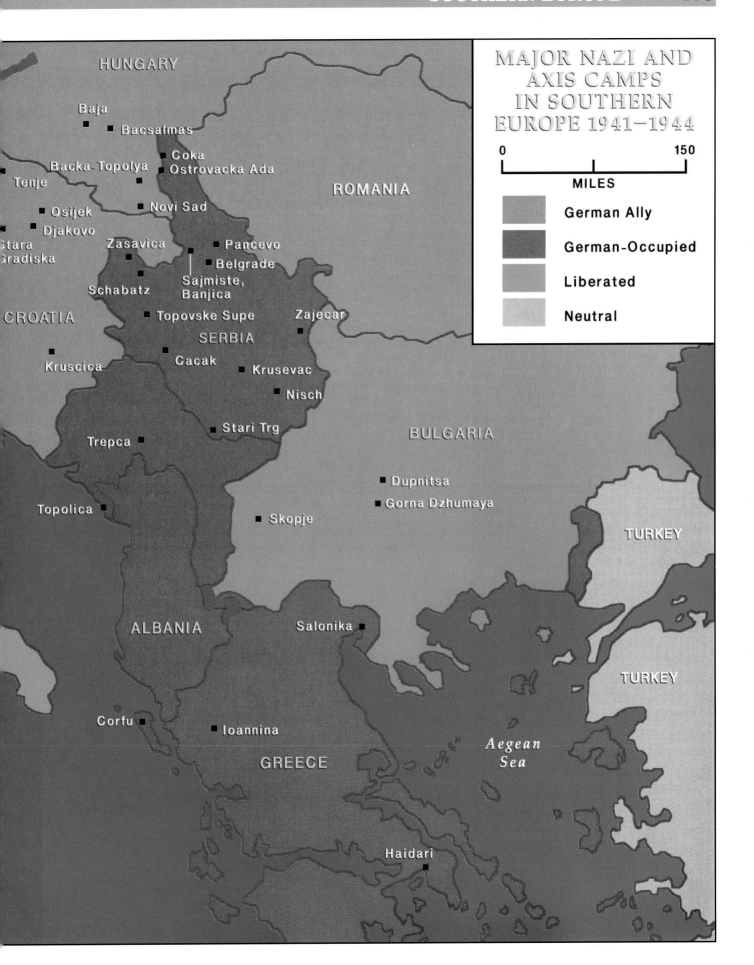

MAJOR NAZI AND
AXIS CAMPS
IN SOUTHERN
EUROPE 1941–1944

0   150

MILES

German Ally

German-Occupied

Liberated

Neutral

HUNGARY

Baja

Bacsalmas

Coka
Backa-Topolya   Ostrovacka Ada

Tenje

ROMANIA

Osijek   Novi Sad

Djakovo

Stara   Zasavica   Pancevo
Gradiska

Belgrade

Sajmiste,
Schabatz   Banjica

CROATIA   Topovske Supe   Zajecar

SERBIA

Kruscica   Cacak

Krusevac

Nisch

Stari Trg

BULGARIA

Trepca

Dupnitsa

Gorna Dzhumaya

Topolica

Skopje

TURKEY

ALBANIA   Salonika

TURKEY

Corfu

Ioannina   Aegean
Sea

GREECE

Haidari

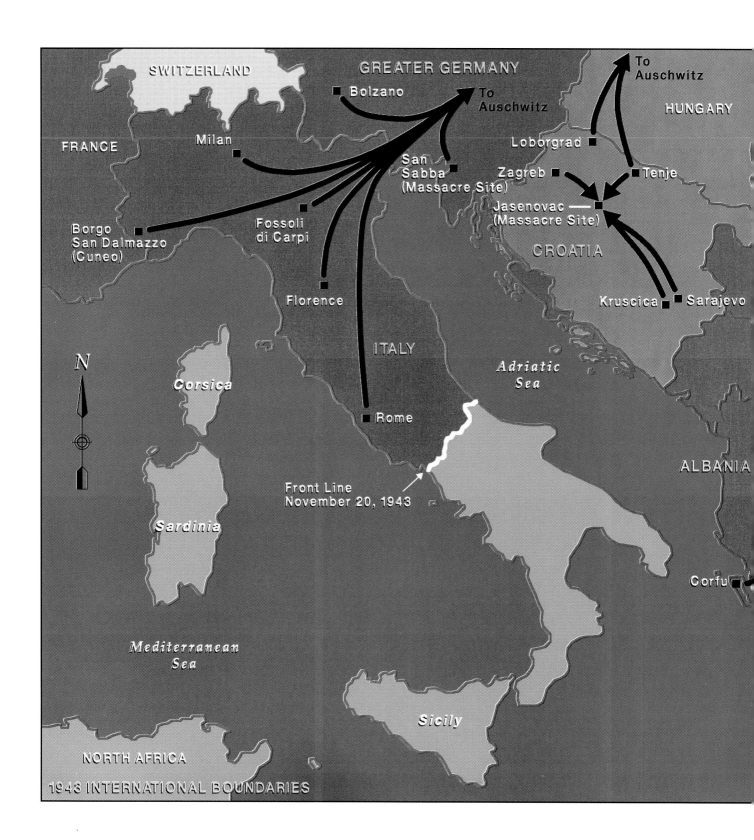

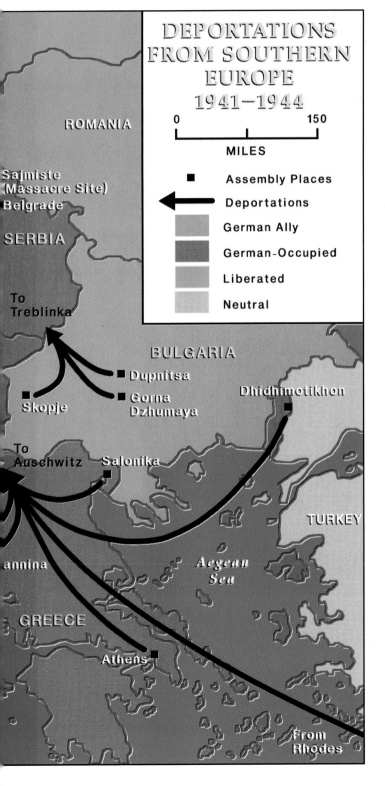

DEPORTATIONS FROM SOUTHERN EUROPE 1941–1944

0   150
MILES

■ Assembly Places

← Deportations

German Ally

German-Occupied

Liberated

Neutral

ROMANIA

Sajmiste (Massacre Site) Belgrade

SERBIA

To Treblinka

BULGARIA

■ Dupnitsa

■ Gorna Dzhumaya

Skopje

Dhidhimotikhon

To Auschwitz   Salonika

annina

TURKEY

Aegean Sea

GREECE

Athens

From Rhodes

had been interned. At least 8,000 Jewish women and children were killed by the end of May.

In the German puppet state of Croatia (established in April 1941), the Ustasa (Croatian fascists) instituted a reign of terror and began the systematic murder of Serbs, Jews, and Roma (Gypsies). The Ustasa killed hundreds of thousands of Serbs and expelled more than 200,000 from Croatia. They employed particularly cruel measures to terrorize the Serbs: whole villages were burned down and the inhabitants killed; Serb women were raped; Serb men were tortured.

About two-thirds of the Jews of Croatia were imprisoned in camps throughout Croatia (Jadovno, Kruscica, Loborgrad, Djakovo, Tenje, Osijek, and Jasenovac) by the end of 1941. The Ustasa killed more than 20,000 Jews in the Jasenovac concentration camp, near Zagreb. In 1942 and 1943, about 7,000 Jews were deported from Croatia to the killing centers in German-occupied Poland, mainly to Auschwitz-Birkenau.

Most of the Croatian Jews who survived the war were saved by seeking refuge in the Italian-occupied areas. Rejecting German demands to hand over Jews in these areas, the Italians instead assembled many of those in Italian-occupied Yugoslavia in the Rab island camp, which was in the Italian zone. After the Italian armistice with the Allies in September 1943, Germany occupied the Italian zone of Yugoslavia. Yugoslav partisans helped many former prisoners of Rab avoid capture by German forces.

The largest Jewish community in Greece was in Salonika, located in northern Greece in the German occupation zone. In February 1943, the Jews of Salonika were concentrated in the Baron de Hirsch quarter of the city. More than 40,000 were deported to Auschwitz-Birkenau between March and August 1943, and most were gassed on arrival. In 1944 the Germans began deportations from the former Italian zone in Greece: 800 Jews from Athens, almost 2,000 from the island of Corfu, and almost 2,000 from Rhodes were deported to Auschwitz-Birkenau. The vast majority were killed upon arrival.

In September 1944, the Germans withdrew from Yugoslavia and the Greek mainland. Approximately 60,000 Yugoslav Jews and more than 50,000 Greek Jews died in the Holocaust. Thousands of Greek and Yugoslav Jews survived by hiding with friends or neighbors or by joining the partisans.

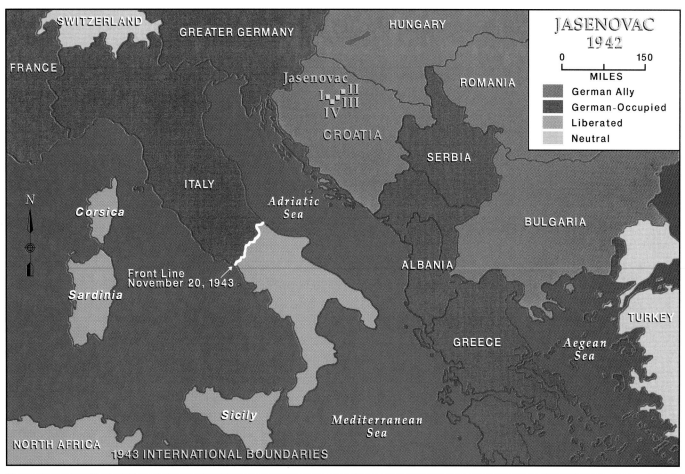

JASENOVAC
1942

0 ——— 150
MILES

German Ally
German-Occupied
Liberated
Neutral

SWITZERLAND
FRANCE
GREATER GERMANY
HUNGARY
ROMANIA
Jasenovac
I ▪ II
III
IV
CROATIA
SERBIA
ITALY
Corsica
Adriatic
Sea
BULGARIA
N
Front Line
November 20, 1943
Sardinia
ALBANIA
TURKEY
GREECE
Aegean
Sea
Sicily
Mediterranean
Sea
NORTH AFRICA   1943 INTERNATIONAL BOUNDARIES

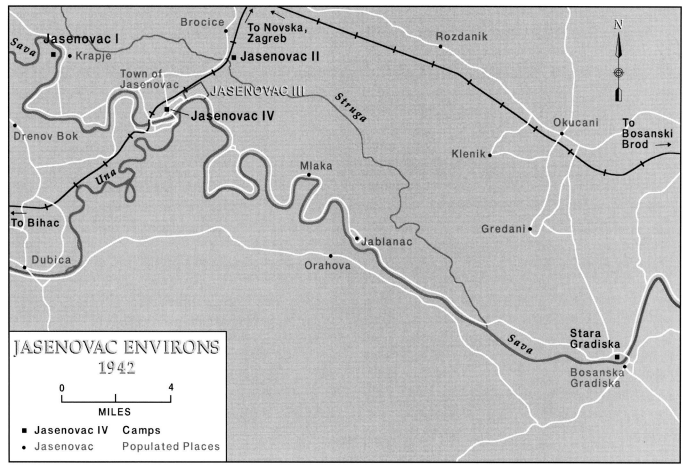

JASENOVAC ENVIRONS
1942

0 ——— 4
MILES

▪ Jasenovac IV   Camps
• Jasenovac   Populated Places

Brocice
To Novska,
Zagreb
Rozdanik
Sava
Jasenovac I
▪ • Krapje
Jasenovac II
Town of
Jasenovac
JASENOVAC III
Jasenovac IV
Struga
Okucani
To
Bosanski
Brod →
Drenov Bok
Klenik
Una
Mlaka
To Bihac
Gredani
Jablanac
Dubica
Orahova
Sava
Stara
Gradiska
Bosanska
Gradiska
N

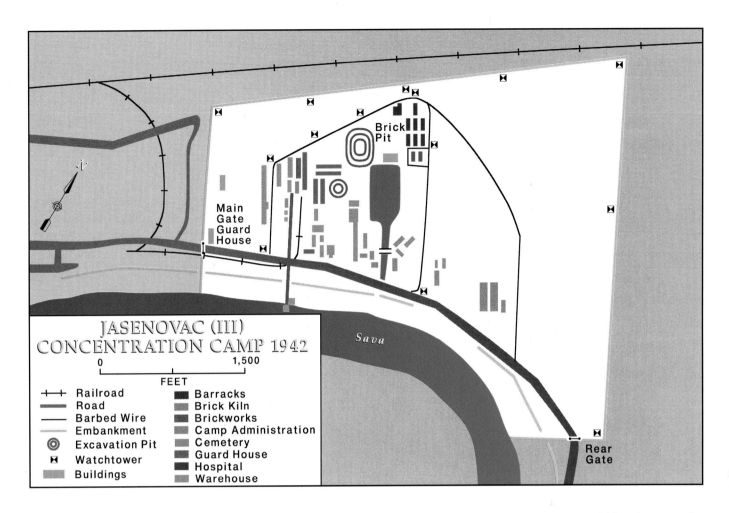

JASENOVAC (III)
CONCENTRATION CAMP 1942

0   1,500
FEET

++ Railroad
── Road
── Barbed Wire
─── Embankment
◎ Excavation Pit
⊠ Watchtower
▨ Buildings

■ Barracks
▨ Brick Kiln
▨ Brickworks
▨ Camp Administration
▨ Cemetery
▨ Guard House
■ Hospital
▨ Warehouse

Brick Pit

Main
Gate
Guard
House

Sava

Rear
Gate

JASENOVAC CONCENTRATION CAMP

Jasenovac was a complex of camps established in Croatia by the Croatian security police in 1941. It was built along the Sava River, about 62 miles south of the Croatian capital of Zagreb. Members of the Ustasa (Croatian fascists) staffed the camp. Stara Gradiska, a concentration camp for women, was attached to Jasenovac.

The largest camp in Croatia, Jasenovac was a center of the genocide perpetrated by the Ustasa. Tens of thousands of people, mostly Serbs, were killed at Jasenovac. Other victims included Jews, Roma (Gypsies), and political opponents of the Ustasa regime.

Jews from Croatia, Bosnia, and, after the Italian armistice, Dalmatia, were deported to Jasenovac. They were usually killed upon arrival at massacre sites, such as Granik and Gradina, near the camp. Only those Jews with needed skills—for example, doctors, electricians, and carpenters—remained in the camp, where they were employed in camp services and workshops. More than 20,000 Jews were killed in Jasenovac, mostly in 1942.

Conditions in Jasenovac were very primitive. Prisoners received little food and poor shelter, and sanitary facilities were inadequate. Ustasa guards instituted a reign of terror in the camp, where killings and torture were a feature of daily life.

In April 1945, as Yugoslav partisan troops approached the camp, several hundred prisoners took part in an uprising against the Ustasa guards. Only a few prisoners managed to escape. The Ustasa demolished the camp and killed the remaining inmates. Yugoslav partisans liberated the camp area on April 30, 1945.

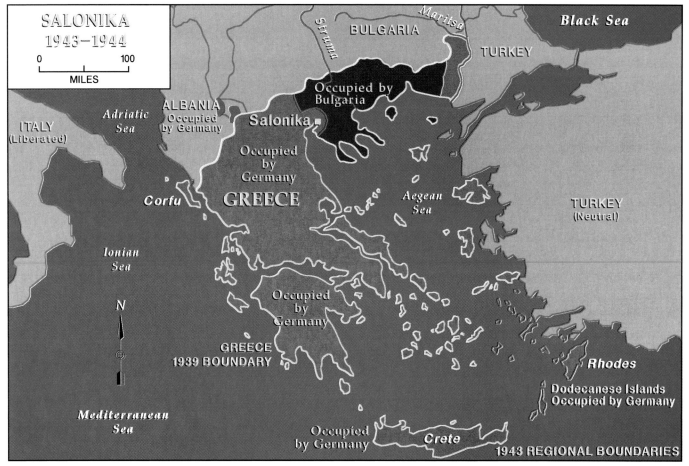

SALONIKA
1943–1944

0   100
MILES

ITALY
(Liberated)

*Adriatic
Sea*

ALBANIA
Occupied
by Germany

Struma

BULGARIA

Maritsa

Black Sea

TURKEY

Salonika

Occupied by
Bulgaria

Occupied
by
Germany

GREECE

Corfu

*Aegean
Sea*

TURKEY
(Neutral)

*Ionian
Sea*

N

Occupied
by
Germany

GREECE
1939 BOUNDARY

Rhodes

Dodecanese Islands
Occupied by Germany

*Mediterranean
Sea*

Occupied
by Germany   *Crete*

1943 REGIONAL BOUNDARIES

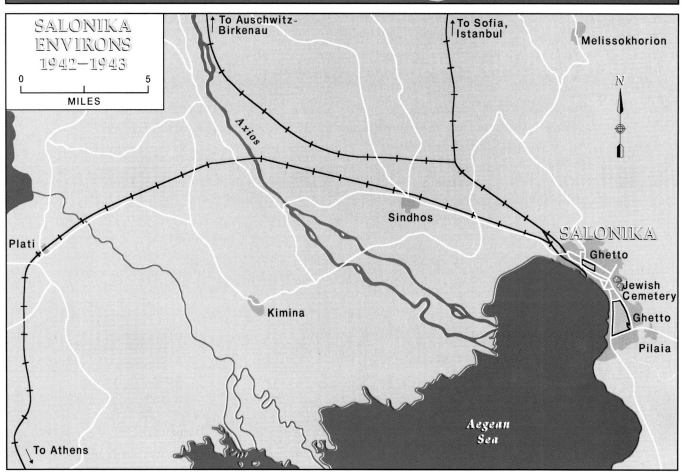

SALONIKA
ENVIRONS
1942–1943

0   5
MILES

To Auschwitz-
Birkenau

To Sofia,
Istanbul

Melissokhorion

N

Axios

Sindhos

SALONIKA

Ghetto

Plati

Jewish
Cemetery

Ghetto

Kimina

Pilaia

*Aegean
Sea*

To Athens

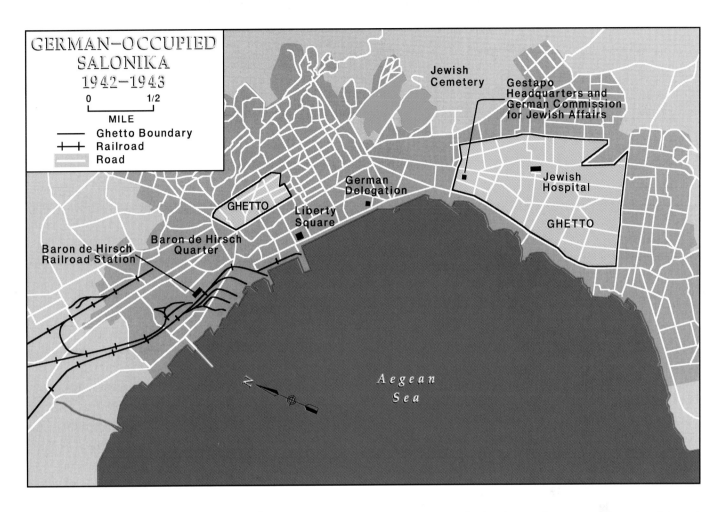

GERMAN–OCCUPIED
SALONIKA
1942–1943
0   1/2
MILE
——— Ghetto Boundary
+—+—+ Railroad
Road

Jewish
Cemetery
Gestapo
Headquarters and
German Commission
for Jewish Affairs

German
Delegation

GHETTO

Liberty
Square

Jewish
Hospital

GHETTO

Baron de Hirsch
Railroad Station

Baron de Hirsch
Quarter

Aegean
Sea

THE DEPORTATION OF THE JEWS
OF SALONIKA

The city of Salonika (Thessaloniki) is located in northern Greece. After the invasion and occupation of Greece in April 1941, Salonika was included in the German occupation zone. The city was occupied by German forces in early April.

Before the war, Salonika had the largest Jewish community in Greece. At the time of the German occupation, the Jewish population was about 50,000. Within a week of the occupation, the Germans arrested the Jewish leadership, evicted hundreds of Jewish families and confiscated their apartments, and expropriated the Baron de Hirsch Jewish hospital for use by the German army.

In mid-July 1942, the Germans forced 9,000 Jewish men to assemble at Liberty Square (Plateia Eleftheria), where they were registered for forced-labor assignments. Two thousand of them were assigned to forced-labor projects for the German army. Their release was ransomed by the Jewish community in Salonika, which collected money in Salonika and Athens and sold the Jewish cemetery in Salonika to raise the required sum. (The cemetery was purchased by the city administration,

which broke up the headstones for construction materials and built a university at the site.)

In February 1943, the Jews of Salonika were concentrated in two ghettos: one in the east of Salonika and one in the western, Baron de Hirsch quarter of the city. Jews were concentrated in the Baron de Hirsch quarter, near the railway station, in preparation for impending deportations. Between March and August 1943, more than 40,000 Jews were deported from Salonika to the Auschwitz-Birkenau killing center. Most of the deportees were gassed on arrival in Auschwitz.

Jews holding identity papers or visas issued by neutral governments were not deported. More than 300 Jews holding Spanish papers were transferred to Spain via the Bergen-Belsen camp in northern Germany. Some Jews escaped from German-occupied Greece to the Italian occupation zone or to Palestine. About 500 Jews from Salonika avoided the deportations by escaping to the nearby mountains, where they joined partisan units that fought the Germans.

Only about 1,000 Jews returned to Salonika after the war. The ancient Jewish community of Salonika was destroyed.

ITALY 1939

0   150
MILES

SWITZERLAND   GREATER GERMANY   Budapest   *Tisza*
Drava   HUNGARY
Bolzano
FRANCE   Milan   •Udine   •Szeged
Turin   Trieste   Subotica   •Timisoara
Cuneo   Carpi   Venice   Zagreb   *Sava*   ROMANIA
Genoa   Modena   Ferrara   •Bucharest
Nice   La Spezia   Bologna   YUGOSLAVIA   Belgrade
•Florence   Sarajevo   BULGARIA
Po
Siena   Sofia   *Tundzha*
Tiber   *Adriatic*   *Drina*   Skopje   *Maritsa*
Elba   *Sea*
Corsica   N   *Struma*
•Rome   ITALY   Foggia   ALBANIA   Tirana   TURKEY
(Occupied by
Naples   Italy April 1939)   Salonika
Sardinia   •Salerno   GREECE   TURKEY
Cagliari   Taranto
Corfu   *Aegean*
Sea
Mediterranean   Athens   *Dodecanese*
Sea   Palermo   Patras   *Islands*
Reggio
Sicily   Catania   ITALY
Tunis

ITALIAN–OCCUPIED AREAS
IN SOUTHERN EUROPE
1942

0   150
MILES

SWITZERLAND   GREATER GERMANY   Budapest   ITALIAN–OCCUPIED AREAS
Drava   Kaposvar
Occupied   Milan
by Italy   Trieste   Subotica
FRANCE   Venice   Zagreb   *Sava*
Po   Belgrade   ROMANIA   Bucharest
Genoa   CROATIA   SERBIA
Nice   •Florence   Sarajevo   Occupied by   *Danube*
Occupied   Split   Germany
by   Corsica   *Adriatic*   •Nis
Germany   Occupied   Elba   *Sea*   *Drina*   BULGARIA
by   Occupied by Italy   Sofia   *Tundzha*
Italy   •Rome   Skopje   *Maritsa*   Burgas
ITALY   *Tiber*   *Struma*   TURKEY
•Naples   Tirana •Bitola
ALBANIA   Occupied by
Sardinia   Germany
N   Salonika
ITALY   TURKEY
1939 BOUNDARY   *Corfu*
GREECE   *Aegean*
Sea
Sicily   Athens
Mediterranean Sea   Joint Occupation
Tunis   by Germany
TUNISIA   and Italy   ITALY

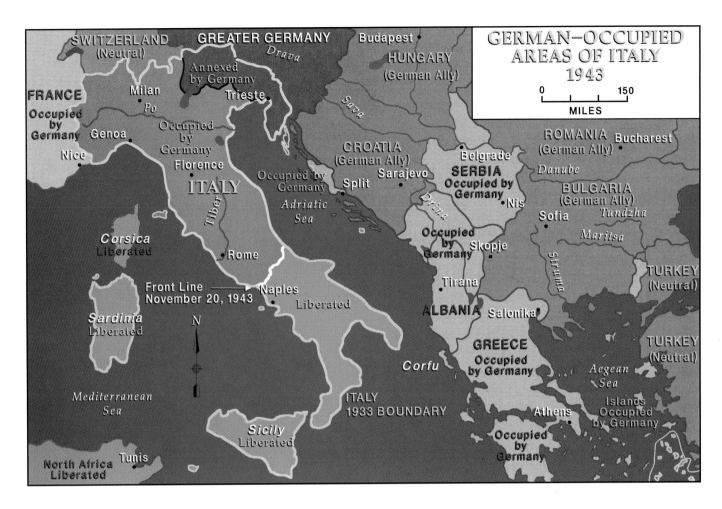

GERMAN–OCCUPIED
AREAS OF ITALY
1943

0   150
MILES

THE HOLOCAUST IN ITALY

In October 1922, King Victor Emmanuel III appointed the Italian Fascist leader, Benito Mussolini, prime minister of Italy. Shortly thereafter, Mussolini established a Fascist dictatorship.

The Italian Jewish community, one of the oldest in Europe, numbered about 50,000 in 1933. Jews had lived in Italy for more than 2,000 years; by the 1930s, Italian Jews were thoroughly assimilated into Italian culture and society. There was relatively little antisemitism among Italians. Italian Fascism was generally not an antisemitic ideology.

However, in 1938, Italy passed antisemitic laws. These laws forbade marriage between Jews and non-Jews and removed Jewish teachers from the public schools. Further, foreign refugee Jews living in Italy were confined in internment camps, although under relatively good conditions: families lived together and the camps provided schools, cultural activities, and social events.

Italy entered World War II in 1940 as a German ally, hoping to establish a new Italian empire. Italy occupied territory in Yugoslavia (1941), Greece (1941), and a small portion of southern France (1942). Although allied with Germany, Fascist Italy did not willingly cooperate in the Nazi plan to kill the Jews of Europe. Italians generally refused to participate in genocide or permit deportations from Italy or the Italian occupation zones in Yugoslavia, Greece, and France to the Nazi killing centers. Italian military officers and officials usually protected Jews and Italian-occupied areas were relatively safe for Jews. Between 1941 and 1943, thousands of Jews escaped to Italy.

Military reversals in northern Africa and the Allied invasion of Sicily and southern Italy in 1943 contributed to the overthrow of Mussolini's dictatorship. The king ordered Mussolini imprisoned. Pietro Badoglio, the new prime minister, negotiated a cease-fire with the Allies in early September 1943. That same month, German paratroopers freed Mussolini from prison. German forces occupied most of northern and central Italy and installed Mussolini as the head of a pro-German puppet government. German forces also occupied the Italian zones in Yugoslavia, Greece, and France.

The German occupation of northern Italy radically altered the situation for Italian Jews, especially since most Italian Jews lived in the north. Deportations began almost immediately from both the German-occupied areas of Italy

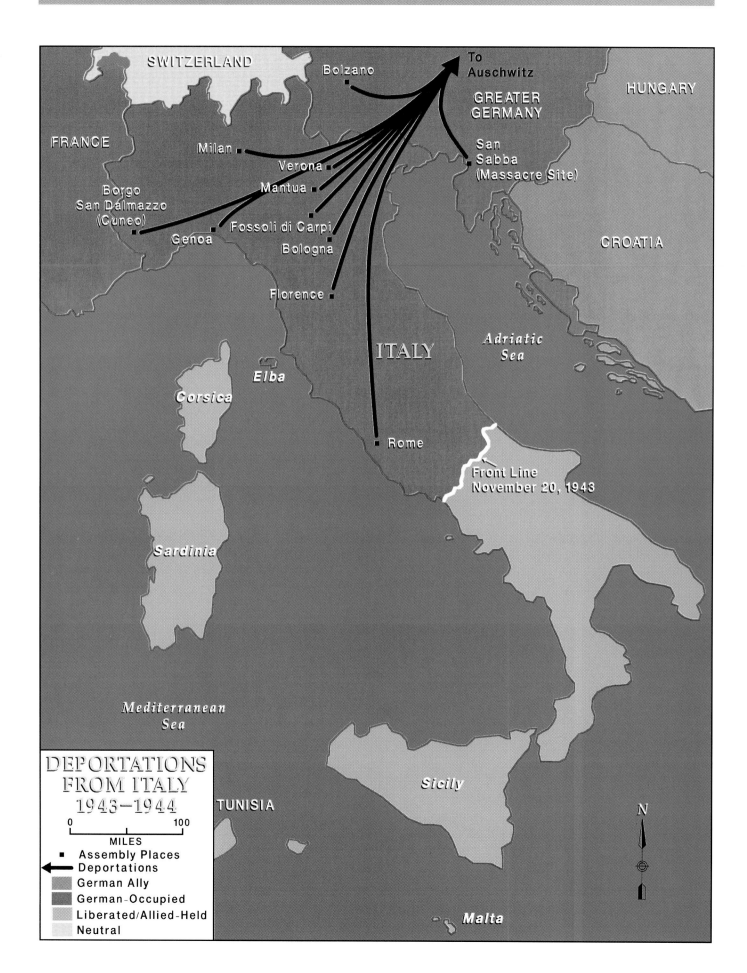

SWITZERLAND

Bolzano

To
Auschwitz

GREATER
GERMANY

HUNGARY

FRANCE

Milan

Verona

San
Sabba
(Massacre Site)

Mantua

CROATIA

Borgo
San Dalmazzo
(Cuneo)

Fossoli di Carpi

Genoa

Bologna

Florence

ITALY

*Adriatic
Sea*

Elba

Corsica

Rome

Front Line
November 20, 1943

Sardinia

*Mediterranean
Sea*

DEPORTATIONS
FROM ITALY
1943–1944

0   100

MILES

■   Assembly Places
←   Deportations
   German Ally
   German-Occupied
   Liberated/Allied-Held
   Neutral

TUNISIA

Sicily

N

Malta

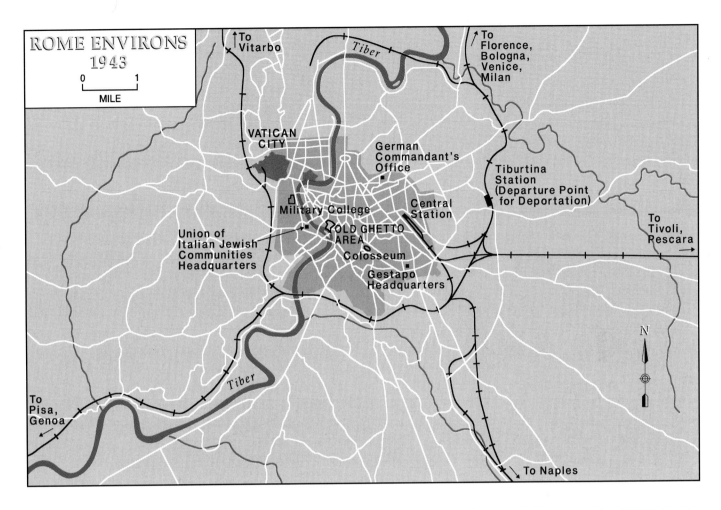

ROME ENVIRONS 1943

0   1
MILE

To Vitarbo

Tiber

To Florence, Bologna, Venice, Milan

VATICAN CITY

German Commandant's Office

Tiburtina Station (Departure Point for Deportation)

Military College

Central Station

Union of Italian Jewish Communities Headquarters

OLD GHETTO AREA

Colosseum

To Tivoli, Pescara

Gestapo Headquarters

N

Tiber

To Pisa, Genoa

To Naples

and the former Italian occupation zones in southern Europe.

In October and November 1943, the Germans rounded up Jews in Rome, Milan, Genoa, Florence, Trieste, and other major cities in northern Italy. They were interned in transit camps, particularly the Fossoli di Carpi camp, originally an Italian-run internment camp approximately 12 miles north of Modena, and the Bolzano camp in northeastern Italy, established in late 1943. Periodically, trains carrying Jews left both camps for the Auschwitz-Birkenau killing center. In Trieste, about 5,000 people, mostly non-Jews, were tortured to death or executed in La Risiera di San Sabba, which was primarily a police detention camp. Some Jews were deported from San Sabba and several dozen Jews were killed there. Mantua, Milan, and Borgo San Dalmazzo were other assembly points for Jews during the deportations from Italy.

During the German occupation, about 8,000 Jews were deported from Italy to Auschwitz-Birkenau and other Nazi camps. Almost 2,000 Jews were deported from Rhodes, an Aegean Sea island that had been part of Italy before the war. About 7,600 of those deported died.

Because Italian authorities obstructed the deportations and many Italian Jews were able to hide or escape southward to Allied-occupied areas of Italy, more than 40,000 Jews in Italy survived the Holocaust.

In late April 1945, Communist partisans captured and executed Mussolini. German forces in Italy surrendered to the Allies in early May 1945.

THE DEPORTATION OF THE JEWS IN ROME

At the time of the German occupation of northern and central Italy in 1943, there were approximately 12,000 Jews living in Rome. Under German occupation, Italian Jews became subject to the "Final Solution."

The Gestapo levied a ransom on the Jews of Rome, demanding about 110 pounds of gold in exchange for the safety of the Jewish community. Although the ransom was delivered in late September 1943, the Germans still planned to deport Rome's Jews. The SS confiscated the registry of Roman Jews, which had been kept by the Jewish community at Rome's main synagogue, and deportations began in mid-October 1943. Wherever they lived, Jews were seized by the SS and taken to a military college in the center of Rome. After several days, more than 1,000 Jews were deported to the Auschwitz-Birkenau killing center. Subsequent roundups

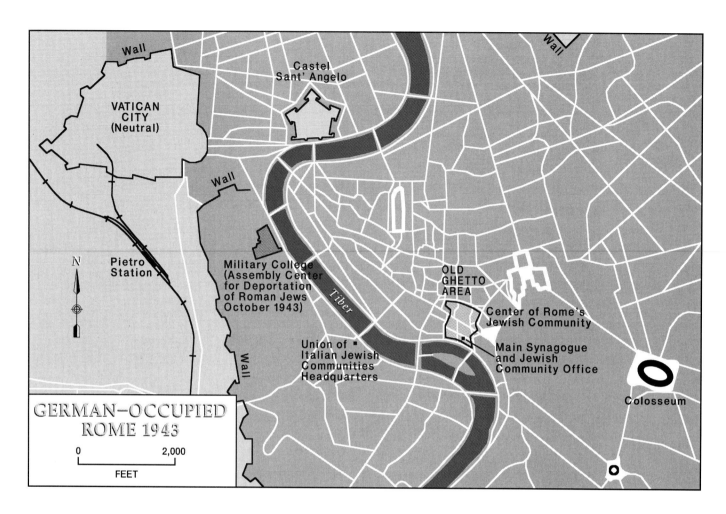

resulted in the arrest and deportation of about another 1,000 Roman Jews.

Because Italian police did not participate in these roundups and most Italians objected to the deportations, many Italian Jews were able to go into hiding. For every Jew caught by the Germans in Rome, at least 10 escaped and hid, many in the Vatican. Located in the heart of Rome, the Vatican was headed by Pius XII, pope of the Roman Catholic Church; it had the status of a neutral sovereign state. During the occupation, Germany recognized and respected the neutrality of the Vatican. While Pope Pius XII refrained from any public denunciation of German policy toward the Jews, Catholic institutions in Rome aided the Jews.

The Germans occupied Rome for nine months. American forces liberated the city on June 5, 1944, and Jews came out of hiding to participate in the liberation ceremony held at Rome's main synagogue.

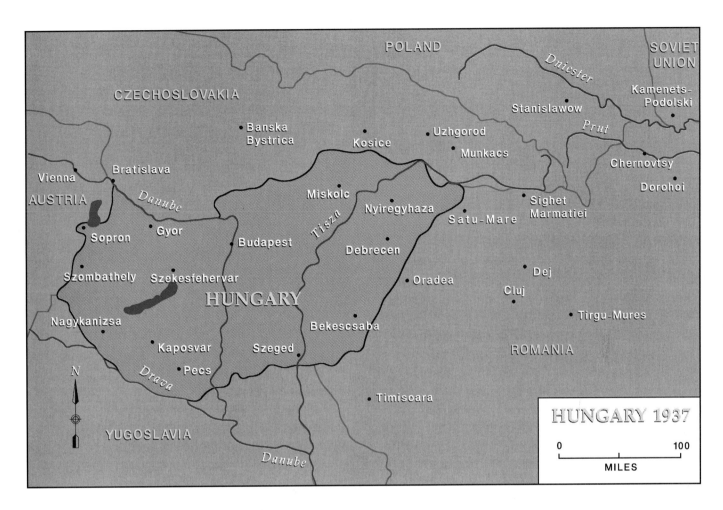

THE HOLOCAUST IN HUNGARY

Soon after World War I, Admiral Miklos Horthy came to power in Hungary, ruling as regent for the crown. In principle, Horthy ruled in the name of a monarchy with a vacant throne. In reality, Horthy was dictator.

During World War II, Horthy allied Hungary with Germany. Hungary joined the Axis alliance in November 1940, declaring war on the Soviet Union in June 1941 and on Great Britain and the United States in December 1941. Germany enticed and then rewarded Hungary with territory, which allowed it to expand greatly—at the expense of its neighbors. With German backing, Hungary received the Transcarpathian Ukraine and sections of southern Slovakia from Czechoslovakia (1938-39), northern Transylvania from Romania (1940), and the Backa region from Yugoslavia (1941). Hungarian forces participated fully in the war in the Balkans and on the eastern front.

According to a 1941 census, Hungary, including the annexed territories, had a Jewish population of about 825,000, less than 6 percent of the total Hungarian population. This figure included 100,000 converts to Christianity who, under race laws, were classified as Jews. Between 1938 and 1941,

Hungary had introduced antisemitic legislation resembling Germany's Nuremberg Laws. Jews, defined in racial terms, were removed from public life and from the economy. In 1939, Hungary drafted all adult Jewish men for forced-labor service and assigned them to war-related construction work. About 40,000 Hungarian Jews died in the labor-service brigades before the German occupation of Hungary in March 1944.

Horthy generally did not deport Hungarian Jews to German-held territory, where they would have been included in the "Final Solution." However, about 20,000 "foreign" Jews from the territories annexed to Hungary—especially the Transcarpathian Ukraine—were deported in July and August of 1941 to Kamenets-Podolski, in the German-occupied Ukraine, where they were shot by German Einsatzgruppen detachments. Those Jews remaining in Hungary were relatively secure from deportation.

After the German defeat in the battle of Stalingrad of 1942-1943, and with Hungarian war casualties increasing, Horthy recognized that Germany would probably lose the war. He attempted to negotiate an armistice with the Allies. In response, German forces occupied Hungary on March 19,

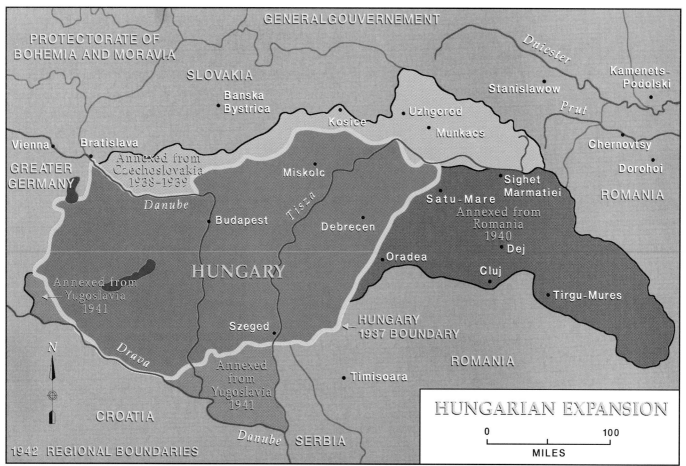

HUNGARIAN EXPANSION

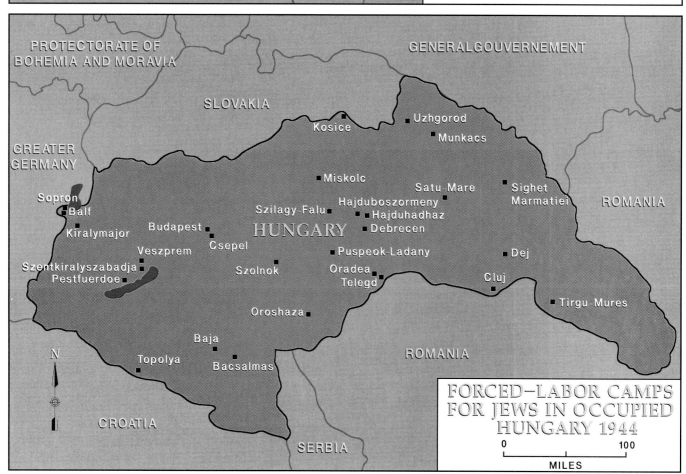

FORCED—LABOR CAMPS FOR JEWS IN OCCUPIED HUNGARY 1944

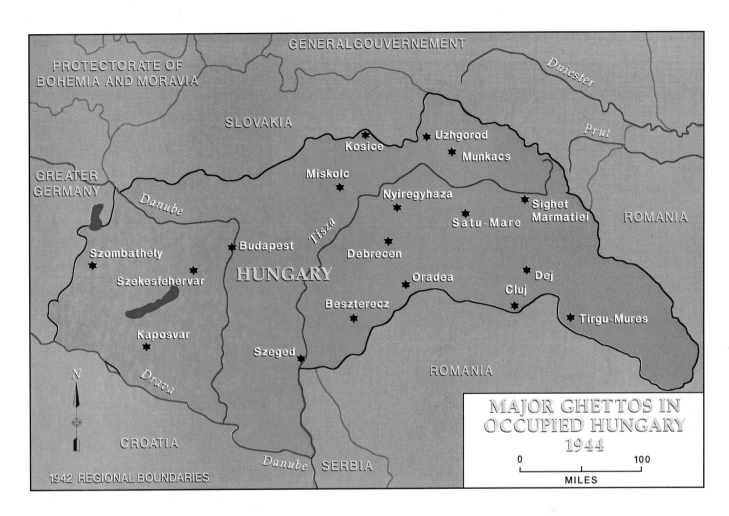

MAJOR GHETTOS IN OCCUPIED HUNGARY 1944

1944, preventing such an armistice. Horthy remained as regent, but the Germans installed a pro-German government under Dome Sztojay. Sztojay committed Hungary to continuing the war against the Soviet Union and cooperated with Germany in the deportation of Jews in Hungary.

In April 1944, all Jews except those in Budapest were ordered into ghettos. Jews from the rural areas were sent to ghettos in Hungary's larger cities. The ghettos were enclosed areas, sometimes in a city's Jewish quarter, or in a nearby factory. In some places, Jews were compelled to live outdoors, without shelter or sanitary facilities. Jews were not permitted to leave the ghetto, and Hungarian police guarded its perimeter. Often, Jews were tortured and forced to turn over valuables to the Hungarian police. As in Poland, ghettoization was generally a temporary measure—but in this case for a matter of weeks, not months or years. Systematic deportations from the ghettos to Auschwitz-Birkenau began the next month, in May 1944.

Adolf Eichmann, the SS officer responsible for organizing the deportations, led a team of German specialists that worked with the Hungarians. The Hungarian police participated fully in the roundups. In less than three months,

nearly 440,000 Jews were deported from Hungary in more than 140 trains. By then, the only remaining Jewish community in Hungary was in Budapest, the capital.

Under Allied pressure and in light of the deteriorating military situation, Horthy halted the deportations of Jews from Hungary to Auschwitz-Birkenau, and in August 1944 dismissed Sztojay's government. In October 1944, Horthy accepted terms for an armistice with the Soviet Union. Before the armistice was signed, the Germans arrested Horthy, took him to Germany, and installed a new Hungarian government dominated by the Hungarian fascist Arrow Cross. Under Ferenc Szalasi, the Arrow Cross regime began a reign of terror, especially against the Jews in Budapest.

Before the Arrow Cross regime, the Jews of Budapest, traditionally Hungary's largest Jewish community, had remained virtually untouched by ghettoization and deportations. Under the Arrow Cross, the killing of Jews in Budapest was a daily occurrence. Thousands of victims were taken to the banks of the Danube, shot, and thrown in the river. More than 70,000 Jews, most of them women, were forced on a death march to Austria, where they were used as forced laborers in Nazi concentration camps and in the construction

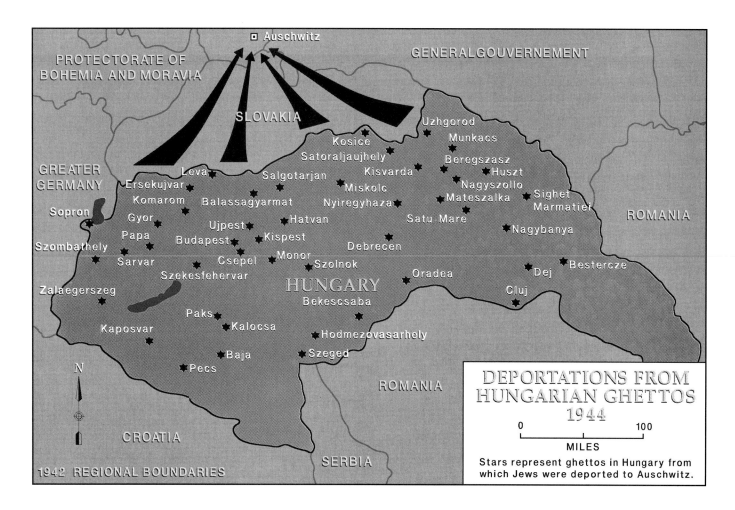

DEPORTATIONS FROM
HUNGARIAN GHETTOS
1944

0   100

MILES

Stars represent ghettos in Hungary from
which Jews were deported to Auschwitz.

of fortifications around Vienna. As the Soviets approached Budapest, the Nazis ordered 70,000 Jews into a ghetto, where thousands died as a result of poor conditions.

Yet there were rescue attempts. Diplomat Raoul Wallenberg of neutral Sweden and other representatives of neutral states were able to rescue many thousands of Jews from the Arrow Cross and the Germans. These diplomats issued false citizenship papers and protective passes to save the Jews from deportation.

In January 1945, Hungary signed an armistice with the Soviet Union. Soviet forces liberated Budapest in February, and by early April all German troops had been forced out of Hungary.

Of the more than 800,000 Jews living in Hungary, more than 60,000 were killed before the German occupation. Almost 620,000 Jews living in Hungary died or were deported or killed before the liberation of Hungary in early 1945. At liberation, about 140,000 Jews remained in Hungary, mostly in Budapest under the protection of a neutral power.

BUDAPEST

Hungary's capital, Budapest, straddles both banks of the

Danube River and is the country's most populous city. Budapest was created by the union of three cities: Buda, Obuda, and Pest.

Before World War II, approximately 200,000 Jews lived in Budapest, making it the center of Hungarian Jewish cultural life. In the late 1930s and early 1940s, Budapest was a safe haven for Jewish refugees. Before the war some 5,000 refugees, primarily from Germany and Austria, arrived in Budapest. With the beginning of deportations of Jews from Slovakia in March 1942, as many as 8,000 Slovak Jewish refugees also settled in Budapest.

Despite discriminatory legislation against the Jews and widespread antisemitism, the Jewish community of Budapest was relatively secure until the German occupation of Hungary in March 1944. With the occupation, the Germans ordered the establishment of a Jewish council in Budapest and severely restricted Jewish life. Hundreds of apartments occupied by Jews were confiscated. Hundreds of Jews were rounded up and interned in the Kistarcsa transit camp, 15 miles northeast of Budapest.

Between April and July 1944, the Germans rounded up and deported Jews from the Hungarian provinces. By the end

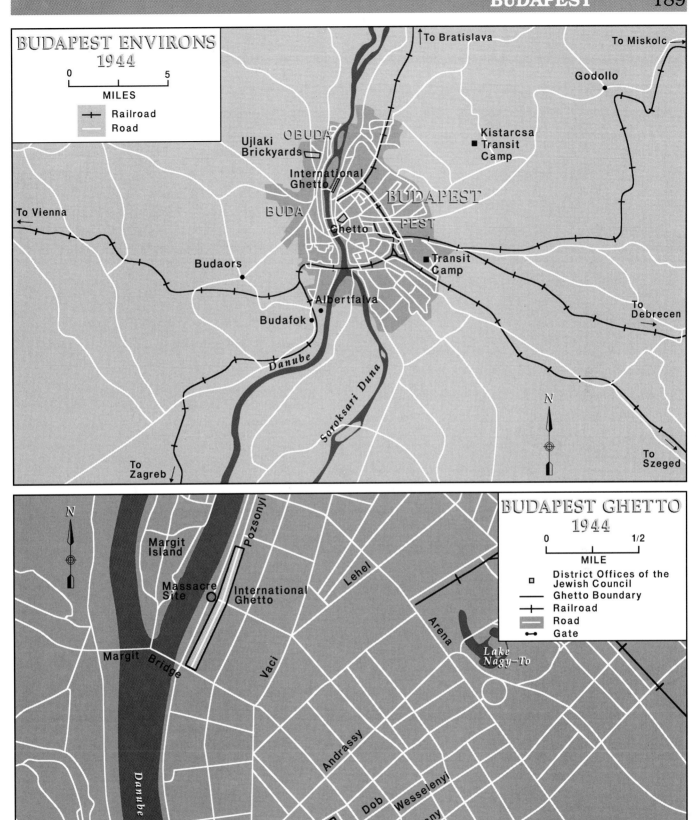

BUDAPEST ENVIRONS 1944

0 — 5
MILES

—†— Railroad
Road

To Bratislava
To Miskolc

Godollo

OBUDA

Ujlaki
Brickyards

Kistarcsa
Transit
Camp

International
Ghetto

BUDAPEST

BUDA

PEST

To Vienna

Ghetto

Transit
Camp

Budaors

Albertfalva

Budafok

To Debrecen

Danube

Soroksari Duna

N

To Zagreb

To Szeged

BUDAPEST GHETTO 1944

0 — 1/2
MILE

▫ District Offices of the
Jewish Council
— Ghetto Boundary
—†— Railroad
Road
•—• Gate

N

Margit
Island

Pozsonyi

Massacre
Site

International
Ghetto

Lehel

Margit Bridge

Vaci

Arena

*Lake
Nagy-To*

Danube

Andrassy

Dob

Wesselenyi

Dohany

Massacre
Site

Kiraly

Ghetto

Mosonyi

Police
Headquarters

Szechenyi
Bridge

Karoly

Rakoczi

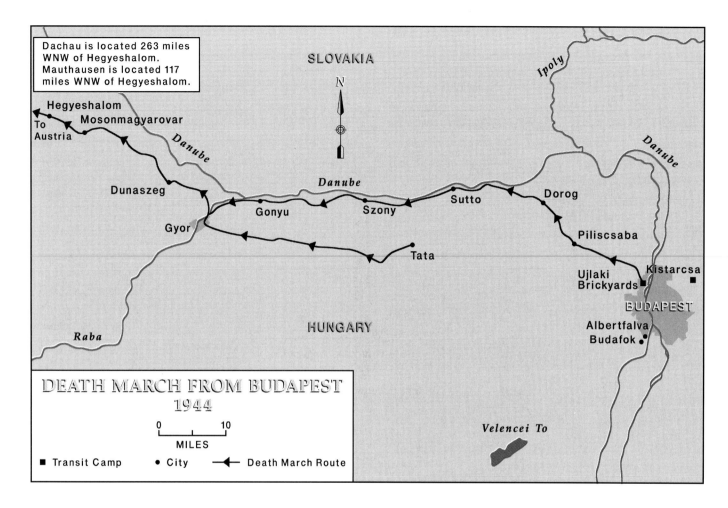

Dachau is located 263 miles WNW of Hegyeshalom. Mauthausen is located 117 miles WNW of Hegyeshalom.

SLOVAKIA

N

DEATH MARCH FROM BUDAPEST
1944

0   10
MILES

■ Transit Camp   ● City   ◄── Death March Route

of July, the Jews in Budapest were the only Jews remaining in Hungary. They were not immediately ghettoized. Instead, in June 1944, Hungarian authorities ordered the Jews into over 2,000 designated buildings scattered throughout the city. The buildings were marked with Stars of David. Further, about 25,000 Jews from the suburbs of Budapest were rounded up and deported to the Auschwitz-Birkenau killing center. Hungarian authorities suspended the deportations in July 1944, sparing the remaining Jews of Budapest, at least temporarily.

Many Jews searched for places of hiding or for protection, should the deportations be renewed. They were aided by the Swedish diplomat Raoul Wallenberg and other diplomats who organized false papers and safe houses for them. These actions saved tens of thousands of Jews.

In October 1944, Germany installed a new Hungarian government dominated by the Hungarian fascist Arrow Cross. The remaining Jews of Budapest were again in grave danger. The Arrow Cross instituted a reign of terror in Budapest. Jews were drafted for forced labor, fortifying the city. Hundreds of Jews were shot.

On November 8, the Hungarians concentrated more than 70,000 Jews—men, women, and children—in the Ujlaki brickyards in Obuda, and from there forced them on a death march to camps in Austria. Thousands were shot along the way and thousands more died as a result of starvation or exposure to the bitter cold. The prisoners who survived the death march reached Austria in late December 1944. There, the Germans took them to various concentration camps, especially Dachau in southern Germany and Mauthausen in northern Austria, and to Vienna, where they were employed in the construction of fortifications around the city.

In November 1944, the Arrow Cross ordered the remaining Jews in Budapest into a closed ghetto. Jews who did not have protective papers issued by a neutral power were to move to the ghetto by early December. Between December 1944 and the end of January 1945, the Arrow Cross took as many as 20,000 Jews from the ghetto, shot them along the banks of the Danube, and threw their bodies into the river.

Soviet forces liberated Budapest on February 13, 1945. More than 100,000 Jews remained in the city at liberation.

RESCUE AND JEWISH ARMED RESISTANCE

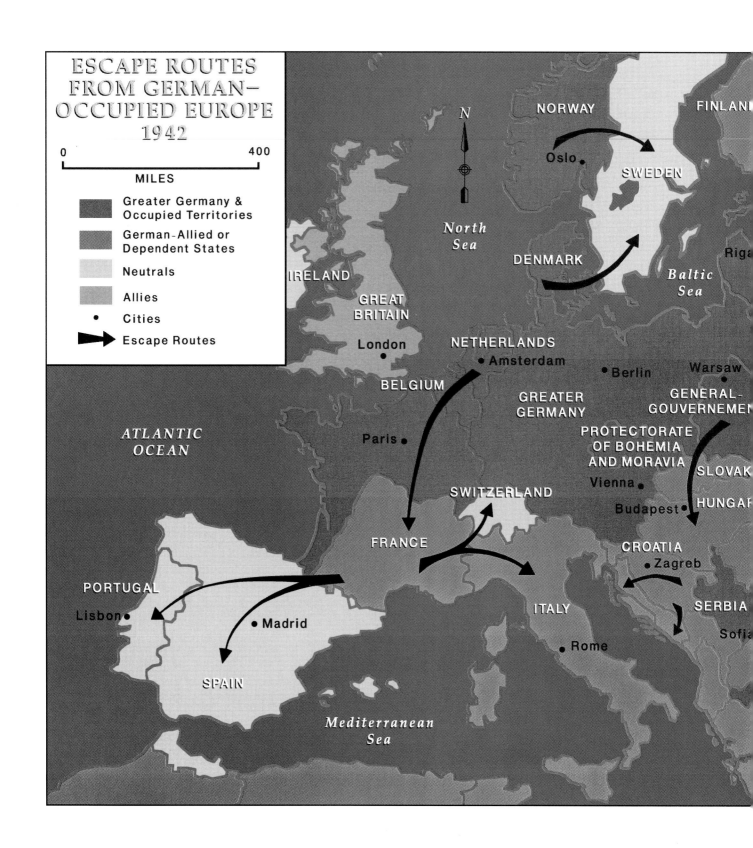

ESCAPE ROUTES
FROM GERMAN-
OCCUPIED EUROPE
1942

0   400
MILES

Greater Germany &
Occupied Territories

German-Allied or
Dependent States

Neutrals

Allies

• Cities

➤ Escape Routes

Fleeing Advancing
German Forces
1941–1942

Moscow

SOVIET
UNION

OSTLAND

•Rovno

UKRAINE

ROMANIA

•Bucharest   Black Sea

BULGARIA

TURKEY

To Palestine

RESCUE AND ESCAPE

At its height, German-occupied Europe extended from the Pyrenees Mountains in the west to the city of Stalingrad on the Volga in the east; from the Arctic reaches of Norway in the north to the desert sands of Egypt in the south. Throughout most of German-occupied Europe, the Germans sought to round up and deport Jews to killing centers in occupied Poland. Some survived the "Final Solution" by hiding or escaping from German-controlled Europe.

Most non-Jews neither aided nor hindered the "Final Solution." Relatively few people helped Jews escape. Those who did aid Jews were motivated by opposition to Nazi racism, by compassion, or by religious or moral principle. In a few rare instances, entire communities as well as individuals helped save Jews from the Nazis. They did so at tremendous risk. In many places, providing shelter to Jews was punishable by death.

Between 1941 and 1944, the residents of Le Chambon-sur-Lignon, a Protestant village in southern France, helped thousands of refugees, including about 5,000 Jews, escape Nazi persecution. Though the villagers' actions placed them in grave danger, they were resolute, inspired by religious conviction and a sense of moral duty. Refugees were hidden in private homes throughout the community. Nearby Catholic convents and monasteries also provided shelter. Beginning in 1943, the townspeople also helped smuggle refugees to neutral Switzerland.

Some escape routes out of occupied Europe led to belligerent states (such as the Soviet Union), neutral states (such as Switzerland, Spain, Sweden, and Turkey), and even to states allied with Germany (such as Italy and Hungary before they were occupied by Germany).

Between 1939 and 1941 nearly 300,000 Polish Jews, almost 10 percent of the entire Polish-Jewish population, fled German-held western Poland and crossed into Soviet-occupied Poland. Soviet authorities deported tens of thousands of Jews from Poland and the Baltic states to Siberia far to the east. Although these Jews faced extreme hardship, remaining in the Soviet Union meant that they survived the "Final Solution." After the German attack on the Soviet

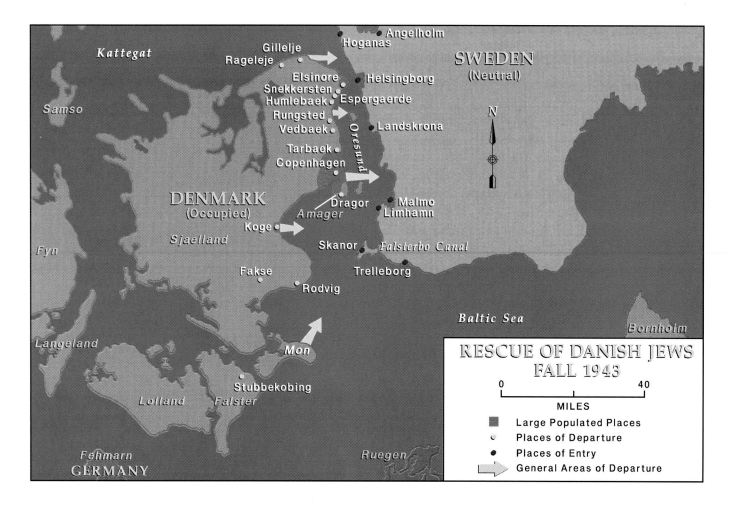

RESCUE OF DANISH JEWS
FALL 1943

0   40
MILES
■ Large Populated Places
◦ Places of Departure
● Places of Entry
⇨ General Areas of Departure

Union, more than a million Soviet Jews escaped eastward, fleeing the advancing German army and again avoiding almost certain death.

During World War II, close to 30,000 Jews managed to enter neutral Switzerland. Although most were interned in Swiss detention camps, thousands more were turned back into German-occupied territory. Tens of thousands of Jews escaped to Spain and Portugal. Spain usually permitted refugees escaping from France, many of whom came across the Pyrenees Mountains, to enter the country. However, it sought to ensure the immediate emigration of Jewish refugees to other countries. Most Jews who escaped to Spain continued on to the Portuguese port of Lisbon, hoping to leave from there for other countries of refuge. Thousands went on to the United States.

In the north, neutral Sweden provided sanctuary for Jews fleeing German-occupied Denmark and Norway. More than 7,000 Danish Jews fled from Denmark to Sweden in October 1943.

Thousands of Jews managed to leave Black Sea ports in Bulgaria and Romania. To reach Palestine, their ultimate destination, the boats needed to refuel in Turkish ports.

Turkey, however, sought to prevent these boats from using its ports and Jews from entering Turkey. Thus, Turkish policy was an obstacle to the rescue of Jews and ultimately led to tragedy. The most poignant instance was the sinking, off the Turkish coast, of the *Struma*, one of the boats that carried refugees attempting to reach Palestine.

Italian forces protected Jews in the Italian occupation zones in Yugoslavia, Greece, and France, and avoided deporting Jews to German-occupied territory. Not until Germany occupied Italy and the Italian territories did Jews there become subject to deportation. Hungary tolerated the entry of Jewish refugees from neighboring Poland and Slovakia and generally did not deport Hungarian Jews to German-occupied territory. After the German occupation of Hungary in 1944, Jews there were subject to deportation.

THE RESCUE OF DANISH JEWS

When Germany occupied Denmark in 1940, the Jewish population was approximately 7,500. About 6,000 of them were Danish citizens and about 1,500 were Jewish refugees. Most of them lived in the country's capital, Copenhagen.

Until 1943, the German occupation of Denmark was

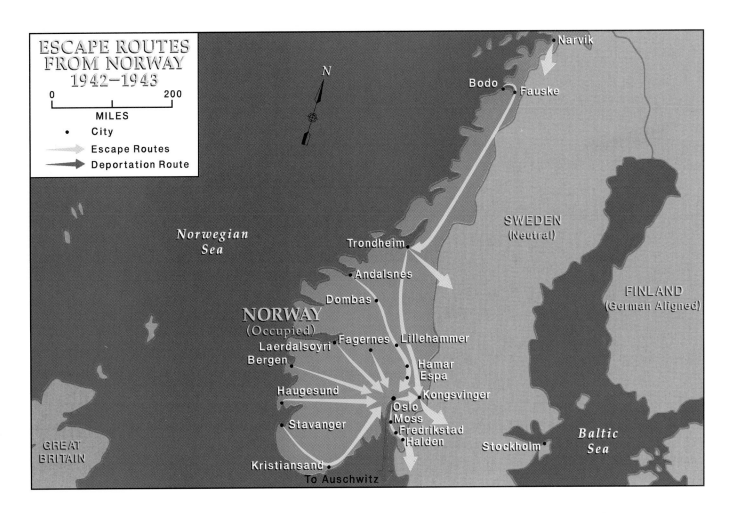

ESCAPE ROUTES
FROM NORWAY
1942–1943

0   200
MILES
•   City
    Escape Routes
    Deportation Route

N

Norwegian
Sea

Narvik

Bodo   Fauske

SWEDEN
(Neutral)

FINLAND
(German Aligned)

Trondheim

Andalsnes

Dombas

NORWAY
(Occupied)

Fagernes Lillehammer

Laerdalsoyri
Bergen

Hamar
Espa

Haugesund

Kongsvinger

Oslo
Moss

Stavanger

Fredrikstad
Halden

Stockholm

Baltic
Sea

GREAT
BRITAIN

Kristiansand

To Auschwitz

relatively benign. The Danish government continued to rule the country, but Germany dominated Danish foreign policy. Considering the relatively small Jewish population and the steadfast support Danes gave to their fellow Jewish citizens, Germany decided not to make a major issue of the "Jewish question" in Denmark.

The situation changed dramatically in 1943. Allied victories convinced some Danes that Germany could be defeated and they decided to resist the Germans. Strikes and acts of sabotage strained relations with Germany. The Danish government resigned in August 1943 rather than yield to new German demands to halt the resistance. When the Germans decided to deport Jews from Denmark, a German officer leaked word of the planned deportations and the Danes informed the Jewish community.

German police began arresting Jews in early October 1943, without the help of the Danish police, who refused to cooperate. Danes spontaneously organized a rescue operation and helped Jews reach the coast; fishermen then ferried them to neutral Sweden. The rescue operation expanded to include participation by the Danish resistance, the police, and the government. In little more than three weeks, the Danes ferried

more than 7,000 Jews and close to 700 of their non-Jewish relatives to Sweden, which accepted the Danish refugees.

The Germans seized about 500 Jews in Denmark and deported them to the Theresienstadt ghetto in Bohemia. The Danes demanded information on their whereabouts and Danish government officials visited them in the summer of 1944. Danish Jews remained in Theresienstadt until 1945. As the war ended, the Germans handed them over to the Swedish Red Cross. The vigor of Danish protests perhaps prevented their deportation to the killing centers in occupied Poland.

NORWEGIAN JEWRY IN THE HOLOCAUST

There were approximately 1,700 Jews in Norway, part of Scandinavia, when Germany invaded in April 1940. This included several hundred foreign Jews who had found refuge in Norway in the 1930s.

Mass arrests of Jews began in the fall of 1942. Norwegian police assisted the SS units assigned to round up Jews. In early October, all male Jews in Trondheim, a major Norwegian city, were arrested. In October and November 1942, Jews were arrested in Oslo, Norway's capital. Those caught by the Germans were interned in camps throughout

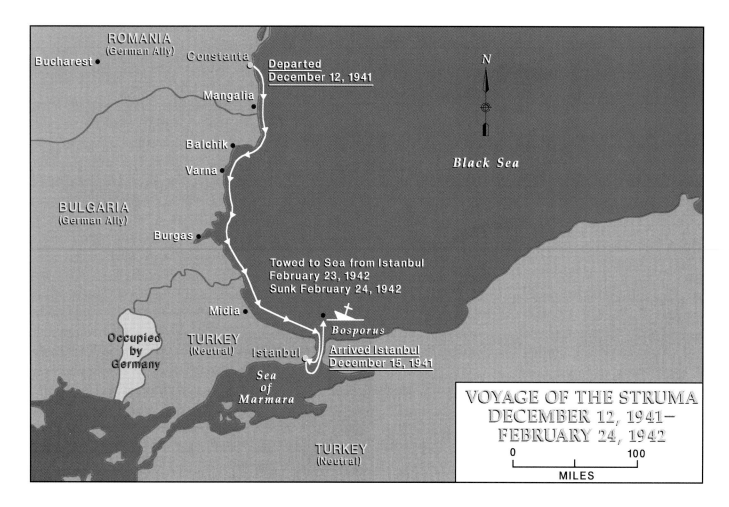

ROMANIA
(German Ally)
Bucharest •
Constanta
Departed
December 12, 1941
Mangalia •
N
Balchik •
Varna •
Black Sea
BULGARIA
(German Ally)
Burgas •
Towed to Sea from Istanbul
February 23, 1942
Sunk February 24, 1942
Midia •
Bosporus
Occupied
by
Germany
TURKEY
(Neutral)   Istanbul
Arrived Istanbul
December 15, 1941
Sea of Marmara
TURKEY
(Neutral)

VOYAGE OF THE STRUMA
DECEMBER 12, 1941–
FEBRUARY 24, 1942
0   100
MILES

southern Norway and then deported to the Auschwitz-Birkenau killing center. Many Jews, however, received warnings of the roundups from Norwegian policemen and members of the underground. The Norwegian underground helped about 900 Jews escape to neutral Sweden. Many others went into hiding. Despite the protests of Norwegian church leaders and the Norwegian population, the deportation of Jews from Norway continued sporadically.

Between 1940 and 1945, the Germans deported more than 750 Jews from Norway; only about 25 returned after the war. The others died in Auschwitz. In early May 1945, German forces in Norway surrendered to the Allies and a civilian Norwegian government was restored.

THE SINKING OF THE *STRUMA*

The Romanian port of Constanta, on the Black Sea, was a major embarkation point for Jews attempting to leave Europe for Palestine. Thousands of Jews, desperate to escape the Germans, took the route by boat from Constanta via Turkey to

Palestine, despite British immigration restrictions. In December 1941, in Constanta, more than 750 Jews boarded a boat named the *Struma*. They planned to travel to Istanbul, apply for visas to Palestine, and then sail to Palestine. The *Struma* was unsafe and overcrowded, and lacked adequate sanitary facilities. Despite engine problems, it reached Istanbul. There, the passengers were informed they would not get visas to enter Palestine and, furthermore, would not be permitted entry into Turkey.

The boat was kept in quarantine in Istanbul's harbor for more than two months. Turkish authorities denied the passengers permission to land without British agreement to their continued journey to Palestine. On February 23, 1942, the Turkish police towed the boat out to sea and abandoned it. Within hours the boat sank. Although the cause of the sinking is not definitively known, it is assumed that it was mistakenly torpedoed by a Soviet submarine. Only one passenger survived. The sinking of the *Struma* led to widespread international protest against Britain's policy on immigration into Palestine.

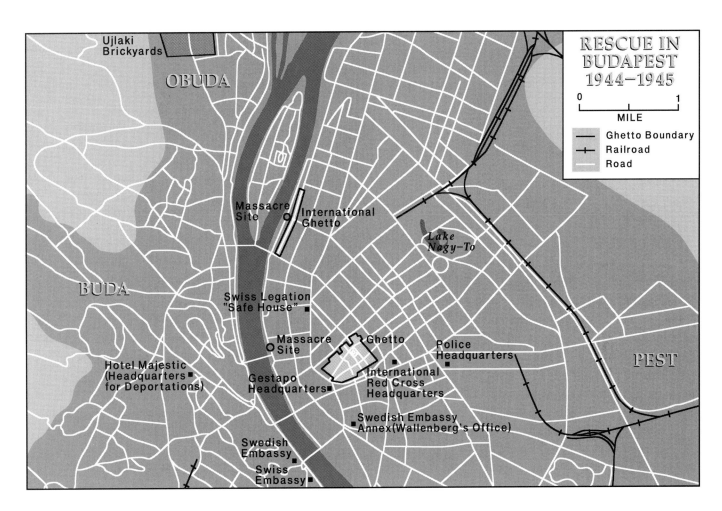

RESCUE IN BUDAPEST

Raoul Wallenberg led one of the most extensive and successful rescue efforts during the Holocaust. A Swedish diplomat, Wallenberg was assigned to the embassy in Budapest, Hungary. He worked with the United States War Refugee Board (WRB) and the World Jewish Congress to protect tens of thousands of Hungarian Jews from deportation to the Auschwitz-Birkenau killing center.

Hungary had been an ally of Germany, but German defeats and mounting Hungarian losses led Hungary to seek an armistice with the Soviet Union. German forces occupied Hungary in March 1944 to prevent Hungary from leaving the war and negotiating such an armistice. Shortly after the occupation, Germany began deporting Hungarian Jews to Auschwitz. By July 1944, the Germans had deported nearly 440,000 Jews from Hungary. Two hundred thousand Jews remained in Budapest, and they too faced deportation.

Wallenberg began distributing Swedish protective passports to the Jews in Budapest in July 1944. He established hospitals, nurseries, and a soup kitchen, and set up more than 30 safe houses that together formed the core of the international ghetto in Budapest. The international ghetto was reserved for those Jews and their families holding protective papers from a neutral country. In November 1944, during the death march of Hungarian Jews from Budapest to labor camps in Austria, Wallenberg secured the release of bearers of protective passports, and forged papers to save as many as possible.

Diplomats from other neutral countries joined the rescue effort. Carl Lutz, a Swiss diplomat, issued certificates of emigration so that nearly 50,000 Jews in Budapest were under Swiss protection as potential emigrants to Palestine. Italian businessman Giorgio Perlasca posed as a Spanish diplomat; he issued forged Spanish visas and established safe houses, including one for Jewish children. When Soviet forces liberated Budapest in February 1945, more than 100,000 Jews remained, mostly because of the efforts of Wallenberg and his colleagues.

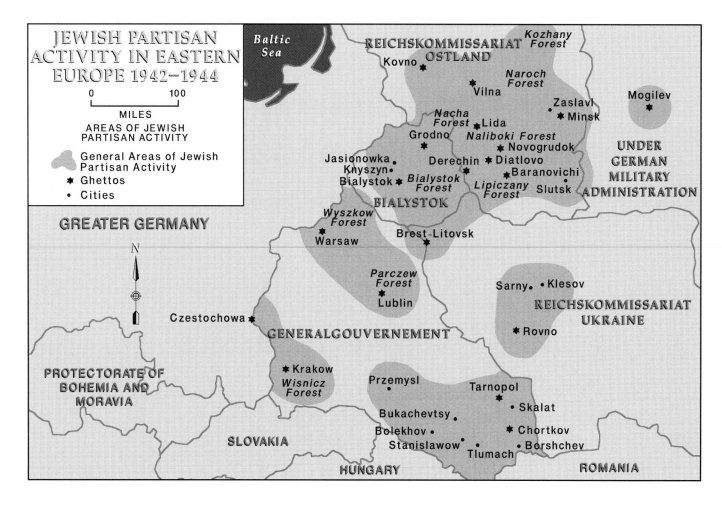

JEWISH PARTISAN
ACTIVITY IN EASTERN
EUROPE 1942–1944

0   100
MILES
AREAS OF JEWISH
PARTISAN ACTIVITY

General Areas of Jewish
Partisan Activity
★ Ghettos
• Cities

JEWISH ARMED RESISTANCE
IN OCCUPIED EUROPE

Despite enormous obstacles, many Jews throughout German-occupied Europe attempted armed resistance against the Germans. Individual Jews or groups of Jews engaged in planned or spontaneous opposition to the Germans and their allies. Jewish partisan units operated in France, Belgium, the Ukraine, Belorussia, Lithuania, and Poland. Large numbers of Jews also fought in non-Jewish French, Italian, Yugoslav, Greek, and Soviet resistance organizations.

Jewish partisans were especially active in the east, where they fought the Germans from bases established behind the front lines in the forests and ghettos. Because antisemitism was widespread, they found little support among the surrounding population. Even so, as many as 20,000 Jews fought the Germans in the forests of eastern Europe.

Jews from Minsk, for example, established seven different partisan units. Thousands of Jews escaped from ghettos such as Bialystok, Kovno, Riga, and Vilna and joined partisan groups operating in the nearby forests. In Krakow, Jewish fighters used the ghetto as a base from which to attack targets throughout Krakow city. Their most important attack was at the Cyganeria cafe, which was frequented by German officers.

Thousands of Jews—including whole families with women and children—took refuge in the extensive forests of eastern Europe. Jewish partisans established camps for non-combatants deep in the forests and swamps surrounding major Jewish population centers. These camps were mostly located in western Belorussia (in the Naliboki Forest) and in the western Ukraine, but also in eastern Poland. In 1943, many of the camps became bases for Soviet partisan operations. Jewish civilians repaired weapons, made clothing, and cooked for the fighters. As many as 10,000 Jews survived the war by taking refuge with Jewish partisan units.

In western Europe, Jewish partisans were particularly active in France. The "Jewish Army," a French Jewish partisan group, was founded in Toulouse in January 1942 and operated especially in Toulouse, Nice, Lyon, and Paris. Members of the "Jewish Army" smuggled millions of francs from Switzerland into France to distribute to Jewish relief organizations. This money helped thousands of Jews who had gone into hiding. The "Jewish Army" assassinated some

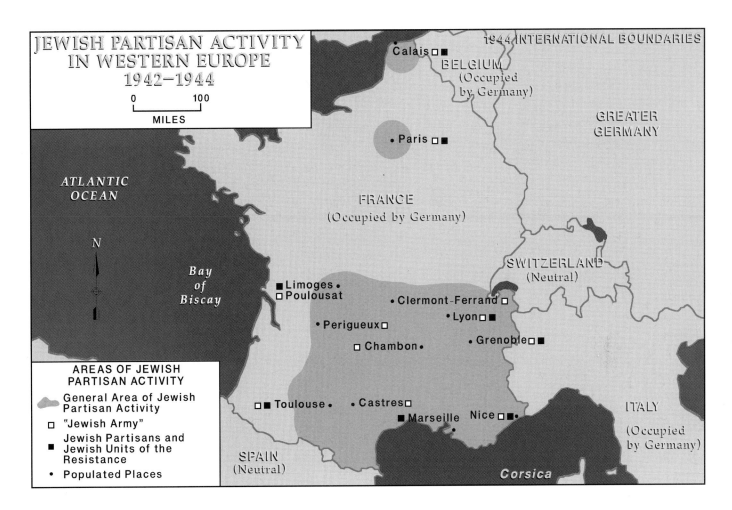

JEWISH PARTISAN ACTIVITY
IN WESTERN EUROPE
1942–1944

0   100
MILES

1944 INTERNATIONAL BOUNDARIES

• Calais □ ■

BELGIUM
(Occupied
by Germany)

GREATER
GERMANY

ATLANTIC
OCEAN

N

Bay
of
Biscay

• Paris □ ■

FRANCE
(Occupied by Germany)

SWITZERLAND
(Neutral)

■ Limoges •
□ Poulousat

• Clermont-Ferrand □

• Lyon □ ■

• Perigueux □

□ Chambon •

• Grenoble □ ■

AREAS OF JEWISH
PARTISAN ACTIVITY

General Area of Jewish
Partisan Activity

□   "Jewish Army"

■   Jewish Partisans and
Jewish Units of the
Resistance

•   Populated Places

□ ■ Toulouse •

• Castres □

■ Marseille   Nice □ ■ •

ITALY
(Occupied
by Germany)

SPAIN
(Neutral)

Corsica

of those who collaborated with the Germans and safely smuggled about 500 Jews and non-Jews alike across the border into neutral Spain. "Jewish Army" units also took part in the 1944 uprisings against the Germans in Paris, Lyon, and Toulouse.

A partisan group of Jews and non-Jews assassinated a collaborationist general in the Netherlands. In Belgium, a Jewish and Belgian partisan group ("Solidarity") derailed a deportation train in April 1943.

Organized armed resistance was the most direct form of Jewish opposition to the Nazis. In many areas of German-occupied Europe, Jewish resistance instead focused on aid, rescue, and spiritual resistance. The preservation of Jewish cultural institutions and the continuance of religious observance were acts of spiritual resistance to the Nazi policy of genocide.

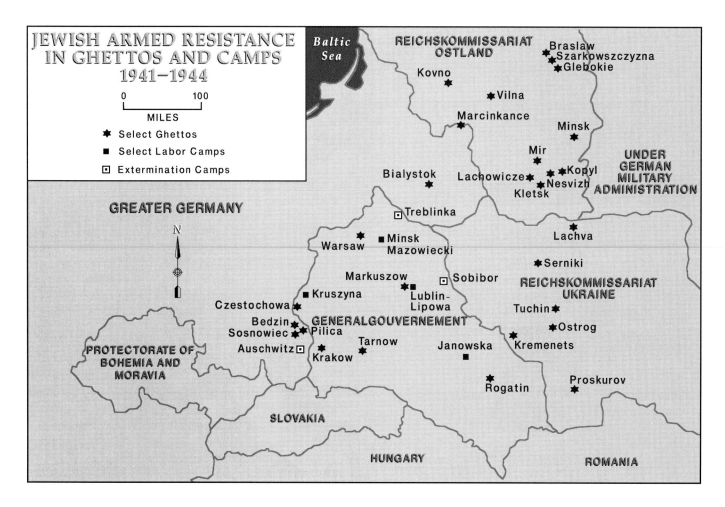

JEWISH ARMED RESISTANCE IN GHETTOS AND CAMPS 1941–1944

0   100
MILES

★ Select Ghettos
■ Select Labor Camps
☐ Extermination Camps

JEWISH RESISTANCE IN GHETTOS AND CAMPS

Between 1941 and 1943, underground resistance movements developed in about 100 Jewish ghettos in Nazi-occupied eastern Europe, especially in Poland, Lithuania, Belorussia, and the Ukraine. Their main goals were to organize uprisings, break out of the ghettos, and join partisan units in the fight against the Germans.

The Jews knew that uprisings would not stop the Germans and that only a handful of fighters would succeed in escaping to join with partisans. Still, Jews made the decision to resist. The ghettos of Vilna, Mir, Lachva, Kremenets, Czestochowa, Nesvizh, Sosnowiec, and Tarnow, among others, rebelled when the Germans announced deportations. In Bialystok, the underground staged an uprising just prior to the final destruction of the ghetto in September 1943. Most of the ghetto fighters, who were young men and women, died during the fighting.

The Warsaw ghetto uprising in the spring of 1943 was the largest single revolt by Jews. Hundreds of Jews fought the Germans and their Ukrainian auxiliaries in the streets of the ghetto. Thousands of Jews refused to obey German orders to

report to an assembly point for deportation. In the end the Nazis burned the ghetto to the ground to force the Jews out. Although they knew defeat was certain, Jews in the ghetto fought desperately and valiantly.

Under the most adverse conditions, Jewish prisoners succeeded in initiating resistance and uprisings in some Nazi concentration camps, and even in the killing centers of Treblinka, Sobibor, and Auschwitz. About 1,000 Jewish prisoners took part in the revolt in Treblinka. On August 2, 1943, they seized what weapons they could find—picks, axes, and some firearms stolen from the camp armory—and set fire to the camp. About 200 managed to escape. The Germans recaptured and killed about half of them almost immediately.

On October 14, 1943, prisoners in Sobibor killed 11 SS guards and set the camp on fire. About 300 prisoners escaped, breaking through the barbed wire and risking their lives in the minefield surrounding the camp. Over 100 were recaptured and later shot.

On October 7, 1944, prisoners assigned to Crematorium IV at Auschwitz-Birkenau rebelled after learning that the Germans were going to kill them. During the uprising, the prisoners killed three guards and blew up the crematoria and connecting

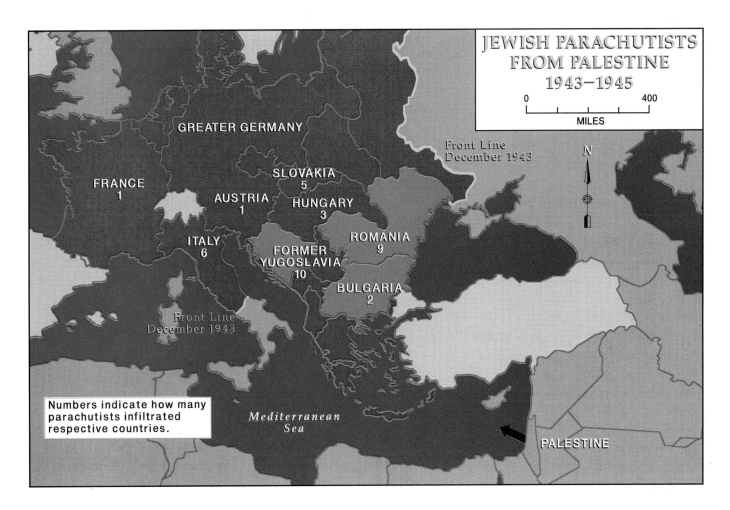

JEWISH PARACHUTISTS
FROM PALESTINE
1943–1945

0   400
MILES

GREATER GERMANY

Front Line
December 1943

N

FRANCE
1

SLOVAKIA
5

AUSTRIA
1

HUNGARY
3

ITALY
6

ROMANIA
9

FORMER
YUGOSLAVIA
10

BULGARIA
2

Front Line
December 1943

Numbers indicate how many
parachutists infiltrated
respective countries.

Mediterranean
Sea

PALESTINE

gas chamber. The prisoners used explosives smuggled into the camp by Jewish women who had been assigned to forced labor in a nearby armaments factory. The Germans crushed the revolt and killed almost all the several hundred prisoners involved in the rebellion. The Jewish women who had smuggled the explosives into the camp were hanged.

Other camp uprisings took place in the Kruszyna (1942), Minsk Mazowiecki (1943), and Janowska (1943) camps. In several dozen camps prisoners organized escapes to join partisan units. Successful escapes occurred, for example, from the Lublin-Lipowa camp.

JEWISH PARACHUTISTS FROM PALESTINE

Between 1943 and 1945, a select group of Jewish men and women from Palestine who had volunteered to join the British army parachuted into German-occupied Europe. Their mission was to organize resistance to the Germans and aid in the rescue of Allied personnel. Of the 250 original volunteers, 110 underwent training. Thirty-two eventually parachuted into Europe and five infiltrated the target countries by other routes. Most of those selected for training were emigres from Europe, with intimate knowledge of the countries to which they would be sent.

Three of the parachutists infiltrated Hungary, five participated in the Slovak national uprising, and six operated in northern Italy. Ten parachutists served with the British liaison missions to the Yugoslav partisans. Nine parachutists operated in Romania. Two others entered Bulgaria, and one each operated in France and Austria.

The Germans captured 12 and executed 7 of the 37 parachutists sent into occupied Europe. Three of those executed were captured in Slovakia. Two were captured in Hungary and one in northern Italy. The Jewish parachutist who entered France was captured and killed after seven missions.

Hannah Szenes, one of the most well-known of the parachutists, was seized in German-occupied Hungary and executed in Budapest in November 1944, at the age of 23. Szenes was a talented poet and her songs are still sung in Israel.

After the war, remains of the seven parachutists who lost their lives during the war, including Szenes, were interred in the National Military Cemetery overlooking Jerusalem in Israel.

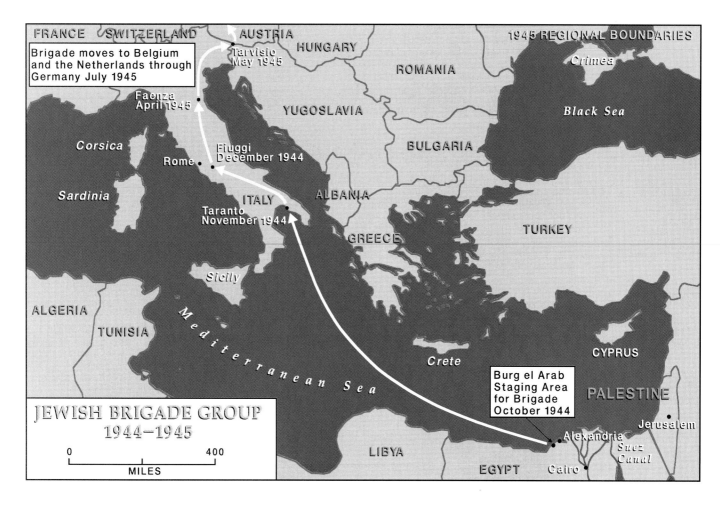

FRANCE   SWITZERLAND   AUSTRIA   HUNGARY

Brigade moves to Belgium
and the Netherlands through
Germany July 1945

Tarvisio
May 1945

1945 REGIONAL BOUNDARIES

Crimea

ROMANIA

Black Sea

Faenza
April 1945

YUGOSLAVIA

BULGARIA

Corsica

Fiuggi
December 1944

Rome

Sardinia

ITALY

ALBANIA

TURKEY

Taranto
November 1944

GREECE

Sicily

Mediterranean Sea

ALGERIA

TUNISIA

Crete

CYPRUS

Burg el Arab
Staging Area
for Brigade
October 1944

PALESTINE

Jerusalem

JEWISH BRIGADE GROUP
1944–1945

0   400
MILES

Alexandria

Suez
Canal

LIBYA

EGYPT   Cairo

THE JEWISH BRIGADE GROUP

In light of opposition to a Jewish homeland in Palestine, the British were at first reluctant to establish, in the framework of the British army, a fighting unit of Jewish volunteers from Palestine. However, the requirements of war led to the formation of Palestinian Jewish units incorporated into the British army as early as September 1940. Many Jews volunteered to serve, and demanded to be transferred to the front. Over 30,000 Jewish volunteers from Palestine served with the British army during the war. Of these, more than 700 were killed on active duty.

The Jewish Brigade Group, the only Jewish unit in the British army to fight under the Jewish flag, was formed in September 1944. It included more than 5,000 Jewish volunteers from Palestine who were organized into three infantry battalions and supporting units. The Jewish Brigade Group fought against the Germans in Italy from March 1945 until the end of the war in May 1945. About 30 soldiers were killed in action and about 70 were wounded.

After Germany's surrender, the Brigade was stationed along the Italian border with Austria and Yugoslavia, and later in Belgium and the Netherlands. Some soldiers from the Brigade helped organize displaced persons' camps for Jewish survivors of the Holocaust. Others became involved in organizing the flight of Jewish refugees from eastern Europe and in the "illegal" immigration of Jews to Palestine. Some soldiers also acquired arms for the Hagana, a Jewish underground organization in Palestine. Britain disbanded the Jewish Brigade Group in the summer of 1946.

DEATH MARCHES AND LIBERATION

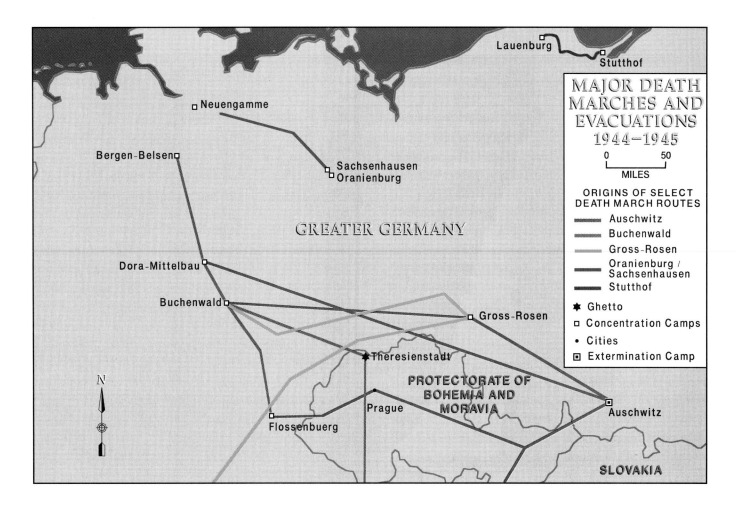

THE EVACUATION OF NAZI CAMPS AND THE DEATH MARCHES OF PRISONERS

In January 1945, the Third Reich stood on the verge of military defeat. Soviet forces stretched across eastern Europe from the cities of Tilsit in the north, Warsaw in the center, and Budapest in the south. After the failure of the surprise German offensive through the Ardennes in December 1944, Allied forces in the west were poised for the invasion of Germany. As Allied forces approached Nazi camps, the SS organized death marches of concentration camp inmates.

The term "death march" was probably coined by concentration camp prisoners. It referred to forced marches of concentration camp prisoners over long distances under heavy guard and extremely harsh conditions. During death marches, SS guards brutally mistreated the prisoners and killed many. Death marches were held throughout the war but were especially common between 1944 and 1945, as the Nazis attempted to prevent significant numbers of prisoners from

falling into the hands of the advancing Allied armies. The largest death marches were launched from Auschwitz and Stutthof. There was also a large death march from the Hungarian city of Budapest.

Soviet forces were the first to reach a major camp, the Majdanek camp near Lublin, Poland, in July 1944. The rapid Soviet advance surprised the Germans, who attempted to demolish the camp in order to destroy evidence of mass murder. However, in the hurry to evacuate the camp, the gas chambers were left standing. Liberated prisoners testified about Nazi crimes before hastily formed tribunals.

In mid-January 1945, the Soviet army began a major offensive into central Poland. Soviet forces advanced toward the city of Koenigsberg, threatening the Stutthof camp system. In the south, Soviet troops advanced toward the city of Krakow, threatening the Auschwitz camp system. The Nazis began to evacuate these and other remaining camps in Poland.

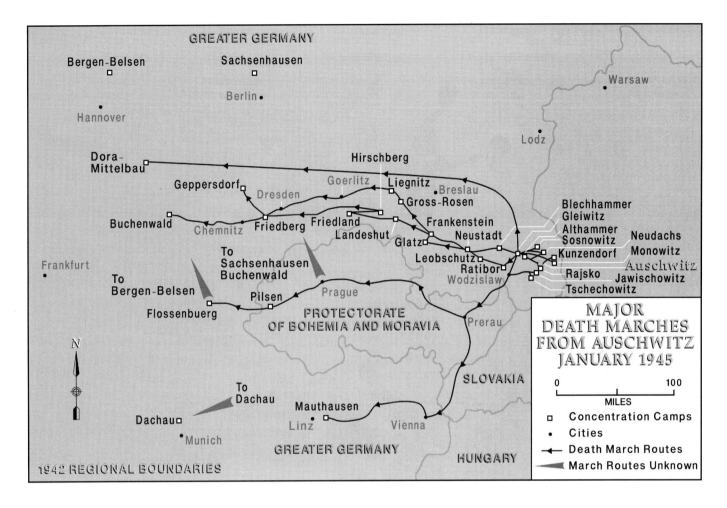

MAJOR DEATH MARCHES FROM AUSCHWITZ JANUARY 1945

0   100

MILES

- □ Concentration Camps
- • Cities
- ← Death March Routes
- ◄ March Routes Unknown

DEATH MARCHES FROM THE AUSCHWITZ CAMP SYSTEM

The SS began evacuating Auschwitz and its satellite camps in mid-January 1945. Nearly 60,000 prisoners were forced on death marches from the Auschwitz camp system. Thousands had been killed in the camps in the days before the death march. Tens of thousands of prisoners, mostly Jews, were forced to march to the city of Wodzislaw in the western part of Upper Silesia. SS guards shot anyone who fell behind or could not continue. More than 15,000 died during the death marches from Auschwitz.

Upon arrival in Wodzislaw, the prisoners were put on unheated freight trains and transported to concentration camps in Germany, particularly to Flossenbuerg, Sachsenhausen, Gross-Rosen, Buchenwald, Dachau, and Mauthausen. The rail journey lasted for days. Without food or water, shelter or blankets, many prisoners did not survive the transport.

In late January 1945, 4,000 prisoners were forced on a death march from Blechhammer, a subcamp of Auschwitz. About 1,000 prisoners died during the march to the Gross-Rosen concentration camp. After a brief delay, the remaining prisoners were moved to the Buchenwald camp in eastern Germany.

On January 27, 1945, the Soviet army entered Auschwitz and liberated over 7,000 remaining prisoners, who were mostly ill and dying.

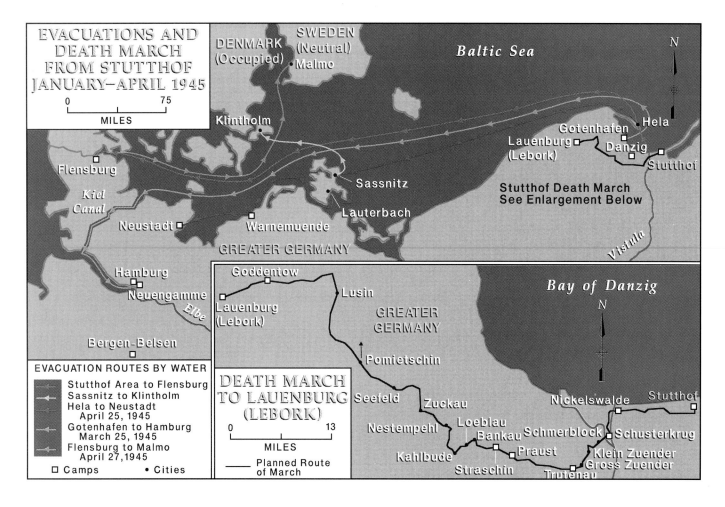

THE EVACUATION AND DEATH MARCH FROM STUTTHOF CONCENTRATION CAMP

The evacuation of prisoners from the Stutthof camp system in northern Poland began in January 1945. When the final evacuation was launched, there were nearly 50,000 prisoners, the overwhelming majority of them Jews, in the Stutthof camp system. About 5,000 prisoners from Stutthof subcamps were marched to the Baltic Sea coast, forced into the water, and machine gunned. The rest of the prisoners were put on a death march to Lauenburg in eastern Germany, where they were cut off by advancing Soviet forces. The Germans forced the surviving prisoners back to Stutthof. Marching in severe winter conditions and treated brutally by SS guards, thousands died during the death march.

In late April 1945, the remaining prisoners were removed from Stutthof by sea, since Stutthof was completely encircled by Soviet forces. Again, hundreds of prisoners were forced into the sea and shot; over 4,000 were sent by small boat to Germany, some to the Neuengamme concentration camp near Hamburg, and some to camps along the Baltic coast. Many drowned along the way. Shortly before the German surrender, some prisoners were transferred to Malmo, Sweden, and

released to the care of that neutral country. It has been estimated that over 25,000 prisoners, one in two, died during the evacuation from Stutthof and its subcamps. Soviet forces liberated Stutthof on May 9, 1945.

THE EVACUATION AND DEATH MARCH FROM GROSS-ROSEN CONCENTRATION CAMP

In late January 1945, with Soviet forces approaching the Oder River, Gross-Rosen subcamps to the east of the Oder were closed and the prisoners forced on death marches. Prisoners from the main camp were evacuated by rail early in February 1945. Many died en route because little if any food or water was provided. Prisoners from Gross-Rosen and its subcamps were sent to the Bergen-Belsen, Buchenwald, Dachau, Flossenbuerg, Mauthausen, Dora-Mittelbau, and Neuengamme concentration camps.

THE DEATH MARCH FROM BUCHENWALD CONCENTRATION CAMP

In late March and early April 1945, as American forces approached, the Nazis began a mass evacuation of prisoners from the Buchenwald concentration camp and its subcamps.

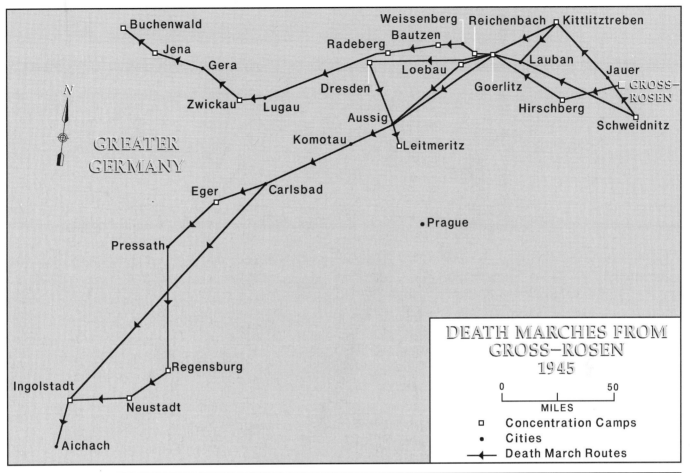

Buchenwald
Jena
Gera
Zwickau
Lugau
Radeberg
Dresden
Loebau
Weissenberg
Bautzen
Reichenbach
Kittlitztreben
Lauban
Jauer
GROSS-ROSEN
Goerlitz
Hirschberg
Schweidnitz
Aussig
Komotau
Leitmeritz
Eger
Carlsbad
Prague
Pressath
Regensburg
Ingolstadt
Neustadt
Aichach

N

GREATER
GERMANY

DEATH MARCHES FROM GROSS-ROSEN 1945

0   50
MILES

☐ Concentration Camps
• Cities
◄— Death March Routes

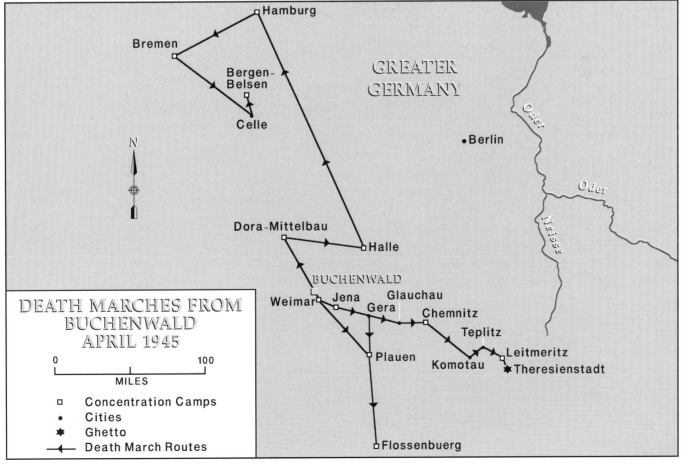

Hamburg
Bremen
Bergen-Belsen
Celle
GREATER GERMANY
Berlin
Oder
Oder
Neisse
Dora-Mittelbau
Halle
BUCHENWALD
Weimar
Jena
Glauchau
Gera
Chemnitz
Teplitz
Plauen
Komotau
Leitmeritz
Theresienstadt
Flossenbuerg

N

DEATH MARCHES FROM BUCHENWALD APRIL 1945

0   100
MILES

☐ Concentration Camps
• Cities
★ Ghetto
◄— Death March Routes

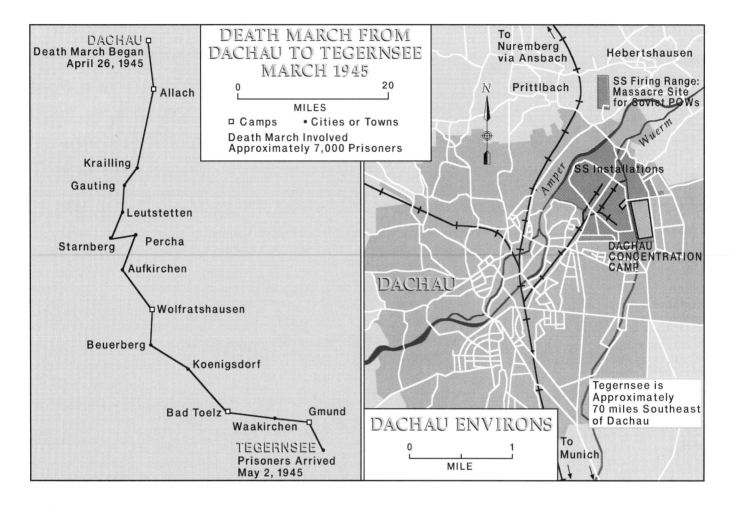

More than 30,000 prisoners were forced on death marches away from advancing American forces. About 8,000 died during the marches. On April 11, 1945, the surviving prisoners took control of the camp, shortly before American forces entered on the same day.

THE DEATH MARCH FROM DACHAU CONCENTRATION CAMP

In late April 1945, just three days before the liberation of the Dachau camp, the SS forced about 7,000 prisoners on a death march from Dachau south to Tegernsee. During the six-day death march, anyone who could not keep up or could no longer continue was shot. Many others died of exposure, hunger, or exhaustion. American forces liberated the Dachau concentration camp on April 29, 1945. In early May 1945, American troops liberated the surviving prisoners from the death march to Tegernsee.

THE LIBERATION OF NAZI CAMPS

As Allied troops moved across Europe in a series of offensives on Germany, they began to encounter and liberate concentration camp prisoners, many of whom had survived death marches into the interior of Germany.

Soviet forces were the first to approach a major Nazi camp, reaching the Majdanek camp near Lublin, Poland, in July 1944. Surprised by the rapid Soviet advance, the Germans attempted to demolish the camp in an effort to hide the evidence of mass murder. The camp staff set fire to the large crematorium, but because of the hasty evacuation, the gas chambers were left standing. The Soviets also overran the sites of the killing centers of Belzec, Sobibor, and Treblinka in the summer of 1944. The Germans had dismantled these camps in 1943, after most of the Jews of Poland had been killed.

The Soviets liberated Auschwitz, the largest extermination and concentration camp, in January 1945. The Nazis had forced almost all of the prisoners of Auschwitz on death marches. Soviet soldiers found only several thousand emaciated prisoners alive when they entered the camp. There was abundant evidence of mass murder in Auschwitz. The retreating Germans had destroyed most of the warehouses in the camp, but in the remaining ones the Soviets found personal belongings of some of the victims killed there. They discovered, for example, hundreds of thousands of men's

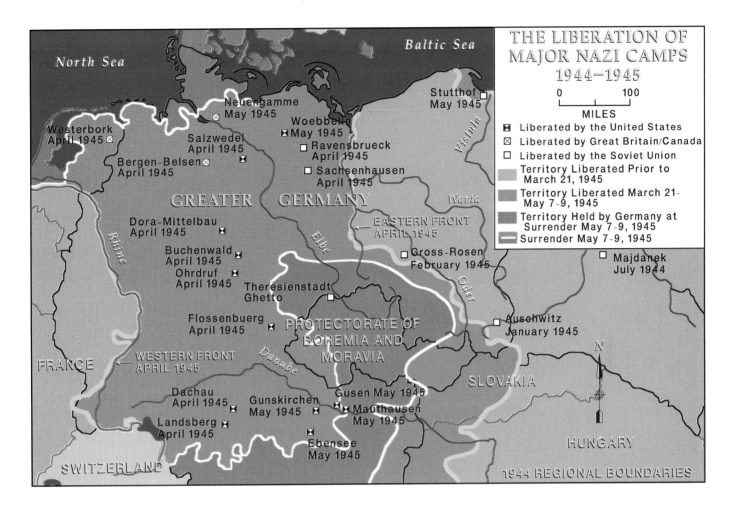

THE LIBERATION OF MAJOR NAZI CAMPS 1944–1945

0   100
MILES

- ☒ Liberated by the United States
- ⊠ Liberated by Great Britain/Canada
- ☐ Liberated by the Soviet Union
- Territory Liberated Prior to March 21, 1945
- Territory Liberated March 21–May 7-9, 1945
- Territory Held by Germany at Surrender May 7-9, 1945
- Surrender May 7-9, 1945

North Sea

Baltic Sea

Stutthof
May 1945

Neuengamme
May 1945

Woebbelin
May 1945

Westerbork
April 1945

Salzwedel
April 1945

Ravensbrueck
April 1945

Bergen-Belsen
April 1945

Sachsenhausen
April 1945

GREATER GERMANY

Warta

Vistula

Dora-Mittelbau
April 1945

EASTERN FRONT
APRIL 1945

Elbe

Gross-Rosen
February 1945

Majdanek
July 1944

Buchenwald
April 1945

Ohrdruf
April 1945

Theresienstadt
Ghetto

Oder

Auschwitz
January 1945

Flossenbuerg
April 1945

PROTECTORATE OF BOHEMIA AND MORAVIA

Rhine

FRANCE

WESTERN FRONT
APRIL 1945

Danube

SLOVAKIA

N

Dachau
April 1945

Gunskirchen
May 1945

Gusen May 1945

Mauthausen
May 1945

Landsberg
April 1945

Ebensee
May 1945

HUNGARY

SWITZERLAND

1944 REGIONAL BOUNDARIES

suits, more than 800,000 women's outfits, and more than 14,000 pounds of human hair.

In the following months, the Soviets liberated additional camps in the Baltic states and in Poland. Shortly before Germany's surrender, Soviet forces liberated the main camps of Stutthof, Sachsenhausen, and Ravensbrueck.

U.S. forces liberated the Buchenwald concentration camp near Weimar, Germany, in April 1945, a few days after the Nazis began evacuating the camp. On the day of liberation, an underground prisoner resistance organization seized control of Buchenwald to prevent atrocities by the retreating camp guards. American forces liberated more than 20,000 prisoners at Buchenwald. They also liberated the main camps of Dora-Mittelbau, Flossenbuerg, Dachau, and Mauthausen.

British forces liberated camps in northern Germany, including Neuengamme and Bergen-Belsen. They entered the Bergen-Belsen concentration camp, near Celle, Germany, in mid-April 1945. Some 60,000 prisoners, most in critical condition because of a typhus epidemic, were found alive. More than 10,000 died of malnutrition or disease within a few weeks.

Only after the liberation of the Nazi camps was the full scope of Nazi horrors exposed to the world. Liberators confronted unspeakable conditions in the camps, where piles of corpses lay unburied. Those who survived resembled skeletons because of forced labor and the lack of food. Many were so weak that they could hardly move. Disease remained an ever-present danger, and many of the camps had to be burned down to prevent the spread of epidemics. Survivors of the camps faced a long and difficult road to recovery.

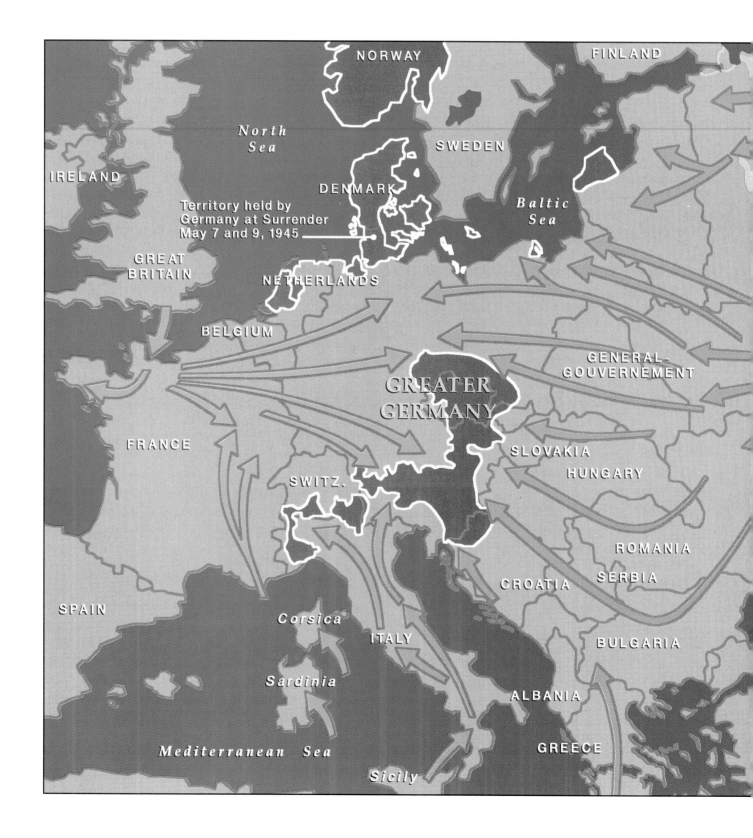

IRELAND

NORWAY

FINLAND

North Sea

SWEDEN

DENMARK

Territory held by Germany at Surrender May 7 and 9, 1945

Baltic Sea

GREAT BRITAIN

NETHERLANDS

BELGIUM

GENERAL-GOUVERNEMENT

GREATER GERMANY

SLOVAKIA

FRANCE

HUNGARY

SWITZ.

ROMANIA

SPAIN

SERBIA

CROATIA

Corsica

ITALY

BULGARIA

Sardinia

ALBANIA

GREECE

Mediterranean Sea

Sicily

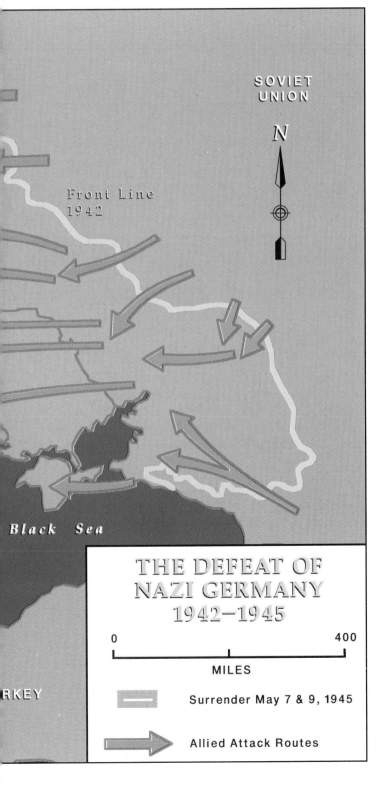

SOVIET
UNION

N

Front Line
1942

Black Sea

THE DEFEAT OF
NAZI GERMANY
1942–1945

0   400

MILES

Surrender May 7 & 9, 1945

Allied Attack Routes

RKEY

THE DEFEAT OF GERMANY 1942-1945
The Eastern Front 1942-1944

Until the winter of 1942-1943, the German army was victorious, achieving an almost unbroken chain of successes. Europe lay under German domination, from France in the west to the Volga River in the east; from northern Norway to the shores of North Africa. The battle for the city of Stalingrad proved a decisive turning point, ending the German series of victories and campaign of conquest in the east. After defeat at Stalingrad, German troops were forced on the defensive, beginning the retreat westward that was to end with Germany's surrender in May 1945, some three years later.

The Soviet army launched a counteroffensive at Stalingrad in mid-November 1942. They quickly encircled an entire German army, some 250,000 soldiers. In February 1943, after months of fierce fighting and heavy casualties, the surviving German forces, now only about 91,000 soldiers, surrendered. After Stalingrad, the Soviet army remained on the offensive, despite some temporary setbacks. Soviet forces pushed the Germans back to the banks of the Dnieper in 1943 and then, by the end of 1944, to the borders of East Prussia. In January 1945, a new offensive brought Soviet forces to the banks of the Oder, in eastern Germany. From their bridgehead across the Oder River, they launched the final offensive on Berlin in mid-April 1945.

D-Day: The Normandy Invasion and the Battle for France

On June 6, 1944 (known as D-Day), more than 150,000 Allied soldiers under the command of U.S. General Dwight D. Eisenhower landed on the beaches of Normandy, France, opening a long-awaited second front against the Germans in Europe. After the beachhead was secured, more than two million Allied soldiers poured into France. In July, Allied forces broke out of the Normandy beachhead, forcing a German withdrawal. The Allies entered Paris on August 25, 1944, and liberated most of France by the end of the month.

The western Allies were surprised in December 1944 when German forces attacked through the Ardennes Forest in Belgium in an attempt to divide and destroy Allied forces.

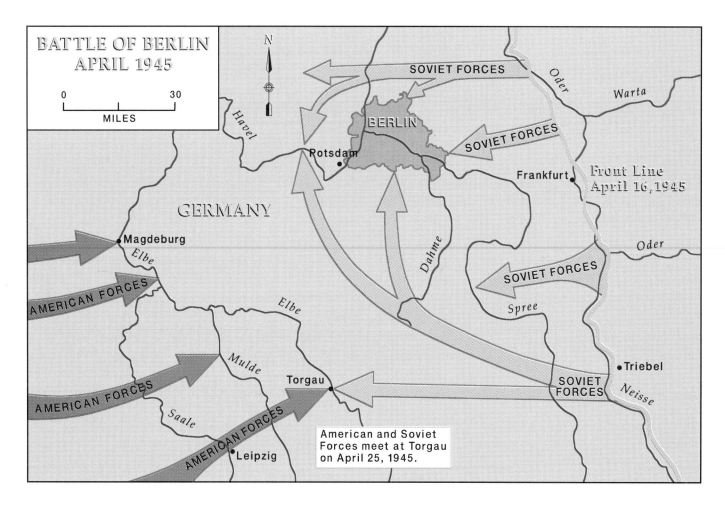

BATTLE OF BERLIN
APRIL 1945

0   30
MILES

American and Soviet
Forces meet at Torgau
on April 25, 1945.

Allied air forces, together with a fierce American defense, blocked the advance of German troops and forced them into a general retreat. The Allies won a decisive victory in what became known as the Battle of the Bulge, and continued the attack into Germany itself, occupying the left bank of the Rhine in February 1945. In March 1945, Allied forces crossed the Rhine, advancing into the heart of Germany.

The Battle of Berlin and the Surrender of Germany

In mid-April 1945, Soviet forces launched a massive offensive toward Berlin, which was encircled on April 25.

That same day, Soviet forces linked up with American forces attacking from the west at Torgau, on the Elbe River in central Germany. In Berlin, heavy fighting took place in the northern and southern suburbs of the city. As Soviet forces neared his command bunker in central Berlin on April 30, 1945, Adolf Hitler committed suicide. Berlin surrendered to Soviet forces on May 2, 1945.

World War II ended in Europe when the German armed forces surrendered unconditionally in the west on May 7 and in the east on May 9, 1945. May 8, 1945, was proclaimed Victory in Europe Day (V-E Day).

POSTWAR EUROPE 1945-1950

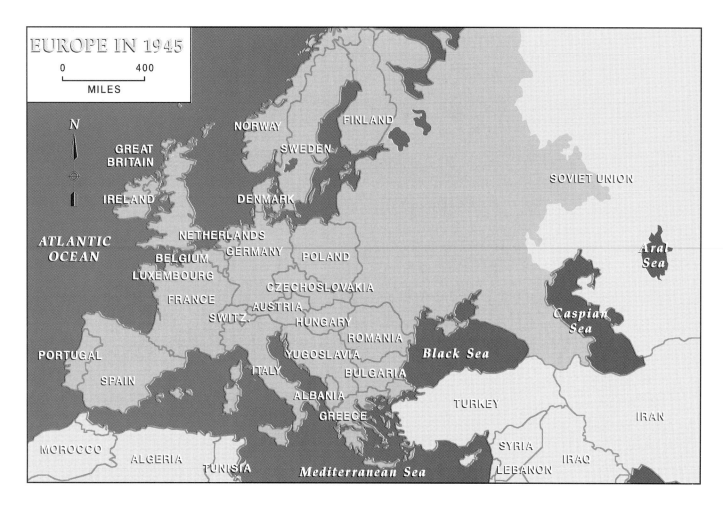

EUROPE IN 1945

Continental Europe emerged from German domination in 1945, shattered and transformed. After the German surrender, Great Britain, the United States, France, and the Soviet Union divided Germany and Austria into four occupation zones, each to be administered by a victorious power. The cities of Berlin and Vienna were similarly divided and occupied. Poland occupied and later annexed German territory east of the Oder-Neisse rivers.

The Allies ended the occupation of Austria in 1955 and Austria pledged unconditional neutrality. Germany remained under Allied occupation. In 1949, the western zones were combined into the Federal Republic of Germany (West Germany), and the Soviet zone became a Soviet-style dictatorship, the German Democratic Republic (East Germany). In 1989, the East German government collapsed and in 1990, West Germany and East Germany were united into one state. The newly united Germany formally recognized the Polish annexation of Germany's former eastern territories and pledged to be a force for peace and stability in Europe.

The year 1945 also marked the rapid expansion of Soviet power and influence in Europe. The Soviet Union retained and added to the gains made in eastern Europe under the terms of the German-Soviet Pact of 1939. The Soviets annexed the Baltic states (Latvia, Lithuania, and Estonia), most of eastern Poland, the Transcarpathian Ukraine, northern Bukovina, and Bessarabia. Further, they gradually installed pro-Soviet Communist regimes in Poland, Romania, Hungary, Bulgaria, and East Germany. By 1946, they were opposed by democratic states in Western Europe, under the leadership of the United States. Europe became a major battleground during this period of heightened tension, known as the cold war, between East and West. Beginning in the mid 1970s, East-West tensions lessened under the policy of detente, but the cold war continued until the collapse of Soviet power and the breakup of the Soviet Union in 1989.

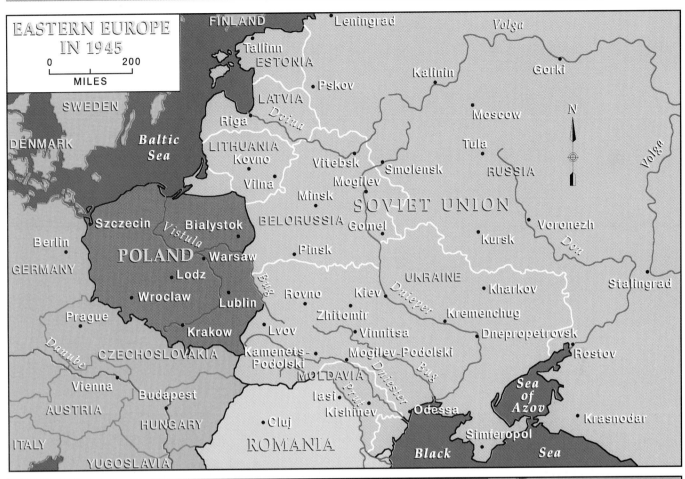

EASTERN EUROPE
IN 1945

0   200
MILES

SWEDEN

DENMARK

Baltic
Sea

FINLAND

Leningrad

Volga

Tallinn
ESTONIA

Pskov

Kalinin

Gorki

LATVIA

Riga

Dvina

Moscow

LITHUANIA
Kovno

Vilna

Vitebsk

Mogilev

Minsk

Smolensk

Tula

RUSSIA

SOVIET UNION

Berlin

GERMANY

Szczecin

POLAND

Bialystok

Vistula

Warsaw

Lodz

BELORUSSIA

Gomel

Pinsk

Bug

Voronezh

Kursk

Don

Stalingrad

Wroclaw

Lublin

Rovno

Kiev

Dnieper

UKRAINE

Kharkov

Prague

Krakow

Lvov

Zhitomir

Kremenchug

Dnepropetrovsk

Rostov

Danube

CZECHOSLOVAKIA

Kamenets-
Podolski

Vinnitsa

Mogilev-Podolski

Bug

Dniester

Vienna

AUSTRIA

Budapest

HUNGARY

MOLDAVIA

Iasi

Prut

Kishinev

Sea
of
Azov

Krasnodar

ITALY

Cluj

ROMANIA

Odessa

Simferopol

YUGOSLAVIA

Black

Sea

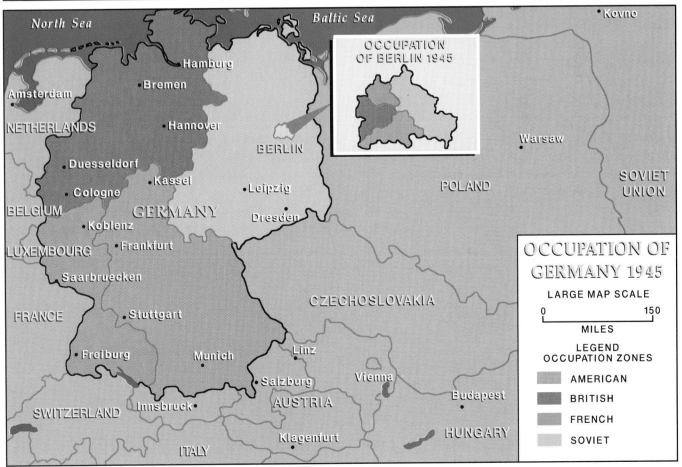

North Sea

Baltic Sea

Kovno

Hamburg

OCCUPATION
OF BERLIN 1945

Amsterdam

Bremen

NETHERLANDS

Hannover

BERLIN

Warsaw

Duesseldorf

Kassel

Cologne

GERMANY

Leipzig

POLAND

SOVIET
UNION

BELGIUM

Koblenz

Dresden

LUXEMBOURG

Frankfurt

Saarbruecken

FRANCE

Stuttgart

CZECHOSLOVAKIA

OCCUPATION OF
GERMANY 1945

LARGE MAP SCALE

0   150

MILES

LEGEND
OCCUPATION ZONES

Freiburg

Munich

Linz

Vienna

AMERICAN

Salzburg

Budapest

BRITISH

SWITZERLAND

Innsbruck

AUSTRIA

FRENCH

Klagenfurt

HUNGARY

SOVIET

ITALY

MAJOR EUROPEAN
WAR CRIMES TRIALS
1943–1947

Solid dots represent select sites of war crime trials.

1945 INTERNATIONAL BOUNDARIES

TRIALS OF WAR CRIMINALS IN EUROPE

Even before the end of World War II, some of those accused of war crimes stood trial in a variety of courts. Following the war, the best known war crimes trial was the trial of "major" war criminals in Nuremberg, Germany. These leading German officials were tried before the International Military Tribunal (IMT), which consisted of judges from Great Britain, France, the Soviet Union, and the United States. Between October 18, 1945, and October 1, 1946, the IMT tried 22 "major" war criminals on charges of conspiracy, crimes against peace, war crimes, and crimes against humanity. Twelve of the defendants were sentenced to death; three were sentenced to life imprisonment; and four

received prison terms ranging from 10 to 20 years. The IMT acquitted three of the defendants.

The overwhelming majority of post-1945 war crimes trials involved lower-level officials and officers. They included concentration camp guards and commandants, police officers, members of the Einsatzgruppen, and doctors who participated in medical experiments. These war criminals were tried by military courts in the British, American, French, and Soviet zones of occupied Germany and Austria; and in Italy. Others were tried by the courts of those countries where they had committed their crimes. Many war criminals, however, were never brought to trial or punished.

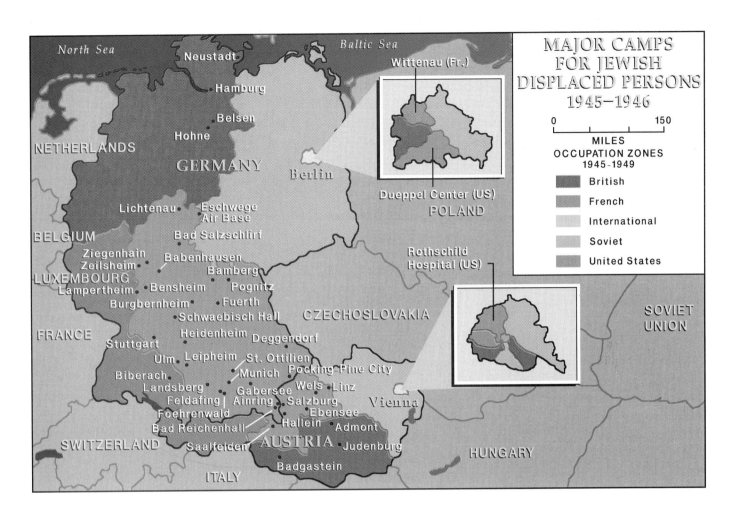

THE POSTWAR REFUGEE CRISIS AND THE ESTABLISHMENT OF THE STATE OF ISRAEL

Between seven and nine million Europeans were uprooted during World War II. Within several months, the Allies repatriated to their countries of origin more than six million displaced persons (DPs; wartime refugees). Between 1.5 million and two million DPs refused to return to their home countries. Several hundred thousand Jewish survivors gathered in camps for displaced persons. The Allies established such camps in Allied-occupied Germany, Austria, and Italy for refugees waiting to leave Europe. Most Jewish DPs preferred to emigrate to Palestine but many also sought entry into the United States. They decided to remain in the DP camps until they could leave Europe. At the end of 1946 the number of Jewish DPs was estimated at 250,000, of whom 185,000 were in Germany, 45,000 in Austria, and 20,000 in Italy. Most of the Jewish DPs were refugees from Poland, many of whom had fled the Germans into the interior of the Soviet Union during the war. Other Jewish DPs came from Czechoslovakia, Hungary, and Romania.

While most Jewish DPs sought to emigrate to Palestine, Great Britain sharply restricted Jewish entry there. In 1920,

Britain had received a mandate from the League of Nations to administer Palestine and continued to administer the territory after World War II. Despite British restrictions, about 70,000 Jewish Holocaust survivors risked the trip across the Mediterranean Sea in the attempt to enter Palestine between 1945 and May 1948.

Beginning in August 1946, the British attempted to halt this "illegal" immigration by deporting would-be immigrants to the island of Cyprus. By 1948, the British had intercepted and deported about 50,000 Jews to 12 detention camps established on Cyprus. Five of these camps were tent camps while the remaining camps housed prisoners in tin huts. The British use of detention camps as a deterrent failed, and the flood of immigrants attempting entry into Palestine continued unabated. Further, the internment of Jewish refugees—most of them Holocaust survivors—turned world opinion against the British policy. Jewish detainees remained in the camps until after the establishment of the State of Israel in 1948.

The fate of the refugee ship *Exodus* dramatized the plight of Holocaust survivors in the DP camps. In July 1947, the *Exodus* left southern France for Palestine, carrying 4,500 Jewish refugees from the DP camps in Germany. The British

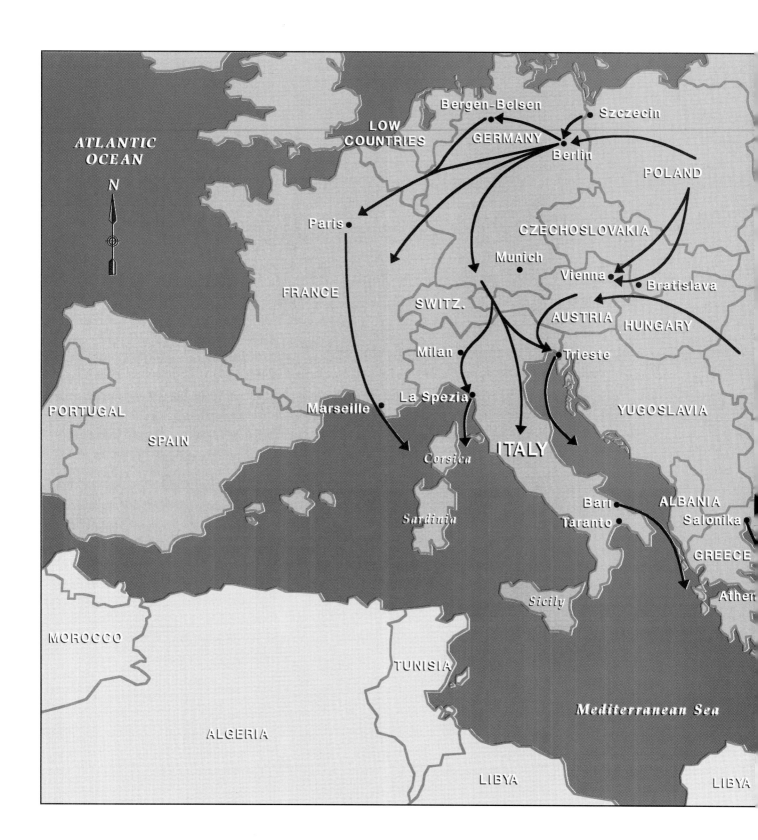

JEWISH "ILLEGAL" IMMIGRATION 1945–1947

0   400

MILES

→ Immigration Routes

SOVIET UNION

ROMANIA

Constanta

Varna

BULGARIA

Black Sea

TURKEY

SYRIA

Cyprus

Internment

LEBANON

British Naval Blockade →

Haifa

Tel Aviv

PALESTINE

JORDAN

EGYPT

Suez Canal

intercepted the ship even before it entered territorial waters off the coast of Palestine. Three Jews died during the forcible transfer of the passengers to British ships. The passengers were deported not to the Cyprus camps but back to their port of origin in France. For almost a month the British held the refugees aboard ship, at anchor off the French coast, because the French rejected the British demand to land the passengers. Ultimately, the British took the refugees to Hamburg, Germany, and forcibly returned them to DP camps. This sparked massive protests against British policy and its brutal application. Great Britain came under increasing international pressure to allow unrestricted Jewish immigration into Palestine and to create a homeland for Jewish displaced persons of Europe.

In a special session, the United Nations General Assembly voted on November 29, 1947, to partition Palestine into two new states, one Jewish and the other Arab. In early April 1948, Great Britain began the withdrawal of British forces from Palestine. On May 14, 1948, prominent Zionist leader David Ben-Gurion announced the establishment of the State of Israel and declared that Jewish immigration to the new state would be unrestricted.

Ships carrying Jewish refugees began landing in Haifa, Israel. Holocaust survivors, the passengers from the *Exodus*, DPs from central Europe, and Jewish detainees from the British detention camps on Cyprus were welcomed to the Jewish homeland. Between 1948 and 1951, almost 700,000 Jews emigrated to Israel, including more than two-thirds of the Jewish displaced persons in Europe.

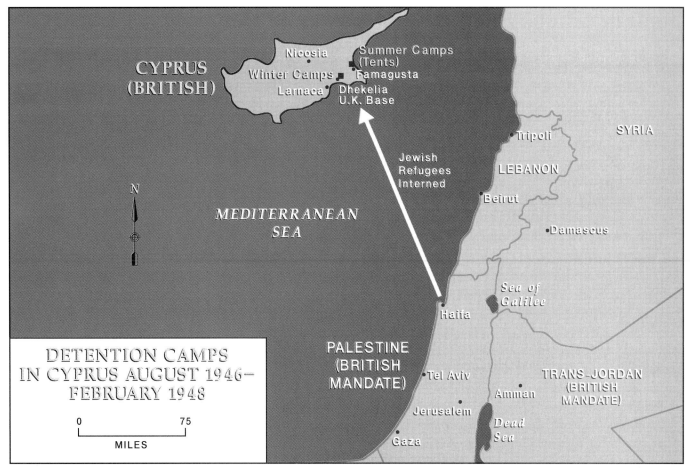

CYPRUS (BRITISH)

Nicosia

Summer Camps (Tents)

Winter Camps
Famagusta

Larnaca
Dhekelia
U.K. Base

Jewish
Refugees
Interned

Tripoli

SYRIA

LEBANON

Beirut

Damascus

MEDITERRANEAN SEA

N

Sea of Galilee

Haifa

DETENTION CAMPS IN CYPRUS AUGUST 1946– FEBRUARY 1948

0 — 75

MILES

PALESTINE (BRITISH MANDATE)

Tel Aviv

Jerusalem

Gaza

Amman

Dead Sea

TRANS-JORDAN (BRITISH MANDATE)

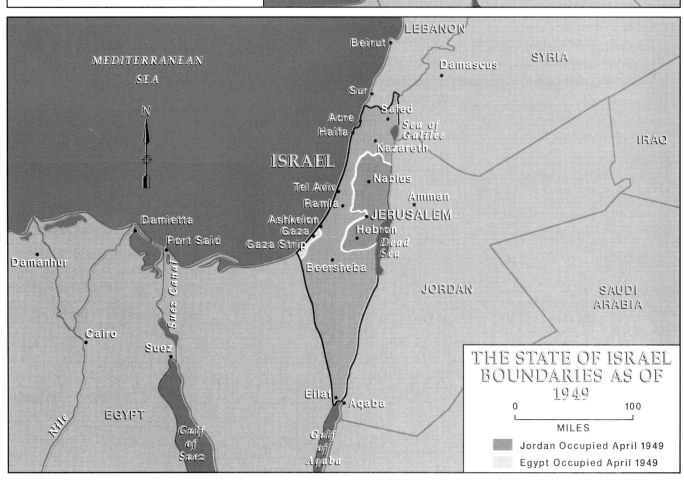

LEBANON

Beirut

Damascus

SYRIA

MEDITERRANEAN SEA

N

Sur

Safed

Acre
Haifa

Sea of Galilee

Nazareth

IRAQ

ISRAEL

Nablus

Tel Aviv

Ramla

Amman

Ashkelon
Gaza
Gaza Strip

JERUSALEM

Hebron

Dead Sea

Damietta

Port Said

Beersheba

Damanhur

Suez Canal

JORDAN

SAUDI ARABIA

Cairo

Suez

THE STATE OF ISRAEL BOUNDARIES AS OF 1949

0 — 100

MILES

Eilat
Aqaba

Nile

EGYPT

Gulf of Suez

Gulf of Aqaba

◼ Jordan Occupied April 1949

◻ Egypt Occupied April 1949

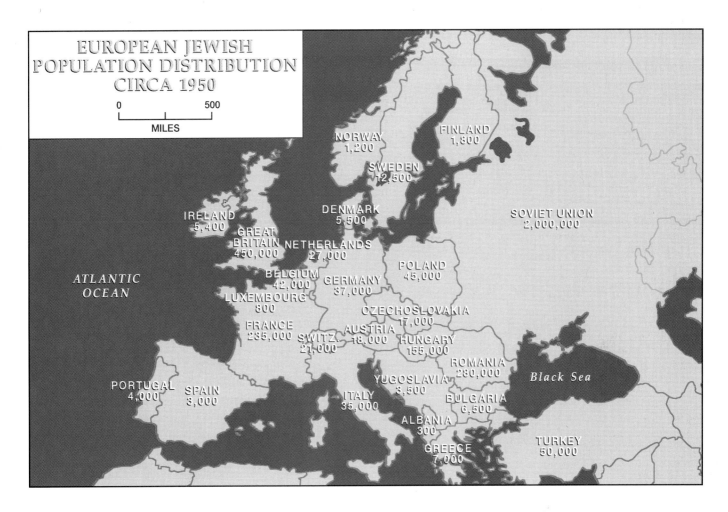

EUROPEAN JEWISH
POPULATION DISTRIBUTION
CIRCA 1950

0   500
MILES

NORWAY 1,200
FINLAND 1,800
SWEDEN 12,500
DENMARK 5,500
SOVIET UNION 2,000,000
IRELAND 5,400
GREAT BRITAIN 450,000
NETHERLANDS 27,000
POLAND 45,000
ATLANTIC OCEAN
BELGIUM 42,000
GERMANY 37,000
LUXEMBOURG 800
CZECHOSLOVAKIA 17,000
FRANCE 235,000
SWITZ. 21,000
AUSTRIA 18,000
HUNGARY 155,000
ROMANIA 280,000
Black Sea
YUGOSLAVIA 3,500
PORTUGAL 4,000
SPAIN 3,000
ITALY 35,000
BULGARIA 6,500
ALBANIA 300
GREECE 7,000
TURKEY 50,000

THE JEWISH POPULATION OF EUROPE 1950

About six million Jews died in the Holocaust. Jewish communities across Europe were shattered. Many of those who survived were determined to leave Europe and start new lives in Israel or the United States. The population shifts brought on by the Holocaust and by Jewish emigration were astounding.

According to the *American Jewish Yearbook*, the Jewish population of Europe was about 9.5 million in 1933. In 1950, the Jewish population of Europe was about 3.5 million. In 1933, 60 percent of all Jews lived in Europe. In 1950, most Jews (51 percent) lived in America (North and South combined), while only a third of the world's Jewish population lived in Europe.

The Jewish communities of eastern Europe were devastated. In 1933, Poland had the largest Jewish population in Europe, numbering about three million. By 1950, the Jewish population of Poland was reduced to about 45,000. The Soviet Union had the largest remaining Jewish population, with some two million Jews. Romania's Jewish population fell from about 980,000 in 1933 to about 280,000 in 1950.

The Jewish population of central Europe was also decimated. Germany had a Jewish population of 565,000 in 1933 and just 37,000 in 1950. Hungary had a Jewish population of 445,000 in 1933 and 155,000 in 1950. Czechoslovakia's Jewish population was reduced from about 357,000 in 1933 to 17,000 in 1950 and Austria's from about 250,000 to just 18,000.

In western Europe, the largest Jewish communities remained in Great Britain, with approximately 450,000 Jews (300,000 in 1933) and France, with 235,000 (225,000 in 1933). In southern Europe, the Jewish population fell dramatically: in Greece from about 100,000 in 1933 to just 7,000 in 1950; in Yugoslavia from about 70,000 to 3,500; in Italy from about 48,000 to 35,000; and in Bulgaria from 50,000 in 1933 to just 6,500 in 1950.

Before the Nazi takeover of power in 1933, Europe had a vibrant and mature Jewish culture. By 1945, most European Jews—two out of every three—had been killed. Most of the surviving remnant of European Jewry decided to leave Europe. Hundreds of thousands established new lives in Israel and the United States.

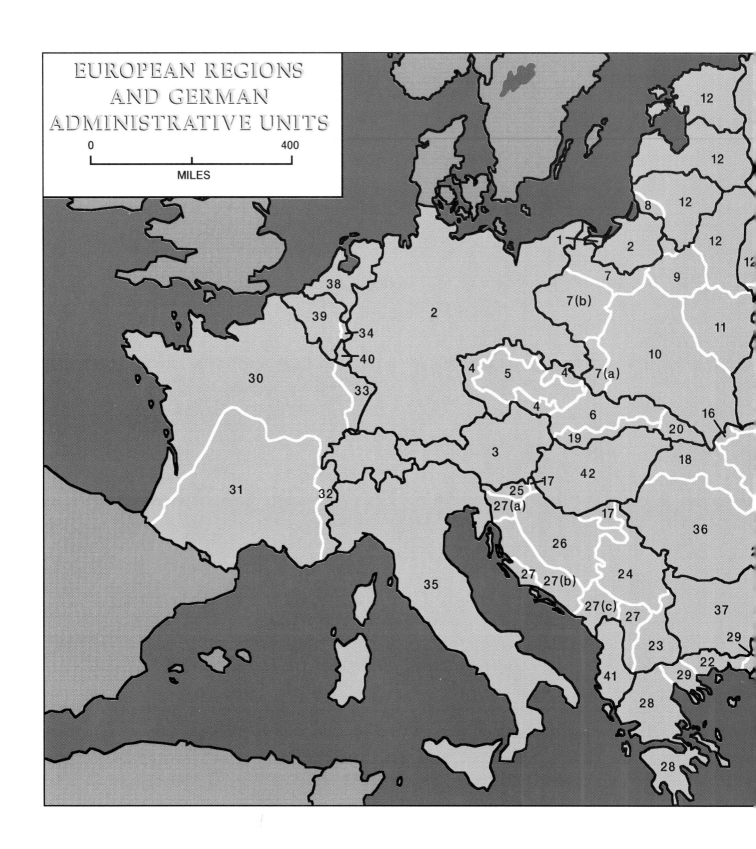

EUROPEAN REGIONS
AND GERMAN
ADMINISTRATIVE UNITS

0   400
MILES

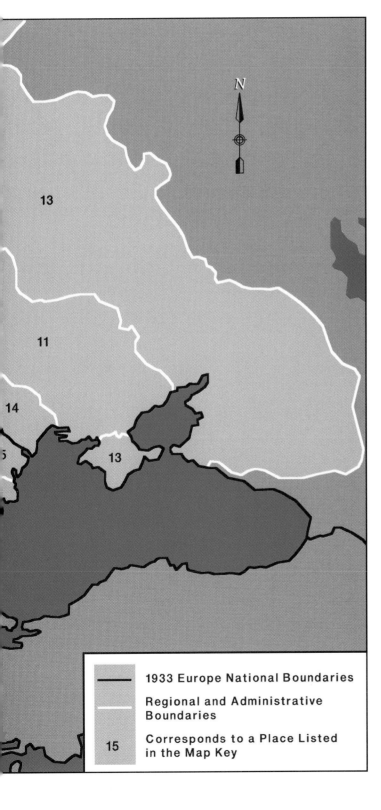

MAP KEY

1. Free City of Danzig
2. Germany 1933
3. Austria
4. Sudetenland
5. Reich Protectorate of Bohemia and Moravia
6. Slovakia
7. Western Poland, Annexed by Germany 1939
7(a). Eastern Upper Silesia
7(b). Warthegau
8. Memel Territory
9. Bialystok District
10. Generalgouvernement of Poland
11. Reichskommissariat Ukraine
12. Reichskommissariat Ostland
13. Soviet Territory-German Military Government
14. Transnistria
15. Bessarabia
16. Northern Bukovina
17. Hungarian-Occupied Yugoslavia
18. Northern Transylvania
19. Hungarian-Occupied Slovakia
20. Transcarpathian Ukraine
21. Southern Dobruja
22. Bulgarian-Occupied Thrace
23. Bulgarian-Occupied Macedonia
24. Serbia and the Banat
25. Northern Slovenia
26. Croatia 1941 (including Bosnia and Herzegovina)
27. Italian-Occupied Yugoslavia 1941
27(a). Southern Slovenia
27(b). Dalmatia
28. Italian-Occupied Greece 1941
29. German-Occupied Greece 1941
30. German-Occupied France 1940
31. Southern Zone of France, Occupied 1942
32. Italian-Occupied France 1942-1943
33. Alsace-Lorraine
34. Eupen and Malmedy
35. Italy
36. Romania
37. Bulgaria
38. Netherlands
39. Belgium
40. Luxembourg
41. Albania
42. Hungary

Aktion 1005 (Operation 1005): Code name for the German plan to obliterate evidence of mass murder. The Germans forced prisoners to reopen mass graves and cremate the bodies.

Aktion Reinhard (Operation Reinhard): Code name for the German plan to kill more than two million Jews living in the Generalgouvernement.

Alsace-Lorraine: Territories in eastern France along the border with Germany. They were incorporated de facto into Germany in 1940. After World War II, they were returned to France.

American Jewish Joint Distribution Committee (JDC or Joint): Organization founded in 1914 by American Jews to provide financial and material aid to Jews overseas. During World War II, the JDC sought to aid Jews across German-occupied Europe. After the war, it cared for Jewish displaced persons, detainees on Cyprus, and emigrants to Israel.

Anschluss (Union): German term referring to the incorporation of Austria into Germany in March 1938.

Arrow Cross Party: Pro-German Hungarian fascist party founded by Ferenc Szalasi in 1937.

"Aryanization": Term referring to the seizure of Jewish-owned property, businesses, and other economic enterprises, and the transfer of such property from Jews to non-Jews.

B.C.E.: Abbreviation for "Before the Common Era." Also referred to as B.C.

Bessarabia: Territory in eastern Romania located between the Prut and Dniester rivers; occupied by the Soviet Union in 1940.

Bialystok District: Territory in northern Poland established after the German invasion of the Soviet Union in 1941 (the Soviet Union had previously annexed the region under the terms of the German-Soviet Pact of 1939).

Blitzkrieg (Lightning War): Term referring to military tactics that entailed the concentration of offensive weapons to breach enemy defenses and the swift advance deep into enemy territory.

Bukovina: Territory in northeastern Romania, along the Carpathian Mountains. The Soviet Union occupied the northern part of Bukovina in 1940.

C.E.: Abbreviation for "Common Era." Also referred to as A.D.

Concentration camps (Konzentrationslager; KL): Places of incarceration in which people are detained without regard to due process and the legal norms of arrest and detention. The extensive German camp system also included labor camps, transit camps, prisoner-of-war camps, and extermination camps.

Croatia: Before World War II, Croatia was a province of Yugoslavia. After the German invasion in 1941, Germany and Italy established the fascist satellite state of Croatia. It included the provinces of Croatia and Bosnia-Herzegovina and was ruled by the Ustasa (Croatian fascists) under Ante Pavelic.

Death marches: Term probably coined by concentration camp prisoners, referring to forced marches of prisoners over long distances, under heavy guard and extremely harsh conditions.

Einsatzgruppen (sing., Einsatzgruppe): Mobile killing units; German special duty squads, composed mainly of SS and police personnel, assigned to kill Jews in eastern Europe following the German invasion of the Soviet Union in June 1941.

"Erntefest" ("Harvest Festival"): Code name for the German operation to kill Jews in the Generalgouvernement in November 1943.

Eupen and Malmedy: Territories in western Belgium, annexed de facto by Germany in 1940.

Extermination camps: The six killing centers—Chelmno, Belzec, Sobibor, Treblinka, Auschwitz-Birkenau, and Majdanek—established by the Germans in occupied Poland.

"Final Solution": Nazi euphemism referring to the Nazi plan to kill the Jews of Europe.

Gas Van: Truck with a hermetically sealed compartment that served as a mobile gas chamber. Gas vans were used especially in the Chelmno killing center.

Generalgouvernement (General Government): Territory in central and southern Poland established after the defeat of Poland in September 1939; it had a German civilian administration.

German Armament Works (Deutsche Ausruestungswerke; DAW): An SS-owned company that utilized forced labor from concentration camps for armament production. DAW plants were built at Dachau, Sachsenhausen, Buchenwald, Auschwitz, Janowska, Ravensbrueck, Stutthof, and elsewhere.

Gestapo (Geheime Staatspolizei): German secret state police, responsible for state security and the consignment of individuals to concentration camps. Members of the Gestapo were often also members of the SS.

Ghetto: An enclosed district of a city where the Germans forced the Jewish population to live. Ghettos were established in Poland, the Baltic states, the Soviet Union, the Protectorate of Bohemia and Moravia, and Hungary.

Greater Germany: Term referring to Germany and its annexed territories. It came into common German usage after the incorporation of Austria in 1938.

Iron Guard: Romanian fascist and antisemitic organization sympathetic to the Nazis.

Jewish councils (Judenraete; sing., Judenrat): Governing bodies established on German orders in the Jewish communities of occupied Europe.

"Judenfrei" (free of Jews): Nazi euphemism used to describe areas from which all Jews had been deported or killed.

"Kristallnacht" ("Crystal Night" or "Night of Broken Glass"): The violent anti-Jewish pogrom of November 9 and 10, 1938, in Germany, Austria, the Sudetenland, and the Free City of Danzig.

Low Countries: Region of northwestern Europe consisting of the small states of Belgium, the Netherlands, and Luxembourg.

Munich agreement: International agreement sanctioning the German annexation of the Sudetenland in western Czechoslovakia, signed September 29-30, 1938, in Munich, Germany.

Nacht und Nebel Decree (Night and Fog Decree): Order establishing the German policy of arrest and deportation to Germany of those individuals suspected of anti-German resistance activities in western Europe. Those arrested were not permitted to contact family members and simply disappeared into the "night and fog."

Nazi party: Abbreviated term for the National Socialist German Workers' Party (Nationalsozialistische Deutsche Arbeiterpartei; NSDAP), the party headed by Hitler and the only political party legally permitted in Germany from 1934 to 1945.

Northern Transylvania: Region in northwestern Romania transferred to Hungary in 1940 as part of the Vienna Arbitration Awards. It reverted to Romanian rule following World War II.

Nuremberg Laws: Antisemitic legislation enacted at the Nuremberg Nazi Party Congress in September 1935, depriving Jews of civil rights and prohibiting marriage or sexual relations between German non-Jews and Jews.

Operation 14f13 (also called "Invalid Operation"): Code name for the killing of concentration camp prisoners deemed by the Germans "unfit" to perform forced labor.

Operation Reinhard: *see* Aktion Reinhard

Organisation Schmelt: System of forced-labor camps that operated from 1940 to 1944 for Jews in Eastern Upper Silesia, a small territory annexed by Germany from Poland in 1939.

Palestine: Area of the Middle East bordered today by Egypt, Jordan, Syria, and Lebanon; a province of the Ottoman Empire from the sixteenth century until 1920. After the defeat and collapse of the Ottoman Empire in World War I, the League of Nations granted Great Britain a mandate to govern Palestine. In May 1948, Britain ended the mandate and withdrew from Palestine, leading to the proclamation of the State of Israel that same month.

Pogrom: Violent, organized attack on helpless civilians, usually with the connivance of government officials.

Protectorate of Bohemia and Moravia: German protectorate established after the partition of Czechoslovakia in 1939, in violation of the Munich agreement.

Reichskommissariat Ostland: Territory established after the German invasion of the Soviet Union in June 1941. It encompassed Lithuania, Latvia, Estonia, most of Belorussia, and part of northeastern Poland, and had a German civilian administration.

Reichskommissariat Ukraine: Territory established after the German invasion of the Soviet Union in June 1941. It encompassed part of eastern Poland and most of the Ukraine, as far east as the area around the cities of Kiev and Dnepropetrovsk, and had a German civilian administration.

SA (Sturmabteilung; Storm Troopers): Street fighters of the Nazi party before Hitler's rise to power; after 1934, the SS supplanted the SA as the paramilitary organization of the Nazi party. The SA played a key role in "Kristallnacht."

SD (Sicherheitsdienst des Reichsfuehrers-SS): Security Service of the SS and the intelligence gathering agency of the Nazi party. The SD played an important role in carrying out the "Final Solution"; SD officers served in Einsatzgruppen, police, and other security units.

Sonderkommando: German term for a prisoner forced-labor detachment assigned to work in the killing area of an extermination camp.

Southern Dobruja: Region in southeastern Romania transferred to Bulgaria in 1940 as part of the Vienna Arbitration Awards. It reverted to Romanian rule following World War II.

SS (Schutzstaffel; Protection Squad): Originally Hitler's bodyguard, it became the elite guard of the Nazi state, responsible for carrying out the "Final Solution."

Statut des Juifs (Jewish Law): Two laws in Vichy France, one passed in October 1940 and the second in June 1941. The legislation provided the legal foundation for the persecution of Jews in France.

Subcamp: Work detail or auxiliary forced-labor camp linked administratively to one of the major concentration camps. Subcamps were usually established near factories or mining operations and functioned anywhere from a few weeks to several years.

Sudetenland: Border region of Czechoslovakia with a large ethnic German population. It was transferred to Germany by international agreement (the Munich agreement) in 1938. It reverted to Czechoslovakia following World War II.

Transcarpathian Ukraine: Region in eastern Czechoslovakia annexed by Hungary according to the first Vienna Award of November 1938. It became part of the Soviet Union after World War II.

Transnistria: Territory transferred to Romanian rule after the invasion of the Soviet Union in 1941. It was located between the Bug and Dniester rivers in the western Ukraine.

Ustasa: Croatian fascists allied with Germany. The Ustasa instituted a reign of terror in Croatia after the establishment of the independent pro-German state of Croatia in April 1941.

Vichy France: Nationalist regime established in the French spa town of Vichy after the defeat of France in June 1940. Headed by Marshal Henri Philippe Petain, the Vichy regime declared neutrality in the war, but cooperated closely with Germany.

Vienna Arbitration Awards: Settlement of Hungarian demands for territory from Czechoslovakia and Hungarian and Bulgarian demands for Romanian territory. Sponsored by Germany and Italy, the first Vienna Award in November 1938 gave Hungary the Transcarpathian Ukraine and a strip of territory from southern Slovakia. In the second Vienna Award in August and September 1940, Romania was forced to cede northern Transylvania to Hungary and southern Dobruja to Bulgaria.

Wehrmacht (literally, military or defense power): Term referring to Germany's military forces from 1935 to 1945.

Zyklon B: Commercial name for crystalline hydrogen cyanide gas; used normally as an insecticide but employed, especially at the Auschwitz-Birkenau killing center, as the killing agent in gas chambers.

MAPPING AGENCIES

Following is a select list of organizations that issued maps used in the compilation of this atlas.

U.S.
United States Army, Corps of Engineers
United States Army Map Service
United States Defense Mapping Agency
United States Department of State, Division of Map Intelligence
United States Office of Strategic Service (OSS)
United States War Office, General Staff, Geographical Section

GERMAN
Bayerisches Landesvermessungsamt, Muenchen
Generalstab der Luftwaffe, Berlin
Kriegskarten- und Vermessungsamt, Berlin
Kursbuchburo der Generalbetriebsleitung Ost
Lithographisches Institut, Berlin
Militargeographisches Institut, Wien
Niedersaechsischen Landesverwaltungsamt-Landesvermessung
OKH, GenStdH, Abteilung Fuer Kriegskarten- und Vermessungswesens
Preussischen Landesaufnahme, Berlin
Reichsamt fuer Landesaufnahme, Berlin
Reichsbahnzentrale fuer den Deutschen Reisverkehr
Reichsministerium des Innern, Publikationsstelle, Berlin-Dahlem
Stadtvermessungsamt, Riga
Statistisches Reichsamt, Berlin
Vermessungskommissar fuer die Reichshauptstadt, Berlin
Vermessungswesen (Landesaufnahme), Wien
Wehrmacht, Militar-Geographische, Gruppe Radom
Wirtschaftsstab Ost, Chefgruppe Berlin

POLISH
Generalne Przedstawicielstwo Sprzedazy
Polish General Staff, Geographic Section
Polskie Tow, Ksiegarni Kolejowych, Warszawa
Rzeczpospolita Polska
Sekcja Geograficzna Towarzystwa Wiedzy Wojskowej w Warszawie
Wojskowy Instytut Geograficzny, Warszawa
Wydawnictwo A. J. Ostrowski Lodz-Warszawa
Wydawnictwo Min, Komunikacji W Warszawie
Wydawnictwo Wojskowego Instytutu Naukowo-Wydawniczego-Lodz
Zarzad Miejski m Lodzi

OTHER
Instituto Geografico d'Agostini, Novara
Institut Cartographique Militaire
Ukrainischen geodatichen Institut

SELECT BIBLIOGRAPHY

Adler, H. G. *Die verheimlichte Wahrheit: Theresienstaedter Dokumente.* Tuebingen: Mohr, 1958.

—. *Theresienstadt, 1941-1945: das Antlitz einer Zwangsgemeinschaft; Geschichte, Soziologie, Psychologie.* Tuebingen: Mohr, 1960.

Adler, Jacques. *The Jews of Paris and the Final Solution: Communal Response and Internal Conflicts, 1940-1944.* New York: Oxford University Press, 1987.

Ainsztein, Reuben. *Jewish Resistance in Nazi-Occupied Eastern Europe, with a Historical Survey of the Jew as Fighter and Soldier in the Diaspora.* New York: Barnes & Noble, 1974.

—. *The Warsaw Ghetto Revolt.* New York: Holocaust Library, 1979.

American Jewish Committee. *American Jewish Yearbook.* Philadelphia: American Jewish Committee, 1933-1951.

Arad, Yitzhak. *Ghetto in Flames: The Struggle and Destruction of the Jews in Vilna in the Holocaust.* Jerusalem: Yad Vashem, Martyrs' and Heroes' Remembrance Authority, 1981.

—. *Belzec, Sobibor, Treblinka: The Operation Reinhard Death Camps.* Bloomington: Indiana University Press, 1987.

Arad, Yitzhak, Shmuel Krakowski, and Shmuel Spector, eds. *The Einsatzgruppen Reports: Selections from the Dispatches of the Nazi Death Squads' Campaign against the Jews, July 1941-January 1943.* Translated by Stella Schossberger. New York: Holocaust Library, 1989.

Archivdirektion Stuttgart. *Die Opfer der nationalsozialistischen Judenverfolgung in Baden-Wuerttemberg, 1933-1945: ein Gedenkbuch.* Stuttgart: W. Kohlhammer, 1969.

Auschwitz Hefte. *Die Auschwitz-Hefte: Texte der polnischen Zeitschrift "Przeglad Lekarski" ueber historische, psychische und medizinische Aspekte des Lebens und Sterbens in Auschwitz.* Weinheim: Beltz, 1987.

Avni, Haim. *Spain, the Jews and Franco.* Philadelphia: Jewish Publication Society of America, 1982.

Bartel, Walter, Pierre Durand, Paul Gruenewald, Vojtech Holecek, Nikolai Kjung, Henryk Sokolak, Rudi Supek, and Ferdinanda Zidar, eds. *Buchenwald: Mahnung und Verpflichtung: Dokumente und Berichte.* Berlin: Deutscher Verlag der Wissenschaften, 1983.

Bauminger, Arieh L. *The Fighters of the Cracow Ghetto.* Jerusalem: A.L. Bauminger, 1986.

Bensimon, Doris, and Sergio Della Pergola. *La population juive de France: socio-demographie et identite.* Jerusalem: Institute of Contemporary Jewry, Hebrew University of Jerusalem; Paris: Centre national de la recherche scientifique, 1984.

Benz, Wolfgang, ed. *Die Juden in Deutschland, 1933-1945: Leben unter nationalsozialistischer Herrschaft.* Munich: Beck, 1988.

—, ed. *Dimension des Voelkermords: die Zahl der juedischen Opfer des Nationalsozialismus.* Munich: Oldenbourg, 1991.

Berenbaum, Michael. *The World Must Know: The History of the Holocaust as Told in the United States Holocaust Memorial Museum.* Boston: Little, Brown, 1993.

Berlin Museum. *Synagogen in Berlin: zur Geschichte einer zerstoerten Architektur.* Berlin: Verlag Willmuth Arenhoevel, 1983.

Bialystoker Center. *The Bialystoker Memorial Book.* New York: Bialystoker Center, 1982.

Bierman, John. "How Italy Protected the Jews in the Occupied South of France, 1942-1943." In *The Italian Rescue: Rescue of Jews During the Holocaust,* edited by Ivo Herzer. Washington, D.C.: Catholic University of America Press, 1989.

Boas, Jacob. *Boulevard des Miseres: The Story of Transit Camp Westerbork.* Hamden, Conn.: Archon, 1985.

Botz, Gerhard, Ivar Oxaal, and Michael Pollak, eds. *Eine zerstoerte Kultur: Juedisches Leben und Antisemitismus in Wien seit dem 19. Jahrhundert.* Buchloe: Obermeyer, 1990.

Braham, Randolph L. *The Politics of Genocide: The Holocaust in Hungary.* New York: Columbia University Press, 1981.

—. *Studies on the Holocaust in Hungary.* Boulder, Colo.: Social Science Monographs, 1990.

—, ed. *The Destruction of Hungarian Jewry: A Documentary Account.* New York: Pro Arte for the World Federation of Hungarian Jews, 1963.

Bridgman, Jon. *The End of the Holocaust: The Liberation of the Camps.* Portland, Oregon: Areopagitica Press, 1990.

Bromberger, Barbara, Hanna Elling, Julta von Freyberg, and Ursula Krause-Schmitt. *Schwestern, vergesst uns nicht. Frauen im Konzentrationslager: Moringen, Lichtenburg,* *Ravensbrueck, 1933-1945.* Frankfurt am Main: VAS-Verlag fuer Akademische Schriften, 1988.

Buchheim, Hans, Martin Broszat, Hans-Adolf Jacobsen, and Helmut Krausnick. *Anatomie des SS-Staates.* Munich: Deutscher Taschenbuch Verlag, 1967.

Buechner, Howard A. *Dachau: The Hour of the Avenger (An Eyewitness Account).* Metairie, La.: Thunderbird, 1986.

Bullinger, Thomas, ed. *Gurs, 1939-1943: ein Internierungslager in Suedfrankreich: Zeichnungen, Aquarelle, Fotografien.* Hamburg: Hamburger Stiftung zur Foerderung von Wissenschaft und Kultur, 1993.

Burleigh, Michael and Wolfgang Wippermann. *The Racial State: Germany, 1933-1945.* New York: Cambridge University Press, 1991.

Butnaru, I. C. *The Silent Holocaust: Romania and Its Jews.* New York: Greenwood, 1992.

—. *Waiting for Jerusalem: Surviving the Holocaust in Romania.* Westport, Conn.: Greenwood, 1993.

Carlebach, Emil, Paul Gruenewald, Helmut Roder, and Willy Schmidt. *Buchenwald: ein Konzentrationslager.* Berlin: Dietz, 1986.

Carp, Matatias. *Holocaust in Romania: Facts and Documents on the Annihilation of Romania's Jews, 1940-44.* Budapest: Primor, 1994.

Cohen, Marcel, Diane Kolnokoff, Jacques Kolkikoff, Robert Linhart, Genevieve Mouillaud-Fraisse, Sylvia Ostrowiecki, Eric Didier, and Gerard Conio. *Les camps en Provence: exil, internement, deportation, 1933-1944.* Aix-en-Provence: Editions Alinea et L.L.C.G., 1984.

Comite national pour l'erection et la conservation d'un memorial de la deportation au Struthof. *Natzweiler Struthof.* Paris: Commission executive du comite national du Struthof, 1964.

Czech, Danuta. *Auschwitz Chronicle, 1939-1945.* New York: Henry Holt, 1990.

Czerniakow, Adam. *The Warsaw Diary of Adam Czerniakow: Prelude to Doom.* New York: Stein and Day, 1979.

Dachauer Hefte. *Dachauer Hefte.* Dachau: Verlag Dachauer Hefte, 1985-1995.

Dekel, Ephraim. *B'riha: Flight to the Homeland.* New York: Herzl, 1973.

Diamant, David. *Les juifs dans la resistance francaise, 1940-1944*. Paris: Le Pavillon, 1971.

Diament, Adolf, ed. *Deportationsbuch der von Frankfurt am Main aus gewaltsam verschickten Juden in den Jahren 1941 bis 1944*. Frankfurt am Main: Juedische Gemeinde Frankfurt am Main, 1984.

—, ed. *Deportationsbuch der in den Jahren 1942 bis 1945 von Leipzig aus gewaltsam verschickten Juden*. Frankfurt am Main: Selbstverlag, 1991.

Distel, Barbara, and Ruth Jakusch, eds. *Concentration Camp Dachau, 1933-1945*. Brussels: Comite International de Dachau, 1978.

Dobroszycki, Lucjan, ed. *The Chronicle of the Lodz Ghetto, 1941-1944*. New Haven: Yale University Press, 1984.

Donati, Giuliana. *Ebrei in Italia: Deportazione, Resistenza*. Milano: Centro di Documentazione Ebraica Contemporanea, 1974.

Durand, Pierre. *La chienne de Buchenwald*. Paris: Temps actuels, 1982.

Durin, Jacques. *Drancy, 1941-1944*. Le Bourget: GM imprimerie, 1988.

Ehmann, Annegret, Wolf Kaiser, Christiane Klingspor, Michael Metto, Horst Neumann, Pim Richter, Ewa M. Runge, and Martina Voigt. *Die Grunewald-Rampe: die Deportation der Berliner Juden*, 2d ed. Berlin: Edition Colloquium, 1993.

Eisfeld, Rainer. *Die unmenschliche Fabrik: V2-Produktion und KZ "Mittelbau-Dora."* Nordhausen: KZ-Gedenkstaette Mittelbau-Dora, 1991.

Elazar, Daniel Judah. *The Jewish Communities of Scandinavia—Sweden, Denmark, Norway, and Finland*. Lanham, Md.: University Press of America, 1984.

Encyclopedia Judaica. Vol. 14, 699-707. New York: Macmillan, 1972.

Exenberger, Herbert. *Guide to Vienna in Resistance, 1938-1945*. Vienna: Austria Today, 1985.

Fayol, Pierre. *Le Chambon-sur-Lignon sous l'occupation*. Paris: Editions l'Harmattan, 1990.

Fein, Erich, and Karl Flanner. *Rot-weiss-rot in Buchenwald. Die oesterreichischen politischen Haeftlinge im Konzentrationslager am Ettersberg bei Weimar 1938-1945*. Vienna: Europaverlag, 1987.

Fittko, Lisa. *Escape through the Pyrenees*. Evanston, Ill.: Northwestern University Press, 1991.

Flender, Harold. *Rescue in Denmark*. New York: Simon and Schuster, 1963.

Frank, Anne. *Anne Frank: The Diary of a Young Girl*. New York: Pocket Books, 1972.

Frank, Anne. *The Diary of Anne Frank: The Critical Edition*. New York: Doubleday, 1989.

Fuellberg-Stolberg, Claus, Martina Jung, Renate Riebe, and Martina Scheitenberger, eds. *Frauen in Konzentrationslagern: Bergen-Belsen; Ravensbrueck*. Bremen: Edition Temmen, 1994.

Genee, Pierre. *Synagogen in Oesterreich*. Vienna: Loecker, 1992.

Genee, Pierre, Ruth Burstyn, and Walter Lindner. *Wiener Synagogen 1825-1938*. Vienna: Loecker, 1987.

Goldberger, Leo. *The Rescue of the Danish Jews: Moral Courage under Stress*. New York: New York University Press, 1987.

Grabitz, Helge. *Letzte Spuren: Ghetto Warschau, SS-Arbeitslager Trawniki, Aktion Erntefest: Fotos und Dokumente ueber Opfer des Endloesungswahns im Spiegel der historischen Ereignisse*. Berlin: Edition Hentrich, 1988.

Grabowska, Janina. *K.L. Stutthof. Ein historischer Abriss*. Translated by Leon Lendzion. Bremen: Edition Temmen, 1990.

Graf, Malvina. *The Krakow Ghetto and the Plaszow Camp Remembered*. Tallahassee: Florida State University Press, 1989.

Greiss, Thomas, ed. *Atlas for the Second World War: Europe and the Mediterranean*. Wayne, N.J.: Avery Publishing Group, n.d.

Grynberg, Anne. *Les camps de la honte: les internes juifs des camps francais (1939-1944)*. Paris: La Decouverte, 1991.

Gutman, Israel. *The Jews of Warsaw, 1939-1943: Ghetto, Underground, Revolt*. Bloomington: Indiana University Press, 1982.

—. *Resistance: The Warsaw Ghetto Uprising*. Boston: Houghton Mifflin, 1994.

—, ed. *Encyclopedia of the Holocaust*. 4 vols. New York: Macmillan, 1990.

Gutman, Israel, and Efraim Zuroff, eds. *Rescue Attempts during the Holocaust; Proceedings of the Second Yad Vashem International Historical Conference, Jerusalem, April 8-11, 1974*. New York: Ktav, 1978.

Gutman, Israel, and Michael Berenbaum, eds. *Anatomy of the Auschwitz Death Camp*. Bloomington: Indiana University Press in association with the United States Holocaust Memorial Museum, 1994.

Hahn, Joachim. *Synagogen in Baden-Wuerttemberg*. Stuttgart: K. Theiss, 1987.

Herzer, Ivo, Klaus Voigt, and James Burgwyn, eds. *The Italian Refuge: Rescue of Jews during the Holocaust*. Washington, D.C.: Catholic University of America Press, 1989.

Hilberg, Raul. *The Destruction of the European Jews*. New York: Holmes & Meier, 1985.

Hohmann, Joachim Stephan. *Geschichte der Zigeunerverfolgung in Deutschland*. New York: Campus Verlag, 1988.

Houwaart, Dick. *Westerbork: Het Begon in 1933*. The Hague: Omniboek, 1983.

International Tracing Service. *Verzeichnis der Haftstaetten unter dem Reichsfuehrer-SS (1933-1945)*. 2 vols. Arolsen, Germany: International Committee of the Red Cross, 1979.

Jewish Historical Museum of Amsterdam. *Documents of the Persecution of the Dutch Jewry, 1940-1945*. Amsterdam: Athenaeum-Polak & Van Gennep, 1979.

Jong, Louis de. *The Netherlands and Nazi Germany*. Cambridge: Harvard University Press, 1990.

Katz, Robert. *Black Sabbath: A Journey through a Crime against Humanity*. New York: Macmillan, 1969.

Kaufmann, Max. *Die Vernichtung des Juden Lettlands: Churbn Lettland*. Munich: Im Selbstverlag, 1947.

Kermish, Joseph, ed. *To Live with Honor and Die with Honor!: Selected Documents from the Warsaw Ghetto Underground Archives "O.S." ("Oneg Shabbath")*. Jerusalem: Yad Vashem, 1986.

Klarsfeld, Serge. *Le memorial de la deportation des juifs de France*. Paris: Klarsfeld, 1978.

—. *The Children of Izieu: A Human Tragedy*. New York: Harry N. Abrams, 1985.

—. *Le calendrier de la persecution des juifs en France, 1940-1944*. Paris: L'association "Les fils et filles des deportes juifs en France" and the Beate Klarsfeld Foundation, 1993.

Klarsfeld, Serge, and Maxime Steinberg. *Memorial de la deportation des juifs de Belgique*. New York: Beate Klarsfeld Foundation, 1982.

Klee, Ernst, Willi Dressen, and Volker Reiss, eds. *"The Good Old Days": The Holocaust as Seen by Its Perpetrators and Bystanders*. New York: Free Press, 1991.

Knout, David. *Contribution a l'histoire de la resistance juive en France: 1940-1944*. Paris: Editions du centre, 1947.

Koenig, Ulrich. *Sinti und Roma unter dem Nationalsozialismus: Verfolgung und Widerstand*. Bochum: N. Brockmeyer, 1989.

Kogon, Eugen. *Nationalsozialistische Massentoetungen durch Giftgas: eine Dokumentation*. Frankfurt am Main: S. Fischer, 1983.

Kolb, Eberhard. *Bergen-Belsen: Geschichte des "Aufenthaltslager," 1943-1945*. Hannover: Verlag fuer Literatur und Zeitgeschehen, 1962.

—. *Bergen-Belsen: vom "Aufenthaltslager" zum Konzentrationslager, 1943-1945*. Goettingen: Vandenhoeck & Ruprecht, 1985.

Konieczny, Alfred. "Das Konzentrationslager Gross-Rosen." *Dachauer Hefte* 5. Jahrgang, Heft 5 (November 1989): 15-27.

Kowalski, Isaac, ed. and comp. *Anthology on Armed Jewish Resistance*. Vol. 2. Brooklyn, N.Y.: Jewish Combatants Publisher's House, 1984.

Krakowski, Shmuel. "Massacre of Jewish Prisoners on the Samland Peninsula—Documents." *Yad Vashem Studies* 24 (1994): 349-387.

Kugelmass, Jack, and Jonathan Boyarin, eds. *From a Ruined Garden: The Memorial Books of Polish Jewry*. New York: Schocken, 1983.

Laharie, Claude. *Le camp de Gurs: 1939-1945. Un aspect meconnu de l'histoire du Bearn*. Biarritz: Societe Atlantique d'impression, 1985.

Lasry, Jean-Claude, and Claude Tapia. *Les Juifs du Maghreb: diasporas contemporaines*. Paris: Editions l'Harmattan, 1989.

Latour, Anny. *The Jewish Resistance in France, 1940-1944*. New York: Schocken, 1981.

Laub, Morris. *Last Barrier to Freedom: Internment of Jewish Holocaust Survivors on Cyprus, 1946-1949.* Berkeley, Calif.: J.L. Magnes Museum, 1985.

Levy, Claude. *La grande rafle du Vel d'Hiv (16 Juillet 1942).* Paris: R. Laffont, 1967.

Lichtenstein, Heiner. *Mit der Reichsbahn in den Tod: Massentransporte in den Holocaust 1941 bis 1945.* Koeln: Bund-Verlag, 1985.

Lindwer, Willy. *The Last Seven Months of Anne Frank.* New York: Pantheon, 1991.

Lipschitz, Chaim U. *Franco, Spain, the Jews, and the Holocaust.* New York: Ktav, 1984.

Madajczyk, Czeslaw. *Die Okkupationspolitik Nazideutschlands in Polen, 1939-1945.* Translated by Berthold Puchert. Berlin: Akademie-Verlag, 1987.

Marrus, Michael Robert, and Robert O. Paxton. *Vichy France and the Jews.* New York: Basic, 1981.

Marsalek, Hans. *Die Geschichte des Konzentrationslagers Mauthausen: Dokumentation.* Vienna: Oesterreichische Lagergemeinschaft Mauthausen, 1980.

—. *Die Vergasungsaktionen im Konzentrationslager Mauthausen: Gaskammer, Gaswagen, Vergasungsanstalt Hartheim, Tarnnamen.* Vienna: Dokumentation, 1988.

Marshall, Robert. *In the Sewers of Lvov: A Heroic Story of Survival from the Holocaust.* New York: Maxwell Macmillan International, 1991.

Marszalek, Jozef. *Majdanek: The Concentration Camp in Lublin.* Warsaw: Interpress, 1986.

Mogilanski, Roman, ed. *The Ghetto Anthology: A Comprehensive Chronicle of the Extermination of Jewry in Nazi Death Camps and Ghettos in Poland.* Los Angeles: American Congress of Jews from Poland and Survivors of Concentration Camps, 1985.

Mokotoff, Gary, and Sallyann Amdur Sack. *Where Once We Walked: A Guide to the Jewish Communities Destroyed in the Holocaust.* Teaneck, N.J.: Avotaynu, 1991.

Molho, Michael. *In Memoriam: Hommage aux victimes juives des nazis en Grece.* Thessalonique: Communaute israelite de Thessalonique, 1973.

Mueller-Hill, Benno. *Murderous Science: Elimination by Scientific Selection of Jews, Gypsies, and Others; Germany, 1933-1945.* Translated by George R. Fraser. New York:

Oxford University Press, 1988.

Novitch, Miriam. *The Passage of the Barbarians.* Hull, England: Wilberforce Council, 1989.

Ofer, Dalia. *Escaping the Holocaust: Illegal Immigration to the Land of Israel, 1939-1944.* New York: Oxford University Press, 1990.

Office of Geography, Department of the Interior. *Official Standard Names Gazetteer: Approved by the U.S. Board on Geographic Names.* Washington, D.C.: Department of the Interior, 1960-1988.

Pehle, H., ed. *November 1938: From "Reichskristallnacht" to Genocide.* New York: Berg, 1991.

Peleg, Miryam. *Witnesses: Life in Occupied Krakow.* New York: Routledge, 1991.

Poliakov, Leon, and Jacques Sabille. *Jews under the Italian Occupation.* New York: Howard Fertig, 1983.

Press, Bernhard. *Judenmord in Riga, 1941-1945.* Berlin, 1988.

Presser, Jacob. *The Destruction of the Dutch Jews.* New York: E.P. Dutton, 1969.

Proudfoot, Malcolm Jarvis. *European Refugees: 1939-1952. A Study in Forced Population Movement.* Evanston, Ill.: Northwestern University Press, 1956.

Puvogel, Ulrike. *Gedenkstaetten fuer die Opfer des Nationalsozialismus: eine Dokumentation.* Bonn: Bundeszentrale fuer Politische Bildung, 1987.

Rol, Rund van der. *Anne Frank: Beyond the Diary—A Photographic Remembrance.* New York: Viking, 1993.

Rueter, C.F., and Adelheid L. Rueter-Ehlermann, eds. *Justiz und NS-Verbrechen: Sammlung deutscher Strafurteile wegen Nationalsozialistischer Toetungsverbrechen.* 22 vols. Amsterdam: University Press, 1968-81.

Sacerdoti, Annie. *Guide to Jewish Italy.* Brooklyn, N.Y.: Israelowitz, 1989.

Sanders, Ronald. *Shores of Refuge: A Hundred Years of Jewish Emigration.* New York: Henry Holt, 1988.

Schmid, Kurt, and Robert Streibel, eds. *Der Pogrom 1938: Judenverfolgung in Oesterreich und Deutschland: Dokumentation eines Symposiums der Volkshochschule Brigittenau.* Vienna: Picus, 1990.

Schneider, Gertrude. *Journey into Terror: The Story of the Riga Ghetto.* New York: Ark House, 1979.

—, ed. *Muted Voices: Jewish Survivors of Latvia Remember.* New York: Philosophical Library, 1987.

—, ed. *The Unfinished Road: Jewish Survivors of Latvia Remember.* New York: Praeger, 1991.

Schroeter, Kurt. *Tage, die so quaelend sind: Aufzeichnungen eines juedischen Buergers aus Groebenzell im besetzten Amsterdam, September 1942-Januar 1943.* Munich: R. Kovar, 1993.

Schur, Maxine. *Hannah Szenes: A Song of Light.* Philadelphia: Jewish Publication Society of America, 1986.

Schwarz, Gudrun. *Die nationalsozialistischen Lager.* New York: Campus, 1990.

Schwarz, Stefan. *Die juedische Gedenkstaette in Dachau.* Munich: Landesverband der Israelitischen Kultusgemeinden in Bayern, 1972.

Smolar, Hersh. *The Minsk Ghetto: Soviet-Jewish Partisans against the Nazis.* New York: Holocaust Publications, 1989.

Steen, Juergen, and Wolf von Wolzogen. *Anne aus Frankfurt: Leben und Lebenswelt Anne Franks.* Frankfurt am Main: Historisches Museum Frankfurt am Main, 1990.

Stein, Harry. *Juden in Buchenwald, 1937-1942.* Weimar: Gedenkstaette Buchenwald, 1992.

Steinbacher, Sybille. *Dachau—die Stadt und das Konzentrationslager in der NS-Zeit. Die Untersuchung einer Nachbarschaft.* (Muenchner Studien zur neueren und neuesten Geschichte, Band 5), Frankfurt am Main: Peter Lang, 1994.

Stock, Ernest. *Chosen Instrument: The Jewish Agency in the First Decade of the State of Israel.* New York: Herzl, 1988.

Thomas, Gordon. *Voyage of the Damned.* Greenwich, Conn.: Fawcett, 1974.

Tillion, Germaine. *Ravensbrueck.* Garden City, N.Y.: Anchor, 1975.

Tory, Avraham. *Surviving the Holocaust: The Kovno Ghetto Diary.* Cambridge: Harvard University Press, 1990.

Trial of the Major War Criminals before the International Military Tribunal, Nuremberg 14 November 1945-1 October 1946. Nuremberg: 1947-1949.

Trials of War Criminals before the Nuernberg Military Tribunals under Control Council Law no. 10. October 1946-April 1949. Washington, D.C.: U.S.G.P.O., 1949-1953.

Trunk, Isaiah. *Judenrat: The Jewish Councils in Eastern Europe under Nazi Occupation.* New York: Stein and Day, 1977.

Warmbrunn, Werner. *The German Occupation of Belgium, 1940-1944.* New York: Peter Lang, 1993.

Weglein, Resi. *Als Krankenschwester im KZ Theresienstadt: Erinnerungen einer Ulmer Juedin.* Stuttgart: Silberburg-Verlag, 1988.

Weinberg, Gerhard L. *A World at Arms: A Global History of World War II.* Cambridge and New York: Cambridge University Press, 1994.

Weinmann, Martin, ed. *Das nationalsozialistische Lagersystem.* Frankfurt am Main: Zweitausendeins, 1990.

Wiehn, Erhard, ed. *Oktoberdeportation 1940: die sogenannte "Abschiebung" der badischen und saarpfaelzischen Juden in das franzoesische Internierungslager Gurs und andere Vorstationen von Auschwitz: 50 Jahre danach zum Gedenken.* Konstanz: Hartung-Gore, 1990.

Wistrich, Robert S., ed. *Austrians and Jews in the Twentieth Century: From Franz Joseph to Waldheim.* New York: St. Martin's, 1992.

Yahil, Leni. *The Rescue of Danish Jewry: Test of a Democracy.* Translated by Morris Gradel. Philadelphia: Jewish Publication Society of America, 1969.

—. *The Holocaust: The Fate of European Jewry, 1932-1945.* Translated by Ina Friedman and Haya Galai. New York: Oxford University Press, 1990.

Zentner, Christian, and Friedemann Beduerftig, eds. *The Encyclopedia of the Third Reich.* 2 vols. New York: Macmillan, 1991.

Zoerner, G. *Frauen-KZ Ravensbrueck.* Berlin: Deutscher Verlag der Wissenschaften, 1982.

Zucotti, Susan. *The Holocaust, the French, and the Jews.* New York: Basic, 1993.

This gazetteer is a comprehensive listing of place names found on the maps in the *Historical Atlas of the Holocaust*. Cities and towns are generally named according to the language of the country in which they were located before World War II. However, because national boundaries shifted radically before, during, and after World War II, extensive cross referencing with alternate spellings of many eastern European places is also included. German designations are used for Nazi concentration camps: in cases where a camp is listed by its German name and the nearby town by another name, *see also* references direct the reader from one term to the other. Many alternate place-name spellings come from sources such as the United States Board on Geographic Names *Official Standard Names Gazetteer* for each European country covered and from Gary Mokotoff and Sallyann Amdur Sack's *Where Once We Walked: A Guide to the Jewish Communities Destroyed in the Holocaust*. Camp names come largely from *Verzeichnis der Haftstaetten unter dem Reichsfuehrer-SS (1933-1945)* of the International Committee of the Red Cross.

The gazetteer uses the following conventions for ease of use. Alternate spellings appear in parentheses after a term; for example, *Belchatow, (Belchatov, Belkhatov) 36, 42, 54-55, 82*.

Where the same term actually refers to more than one location, the entries are distinguished from each other by a bracketed term identifying the larger town or camp with which each distinct location is associated in the atlas; for example, *Brezeziny [Belzec] 84* and *Brezeziny [Lodz] 42-43*.

The letter *t* following a page reference indicates that the term will be found on the map at the top of that page; the letter *b* that it will be found on the map at the bottom of the page.

The extensive Table of Contents found at the front of this atlas is a thematic and regional guide to the maps.

A

Aachen, (Aix la Chapelle) 121

Aalst, 116, 124

Aarschot, 124

Acre, 220b

Adamczuki, 87

Admont, 217

Aflenz, 152

Agen, 110

Agram, *see* Zagreb

Agustov, *see* Augustow

Aichach, 207t

Ainring, 217

Aix la Chapelle, *see* Aachen

Akhmetchetka, 71, 72b

Akovo, *see* Djakovo

Albania, 14, 16, 170-71, 180-181, 221

Albertfalva, 189t, 190

Alexsander, *see* Aleksandrow

Aleksandrov, *see* Aleksandrow

Aleksandrow, (Aleksander, Aleksandrov, Aleksandrow Lodzki) 43

Aleksandrow Lodski, *see* Aleksandrow

Aleksat, *see* Aleksotas

Aleksotas, (Aleksat) 68

Alexandru-Cel-Bun, 71

Alexoten, 65

Alkmaar, 116, 119

Allach, 146, 208

Allendorf, (Allendorf an der Lumda) 149

Allendorf an der Lumda, *see* Allendorf

Allenstein, (Olsztyn) 24

Alsace-Lorraine, 106, 112, 115

Alsobudak, *see* Bistrita

Alt Lesle, *see* Wloclawek

Alt Ofen, *see* Budapest

Altdamm, *see* Dabie

Altdorf, 99b

Altenburg, 155

Altenhofen, 150

Althammer, 99b, 205

Amager, 194

Amersfoort, 117, 119

Amman, 220b

Ampermoching, 146

Ampfing, 146

Amsterdam, 78-79, 116, 119-121

Amstetten, 152

Andalsnes, 195

Andrespol, 43

Andrichov, *see* Andrychow

Andrikhov, *see* Andrychow

Andrychow, (Andrichov, Andrikhov, Yendrikhov) 98

Angelholm, 194

Angers, 99t, 107

Anninmuiza, 66

Antwerp, 25, 99t, 116-117, 124

Apeldoorn, 116

Apolda, 147

Aqaba, 220b

Aranzenii Vechi, *see* Bratislava

Aren, 110

Argenau, (Gnevkovy, Gniewkowo, Nefcover) 161

Argentina, 26-27

Arnhem, 116-117

Arnstadt, 147

Arolsen, 149

Arras, 112

Artern, 164

Asbach, 115

Aschersleben, 149

Aseri, 65

Ashkelon, 220b

Aslau, 158

Assen, 116

Asten, 150

Andrikhov, *see* Andrychow

Asti, 172-173

Athens, 99t, 168, 169b, 170-171, 174-175, 180b-181, 218-219

Aufkirchen, 208

Augsburg, 24, 146

Augsburg-Pfersee, 146

Augustov, *see* Augustow

Augustow, (Agustov, Augustov, Oygstova, Yagestov, Yagistov, Yagustova) 58

Aumale, 112

Auschwitz, 45, 76-77, 93-99, 121, 128-129, 136b, 138-143, 188, 200, 204-205, 209, 216

Auschwitz I, 93-95

Auschwitz II (Birkenau), 93-94, 96

Auschwitz III (Monowitz), 93-94, 97, 205

Aushvits, *see* Oswiecim

Aussig, (Usti nad Labem) 207t

Austria, 14-16, 18t, 20, 24, 201, 216-219, 221

B

Babenhausen, 217

Babi Yar, 51, 53

Babitz, 93-94, 99b

Bachern, 144

Bachmanning, 152

Backa-Topolya, 172-173

Bacsalmas, 172-173, 186b

Bad Berka, 147, 149

Bad Gandersheim, (Gandersheim) 149

Bad Ischl, 146

Bad Lauchstadt, *see* Langensalza

Bad Oberdorf, 146

Bad Rappenau, (Rappenau) 115

Bad Reichenhall, 217

Bad Salzbrunn, 158

Bad Salzschlirf, (Salzschlirf) 217

Bad Salzungen, 149

Bad Toelz, 146, 208

Bad Warmbrunn, 158

Badgastein, 217

Baeumenheim, 146

Baia Mare, *see* Nagybanya

Baja, 172-173, 186b, 188

Balashadzharmat, *see* Balassagyarmat

Balassagyarmat, (Balashadzharmat, Boloshodyormot, Dyormot, Dzhormot) 188

Balchik, 196

Balf, 186b

Balingen, 115

Ballenstedt, 164

Balti, (Beltsy, Beltz, Belzy, Bielce) 71, 72b

Baltic countries, 64-65

Baltoja Voke, *see* Biala Waka

Bamberg, 217

Banjica, 172-173

Bankau, 206

Banska Bystrica, (Besztercebanya, Neusohl) 18b-19

Bar, (Ber) 71

Baranovich, *see* Baranovichi

Baranovichi, (Baranovich, Baranovitch, Baranovitsh, Baranowicze) 51, 54-56, 198

Baranovitch, *see* Baranovichi

Baranovitsh, *see* Baranovichi

Baranowicze, *see* Baranovichi

Bardichev, *see* Berdichev

Bari, 218-219

Barneveld, 117

Barsad, *see* Bersad

Barth, 155

Barzan, *see* Berezhany

Bastogne, 116

Bauschowitz, *see* Bohusovice nad Ohri

Bautzen, 207t

Baven, 165

Bayonne, 110

Bayrischzell, 146

Beaune-la-Rolande, 99t, 106-107, 112

Beckedorf, 165

Becklingen, 165

Bedzin, (Bendin, Bendzin) 36, 54-55, 98, 200

Beelitz, 130

Beersheba, 220b

Beilen, 122

Bekescsaba, 185, 188

Belaya Vaka, *see* Biala Waka

Belchatov, *see* Belchatow

Belchatow, (Belchatov, Belkhatov) 36, 42, 54-55, 82

Belgium, 14, 16-17, 25-27, 33, 104-105, 116-118, 221

Belgrade, (Beograd, Nandorfehervar) 32, 168-169t, 170-175, 216

Belkhatov, *see* Belchatow

Belmont, 113

Belorussia, 56, 215t

Belostok, *see* Bialystok

Belsen, 165, 217

Beltsy, *see* Balti

Beltz, *see* Balti

Belzec, (Belzhets, Belzhetz) 45, 76-77, 83-86, 128-129, 140-142

Belzhets, *see* Belzec

Belzhetz, *see* Belzec

Belzig, 155

Belzy, *see* Balti

Bendin, *see* Bedzin

Bendzin, *see* Bedzin

Bensheim, 217

Bensheim-Auerbach, 115

Beograd, *see* Belgrade

Ber, *see* Bar

Berchan, *see* Briceni

Berck Plage, 112

Berdichev, (Bardichev, Berditchev, Berditchov, Berdyczow) 51, 54-55, 78-79

Berditchev, *see* Berdichev

Berditchov, *see* Berdichev

Berdyczow, *see* Berdichev

Beregovo, *see* Beregszasz

Beregszasz, (Beregovo, Berehovo, Berehowo, Sachsisch-Bereg) 188

Berehovo, *see* Beregszasz

Berehowo, *see* Beregszasz

Beresovka, *see* Berezovka

Berezany, *see* Berezhany

Berezhany, (Barzan, Berezany, Berson, Berzhan, Brezan, Brzesciany, Brzezany, Brzezhany, Bzezan, Bzhezhani) 51, 54-55, 86

Berezovca, *see* Berezovka

Berezovka, (Beresovka, Berezovca, Berozovka) 71

Berg, 140-141

Bergen, 165, 195

Bergen-Belsen, 121, 138-142, 165-166, 204-206, 207b, 209, 218-219

Bergkirchen, 144

Berlin, 15, 24, 42, 78-79, 99t, 128-130, 212, 215b, 217-219

Berlstedt, 147

Bernau, 130

Bernburg, 28, 149

Bernsdorf, 158

Berozovka, *see* Berezovka

Bersad, (Barsad, Bershad, Berszad, Berszada) 71

Bersdorf, 156

Bershad, *see* Bersad

Berson, *see* Berezhany

Berszad, *see* Bersad

Berszada, *see* Bersad

Berzhan, *see* Berezhany

Bessarabia, 31, 72

Bestercze, 188

Besztece, *see* Bistrita

Besztercebanya, *see* Banska Bystrica

Beszterecz, 187

Beuerberg, 208

Biala D'lita, *see* Biala Podlaska

Biala Gadol, *see* Biala Podlaska

Biala Podlaska, (Biala D'lita, Biala Gadol, Podlyashe) 89

Biala Waka, (Baltoja Voke, Belaya Vaka) 65

Bialistok, *see* Bialystok

Bialystok, (Belostok, Bialistok) 31, 34, 50-51, 54-55, 58-59, 92, 98, 102, 128-129, 142, 198, 200, 215t, 216

Bialystok District, 34-35, 58, 198

Bialystok Forest, 198

Biberach, (Biberach an der Riss) 217

Biberach an der Riss, *see* Biberach

Bidgoshch, *see* Bromberg

Bielany, 94

Bielawa Dolna, *see* Langenbielau

Bielce, *see* Balti

Bielsk Podlaski, (Bielsko Podlaskie, Bilsk, Byelsk, Byelsk Podlaski) 58

Bielsko Podlaskie, *see* Bielsk
Podlaski

Bikernieki, 66

Billroda, 149

Bilsk, *see* Bielsk Podlaski

Binau, 115

Birkenau, *see* Auschwitz II
(Birkenau); Brzezinka

Bischofferode, 162, 164

Bisingen, 115

Bismarckhuette, 99b

Bistrita, (Alsobudak, Besztece)
70

Bitola, (Bitolj, Bitolja,
Monastir) 168

Bitolj, *see* Bitola

Bitolja, *see* Bitola

Blagoevgrad, *see* Gorna
Dzhumaya

Blaichach, 146

Blankenburg, 149. *See also*
Blankenburg am Harz

Blankenburg am Harz, 164. *See
also* Blankenburg

Blankenhain, 147

Blechhammer, 99b, 205

Bleckmar, 165

Bledov, *see* Bledow

Bledow, (Bledov, Blendov) 39

Bleicherode, 164

Blendov, *see* Bledow

Blonie, (Bloyna) 39

Bloyna, *see* Blonie

Bobrek, (Bobrek Karf) 99b

Bobrek Karf, *see* Bobrek

Bochnia, (Bokhnia, Kolanow,
Salzberg) 98

Bochum, 149

Bockfliess, 132

Bodo, 195

Bogdanovka, 71, 72b

Bohnsack, 159

Bohrauseifersdorf, 156

Bohusovice nad Ohri, 134

Bohusowice, *see* Bohusovice
nad Ohri

Bojewo, 90

Bokhnia, *see* Bochnia

Bolderaja, 66

Bolechov, *see* Bolekhov

Bolechow, *see* Bolekhov

Bolechow Ruski, *see* Bolekhov

Bolekhov, (Bolechov,
Bolechow, Bolechow
Ruski) 198

Bolimov, *see* Bolimow

Bolimow, (Bolimov) 39

Bolivia, 26-27

Bolkenhain, 158

Bologna, 180t, 182

Boloshodyormot, *see*
Balassagyarmat

Bolshoi Trostinets, 56

Bolzano, 99t, 140-141, 172-
175, 180t, 182

Bonn, 24

Bonstorf, 165

Bordeaux, 110

Borgo San Dalmazzo, 174-175,
182

Born, 155

Bornholm, 194

Borshchev, (Borshchov,
Borshtchev, Borszczow)
198

Borshchov, *see* Borshchev

Borshtchev, *see* Borshchev

Borszczow, *see* Borshchev

Bosanska Gradiska, 176b

Bosna Serai, *see* Sarajevo

Boszormeny, *see*
Hajduboszormeny

Brandenburg, 28, 130

Brandhofen, 158

Bransk, (Braynsk, Breinsk) 58

Braslav, *see* Braslaw

Braslaw, (Braslav, Breslav,
Breslev) 200

Bratislava, (Aranzenii Vechi,
Bratyslawa, Pozsony,
Pressburg) 18b-19, 99t,
216, 218-219

Bratyslawa, *see* Bratislava

Braunschweig, *see* Brunswick

Braynsk, *see* Bransk

Brazil, 26-27

Breda, 116-117

Bredtveit, 140-141

Breendonk, 99t, 117-118, 124,
126, 140-141

Breinsk, *see* Bransk

Breitenau, 21, 144

Bremen, 24, 207b, 215b

Brens, 106, 112

Breslau, (Bress2au, Wroclaw)
15, 24, 128-129, 158, 205,
215t

Breslav, *see* Braslaw

Breslev, *see* Braslaw

Bresslau, *see* Breslau

Brest, 104t, 112

Brest Kujavsk, *see* Brzesc
Kujawski

Brest Litovsk, *see* Brest-Litovsk

Brest-Litovsk, (Brest Litovsk,
Brest Litowsk, Brisk,
Brisk D Lita, Brisk Dlita,
Brist nad Bugie, Brzesc
Litewski, Brzesc nad
Bugiem, Bzheshch
nad Bugyem) 51, 54-55,
198

Brest Litowsk, *see* Brest-
Litovsk

Bretstein, 152

Brezan, *see* Berezhany

Briceni, (Berchan, Briceni Sat,
Briceni Targ, Brichany,
Bricheni, Bricheni Sat,
Bricheni Targ, Britshan,
Britshani, Britsiteni) 71,
72b

Briceni Sat, *see* Briceni

Briceni Targ, *see* Briceni

Brichany, *see* Briceni

Bricheni, *see* Briceni

Bricheni Sat, *see* Briceni

Bricheni Targ, *see* Briceni

Brieg, (Brzeg, Bzheg) 158

Brisk, *see* Brest-Litovsk

Brisk D Koya, *see* Brzesc

Kujawski

Brisk D Lita, *see* Brest-Litovsk

Brisk Dlita, *see* Brest-Litovsk

Brisk Kuyavsk, *see* Brzesc
Kujawski

Brist nad Bugie, *see* Brest-
Litovsk

Britshan, *see* Briceni

Britshani, *see* Briceni

Britsiteni, *see* Briceni

Brno, (Bruenn, Brunn) 136t

Brocice, 176

Brod, *see* Brody

Brod Uhersky, *see* Uhersky
Brod

Broda, *see* Uhersky Brod

Brody, (Brod, Prode) 51, 54-55,
86, 102

Brok, 90

Bromberg, (Bidgoshch,
Bydgoszcz) 161

Brueckhofen, 142

Bruenn, *see* Brno

Bruennlitz, 158

Brugge, 116

Brunn, *see* Brno

Brunswick, (Braunschweig)
216

Brussels, 116, 124

Brzeg, *see* Brieg

Brzeg Dolny, *see* Dyhernfurth

Brzegi, *see* Dyhernfurth

Brzesc Kujawski, (Brest
Kujavsk, Brisk D Koya,
Brisk Kuyavsk) 42

Brzesc Litewski, *see* Brest-
Litovsk

Brzesc nad Bugiem, *see* Brest-
Litovsk

Brzesciany, *see* Berezhany

Brzeszcze, 94

Brzezany, *see* Berezhany

Brzezhany, *see* Berezhany

Brzezinka (Birkenau), 93-94.
See also Auschwitz II
(Birkenau)

Brzeziny [Belzec] 84

Brzeziny [Lodz] 42-43,

Bucharest, (Bucuresti) 70, 78-
79, 196, 216

Buchenwald, 22, 138-143, 147-
149, 204-205, 207, 209

Buchwald-Hohenwiese, 158

Bucuresti, see Bucharest

Buda, see Budapest

Budafok, 189-190

Budaors, 189t

Budapest, (Alt Ofen, Buda,
Budon, Kobanya, Obuda,
Ofen, Pest) 78-79, 99t,
185-190, 197, 216

Budi, see Budy

Budon, see Budapest

Budy, (Budi) 93-94, 99b

Budzhin, see Budzyn

Budzin, see Budzyn

Budzyn, (Budzhin, Budzin) 45,
140-141

Buialyk, 73

Bukachevtsy, (Bukaczowce,
Bukotchovitz, Bukshevitz)
198

Bukaczowce, see Bukachevtsy

Bukotchovitz, see Bukachevtsy

Bukovina, (Gugel) 72

Bukshevitz, see Bukachevtsy

Bulgaria, 14, 16, 30, 33, 169b-
175, 196, 201, 218-219,
221

Bullenhof, 66

Bumsla, see Mlada Boleslav

Bunzlau, 158

Burdujeni, 71

Burg el Arab, 202

Burgas, 196

Burgau, 146

Burgbernheim, 217

Buttelstedt, 147, 149

Bydgoszcz, see Bromberg

Byelsk, see Bielsk Podlaski

Byelsk Podlaski, see Bielsk
Podlaski

Bzezan, see Berezhany

Bzheg, see Brieg

Bzheshch nad Bugyem, see
Brest-Litovsk

Bzhezhani, see Berezhany

C

Cacak, 172-173

Cagliari, 180t

Calais, 112, 199

Calarasi, (Calarasi Sat, Calarasi
Targ, Kalaras, Kalarash,
Tuzora) 71

Calarasi Sat, see Calarasi

Calarasi Targ, see Calarasi

Calw, 115

Cambrai, 112

Cannstatt, see Stuttgart

Caracal, 71

Carlsbad, (Karlovy Vary,
Karlsbad, Karlzbad) 24,
207t

Carpathian Ruthenia, see
Transcarpathian Ukraine

Carpi, 180t

Cassel, see Kassel

Castres, 199

Catania, 180t

Celle, 207b

Central America, 26-27

Central Europe, see Europe,
central

Cernauti, see Chernovtsy

Cernovcy, see Chernovtsy

Cernowitze Bukovina, see
Chernovtsy

Ceske Kopisty, 134

Channel Islands, 104t

Charkow, see Kharkov

Charleroi, 116

Charlottengrube, 99b

Chechinov, see Ciechanow

Chekhanov, see Ciechanow

Chekhanove, see Ciechanow

Chelem, see Chelm

Chelm, (Chelem, Khelem,
Khelm, Kholm) 89

Chelmek, 99b

Chelmno, 45, 76-77, 80-82,

138-142

Chelodz, see Czeladz

Chemnitz, (Karl-Marx-Stadt)
21, 24, 205, 207b

Chenstchov, see Czestochowa

Chenstochov, see Czestochowa

Chenstokhov, see Czestochowa

Cherbourg, 25

Chernovitsy, see Chernovtsy

Chernovitz, see Chernovtsy

Chernovtsky, see Chernovtsy

Chernovtsy, (Cernauti,
Cernovcy, Cernowitze
Bukovina, Chernovitsy,
Chernovitz, Chernovtsky,
Czerniowce, Czernovitz,
Czernowitz) 51, 54-55, 70-
72, 78-79

Cherson, see Kherson

Chervonoarmeyskoye, see
Cubei

Chestokhova, see Czestochowa

Chile, 26-27

Chisinau, see Kishinev

Chmelnitski, see Proskurov

Chmielnicki, see Proskurov

Chomutov, see Komotau

Chortkev, see Chortkov

Chortkov, (Chortkev,
Czortkow, Czortkow
Stary) 54-55, 198

Chortkow, 86

Chrastava, see Kratzau

Christianstadt, (Krzystkowice)
158

Chruscin, 80

Chrzanow, (Hrycowola, K
Shonev, Keshanov,
Khshanov, Khshanuv,
Krashanov, Kreshanov,
Kshanev, Kshanov) 98

Chust, see Huszt

Cichow, 80

Ciechanow, (Chechinov,
Chekhanov, Chekhanove,
Tshekhanov, Ziechenau)
98

Clermont-Ferrand, 199

Clervaux, 116

Cluj, (Cluj Napoca,
Klausenberg, Klausenburg,
Kluyzenburg, Kluzh,
Kolozhvar, Kolozsvar,
Kolozvar) 70, 99t, 185-
188, 215t

Cluj Napoca, see Cluj

Coblenz, see Koblenz

Cochem-Bruttig, 115

Coka, 172-173

Colditz, 21

Colmar, 115

Coln, see Cologne

Cologne, (Coln, Kelin, Keln,
Klunya, Koeln, Koln) 15,
24, 42, 128-129, 215b

Colonia Umberto I di Tonezza,
172-173

Columbia Haus, 21, 130

Compiegne, 99t, 106-107, 112,
140-141

Constanta, (Kuestendje) 196,
218-219

Copenhagen, 194, 216

Corfu, (Kerkira) 99t, 169b-175,
180-181

Corsica, 170-171, 180-181

Cracow, see Krakow

Crawinkel, 147, 149

Cremenciuc, see Kremenchug

Crete, 32, 169b

Croatia, 33, 169t, 170-175, 186

Csepel, 186b, 188

Cuba, 25, 26-27

Cubei, (Chervonoarmeyskoye)
71

Cuneo, 180t, 182

Cyprus, 218-220t

Czechoslovakia, 14-15, 17,
18b-20, 185, 216, 218-219,
221

Czeladz, (Chelodz) 98

Czerniowce, see Chernovtsy

Czernovitz, see Chernovtsy

Czernowitz, see Chernovtsy

Czestochowa, (Chenstchov, Chenstochov, Chenstokhov, Chestokhova, Tshenstokhov) 36, 54-55, 92, 198, 200

Czortkow, *see* Chortkov

Czortkow Stary, *see* Chortkov

D

Dabelow, 155

Dabie, (Altdamm, Dabie Miasto, Dambia, Dambye, Dombe, Dombie, Dombye) 80

Dabie Miasto, *see* Dabie

Dachau, 21-22, 138-146, 205, 208- 209, 216

Daetzdorf, 156

Dakovo, *see* Djakovo

Dalnik, 72b-73

Dambia, *see* Dabie

Dambye, *see* Dabie

Damerau, 159

Damshoehe, 155

Danica, 172-173

Daniszew, 80

Danzig, (Gdansk) 14-15, 17, 24, 31, 159, 161, 206

Danzig-West Prussia, 34-35

Darmstadt, 115t

Daugapils, *see* Dvinsk

Daugava, *see* Dvinsk

Daugavgriva, 66

Daugavpils, *see* Dvinsk

Dautmergen, (Schomberg Dautmergen) 115

Debrecen, (Debretsin) 99t, 185- 188

Debretsin, *see* Debrecen

Deelen, 117

Deggendorf, 217

Dej, (Des) 70, 99t, 185-188

Dendermonde, 124

Denmark, 14, 32, 194, 216, 221

Derechin, (Dereczyn, Deretchin, Derhichin,

Dretchin) 51, 54-55, 198

Dereczyn, *see* Derechin

Deretchin, *see* Derechin

Derhichin, *see* Derechin

Derpt, *see* Tartu

Des, *see* Dej

Dessau, 149

Deutsch Wagram, 132

Deutschoth, 112, 115

Dhekelia, 220t

Dhidhimotikhon, 174-175

Diatlovo, 51, 54-55, 198

Diekirch, 116

Diesten, 165

Dinaburg, *see* Dvinsk

Dinskivola, *see* Zdunska Wola

Dippoldsau, 152

Dirchau, *see* Dirschau

Dirschau, (Dirchau, Dirschaw, Strzewo, Tczew) 159

Dirschaw, *see* Dirschau

Djakovo, (Akovo, Dakovo) 172-173

Dnepropetrovsk, (Dniepropetrovsk, Ekaterinoslav, Jekaterynoslaw, Keterinoslav, Secheslav, Siczeslaw, Yekaterinoslav) 35, 50-51, 54-55, 215t

Dniepropetrovsk, *see* Dnepropetrovsk

Doaga, 71

Dobrovlyany, *see* Drogobych

Dobrow, 80

Dobrowlany, *see* Drogobych

Dodecanese Islands, 180

Domanevka, (Domanovca, Domonovca, Dumanovka) 71, 72b

Domanovca, *see* Domanevka

Dombas, 195

Dombe, *see* Dabie

Dombie, *see* Dabie

Dombye, *see* Dabie

Domonovca, *see* Domanevka

Dondangen, 65

Dora-Mittelbau, 138-142, 162- 164, 204-205, 207b, 209

Dormettingen, 115

Dornberg, 156

Dornburg, 149

Dorog, 190

Dorohoi, 70

Dorpa, *see* Tartu

Dorpat, 65. *See also* Tartu

Dortmund, 149

Dragor, 194

Drancy, 99t, 106-109, 112, 140-141

Drenov Bok, 176b

Dresden, (Drezden) 24, 205, 207t, 215b

Dretchin, *see* Derechin

Drezden, *see* Dresden

Drobich, *see* Drogobych

Droegen, 155

Drogobich, *see* Drogobych

Drogobych, (Dobrovlyany, Dobrowlany, Drobich, Drogobich, Drogobycz, Drohobich, Drohobitch, Drohobycz) 54-55, 86

Drogobycz, *see* Drogobych

Drohobich, *see* Drogobych

Drohobitch, *see* Drogobych

Drohobycz, *see* Drogobych

Dubeczno, (Dubetchna) 87

Dubetchna, *see* Dubeczno

Dubica, 176b

Duenaburg, 65. *See also* Dvinsk

Duenawerke, 65

Dueppel Center, 217

Duesseldorf, (Dusseldorf) 24, 42, 128-129, 149, 215b

Duffel, 124

Dumanovka, *see* Domanevka

Dunaberg, *see* Dvinsk

Dunaburg, *see* Dvinsk

Dunaszeg, 190

Dunkerque, 104t

Dupnitsa, (Marek, Stanke Dimitrov) 172-175

Dusseldorf, *see* Duesseldorf

Dvart, *see* Warta

Dvinsk, (Daugapils, Daugava, Daugavpils, Dinaburg, Duenaburg, Dunaberg, Dunaburg, Dwinsk, Dzvinsk) 51, 54-55, 64

Dvurt, *see* Warta

Dwinsk, *see* Dvinsk

Dwory, 93-94

Dyhernfurth, (Brzeg Dolny, Brzegi) 158

Dyormot, *see* Balassagyarmat

Dzhormot, *see* Balassagyarmat

Dzvinsk, *see* Dvinsk

E

East Prussia, 21, 24, 34-35

Eastern Europe, *see* Europe, eastern

Ebensee, 142, 152, 209, 217

Eberswalde, 130, 155

Echterdingen, 115

Ecrouves, 107, 112

Edineti, (Edineti Sat, Edineti Targ, Edinita, Edinita Targ, Jedincy, Yedinets, Yedintsy) 70-72

Edineti Sat, *see* Edineti

Edineti Targ, *see* Edineti

Edinita, *see* Edineti

Edinita Targ, *see* Edineti

Eger, 207t

Egypt, 202

Eilat, 220b

Eindhoven, 116-117

Eintrachthuette, 99b

Eisenerz, 152

Eisenhuttenstadt, *see* Fuerstenberg

Ekaterinoslav, *see* Dnepropetrovsk

Elba, 180, 182

Elberfeld, *see* Wuppertal

Elbing, (Elblag) 159, 161

Elblag, *see* Elbing

Elkush, *see* Olkusz

Eller-Meiten, 65

Ellrich, 164

Ellwangen, 115

Elp, 122

Elsdorf, 156

Elsinore, 194

Emden, 24

England, *see* Great Britain

Enkhuizen, 119

Enns, 150, 152

Ennsdorf, 150, 152

Enschede, 116

Erfurt, 147

Ersekujvar, (Nove Zamky) 188

Erzingen, 115

Eschershausen, 149

Eschwege, 217

Espa, 195

Espergaerde, 194

Esseg, *see* Osijek

Essen, 149

Esterwegen, 21

Estonia, 14, 16, 31-32, 56, 64-
    65, 215t

Eszek, *see* Osijek

Europe, 12-14, 30, 32-33, 78-
    79, 99t, 140-141, 192-193,
    214, 216, 221

Europe, central 15, 129, 209

Europe, eastern, 31, 35, 50-51,
    54-55, 198, 215t

Europe, southern, 168-175

Europe, western, 104-105, 199

Eutin, 21

Eversen, 165

F

Faenza, 202

Fagernes, 195

Fakse, 194

Falkenberg, 158

Falster, 194

Falticeni, (Palticeni) 71

Famagusta, 220t

Fauske, 195

Fehebeutel, 156

Feldafing, 146, 217

Feldberg, 155

Feldgeding, 144

Ferrara, 180t

Festerevo, 73

Finland, 14, 30, 221

Finow, 155

Fischamend Markt, 132

Fischbachau, 146

Fischen, 146

Fischhorn, 146

Fiuggi, 202

Flensburg, 206

Florence, 170-171, 174-175,
    180-182

Floridsdorf, 152

Flossenbuerg, 22, 138-142,
    204-205, 207b, 209

Focsani, 71

Foehrenwald, 217

Foggia, 180t

Fort de Romainville, 106, 108t,
    112

Fossoli di Carpi, 99t, 140-141,
    172-175, 182

Fouday, 113

France, 14, 16-17, 25-27, 32-
    33, 104-107, 112, 180b-
    181, 199, 201, 216, 218-
    219, 221

Frankenstein, 205

Frankfurt am Main, 15, 24, 42,
    115, 121, 128-129, 215b

Frankfurt an der Oder, 212

Frankfurt on the Main, *see*
    Frankfurt am Main

Fredrikstad, 195

Freiburg, (Freiburg im
    Breisgau) 24, 158, 215b

Freiburg im Breisgau, *see*
    Freiburg

Freienwalde, 130

Freising, 146

Freudendorf, 161

Freudenthal, 99b

Friedberg, 205

Friedland, (Korfantow) 158,
    205

Friedrichshafen, 146

Friesack, 130

Frommern, 115

Fuenfbrunnen, 117-118, 140-
    141

Fuerstenberg,
    (Eisenhuttenstadt) 155

Fuerstenberg, (Furstenberg) 153

Fuerstengrube, 99b

Fuerth, (Furth) 217

Funfkirchen, *see* Pecs

Furstenberg, *see* Fuerstenberg

Furth, *see* Fuerth

Fyn, 194

G

Gabersdorf, 158

Gabersee, 217

Gablingen, 146

Gablonz, 158

Galati, (Galatz) 71

Galatz, *see* Galati

Gandersheim, *see* Bad
    Gandersheim

Garmisch-Partenkirchen, 146

Gassen, 158

Gauting, 208

Gawesen, 65

Gaza, 220

Gdansk, 216. *See also* Danzig

Geisenheim, 115

Geislingen, 115

Gelsenkirchen, 149

Gendorf, 146

Generalgouvernement, 34-36,
    39, 49, 54-55, 77, 83, 86,
    89, 92, 102, 128-129, 198,
    200

Genoa, 170-171, 180-182

Genthin, 155

Geppersdorf, 158, 205

Ger, *see* Gora Kalwaria

Gera, 207

Germany, 14-22, 26-27, 30, 32,
    138-139, 215b-219, 221.
    See also Greater Germany

Ghent, 116-117

Gier, *see* Gora Kalwaria

Giessen, 149

Gillelje, 194

Gilze Rijen, 117

Girlachsdorf, 156

Glatz, (Klodzko) 205

Glauchau, 207b

Glayvits, *see* Gleiwitz

Glebokie, (Glebokoye,
    Glembokie, Glubokie) 200

Glebokoye, *see* Glebokie

Gleiwitz, (Glayvits, Gliwice)
    24, 99b, 205

Glembokie, *see* Glebokie

Gliwice, *see* Gleiwitz

Glovna, *see* Glowno

Glovno, *see* Glowno

Glowno, (Glovna, Glovno) 39

Glubczyce, *see* Leobschutz

Glubokie, *see* Glebokie

Gmund, 146, 208

Gnevkovy, *see* Argenau

Gniewkowo, *see* Argenau

Gniliakova, 73

Goddentow, 206

Godollo, 189

Goeding, *see* Hodonin

Goerlitz, (Goorlitz, Gorlitz,
    Zgorzelec) 158, 205, 207t

Goettingen, (Gottingen) 149,
    164

Golleschau, 99b

Golta, (Halta) 71

Gomel, (Homel, Homiyah) 51,
    54-55, 215t

Gonyu, 190

Goorlitz, *see* Goerlitz

Gora Kalwaria, (Ger, Gier,
    Gora Kalwarja, Gur, Gura
    Kalvaria) 39

Gora Kalwarja, *see* Gora
    Kalwaria

Gorki, 215t

Gorlitz, *see* Goerlitz

Gorna Dzhumaya,
    (Blagoevgrad) 172-175

Gorodenka, (Horodenka) 51,
    54-55, 86

Goslar, 149

Gospic, 172-173

Gostinin, *see* Gostynin

Gostynin, (Gostinin) 42

Gotenhafen, 161, 206

Gotha, 147

Gottingen, *see* Goettingen

Gouda, 119

Grabina Wielka, 80

Grabow, 87

Grabowiec, 89

Graeben, 158

Grafeneck, 28

Graslitz, 155

Graudenz, (Grudziadz) 161

Graz, 24, 152

Great Britain, 14, 25-27, 221

Greater Germany, 24, 28, 33,
     128-129, 137, 143, 209,
     210-211. *See also*
     Germany

Grebinerfeld, 159

Greci, 71

Gredani, 176b

Greece, 14, 32, 168, 169b-175,
     180b-181, 218-219, 221

Grein, 152

Grenoble, 199

Grenzdorf, 159

Grimbergen, 124

Grini, 140-141

Gritsa, *see* Grojec

Gritza, *see* Grojec

Gritze, *see* Grojec

Grodek, 58

Grodne, *see* Grodno

Grodno, (Grodne, Horodne,
     Hurodno) 51, 54-55, 58,
     92, 98, 198

Grodzhisk, *see* Grodzisk
     Mazowiecki

Grodzhisk Mazovyets, *see*
     Grodzisk Mazowiecki

Grodzisk Mazowiecki,
     (Grodzhisk, Grodzhisk
     Mazovyets, Grozitsk) 39

Grojec, (Gritsa, Gritza, Gritze,

Grutse, Gruyets) 39, 94

Groningen, 116

Gross Lesewitz, 159, 161

Gross Mausdorf, 159, 161

Gross Menow, 153

Gross Raming, 152

Gross-Rosen, (Rogoznica) 138-
     142, 156-158, 204-205,
     207t, 209

Gross Saalau, 159

Gross Zuender, 206

Grosswardein, *see* Oradea

Grosswerther, 164

Grozitsk, *see* Grodzisk
     Mazowiecki

Grudziadz, *see* Graudenz

Gruenberg, (Grunberg, Zielona
     Gora) 158

Grulich, 158

Grunberg, *see* Gruenberg

Grutse, *see* Grojec

Gruyets, *see* Grojec

Guben, (Wilhelmpieckstadt
     Guben) 158

Gudehausen, 165

Gudersleben, 162

Guending, 144

Guenthergrube, 99b

Gugel, *see* Bukovina

Gunskirchen, 152, 209

Gur, *see* Gora Kalwaria

Gura Kalvaria, *see* Gora
     Kalwaria

Gurs, 106-107, 110-112, 140-
     141

Gurske, 161

Gusen, 142, 150, 152, 209

Gutschdorf, 156

Guttau, 161

Guttenbach, 115

Guty, 90

Gyor, (Gyorsziget, Raab) 185,
     188, 190

Gyorsziget, *see* Gyor

H

Haaren, 117

Haarlem, 116, 119

Hadamar, 28

Haeslicht, 156

Hagen, 165

Hague, The, 116, 119, 216. *See
     also* 's-Gravenhage

Haidari, 172-173

Haidfeld, 152

Haifa, 218-219, 220

Hailfingen, 115

Hajduboszormeny,
     (Boszormeny) 186b

Hajduhadhaz, (Hajduhodkaz)
     186b

Hajduhodkaz, *see* Hajduhadhaz

Halbau, 158

Halberstadt, 149

Halbstadt, 158

Halden, 195

Hall, *see* Schwaebisch Hall

Halle, (Halle an der Saale)
     149, 207b

Halle an der Saale, *see* Halle

Hallein, 146, 217

Halta, *see* Golta

Hamar, 195

Hamburg, 15, 24-25, 42, 99t,
     128-129, 206, 207b, 215b-
     217

Hamme, 124

Hannover, (Hanover) 15, 24,
     128-129, 215b

Hanover, *see* Hannover

Harka, 65

Harmense, 93-94, 99b

Hartheim, 28, 152

Hartmannsdorf, 158

Harzungen, 162, 164

Haslach, 115

Hassel, 165

Hatvan, 188

Haugesund, 195

Hausdorf, 158

Havana, 25

Hayingen, 112, 115

Hebertshausen, 144, 208

Hebron, 220b

Hegyeshalom, (Strass
     Somerein) 190

Heidemuhle, *see* Kowale
     Panskie

Heidenheim, 146, 217

Heiligenbeil, 161

Hela, 206

Helmbrechts, 155

Helsingborg, 194

Hennigsdorf, 155

Heppenheim, (Heppenheim an
     der Bergstrasse) 115

Heppenheim an der Bergstrasse,
     see Heppenheim

Hermannsburg, 165

Herreden, 162

Herstal, 117

Herzogenbusch, 117, 142. *See
     also* 's-Hertogenbosch

Herzogswaldau, 156

Hessental, 115

Hilversum, 119

Himberg, 132

Hindenburg, (Zabrze) 99b

Hinterbruehl, 152

Hirschberg, (Jelenia Gora) 158,
     205, 207t

Hirtenberg, 152

Hochstedt, 162

Hodmezovasarhely, 188

Hodonin, (Goeding, Hudonin)
     142

Hoerningen, 162

Hoersten, 165

Hoganas, 194

Hoheneck, 161

Hohenlychen, 155

Hohlstedt, 164

Hohne, 165, 217

Hollenstein, 152

Homel, *see* Gomel

Homiyah, *see* Gomel

Hooghalen, 122

Hoorn, 119

Hopfgarten, 142

Horodenka, *see* Gorodenka

Horodne, *see* Grodno

Horseroed, 140-141

Hotin, 72b

Hottelstedt, 147

Hrubieszow, (Hrubishov, Hrubyeshuv, Rubashov, Rubeshov, Rubischoff, Rubishov, Rubishoyv) 89

Hrubishov, *see* Hrubieszow

Hrubyeshuv, *see* Hrubieszow

Hrycowola, *see* Chrzanow

Hubertushuette, 99b

Hudonin, *see* Hodonin

Humlebaek, 194

Hungary, 14, 16, 19, 30-31, 33, 52, 172-173, 185-188, 190, 201, 216, 221

Hurodno, *see* Grodno

Husi, 71

Hust, *see* Huszt

Huste, *see* Huszt

Hustedt, 165

Huszt, (Chust, Hust, Huste, Khust) 52, 188

I

Iacob Deal, 71

Iasi, (Jasi, Jassy) 70, 72b, 78-79, 215t

Iasin, *see* Korosmezo

Iasinia, *see* Korosmezo

Idunum, *see* Judenburg

Iffezheim, 115

Ilfeld, 164

Ilinka, 73

Ilsenburg, 164

Ingolstadt, 207t

Innsbruck, 24, 146

Ioannina, (Janina, Joanina, Yanina) 99t, 172-175

Ireland, 14, 221

Israel, 220b

Istanbul, 196

Italy, 14, 16, 30, 33, 170-175, 180-182, 201-202, 216, 218-219, 221

Ivano Frankovsk, *see* Stanislawow

Iwano Frankowsk, *see* Stanislawow

Izaslaw, *see* Zaslavl

Izbica, (Izbica Lubelska, Izbica Lubelski) 128-129

Izbica Lubelska, *see* Izbica

Izbica Lubelski, *see* Izbica

Iziaslav, *see* Zaslavl

J

Jablanac, 176

Jadovno, 172-173

Janina, *see* Ioannina

Janinagrube, 99b

Janischken, 65

Janowska, 45, 62-63, 140-141, 200

Japan, 30

Jarak, 172-173

Jarczow, (Yartchovka) 84

Jasenovac, 172-177

Jasi, *see* Iasi

Jasienowka, *see* Jasionowka

Jasina, *see* Korosmezo

Jasionowka, (Jasienowka, Yashinovka, Yashinovke, Yashinowka) 198

Jassy, *see* Iasi

Jauer, (Jawor) 207t

Jaunzeen, 66

Jawischowitz, 94, 99b, 205

Jawor, *see* Jauer

Jedincy, *see* Edineti

Jedlsee, 152

Jedrzejewo, *see* Putzig

Jekaterynoslaw, *see* Dnepropetrovsk

Jelenia Gora, *see* Hirschberg

Jena, 147, 149, 207

Jerusalem, 202, 220

Jesau, 161

Jezierna, 84

Jezow, (Yezhov) 39

Jitomir, *see* Zhitomir

Joanina, *see* Ioannina

Judenburg, (Idunum) 217

Jungbunzlau, *see* Mlada

Boleslav

Juriew, *see* Tartu

Jurjew, *see* Tartu

K

K Shonev, *see* Chrzanow

Kaesemark, 159

Kahlberg, 159, 161

Kahlbude, 206

Kaidan, *see* Kedainiai

Kaiserwald, (Mezapark, Mezaparks) 65-66, 140-141

Kaisheim, 115

Kalaras, *see* Calarasi

Kalarash, *see* Calarasi

Kalinin, (Tver) 215t

Kaliningrad, *see* Koenigsberg

Kalisch, *see* Kalisz

Kalisz, (Kalisch, Kolish) 42

Kalisz Pomorski, *see* Kallies

Kalleten, 65

Kallies, (Kalisz Pomorski) 155

Kalocsa, 188

Kalthaus, 156

Kaltwasser, 158

Kamenets Podolsk, *see* Kamenets-Podolski

Kamenets-Podolski, (Kamenets Podolsk, Kamenets Podolskiy, Kamieniec Podolski, Komenitz Podolsk) 35, 50-52, 215t

Kamenets Podolskiy, *see* Kamenets-Podolski

Kamenz, 158

Kamieniec Podolski, *see* Kamenets-Podolski

Kamienna, *see* Skarzysko-Kamienna

Kamienna Gora, *see* Landeshut

Kampen, 116

Kapoli, *see* Kopyl

Kapolia, *see* Kopyl

Kaposvar, 185, 187-188

Kapulye, *see* Kopyl

Karczew, (Kartchev, Kartshev) 39

Karl-Marx-Stadt, *see* Chemnitz

Karlovy Vary, *see* Carlsbad

Karlsbad, *see* Carlsbad

Karlsfeld, 146

Karlshagen, 155

Karlzbad, *see* Carlsbad

Kartchev, *see* Karczew

Kartshev, *see* Karczew

Kaschau, *see* Kosice

Kasha, *see* Kosice

Kashau, *see* Kosice

Kashov, *see* Kosice

Kashoy, *see* Kosice

Kassa, *see* Kosice

Kassel, (Cassel) 24, 149, 164, 215b

Katowice, *see* Kattowitz

Kattowice, 142. *See also* Kattowitz

Kattowitz, (Katowice, Stalinogrod) 99b. *See also* Kattowice

Kauen, *see* Kovno

Kaufbeuren, 146

Kaufering, 146

Kaunas, *see* Kovno

Kazimierz, 46

Kazlu Ruda, (Kozlova Ruda, Kozlowa Ruda) 65

Kedainai, *see* Kedainiai

Kedainiai, (Kaidan, Kedainai, Keidan, Keidany, Keydan, Kiejdany, Kuidany) 51, 54-56, 64-65

Keidan, *see* Kedainiai

Keidany, *see* Kedainiai

Kelbra, 164

Kelin, *see* Cologne

Keln, *see* Cologne

Kelts, *see* Kielce

Keltz, *see* Kielce

Kemna, 21

Kempten, 146

Kerkira, *see* Corfu

Kerstenhof, 65

Keshanov, *see* Chrzanow

Keshenev, *see* Kishinev

Keshinov, *see* Kishinev

Keterinoslav, *see* Dnepropetrovsk

Keydan, *see* Kedainiai

Kharkov, (Charkow) 35, 50-51, 54-55, 78-79, 215t, 216

Khelem, *see* Chelm

Khelm, *see* Chelm

Kherson, (Cherson) 51, 54-55

Khisinau, *see* Kishinev

Khmelnitski, *see* Proskurov

Khmelnitskii, *see* Proskurov

Khmelnitskiy, *see* Proskurov

Kholm, *see* Chelm

Khshanov, *see* Chrzanow

Khshanuv, *see* Chrzanow

Khust, *see* Huszt

Kiejdany, *see* Kedainiai

Kiel, 24

Kielce, (Kelts, Keltz, Kilts, Kiltz) 36, 54-55, 92, 98, 128-129

Kiemieliszki, *see* Proskurov

Kiernozia, 39

Kiev, (Kiyev, Kijew, Kijow, Kjew) 35, 50-51, 53, 78-79, 215t, 216

Kijew, *see* Kiev

Kijow, *see* Kiev

Kilts, *see* Kielce

Kiltz, *see* Kielce

Kimina, 178

Kimlishuk, *see* Proskurov

Kiralymajor, 186b

Kircholm, *see* Salaspils

Kishinev, (Chisinau, Keshenev, Keshinov, Khisinau, Kiszyniow) 51, 54-55, 70-72, 78-79, 215t

Kishvarda, *see* Kisvarda

Kislau, 21

Kispest, 188

Kistarcsa, 99t, 189-190

Kisvarda, (Kishvarda, Klaynvardayn,

Kleinwardein, Virdayn Katan) 188

Kiszyniow, *see* Kishinev

Kittlitztreben, 158, 207t

Kivioli, 65

Kiyev, *see* Kiev

Kjew, *see* Kiev

Klagenfurt, 24, 152

Klatovy, (Klattau) 136t

Klattau, *see* Klatovy

Klausenberg, *see* Cluj

Klausenburg, *see* Cluj

Klaynvardayn, *see* Kisvarda

Kleck, *see* Kletsk

Klein Radisch, 158

Klein Zuender, 206

Kleinbodungen, 164

Kleinwardein, *see* Kisvarda

Klenik, 176

Klesov, (Klesow, Klisov, Klosova) 198

Klesow, *see* Klesov

Kletsk, (Kleck, Kletzk, Klezk) 200

Kletzk, *see* Kletsk

Klezk, *see* Kletsk

Klintholm, 206

Klisov, *see* Klesov

Klodzko, *see* Glatz

Klooga, 65, 140-141

Klosova, *see* Klesov

Klosterneuburg, 132

Kluetzow, 155

Klunya, *see* Cologne

Kluyzenburg, *see* Cluj

Kluzh, *see* Cluj

Knishin, *see* Knyszyn

Knisin, *see* Knyszyn

Kniszyn, *see* Knyszyn

Knyszyn, (Knishin, Knisin, Kniszyn) 58, 198

Kobanya, *see* Budapest

Kobier, 99b

Koblenz, (Coblenz) 24, 149, 215b

Kochendorf, 115

Koeln, *see* Cologne

Koenigs-Wusterhausen, 130

Koenigsberg, (Kaliningrad) 24, 161

Koenigsberg [Ravensbrueck] 155

Koenigsdorf, 208

Koenigszelt, 158

Koge, 194

Kohling, 159

Kolanow, *see* Bochnia

Koldichevo, 45, 140-141

Kolimeya, *see* Kolomyia

Kolimia, *see* Kolomyia

Kolin, (Neukollin) 136t

Kolish, *see* Kalisz

Koln, *see* Cologne

Kolna, *see* Kolno

Kolne, *see* Kolno

Kolno, (Kolna, Kolne) 58

Kolodziaz, 90

Kolomai, *see* Kolomyia

Kolomea, *see* Kolomyia

Kolomey, *see* Kolomyia

Kolomyia, (Kolimeya, Kolimia, Kolomai, Kolomea, Kolomey, Kolomyja, Kolomyya) 52, 54-55, 86

Kolomyja, *see* Kolomyia

Kolomyya, *see* Kolomyia

Kolonie Wertizany, *see* Vertujeni

Kolozhvar, *see* Cluj

Kolozsvar, *see* Cluj

Kolozvar, *see* Cluj

Komarom, (Ujvaros) 188

Komenitz Podolsk, *see* Kamenets-Podolski

Komotau, (Chomutov) 207

Kongsvinger, 195

Konigsberg, *see* Koenigsberg

Konstancin-Jeziorna, 39

Konstantynow, (Konstantynow Lodzki) 43

Konstantynow Lodzki, *see* Konstantynow

Kopil, *see* Kopyl

Kopisty, 134

Kopyl, (Kapoli, Kapolia, Kapulye, Kopil) 200

Korben, 161

Korfantow, *see* Friedland

Korneuburg, 132

Korosmezo, (Iasin, Iasinia, Jasina, Yasinya) 52

Koschedaren, 65

Koshnik, *see* Krasnik

Kosice, (Kaschau, Kasha, Kashau, Kashov, Kashoy, Kassa) 18b-19, 99t, 185-188

Kosintin, *see* Konstantynow

Kosminek, 100

Kosnitin, *see* Konstantynow

Kosow, 90

Kostantin Yashan, *see* Konstantynow

Kostentin, *see* Konstantynow

Koszeg, 99t

Kottern, 146

Kovel, (Kovla, Kovle, Kowel) 51, 54-55

Kovla, *see* Kovel

Kovle, *see* Kovel

Kovno, (Kauen, Kaunas, Kowno) 31, 50-51, 54-55, 64-65, 68-69, 89, 128-129, 198, 200, 215t

Kowale Panskie, (Heidemuhle) 42

Kowel, *see* Kovel

Kowno, *see* Kovno

Kozhany Forest, 198

Kozlova Ruda, *see* Kazlu Ruda

Kozlowa Ruda, *see* Kazlu Ruda

Kozminek, (Kozminka) 42

Kozminka, *see* Kozminek

Krailling, 208

Krakau, *see* Krakow

Krako, *see* Krakow

Krakow, (Cracow, Krakau, Krako, Krakoy, Krakuv, Kroke) 31, 34, 36, 46-47, 54-55, 78-79, 86, 98, 128-

129, 142, 198, 200, 215t, 216

Krakoy, *see* Krakow

Krakuv, *see* Krakow

Kraljevica, 172-173

Kralove Hradec, 136t

Kranichfeld, 147

Krapje, 176

Krashanov, *see* Chrzanow

Krashnik, *see* Krasnik

Krasnik, (Koshnik, Krashnik, Kroshnik, Krushnik) 89

Krasnodar, (Yekaterinodar) 51, 215t, 216

Krasnogvardeisk, 51

Kratzau, (Chrastava) 158

Kremenchug, (Cremenciuc, Kremenchuk, Krementchug, Kremienczuk, Krzemienczuk) 51, 215t

Kremenchuk, *see* Kremenchug

Kremenets, (Kremenits, Kremenitz, Krzemieniec, Kshemyenyets) 200

Kremenits, *see* Kremenets

Kremenitz, *see* Kremenets

Krementchug, *see* Kremenchug

Kremienczuk, *see* Kremenchug

Kreshanov, *see* Chrzanow

Kretinga, *see* Krottingen

Kretingale, *see* Krottingen

Kretinge, *see* Krottingen

Kretingen, *see* Krottingen

Krettingen, *see* Krottingen

Krienek, *see* Krynki

Krimderode, 162

Krinek, *see* Krynki

Krinki, *see* Krynki

Krinok, *see* Krynki

Kristiansand, 195

Kroke, *see* Krakow

Kroshnik, *see* Krasnik

Krottingen, (Kretinga, Kretingale, Kretinge, Kretingen, Krettingen) 65

Krumau, 161

Kruscica, 172-175

Krusevac, 172-173

Krushnik, *see* Krasnik

Kruszyna, 200

Krynki, (Krienek, Krinek, Krinki, Krinok) 58

Krzemienczuk, *see* Kremenchug

Krzemieniec, *see* Kremenets

Krzystkowice, *see* Christianstadt

Kshanev, *see* Chrzanow

Kshanov, *see* Chrzanow

Kshemyenyets, *see* Kremenets

Kubanka, 73

Kudeb, 65

Kuestendje, *see* Constanta

Kuidany, *see* Kedainiai

Kunda, 65

Kunzendorf, 99b, 205

Kursk, 215t

Kutuzova, 73

Kwiatkow, 80

Kwidzyn, *see* Marienwerder

L

La Grand' Combe, 110

La Lande, 106-107, 112

La Spezia, 180t, 218-219

Lachovici, *see* Lachowicze

Lachowicze, (Lachovici, Lechovich, Lechovicz, Lechowitz, Liachovitch, Lyakhoviche, Lyakhovichi) 200

Lachva, (Lachwa, Lakhva, Lakhwa) 51, 54-55, 200

Lachwa, *see* Lachva

Lackenbach, (Lakompak) 142

Ladorudz, 80

Laerdalsoyri, 195

Lagedi, 65, 140-141

Lagischa, 99b

Laibach, *see* Ljubljana

Lakhva, *see* Lachva

Lakhwa, *see* Lachva

Lakompak, *see* Lackenbach

Lambach, 152

Lampertheim, 217

Landeshut, (Kamienna Gora) 158, 205

Landsberg, 146, 209, 217

Landshut, 146

Landskrona, 194

Langeland, 194

Langenbielau, (Bielawa Dolna) 158

Langensalza, (Bad Lauchstadt) 147, 149

Langfuhr, 159

Lanke, 130

Lapi, *see* Lapy

Lapy, (Lapi) 58

Larnaca, 220t

Lask, (Laski, Lusk) 42

Laski, *see* Lask

Latvia, 14, 16, 31-32, 56, 64-65, 215t

Lauban, (Luban) 207t

Lauenberg, *see* Lauenburg

Lauenburg, (Lauenberg, Lebork) 161, 204, 206

Lauingen, 146

Laurahuette, 99b

Lauterbach, 206

Lay-Lamidou, 110

Layptsig, *see* Leipzig

Layptsik, *see* Leipzig

Le Chambon-sur-Lignon, 199

Le Vernet, 106-107, 111-112

Lebork, *see* Lauenburg

Lechovich, *see* Lachowicze

Lechovicz, *see* Lachowicze

Lechowitz, *see* Lachowicze

Leeuwarden, 116-117

Legnica, *see* Liegnitz

Legniszewo, *see* Liegnitz

Leibisch, 161

Leibnitz, 152

Leiden, 119

Leipheim, 217

Leipzig, (Layptsig, Layptsik) 15, 24, 128-129, 149, 212, 215b-216

Leipzig-Schoenefeld, 155

Leitmeritz, 207. *See also* Litomerice

Leki, 94

Lemberg, *see* Lvov

Leningrad, (Peterburg, St. Petersburg) 32, 35, 50, 78-79, 215t

Lenzing, 152

Leobschuetz, *see* Leobschutz

Leobschutz, (Glubczyce, Leobschuetz) 205

Leonberg, 115

Leopol, *see* Lvov

Leopoldsdorf, (Leopoldsdorf im Marchfelde) 132

Leopoldsdorf im Marchfelde, *see* Leopoldsdorf

Leopoldskron, 142

Les Milles, 106-107, 112

Leskie Zasole, 94

Leslau, *see* Wloclawek

Leslo, *see* Wloclawek

Lesluya, *see* Wloclawek

Leszcze, 80

Lety, 142

Leutstetten, 208

Leuven, 116, 124

Leva, (Levice) 188

Levice, *see* Leva

L'Hopital-Saint-Blaise, 110

Liachovitch, *see* Lachowicze

Liban, *see* Liepaja

Libau, *see* Liepaja

Libava, *see* Liepaja

Libawa, *see* Liepaja

Liboi, *see* Liepaja

Libova, *see* Liepaja

Liboya, *see* Liepaja

Lichtenau, 217

Lichtenburg, 21

Lichtewerden, 99b

Lida, 51, 54-56, 89, 102, 198

Lidice, 18b-19

Liebau, *see* Liepaja

Liebau [Gross-Rosen] 158

Liege, 116

Liegnitz, (Legnica, Legniszewo) 205

Liepaja, (Liban, Libau, Libava, Libawa, Liboi, Libova, Liboya, Liebau) 51, 54-56, 64

Lier, 124

Lillehammer, 195

Limbeni Novi, 71

Limhamn, 194

Limoges, 199

Lind, 152

Linz, 24, 152, 205, 217

Lipiczany Forest, 198

Lipisko, 84

Lippstadt, 149

Liskovitz, see Lyszkowice

Lithuania, 14, 16-17, 20, 31-32, 56, 64-65, 215t

Lititov, see Lututow

Litomerice, 134. See also Leitmeritz

Litzmannstadt, see Lodz

Litzmanstadt, see Lodz

Ljubljana, (Laibach, Lubiana) 216

Loborgrad, 99t, 172-175

Lochau, 146

Lodensee, 65

Lodz, (Litzmannstadt, Litzmanstadt, Lodzh) 31, 34, 36, 42-44, 54-55, 78-79, 82, 98, 128-129, 136b, 142, 215t, 216

Lodzh, see Lodz

Loebau, 207t

Loeblau, 206

Loewenberg, 130

Loibl-Pass North, 152

Loibl-Pass South, 152

Lokeren, 124

Lolland, 194

Lomza, (Lomzha) 58

Lomzha, see Lomza

Londerzeel, 124

London, 32, 78-79

Longwy-Thil, 112, 115

Lovich, see Lowicz

Low Countries, 116-118

Lowicz, (Lovich, Loyvitch, Luyvich) 39

Loyvitch, see Lowicz

Luban, see Lauban

Lubeck, see Luebeck

Lubiana, see Ljubljana

Lublin, 31, 34, 36, 54-55, 83, 86, 100, 102, 128-129, 198, 215t, 216

Lublin-Lipowa, 45, 200

Lubycza Krolewska, 84

Luck, see Lutsk

Lucq-de-Bearn, 110

Ludwigsdorf, 158

Luebeck, (Lubeck) 24

Lueneburg, (Luneburg) 216

Luetzkendorf, 149

Lugau, 207t

Lugoj, 71

Luneburg, see Lueneburg

Lungitz, 150, 152

Lusin, 206

Lusk, see Lask

Luta, 87

Lutsk, (Luck, Lutzk, Luytsk, Luytsk Vilka, Luzk) 51, 54-55

Lututov, see Lututow

Lututow, (Lititov, Lututov) 42

Lutzk, see Lutsk

Luxembourg, 14, 16, 42, 104, 116-118, 221

Luytsk, see Lutsk

Luytsk Vilka, see Lutsk

Luyvich, see Lowicz

Luzk, see Lutsk

Lviv, see Lvov

Lvov, (Lemberg, Leopol, Lviv, Lwow) 31, 34, 50-51, 54-55, 62, 78-79, 86, 89, 98, 215t

Lwow, see Lvov

Lyakhoviche, see Lachowicze

Lyakhovichi, see Lachowicze

Lyon, 99t, 199

Lyszkowice, (Liskovitz, Lyszkowicze) 39

Lyszkowicze, see Lyszkowice

M

Maastricht, 116

Machnow, 84

Maehrisch Ostrau, see Moravska Ostrava

Magdeburg, 149, 155, 212

Magnusholm, 66

Magyarovar, see Mosonmagyarovar

Mahrisch Ostrau, see Moravska Ostrava

Mahrish Ostrau, see Moravska Ostrava

Majdan Tatarski, (Maydan Tatarski) 100

Majdanek, 45, 49, 76-77, 100-102, 136b, 138-142, 209

Majdany, 80-81

Malchow, 155

Malic, 134

Maliszewa Nowa, 90

Malken, (Malki) 161

Malki, see Malken

Malkinia, (Malkinia Gorna) 90

Malkinia Gorna, see Malkinia

Malmedy, 116

Malmo, 194, 206

Malta, 182

Maly, 87

Maly Trostinets, (Maly Trostenets, Maly Trostinec, Maly Trostyanets, Malyy Trostenets) 51, 56

Maly Trostenets, see Maly Trostinets

Maly Trostinec, see Maly Trostinets

Maly Trostyanets, see Maly Trostinets

Malyy Trostenets, see Maly Trostinets

Manderode, 162

Mangalia, 196

Manhorn, 165

Mannheim-Sandhofen, 115

Mantua, 182

Marcinkance, (Marcinkonys) 200

Marcinkonys, see Marcinkance

Marculesti, 71, 72

Marek, see Dupnitsa

Margit Island, 189

Maria Lanzendorf, 152

Marienwerder, (Kwidzyn) 161

Markgrafneusiedl, 132

Marki, 39

Markirch, 112, 115

Markkleeberg, 149

Markt Schwaben, 146

Markushev, see Markuszow

Markushov, see Markuszow

Markuszow, (Markushev, Markushov) 200

Marseille, 106, 112, 199, 218-219

Marzahn, 130, 142

Mateszalka, 188

Matzkau, 159

Mauthausen, 22, 138-143, 150-152, 205, 209

Maydan Tatarski, see Majdan Tatarski

Mechelen, 99t, 116-118, 124-125, 140-141

Medininkai, see Varna

Meisserdorf, 165

Melissokhorion, 178

Melk, 152

Merchtem, 124

Merignac, 106-107, 112

Merzdorf, 158

Merzen, 161

Metz, 112, 115

Meuselwitz, 149

Mezapark, see Kaiserwald

Mezaparks, see Kaiserwald

Mezo Telegd, see Telegd

Mezotelegd, see Telegd

Miami, 25

Midia, 196

Miedniki, *see* Varna

Mikaliskes, 54-55, 64

Milan, 170-171, 174-175, 180-182, 218-219

Mildenberg, 155

Milgravis, 66

Minsk, 50-51, 54-57, 78-79, 89, 128-129, 198, 200, 215t

Minsk Khadash, *see* Minsk Mazowiecki

Minsk Mazovyets, *see* Minsk Mazowiecki

Minsk Mazovyetsk, *see* Minsk Mazowiecki

Minsk Mazowiecki, (Minsk Khadash, Minsk Mazovyets, Minsk Mazovyetsk, Novo Minsk, Novominsk) 36, 54-55, 92, 200

Mir, 51, 54-55, 200

Mirnoe, 73

Miskolc, (Miskolcz) 185-188

Miskolcz, *see* Miskolc

Missler, 21

Mistelbach, (Mistelbach an der Zaya) 152

Mistelbach an der Zaya, *see* Mistelbach

Mittelsteine, 158

Mlada Boleslav, (Bumsla, Jungbunzlau) 136t

Mlaka, 176

Modena, 180

Modrzejow, 98

Moedling, 132

Moerbeke, 124

Moerdijk, 117

Mogelnitsa, *see* Mogielnica

Mogelnitse, *see* Mogielnica

Mogelnitza, *see* Mogielnica

Mogielnica, (Mogelnitsa, Mogelnitse, Mogelnitza) 39

Mogilev, (Mohilev, Mohylew, Mohylow, Molev) 51, 54-55, 198, 215t

Mogilev-Podolski, (Mogilev Podolskiy, Mohilev Podolsk) 51, 54-55, 70-72, 215t

Mogilev Podolskiy, *see* ` Mogilev-Podolski

Mohilev, *see* Mogilev

Mohilev Podolsk, *see* Mogilev-Podolski

Mohylew, *see* Mogilev

Mohylow, *see* Mogilev

Moldavia, 215t

Molev, *see* Mogilev

Mon, 194

Monaco, *see* Munich

Monastir, *see* Bitola

Monor, 188

Monowice, 93-94. *See also* Auschwitz III (Monowitz)

Monowitz, *see* Auschwitz III (Monowitz); Monowice

Mons, 116

Mont de Marsan, 110

Montauban, 110

Montpellier, 110

Moosbierbaum, 152

Moravska Ostrava, (Maehrisch Ostrau, Mahrisch Ostrau, Mahrish Ostrau, Morawska Ostrawa, Ostrava) 136t

Morawska Ostrawa, *see* Moravska Ostrava

Morchenstern, (Smrzovka) 158

Morzyczyn, 90

Moscow, (Moskva) 32, 50, 78-79, 215t

Moskva, *see* Moscow

Moson, *see* Mosonmagyarovar

Mosonmagyarovar, (Magyarovar, Moson) 190

Moss, 195

Mostovoi, (Mostovoye) 71, 72b

Mostovoye, *see* Mostovoi

Mueggenhahl, 159

Muehldorf, 146

Muehlhausen [Buchenwald]

147, 149

Muehlhausen (Mulhouse) [Natzweiler-Struthof] 112, 115

Muenchen, *see* Munich

Mukacevo, *see* Munkacs

Mukachevo, *see* Munkacs

Mukaczewo, *see* Munkacs

Mulhouse, *see* Muehlhausen

Munchen, *see* Munich

Munich, (Monaco, Muenchen, Munchen) 20, 24, 99t, 128-129, 146, 215b, 217-219

Munkacs, (Mukacevo, Mukachevo, Mukaczewo, Munkacz, Munkatsch) 18b-19, 52, 185-188

Munkacz, *see* Munkacs

Munkatsch, *see* Munkacs

Murru, 65

N

Naarn, 150

Nablus, 220b

Nacha Forest, 198

Nagy Banya, *see* Nagybanya

Nagy Varad, *see* Oradea

Nagybanya, (Baia Mare, Nagy Banya) 188

Nagykanizsa, 185

Nagyszollo, 188

Nagyvarad, *see* Oradea

Naliboki Forest, 198

Namslau, (Namyslow) 158

Namur, 116

Namyslow, *see* Namslau

Nandorfehervar, *see* Belgrade

Naples, 170-171, 180-181

Narev, *see* Narew

Narew, (Narev) 58

Naroch Forest, 198

Narva, (Narve, Narwa) 65

Narve, *see* Narva

Narvik, 195

Narwa, *see* Narva

Natzweiler, 113-114

Natzweiler-Struthof, 106, 112-114, 138-143

Nauert, 130

Navahredek, *see* Novogrudok

Navaredok, *see* Novogrudok

Nay Sants, *see* Nowy Sacz

Naya Sandets, *see* Nowy Sacz

Nazareth, 220b

Neckarbischofsheim, 115

Neckarelz, 115

Neckargartach-Heilbronn, 115

Neckargerach, 115

Nefcover, *see* Argenau

Neisantz, *see* Nowy Sacz

Neishtat, *see* Neustadt

Neisse, (Nysa) 158

Neshviz, *see* Nesvizh

Nestempehl, 206

Nesvizh, (Neshviz, Niesviez, Nieswiez, Nishviz, Nyeshvyezh) 51, 54-55, 200

Netherlands, 14, 16, 26-27, 33, 104-105, 116-118, 216, 221

Netzkater, 164

Neu Rohlau, 155

Neu Sandez, *see* Nowy Sacz

Neubrandenburg, 155

Neudachs, 99b, 205

Neuengamme, 22, 138-143, 204, 206, 209

Neufahrwasser, 159, 161

Neuhammer, 158

Neukollin, *see* Kolin

Neumarkt, 146

Neuruppin, 130

Neusalz, (Nowa Sol) 158

Neusatz, *see* Novi Sad

Neusohl, *see* Banska Bystrica

Neustadt, 24; [Auschwitz] 99b, 205

Neustadt [Buchenwald] 149, 207t

Neustadt [Ravensbrueck] 155, 207t

Neustadt [Stutthof] 206, 217

Neustift, 146

Neustrelitz-Fuerstensee, 155
Neuviller, 113
Nexon, 106, 112
Nice, 180b-181, 199
Nickelswalde, 159, 161, 206
Nicosia, 220t
Nieder-Zirking, 150
Niedergebra, 164
Niederoderwitz, 158
Niedersachswerfen, 162, 164
Niemcza, *see* Nimptsch
Niesky, 158
Niesviez, *see* Nesvizh
Nieswiez, *see* Nesvizh
Nimptsch, (Niemcza) 158
Nindorf, 165
Ninove, 124
Nis, 169t, 180b
Nisch, 140-141, 172-173
Nishviz, *see* Nesvizh
Nisk, *see* Nisko
Niska, *see* Nisko
Nisko, (Nisk, Niska) 128-129
Noe, 106-107, 111-112
Nordhausen, 149, 162, 164
Northern Bukovina, 31
Northern Transylvania, 70
Norway, 14, 32-33, 195, 216,
    221
Novaredok, *see* Novogrudok
Novaya Aleksandriya, *see*
    Pulawy
Nove Zamky, *see* Ersekujvar
Novi Sach, *see* Nowy Sacz
Novi Sad, (Neusatz, Ujvidek)
    172-173
Novi Sansh, *see* Nowy Sacz
Novo Minsk, *see* Minsk
    Mazowiecki
Novogrudek, *see* Novogrudok
Novogrudok, (Navahredek,
    Navaredok, Novaredok,
    Novogrudek, Novohorodek,
    Novohorodok, Novradok,
    Nowogrodek,
    Nowogrudok) 51, 54-56,
    198

Novohorodek, *see* Novogrudok
Novohorodok, *see* Novogrudok
Novominsk, *see* Minsk
    Mazowiecki
Novradok, *see* Novogrudok
Novy Sacz, *see* Nowy Sacz
Nowa Sol, *see* Neusalz
Nowogrodek, *see* Novogrudok
Nowogrudok, *see* Novogrudok
Nowy Sacz, (Nay Sants, Naya
    Sandets, Neisantz, Neu
    Sandez, Novi Sach, Novi
    Sansh, Novy Sacz,
    Sandets, Sandz, Sants,
    Sanz, Tsants, Tzanz) 54-
    55, 86
Nuremberg, (Nurnberg, Wohrd)
    24, 146, 216
Nurnberg, *see* Nuremberg
Nyeshvyezh, *see* Nesvizh
Nyiregyhaza, 185, 187-188
Nysa, *see* Neisse

O

Ober Altstadt, 158
Ober Hohenelbe, 158
Oberehnheim, 106, 112, 115
Oberhode, 165
Obersalzberg, 146
Obersitz, 161
Oberstdorf-Birgsau, 146
Oberwuestegiersdorf, 158
Obuda, *see* Budapest
Odenburg, *see* Sopron
Odess, *see* Odessa
Odessa, (Odess) 50-51, 54-55,
    70-74, 78-79, 215t
Ofen, *see* Budapest
Offen, 165
Ohrdruf, 147, 149, 209
Okucani, 176
Okuniev, *see* Okuniew
Okuniew, (Okuniev, Okunyev)
    39
Okunyev, *see* Okuniew
Oldendorf, 165
Olkush, *see* Olkusz

Olkusz, (Elkush, Olkush) 98
Olmuetz, *see* Olomouc
Olmutz, *see* Olomouc
Olomouc, (Olmuetz, Olmutz)
    136t
Oloron-Sainte-Marie, 110
Olszanska, 87
Olsztyn, *see* Allenstein
Ommen, 117
Oostende, 116
Opola, *see* Opole Lubelskie
Opole, *see* Oppeln
Opole Lubelski, *see* Opole
    Lubelskie
Opole Lubelskie, (Opola, Opole
    Lubelski) 36, 54-55, 86,
    89, 128-129
Oppein, *see* Oppeln
Oppeln, (Opole, Oppein) 24
Oradea, (Grosswardein, Nagy
    Varad, Nagyvarad) 70, 99t,
    185-188
Orahova, 176
Orange Landing, 122
Oranienburg, 21, 130, 138-139,
    204
Orbke, 165
Orin, 110
Oroshaza, 186b
Orth, 132
Orzelek, 90
Oshmyany, 56
Oshpetzin, *see* Oswiecim
Oshpitsin, *see* Oswiecim
Oshvitsin, *see* Oswiecim
Oshvitzin, *see* Oswiecim
Oshvyentsim, *see* Oswiecim
Osijek, (Esseg, Eszek) 99t, 172-
    173
Oslo, 99t, 195, 216
Osowa, 87
Ospinzi, *see* Oswiecim
Osterode, 162. *See also*
    Osterode am Harz
Osterode am Harz, 164 *See also*
    Osterode
Ostra, *see* Ostrog

Ostraha, *see* Ostrog
Ostrava, *see* Moravska Ostrava
Ostre, *see* Ostrog
Ostrog, (Ostra, Ostraha, Ostre)
    200
Ostrovacka Ada, 172-173
Ostrow, 80
Oswiecim, (Auschwitz,
    Aushvits, Oshpetzin,
    Oshpitsin, Oshvitsin,
    Oshvitzin, Oshvyentsim,
    Ospinzi) 93-94. *See also*
    Auschwitz
Oud Leusden, 117
Oygstova, *see* Augustow
Ozarkov, *see* Ozorkow
Ozolciems, 66
Ozorkov, *see* Ozorkow
Ozorkow, (Ozarkov, Ozorkov)
    42

P

Pabenits, *see* Pabianice
Pabianice, (Pabenits, Pabjanice,
    Pabnitz, Pabyanets,
    Pabyanitse) 42-43
Pabjanice, *see* Pabianice
Pabnitz, *see* Pabianice
Pabyanets, *see* Pabianice
Pabyanitse, *see* Pabianice
Pag, 172-173
Pajeczno, (Payentchno) 42
Paks, 188
Palemaonas, 65
Palermo, 180t
Palestine, 26-27, 201-202, 218-
    220t
Palticeni, *see* Falticeni
Pancevo, (Pancsova) 172-173
Pancsova, *see* Pancevo
Paneriai, *see* Ponary
Papa, 188
Parczew Forest, 198
Pardubice, (Pardubitz) 136t
Pardubitz, *see* Pardubice
Paris, 32, 78-79, 104t, 106-108,
    112, 199, 216, 218-219

Parnu, 56

Parschnitz, 158

Pasieki, 84

Passau, 146, 152

Payentchno, *see* Pajeczno

Pechora, (Peciora, Pecora, Petchora, Potchera) 71

Peciora, *see* Pechora

Pecora, *see* Pechora

Pecs, (Funfkirchen) 185, 188

Peggau, 152

Pellheim, 144

Pelplin, 161

Pelters, 106, 112, 115

Penig, 149

Percha, 208

Peremyshl, *see* Przemysl

Peresyp, 73

Perg, 150

Perigueux, 199

Perpignan, 110

Pest, *see* Budapest

Pestfuerdoe, 186b

Petchora, *see* Pechora

Peterburg, *see* Leningrad

Petersdorf, 162

Petershagen, 159

Peterswaldau, 158

Petrikau, *see* Piotrkow Trybunalski

Petrikov, *see* Piotrkow Trybunalski

Petrinciems, 66

Petrokow, *see* Piotrkow Trybunalski

Petschur, 65

Piaseczno, (Piasetchna) 39

Piasetchna, *see* Piaseczno

Piaski, (Piesk) 62-63, 100

Piesk, *see* Piaski

Pietnoczki, 84

Pilaia, 178

Pilev, *see* Pulawy

Pilgramshain, 156

Pilica, (Pilitsa, Pilitz, Pilts, Piltz) 200

Piliscsaba, 190

Pilitsa, *see* Pilica

Pilitz, *see* Pilica

Pilov, *see* Pulawy

Pilsen, 205. *See also* Plzen

Pilts, *see* Pilica

Piltz, *see* Pilica

Pinsk, 31, 51, 54-55, 215t

Piotrkow, *see* Piotrkow Trybunalski

Piotrkow Trybunalski, (Petrikau, Petrikov, Petrokow, Piotrkow, Piotrkow Trybunaski, Piotrkuv, Pyetrkov, Trybunalski) 36, 54-55, 82, 92, 98

Piotrkow Trybunaski, *see* Piotrkow Trybunalski

Piotrkuv, *see* Piotrkow Trybunalski

Pithiviers, 99t, 106-107, 112

Plansee, 146

Plashuv, *see* Plaszow

Plaszow, (Plashuv) 45-46, 48, 140-141

Plati, 178

Plauen, 207b

Plawy, 93-94, 99b

Pleskau, 65

Plintsk, *see* Plonsk

Ploiesti, 71

Plonsk, (Plintsk, Plunsk) 98

Ploskirow, *see* Proskurov

Plunsk, *see* Plonsk

Plzen, 136t. *See also* Pilsen

Pocaply, 134

Pocking-Pine City, 217

Podgorza, *see* Podgorze

Podgorze, (Podgorza) 46

Podkarpatska Rus, *see* Transcarpathian Ukraine

Podlesina, 84

Podlyashe, *see* Biala Podlaska

Podvini, 134

Poelitz, 161

Pognitz, 217

Poitiers, 106-107, 112

Pokratice, 134

Poland, 14, 16-17, 31-32, 34, 36, 45, 76, 200, 215-216, 218-219, 221

Polesie, 84

Polkau, 156

Poltava, (Poltawa) 51

Poltawa, *see* Poltava

Pomietschin, 206

Ponary, (Paneriai) 51, 60

Ponewesch, 65

Poniatowa, 45, 49, 140-141

Portugal, 14, 221

Posen, *see* Poznan

Potchera, *see* Pechora

Potsdam, 130, 212

Poulousat, 199

Powiercie, 80

Poznan, (Posen, Pozno) 216

Pozno, *see* Poznan

Pozsony, *see* Bratislava

Praga, 37

Prague, (Praha) 15, 18b-20, 42, 136t, 204-205, 216

Praha, *see* Prague

Prashka, *see* Praszka

Prashke, *see* Praszka

Prashki, *see* Praszka

Praska, *see* Praszka

Praszka, (Prashka, Prashke, Prashki, Praska) 42

Praust, 159, 161, 206

Prawienischken, 65

Prechacq-Josbaig, 110

Prechacq-Navarrenx, 110

Premishla, *see* Przemysl

Premisle, *see* Przemysl

Prenzlau, 155

Prerau, 205

Pressath, 207t

Pressburg, *see* Bratislava

Preussisch Stargard, 161

Prezhemisel, *see* Przemysl

Priemhausen, *see* Stargard

Priepert, 153

Prittlbach, 144, 208

Prode, *see* Brody

Proebbernau, 159, 161

Proskurov, (Chmelnitski, Chmielnicki, Khmelnitski, Khmelnitskii, Khmelnitskiy, Kiemieliszki, Kimlishuk, Ploskirow) 200

Prostyn, 90

Protectorate of Bohemia and Moravia, 16, 19-20, 33, 128-129, 136, 209

Prushkov, *see* Pruszkow

Pruszkow, (Prushkov) 39

Pruzana, *see* Pruzhany

Pruzany, *see* Pruzhany

Pruzhana, *see* Pruzhany

Pruzhani, *see* Pruzhany

Pruzhany, (Pruzana, Pruzany, Pruzhana, Pruzhani, Pruzhene, Pruzin) 54-55, 58, 98

Pruzhene, *see* Pruzhany

Pruzin, *see* Pruzhany

Przemysl, (Peremyshl, Premishla, Premisle, Prezhemisel, Pshemishel, Pshemishl, Pshemysl) 54-55, 86, 98, 198

Przeorsk, 84

Przewioka, 84

Przybylow, 80, 81

Pshemishel, *see* Przemysl

Pshemishl, *see* Przemysl

Pshemysl, *see* Przemysl

Pskov, 215t

Puerschkau, 158

Pulav, *see* Pulawy

Pulavi, *see* Pulawy

Pulavy, *see* Pulawy

Pulawy, (Novaya Aleksandriya, Pilev, Pilov, Pulav, Pulavi, Pulavy) 45

Pullhausen, 144

Purkersdorf, 132

Puspeok-Ladany, 186b

Pustelnik, (Pustelnik Struga) 39

Pustelnik Struga, *see* Pustelnik

Putzig, (Jedrzejewo) 161
Pyetrkov, see Piotrkow
    Trybunalski

Q
Quedlinburg, 149, 164

R
Raab, see Gyor
Rab, 99t, 172-173
Rabinowka, 84
Raciborz, see Ratibor
Radeberg, 207t
Radofzell, 146
Radogoszcz, 43
Radom, (Rodem) 36, 54-55, 92,
    98, 102, 142
Rageleje, 194
Rajsko, 93-94, 99b, 205
Rakvere, see Wesenberg
Rambau, 159
Ramla, 220b
Rappenau, see Bad Rappenau
Rascani, 71
Rastatt, 115
Ratibor, (Raciborz) 24, 205
Ratisbon, see Regensburg
Rauscha, 158
Rautel, (Reutsel) 71
Ravensbrueck, 22, 138-143,
    153-155, 209
Raysha, see Rzeszow
Rayshe, see Rzeszow
Rayvits, see Rejowiec
Rayvitz, see Rejowiec
Rebberlah, 165
Reblenitz, 71
Recebedou, 106-107, 111-112
Rechlin, 155
Regensburg, (Ratisbon) 207t
Regenstein, 164
Reggio, 180t
Reichenbach, 207t
Reichshof, see Rzeszow
Reichskommissariat Ostland,
    33-35, 56, 89, 128-129,
    198, 200

Reichskommissariat Ukraine,
    33-35, 198, 200
Reisha, see Rzeszow
Rejowiec, (Rayvits, Rayvitz,
    Reyovyets, Reyvits) 102
Rems, 150
Reutsel, see Rautel
Reval, 65. See also Tallinn
Revel, see Tallinn
Reyovyets, see Rejowiec
Reyvits, see Rejowiec
Rhineland, 17-18t
Rhodes, (Rhodos) 99t, 169b,
    174-175
Rhodos, see Rhodes
Riashov, see Rzeszow
Rieben, 161
Ried, 152
Riga, (Rige) 31, 50-51, 54-55,
    64, 66-67, 78-79, 215t, 216
Rige, see Riga
Risha, see Rzeszow
Rivesaltes, 106-107, 112, 140-
    141
Rodem, see Radom
Rodvig, 194
Rogatin, (Rohatin, Rohatyn,
    Rotin) 54-55, 86, 200
Rogozna, 71
Rogoznica, see Gross-Rosen
Rohatin, see Rogatin
Rohatyn, see Rogatin
Rohnstock, 156
Romania, 14, 16, 30-33, 70-72,
    170-171, 185-186, 196, 201,
    215t, 216, 218-219, 221
Romanow, 80
Rome, 99t, 170-171, 174-175,
    180-184, 216
Roosendaal, 117
Rosenberg, 159, 161
Rosenheim, 146
Rossla, 164
Rostock-Schwarzenforst, 155
Rostov, (Rostov na Donu,
    Rostov On Don, Rostow)
    35, 50-51, 215t

Rostov na Donu, see Rostov
Rostov On Don, see Rostov
Rostow, see Rostov
Rothau, 113
Rothschild Hospital, 217
Rotin, see Rogatin
Rotterdam, 116
Rottleberode, 164
Rovne, see Rovno
Rovno, (Rovne, Rowne, Ruvne)
    31, 34-35, 51, 54-55, 198,
    215t
Rowne, see Rovno
Rozdanik, 176
Rubashov, see Hrubieszow
Rubeshov, see Hrubieszow
Rubischoff, see Hrubieszow
Rubishov, see Hrubieszow
Rubishoyv, see Hrubieszow
Ruda Pabian, 43
Ruda Woloska, (Ruda
    Wolowska) 84
Ruda Wolowska, see Ruda
    Woloska
Ruda Zurawiecka, 84
Rudolstadt, 147
Rueckenau, 159
Ruedigsdorf, 162
Rumbula, 51, 66
Rungsted, 194
Russenschin, 159, 161
Russia, 215t
Ruszkow, 80
Ruthenia, see Transcarpathian
    Ukraine
Ruvne, see Rovno
Rytele, see Rytele Swieckie
Rytele Swieckie, (Rytele) 90
Rzeszow, (Raysha, Rayshe,
    Reichshof, Reisha,
    Riashov, Risha, Zheshov,
    Zheshuv, Zhezhov) 54-55,
    86, 98
Rzuchow, 80

S
Saalfeld, 149

Saalfelden, 217
Saar, 17
Saarbrucken, see Saarbruecken
Saarbruecken, (Saarbrucken,
    Saarland) 24, 215b
Saarland, see Saarbruecken
Sachsenburg, 21
Sachsenhausen, 22, 130, 138-
    143, 204-205, 209
Sachsisch-Bereg, see
    Beregszasz
Sadowna, see Sadowne
Sadowne, (Sadowna) 90
Safed, 220b
St. Aegyd, 152
St. Georgen, 150, 152
St. Gilgen, 146
St. Goin, 110
St. Lambrecht, 152
St. Michielsgestel, 117
St. Niklaas, 124
St. Ottilien, 217
St. Pantaleon, 150
St. Petersburg, see Leningrad
St. Valentin, 150, 152
St. Wolfgang, 146
Sajmiste, (Semlin, Zemun) 140-
    141, 172-175
Sakovchizna, see
    Szarkowszczyzna
Salaspils, (Kircholm) 65
Salerno, 180
Saleux, 112
Salgotarjan, 188
Saliers, 106, 112
Salonika, (Saloniki,
    Thessaloniki) 78-79, 99t,
    140-141, 168, 169b, 170-
    175, 178-179, 218-219
Saloniki, see Salonika
Salos, (Soly) 54-55, 64
Salza, 162
Salzberg, see Bochnia
Salzburg, 24, 146, 217
Salzschlirf, see Bad Salzschlirf
Salzwedel, 209
Samer, 112

Sampeters, 66

Samso, 194

San Sabba, 140-141, 172-173, 174-175, 182

Sanciai, 68

Sandets, *see* Nowy Sacz

Sandz, *see* Nowy Sacz

Sants, *see* Nowy Sacz

Sanz, *see* Nowy Sacz

Sarajevo, (Bosna Serai, Serajevo) 99t, 168-169t, 170-171, 174-175

Sardinia, 170-171, 180-181

Sargorog, *see* Shargorod

Sarkeyschina, *see* Szarkowszczyzna

Sarkeystsene, *see* Szarkowszczyzna

Sarni, *see* Sarny

Sarny, (Sarni) 198

Sarvar, 188

Sassnitz, 206

Satoraljaujhely, (Ujhely) 188

Satu-Mare, 70, 99t, 185-188

Schaarbeek, 117

Schabatz, 140-141, 172-173

Schatzlar, 158

Schaulen, *see* Siauliai

Schavli, *see* Siauliai

Schelde, 124

Schichau, 159, 161

Schierstein, *see* Wiesbaden

Schippenbeil, (Sepopol) 161

Schirkenpass, 161

Schirmeck-Vorbruck, 106, 112, 140-141

Schlachters, 146

Schlieben, 155

Schlier-Redl-Zipf, 152

Schloss Lind, 152

Schloss Mittersill, 152

Schmerblock, 206

Schoemberg, 115

Schoenbrunn, 152

Schoenebeck, 149

Schoeneweide, 155

Schoenhorst, 159

Schoensee, 159

Schoenwarling, 159

Schoerzingen, 115

Schomberg Dautmergen, *see* Dautmergen

Schoorl, 117

Schoten, 117

Schusterkrug, 159, 206

Schwabing, 146

Schwaebisch Hall, (Hall) 217

Schwechat, 132, 152

Schweidnitz, (Swidnica) 158, 207t

Schwertberg, 150

Schwerte, 149

Schwindratzheim, 115

Secheslav, *see* Dnepropetrovsk

Seckerwitz, 156

Secureni, 71-72t

Sedan, 104t

Seefeld, 206

Semlin, *see* Sajmiste

Semyatich, *see* Siemiatycze

Semyatitcha, *see* Siemiatycze

Sennheim, 115

Sepopol, *see* Schippenbeil

Septfonds, 106-107, 112

Seradz, *see* Sieradz

Serajevo, *see* Sarajevo

Serbia, 33, 169t, 170-175, 186

Sernik, *see* Serniki

Serniki, (Sernik, Serniki Pervyye) 200

Serniki Pervyye, *see* Serniki

Servigliano, 172-173

's-Gravenhage, 117. *See also* Hague, The

Shanghai, 26-27

Shargorod, (Sargorog, Sharigrad, Sharigrod, Szarogrod) 71

Sharigrad, *see* Shargorod

Sharigrod, *see* Shargorod

Sharkotsina, *see* Szarkowszczyzna

Sharkovshchina, *see* Szarkowszczyzna

Sharkoyshchina, *see* Szarkowszczyzna

Shaulyai, *see* Siauliai

Shavl, *see* Siauliai

Shawli, *see* Siauliai

Sheradz, *see* Sieradz

Sheredz, *see* Sieradz

's-Hertogenbosch, 116. *See also* Herzogenbusch

Shiaulai, *see* Siauliai

Shiraduv, *see* Zyrardow

Shiradz, *see* Sieradz

Shiroka, 57

Shitomir, *see* Zhitomir

Shpikov, *see* Spikov

Shvintzion, *see* Svencionys

Shvyentsiani, *see* Svencionys

Shvyetsiani, *see* Svencionys

Siauliai, (Schaulen, Schavli, Shaulyai, Shavl, Shawli, Shiaulai, Silaliai, Szawle) 51, 54-56, 64-65, 89

Sicily, 170-171, 180-181

Siczeslav, *see* Dnepropetrovsk

Siemiatycze, (Semyatich, Semyatitcha) 58

Siena, 180t

Sieradz, (Seradz, Sheradz, Sheredz, Shiradz) 42

Sighet Marmatiei, 70, 185-188

Silaliai, *see* Siauliai

Simferopol, (Symferopol) 35, 50-51, 215t

Sindhos, 178

Sisteron, 112

Sjaelland, 194

Skalat, (Skalat Stary) 198

Skalat Stary, *see* Skalat

Skanor, 194

Skape, 80

Skarzysko-Kamienna, (Kamienna) 45, 140-141

Skazhinetz, 71

Skernyevits, *see* Skierniewice

Skidzin, 94

Skierniewice, (Skernyevits, Skiernivitz) 39

Skiernivitz, *see* Skierniewice

Skopje, (Skoplje, Uskub, Uskup) 168-175

Skoplje, *see* Skopje

Slobodka [Kovno] 68

Slobodka [Odessa] 73-74

Slonim, 51, 54-56

Slovakia, 16, 19, 30-31, 33, 186, 201, 209

Sluck, *see* Slutsk

Slupsk, *see* Stolp

Slutsk, (Sluck, Slutzk) 56, 198

Slutzk, *see* Slutsk

Smolensk, 35, 50-51, 54-55, 215t

Smrzovka, *see* Morchenstern

Snekkersten, 194

Sobibor, 45, 76-77, 83, 87-89, 128-129, 136b, 140-142, 200

Sobotka, 80

Sochaczew, (Sochatchev, Sochoczew, Sokhachev) 39

Sochatchev, *see* Sochaczew

Sochoczew, *see* Sochaczew

Soemmerda, 147, 149

Sofia, (Sofiya) 170-171

Sofiya, *see* Sofia

Sokhachev, *see* Sochaczew

Sokolka, (Sokolke) [Bialystok] 58

Sokolka [Treblinka] 90

Sokolke, *see* Sokolka [Bialystok]

Solbach, 113

Sollstedt, 164

Soly, *see* Salos

Sonneberg, 149

Sonnenstein, 28

Sophienwalde, 161

Sopron, (Odenburg) 185, 186b, 188

Soroca, (Soroka, Soroki) 71

Soroka, *see* Soroca

Soroki, *see* Soroca

Sosnovets, *see* Sosnowiec

Sosnovice, *see* Sosnowiec

Sosnovits, *see* Sosnowiec

Sosnovitz, *see* Sosnowiec

Sosnovyets, *see* Sosnowiec

Sosnowiec, (Sosnovets, Sosnovice, Sosnovits, Sosnovitz, Sosnovyets) 36, 54-55, 98, 200

Sosnowitz, 99b, 205. *See also* Sosnowiec

Southern Europe, *see* Europe, southern

Soviet Union, 14, 16, 31-33, 35, 50-51, 215t, 216, 221

Spaichingen, 115

Spain, 14, 221

Spikov, (Shpikov) 71

Split, 180b, 181

Srednie, 80

Stabschlaeger, 153

Stalingrad, (Tsaritsyn, Tsarizin, Volgograd) 32, 35, 50, 215t

Stalinogrod, *see* Kattowitz

Stanislau, *see* Stanislawow

Stanislav, *see* Stanislawow

Stanislavov, *see* Stanislawow

Stanislawow, (Ivano Frankovsk, Iwano Frankowsk, Stanislau, Stanislav, Stanislavov, Stanisle, Stanislo, Stanislowow) 54-55, 86, 198

Stanisle, *see* Stanislawow

Stanislo, *see* Stanislawow

Stanislowow, *see* Stanislawow

Stanke Dimitrov, *see* Dupnitsa

Stara Gradiska, 172-173, 176

Starachowice, (Starakhovits, Strachovitza, Verzhbnik, Verzhbnik Starakhov, Vierzhbinik, Vyerzbnik, Vyerzhbanik, Wierzbnik, Wierzbnik Starachow) 36, 45, 98, 140-141

Starakhovits, *see* Starachowice

Stargard, (Priemhausen, Stargard Szczecinski) 155

Stargard Szczecinski, *see* Stargard

Stari Trg, 172-173

Starnberg, 208

Stavanger, 195

Steegen, 159, 161

Steinamanger, *see* Szombathely

Steinfoerde, 153

Steinort, 159, 161

Stempeda, 164

Stephanskirchen, 146

Stettin, 24. *See also* Szczecin

Steyr-Muenichholz, 152

Stockholm, 195

Stojaciszka, *see* Svencionys

Stolp, (Slupsk) 161

Strachovitza, *see* Starachowice

Straschin, 159, 206

Strass Somerein, *see* Hegyeshalom

Strasshof, 132

Straszkow, 80

Strausberg, 130

Stri, *see* Stry

Stria, *see* Stry

Struthof, 113-114

Stry, (Stri, Stria, Stryj, Stryje, Stryy) 54-55, 86

Stryj, *see* Stry

Stryje, *see* Stry

Stryy, *see* Stry

Strzewo, *see* Dirschau

Stubbekobing, 194

Stulno, 87

Stuttgart, (Cannstatt) 24, 128-129, 146, 215b, 217

Stutthof, (Sztutowo) 45, 138-142, 159-161, 204, 206, 209

Sucha Beskidzka, 98

Sudetenland, 18b-19, 24

Suelze, 165

Suhl, 149

Sulejowek, 39

Sutto, 190

Svenchan, *see* Svencionys

Svencionys, (Shvintzion, Shvyentsiani, Shvyetsiani, Stojaciszka, Svenchan, Sventsian, Sventsiany, Sventzion, Swenziany, Swieciany) 54-55, 64

Sventsian, *see* Svencionys

Sventsiany, *see* Svencionys

Sventzion, *see* Svencionys

Sweden, 14, 194-195, 221

Swenziany, *see* Svencionys

Swidnica, *see* Schweidnitz

Swieciany, *see* Svencionys

Switzerland, 14, 26-27, 221

Symferopol, *see* Simferopol

Szarkowszczyzna, (Sakovchizna, Sarkeyschina, Sarkeystsene, Sharkotsina, Sharkovshchina, Sharkoyshchina) 200

Szarogrod, *see* Shargorod

Szawle, *see* Siauliai

Szczecin, 215t, 218-219. *See also* Stettin

Szeged, (Szegedin) 99t, 185-186t, 187-188

Szegedin, *see* Szeged

Szekesfehervar, 185, 187-188

Szentkiralyszabadja, 186b

Szilagy-Falu, 186b

Szolnok, 186b, 188

Szombathely, (Steinamanger) 185, 187-188

Szony, 190

Sztutowo, *see* Stutthof

T

Tabor, 136t

Tallin, *see* Tallinn

Tallinn, (Reval, Revel, Tallin) 31, 50-51, 56, 215t

Talmach, *see* Tlumach

Talmatch, *see* Tlumach

Tannhausen, 158

Tannroda, 147

Taranto, 170-171, 180t, 202, 218-219

Tarbaek, 194

Tarczyn, (Tartchin) 39

Tarna, *see* Tarnow

Tarnopol, (Ternopol) 51, 54-55, 86, 198

Tarnov, *see* Tarnow

Tarnow, (Tarna, Tarnov, Tarnuv, Torne, Tornen) 36, 54-55, 86, 98, 200

Tarnowka, 80

Tarnuv, *see* Tarnow

Tartchin, *see* Tarczyn

Tartu, (Derpt, Dorpa, Juriew, Jurjew, Tur Ev, Yuriev, Yuryev) 56. *See also* Dorpat

Tarvisio, 202

Tata, (Toti, Totis) 190

Taucha, 149

Tczew, *see* Dirschau

Tegernsee, 208

Tel Aviv, 218-220

Telegd, (Mezo Telegd, Mezotelegd, Tileagd) 186b

Telz, 56

Temesvar, *see* Timisoara

Tenje, 99t, 172-175

Teplice, *see* Teplitz

Teplice Sanov, *see* Teplitz

Teplitz, (Teplice, Teplice Sanov, Teplitz Schoenau, Teplitz Schonau) 207b

Teplitz Schoenau, *see* Teplitz

Teplitz Schonau, *see* Teplitz

Terezin, 18b-19. *See also* Theresienstadt

Ternberg, 152

Ternopol, *see* Tarnopol

Thalheim, 146

Thansau, 146

Theresienstadt, (Terezin) 99t, 128-129, 134-136, 204, 207b, 209

Thessaloniki, *see* Salonika

Thorn, (Torn, Torun) 161

Tiegenhagen, 159

Tiegenhof, 159

Tileagd, see Telegd

Timisoara, (Temesvar, Timiszora) 70

Timiszora, see Timisoara

Tirana, 170-171, 180-181

Tirgu-Jiu, 71

Tirgu-Mures, 70, 99t, 185-187

Tlashch, see Tluszcz

Tlashts, see Tluszcz

Tlomats, see Tlumach

Tlumach, (Talmach, Talmatch, Tlomats, Tlumacz, Tlumatch) 198

Tlumacz, see Tlumach

Tlumatch, see Tlumach

Tlushch, see Tluszcz

Tluszcz, (Tlashch, Tlashts, Tlushch) 39

Tomashov Khadash, see Tomaszow Mazowiecki

Tomashov Lublinski, see Tomaszow Lubelski

Tomashov Pyetirkov, see Tomaszow Mazowiecki

Tomashov Ravski, see Tomaszow Mazowiecki

Tomashuv Lubelski, see Tomaszow Lubelski

Tomashuv Mazovyetsk, see Tomaszow Mazowiecki

Tomashuv Mazovyetski, see Tomaszow Mazowiecki

Tomashuv Pyetirkov, see Tomaszow Mazowiecki

Tomaszow Lubelski, (Tomashov Lublinski, Tomashuv Lubelski) 84

Tomaszow Mazowiecki, (Tomashov Khadash, Tomashov Pyetirkov, Tomashov Ravski, Tomashuv Mazovyetsk, Tomashuv Mazovyetski, Tomashuv Pyetirkov, Tomaszow Piotrkov,

Tomaszow Rawski) 36, 54-55

Tomaszow Piotrkov, see Tomaszow Mazowiecki

Tomaszow Rawski, see Tomaszow Mazowiecki

Tonndorf, 147, 149

Topolica, 172-173

Topolya, 186b

Topovske Supe, 172-173

Torgau, 149, 212

Torn, see Thorn

Torne, see Tarnow

Tornen, see Tarnow

Torun, see Thorn

Tosie, 90

Toti, see Tata

Totis, see Tata

Toulouse, 110, 199

Transcarpathian Ukraine, (Carpathian Ruthenia, Podkarpatska Rus, Ruthenia) 52

Transnistria, 70b, 72

Traunstein, 146

Trautenstein, 164

Travcice, 134

Trawniki, 45, 49, 128-129, 140-141

Trebic, (Trebitsch) 136t

Trebitsch, see Trebic

Treblinka, 45, 76-77, 83, 90-92, 128-129, 136b, 140-142, 200

Treis, 115

Trelleborg, 194

Trepca, 172-173

Triebel, 212

Trieste, 99t, 170-171, 180-181, 218-219

Trondheim, 195

Trostberg, 146

Truetenau, 159

Trunz, 161

Trutenau, 206

Trybunalski, see Piotrkow Trybunalski

Tsants, see Nowy Sacz

Tsaritsyn, see Stalingrad

Tsarizin, see Stalingrad

Tschechowitz, 99b, 205

Tshekhanov, see Ciechanow

Tshenstokhov, see Czestochowa

Tuchin, (Tuczyn, Tuczyn Nowy, Tutchin, Tutchin Kripah, Tutsin) 51, 54-55, 200

Tuczyn, see Tuchin

Tuczyn Nowy, see Tuchin

Tula, 215t

Tulchin, see Tulcin

Tulcin, (Tulchin, Tulczyn, Tultchin) 71

Tulczyn, see Tulcin

Tulln, 132

Tultchin, see Tulcin

Tur Ev, see Tartu

Turcoaia, 71

Turin, 180t

Turkey, 14, 196, 221

Turnhout, 116

Turnu Severin, 71

Tutchin, see Tuchin

Tutchin Kripah, see Tuchin

Tutsin, see Tuchin

Tutzing, 146

Tuzora, see Calarasi

Tver, see Kalinin

Tzanz, see Nowy Sacz

U

Udine, 180t

Ueberlingen, 146

Uhersky Brod, (Brod Uhersky, Broda, Ungarisch Brod) 136t

Ujhely, see Satoraljaujhely

Ujlaki, 189-190, 197

Ujpest, 188

Ujvaros, see Komarom

Ujvidek, see Novi Sad

Ukraine, 215t

Ulm, 24, 146, 217

Tsants, see Nowy Sacz

Umien, 80

Ungarisch Brod, see Uhersky Brod

Ungvar, see Uzhgorod

Ungwar, see Uzhgorod

United States, 25-27

Unna, 149

Unterriexingen, 115

Upper Silesia, 34-35, 77, 99b

Uschurod, see Uzhgorod

Uskub, see Skopje

Uskup, see Skopje

Usti nad Labem, see Aussig

Utrecht, 116, 119

Uzhgorod, (Ungvar, Ungwar, Uschurod, Uzhhorod, Uzhorod) 18b-19, 52, 99t, 185-188

Uzhhorod, see Uzhgorod

Uzhorod, see Uzhgorod

V

Vadeani, 71

Vadovits, see Wadowice

Vadovitse, see Wadowice

Vadovitz, see Wadowice

Vaihingen, (Vaihingen an der Enz) 115

Vaihingen an der Enz, see Vaihingen

Vaivara, 65, 140-141

Valkenburg, 117

Vals-les-Bains, 112

Vapniarka, 70-71, 72b

Varka, see Warka

Varna, (Medininkai, Miedniki, Varniai, Vorna, Vorne, Vorni, Wornie) 196, 218-219

Varniai, see Varna

Varsava, see Warsaw

Varshau, see Warsaw

Varshe, see Warsaw

Vartejeni Colonie, see Vertujeni

Vartejenii Sat, see Vertujeni

Vartuzhen, see Vertujeni

Vatican City, 183-184

Vec, 66

Vedbaek, 194

Velodrome d'Hiver, 108

Velten, 155

Venice, 180

Venissieux, 106, 112

Venlo, 117

Verona, 182

Vertujeni, (Kolonie Wertizany, Vartejeni Colonie, Vartejenii Sat, Vartuzhen, Vertuzhen, Vertyuzhani, Vertyuzhany) 71-72

Vertuzhen, *see* Vertujeni

Vertyuzhani, *see* Vertujeni

Vertyuzhany, *see* Vertujeni

Verushev, *see* Wieruszow

Verzhbnik, *see* Starachowice

Verzhbnik Starakhov, *see* Starachowice

Veszprem, (Weissbrunn) 186b

Vezenberg, *see* Wesenberg

Vienna, (Wien) 15, 20, 24, 42, 78-79, 128-129, 132-133, 152, 216-219

Vierzhbinik, *see* Starachowice

Vilna, (Vilnia, Vilnius, Vilno, Vilnyus, Wilna, Wilno) 31, 34, 50-51, 54-55, 60-61, 64-65, 78-79, 89, 128-129, 198, 200, 215t

Vilnia, *see* Vilna

Vilnius, *see* Vilna

Vilno, *see* Vilna

Vilnyus, *see* Vilna

Vilvoorde, 124

Vinitza, *see* Vinnitsa

Vinnitsa, (Vinitza, Winnica, Winnitsa, Winniza) 51, 54-55, 215t

Virdayn Katan, see Kisvarda

Viroshov, *see* Wieruszow

Vishegrod, *see* Wyszogrod

Vishogrod, *see* Wyszogrod

Vishogrud, *see* Wyszogrod

Viskit, *see* Wiskitki

Vitebsk, (Witebsk) 51, 54-55, 215t

Vittel, 106-107, 112, 140-141

Vladova, *see* Wlodawa

Vlatzlavek, *see* Wloclawek

Vlodava, *see* Wlodawa

Vlodavi, *see* Wlodawa

Vlodeve, *see* Wlodawa

Vlodova, *see* Wlodawa

Vlotslavek, *see* Wloclawek

Vo Eugane, 172-173

Voecklabruck, 152

Volgograd, *see* Stalingrad

Volozhin, (Volozhyn, Woloskin, Wolozyn) 51, 54-56

Volozhyn, *see* Volozhin

Vorke, *see* Warka

Vorna, *see* Varna

Vorne, *see* Varna

Vorni, *see* Varna

Voronezh, (Woronesch, Woronez) 215t

Votslavsk, *see* Wloclawek

Vught, 117-118, 140-142

Vurka, *see* Warka

Vurke, *see* Warka

Vyershuv, *see* Wieruszow

Vyerushov, *see* Wieruszow

Vyerushuv, *see* Wieruszow

Vyerzbnik, *see* Starachowice

Vyerzhbanik, *see* Starachowice

Vygoda, 73

W

Waakirchen, 208

Wadowice, (Vadovits, Vadovitse, Vadovitz) 98

Wagrain, 152

Walbrzych, *see* Waldenburg

Waldenburg, (Walbrzych) 158

Waldersbach, 113

Walldorf, 115

Walle, 165

Wannsee, 130

Wardboehmen, 165

Warka, (Varka, Vorke, Vurka, Vurke) 39

Warnemuende, 206

Warsaw, (Varsava, Varshau, Varshe, Warsawa, Warschau, Warszawa) 31-32, 34-41, 54-55, 78-79, 92, 98, 102, 128-129, 36b, 142, 198, 200, 215t, 216

Warsawa, *see* Warsaw

Warschau, *see* Warsaw

Warszawa, *see* Warsaw

Warta, (Dvart, Dvurt) 39, 42

Warthegau, 34, 35, 77

Wartsch, 159

Wasseralfingen, 115

Watten, 112

Wederau, 156

Weesen, 165

Weilheim, 146

Weimar, 147, 149, 207b

Weiss-See, 146

Weissbrunn, *see* Veszprem

Weissenberg, 207t

Weisswasser, 158

Weisswasser-Hohenstadt, 158

Wels, 152, 217

Wesenberg, (Rakvere, Vezenberg) 65

Wesserling, 112, 115

Wesslinken, 159

Westerbork, 99t, 117-118, 121-123, 140-142, 209

Western Europe, *see* Europe, western

Westerplatte, 159, 161

Wetteren, 124

Wewelsburg, 142, 149

Weyer, 152

Wickerode, 164

Widdernhausen, 165

Wielun, 42

Wien, 152. *See also* Vienna

Wiener Neudorf, 152

Wiener Neustadt, 24, 152

Wienergraben, 150

Wieruszow, (Verushev, Viroshov, Vyershuv, Vurke) 39

Vyerushov, Vyerushuv) 42

Wierzbnik, *see* Starachowice

Wierzbnik Starachow, *see* Starachowice

Wiesau, 158

Wiesbaden, (Schierstein) 24

Wildersbach, 113

Wilhelmpieckstadt Guben, *see* Guben

Willebroeck, 124

Wilna, *see* Vilna

Wilno, *see* Vilna

Wiltz, 116

Winnica, *see* Vinnitsa

Winnitsa, *see* Vinnitsa

Winniza, *see* Vinnitsa

Wiskitki, (Viskit) 39

Wisnicz Forest, 198

Witebsk, *see* Vitebsk

Witten-Annen, 149

Wittenau, 217

Wloclawek, (Alt Lesle, Leslau, Leslo, Lesluya, Vlatzlavek, Vlotslavek, Votslavsk) 42

Wlodawa, (Vladova, Vlodava, Vlodavi, Vlodeve, Vlodova, Wlodowa) 89

Wlodowa, *see* Wlodawa

Wodzislaw, 205

Woebbelin, 209

Woffleben, 162, 164

Wohrd, *see* Nuremberg

Wolczyny, 87

Wolfen, 149, 155

Wolfratshausen, 208

Wolka-Okraglik, 90

Woloskin, *see* Volozhin

Wolozyn, *see* Volozhin

Wornie, *see* Varna

Woronesch, *see* Voronezh

Woronez, *see* Voronezh

Wotzlaff, 159

Wrieze, 130

Wroclaw, 215t. *See also* Breslau

Wuestewaltersdorf, 158

Wuppertal, (Elberfeld, Wuppertal Elberfeld) 149, 216

Wuppertal Elberfeld, *see* Wuppertal

Wusterhausen, 130

Wyszkow Forest, 198

Wyszogrod, (Vishegrod, Vishogrod, Vishogrud) 98

Y

Yagestov, *see* Augustow

Yagistov, *see* Augustow

Yagustova, *see* Augustow

Yanina, *see* Ioannina

Yartchovka, *see* Jarczow

Yashinovka, *see* Jasionowka

Yashinovke, *see* Jasionowka

Yashinowka, *see* Jasionowka

Yasinya, *see* Korosmezo

Yedinets, *see* Edineti

Yedintsy, *see* Edineti

Yekaterinodar, *see* Krasnodar

Yekaterinoslav, *see* Dnepropetrovsk

Yendrikhov, *see* Andrychow

Yezhov, *see* Jezow

Yugoslavia, 14, 16, 32, 168-169t, 185-186t, 201, 216, 221

Yuriev, *see* Tartu

Yuryev, *see* Tartu

Z

Zablocie, 46

Zabrze, *see* Hindenburg

Zagrab, *see* Zagreb

Zagreb, (Agram, Zagrab) 99t, 169t, 170-175, 216

Zahorany, 134

Zajecar, 172-173

Zalaegerszeg, 188

Zalese, *see* Zalesie

Zalesie, (Zalese) 87

Zamosc, (Zamoshch, Zamoshtch, Zamoshtsh, Zamostie, Zamotch) 54-55, 86

Zamoshch, *see* Zamosc

Zamoshtch, *see* Zamosc

Zamoshtsh, *see* Zamosc

Zamostie, *see* Zamosc

Zamotch, *see* Zamosc

Zangberg, 146

Zasavica, 172-173

Zaslavl, (Izaslaw, Iziaslav, Zaslaw) 198

Zaslaw, *see* Zaslavl

Zavertse, *see* Zawiercie

Zavirtcha, *see* Zawiercie

Zavyerche, *see* Zawiercie

Zawadka, 80

Zawiercie, (Zavertse, Zavirtcha, Zavyerche) 98

Zbereze, 87

Zdunska Vola, *see* Zdunska Wola

Zdunska Volye, *see* Zdunska Wola

Zdunska Wola, (Dinskivola, Zdunska Vola, Zdunska Volye, Zdunske Volye) 42

Zdunske Volye, *see* Zdunska Wola

Zdzarka, 87

Zeilsheim, 217

Zelav, *see* Zelow

Zelow, (Zelav) 42

Zemun, *see* Sajmiste

Zeyersniederkampen, 159

Zeyersvorderkampen, 159

Zgerzh, *see* Zgierz

Zgierz, (Zgerzh, Zgyerz) 42-43

Zgorzelec, *see* Goerlitz

Zgyerz, *see* Zgierz

Zheredov, *see* Zyrardow

Zheshov, *see* Rzeszow

Zheshuv, *see* Rzeszow

Zhezhov, *see* Rzeszow

Zhirardov, *see* Zyrardow

Zhitomir, (Jitomir, Shitomir, Zytomierz) 51, 54-55, 215t

Ziechenau, *see* Ciechanow

Ziegenhain, 217

Zielona Gora, *see* Gruenberg

Zittau, 158

Zlobek, 87

Zlochev, *see* Zolochev

Zlochuv, *see* Zolochev

Zloczow, *see* Zolochev

Zlotchev, *see* Zolochev

Zlotki, 90

Zolitude, 66

Zolochev, (Zlochev, Zlochuv, Zloczow, Zlotchev) 54-55, 86

Zossen, 130

Zuckau, 206

Zwickau, 207t

Zwiggelte, 122

Zwodau, 155

Zyrardow, (Shiraduv, Zheredov, Zhirardov) 39

Zytomierz, *see* Zhitomir